PRESIDENTIAL POWER IN RUSSIA

THE NEW RUSSIAN POLITICAL SYSTEM

Series Editor:
Robert Sharlet

Presidential Power in Russia is the first in a series of books examining the evolution of the main political institutions of post-Soviet Russia. Forthcoming volumes will be devoted to legislative politics, courts and the judicial system, constitutionalism, federalism and regional politics.

THE NEW RUSSIAN
POLITICAL SYSTEM

PRESIDENTIAL POWER IN RUSSIA

EUGENE HUSKEY

M.E. Sharpe

Armonk, New York
London, England

Library of Congress Cataloging-in-Publication Data

Presidential power in Russia / by Eugene Huskey.
p. cm.—(The New Russian political system)
Includes bibliographical references (p.) and index.
ISBN 1-56324-536-1 (cloth : alk. paper). ISBN 1-56324-537-X (pbk. : alk. paper)
1. Presidents—Russia (Federation). 2. Executive power—Russia (Federation). 3. Russia
(Federation)—Politics and government—1991– . 4. Yeltsin, Boris Nikolayevich, 1931–
I. Title. II. Series.
JN6696.H87 1999
352.23′0947—dc21   99-20508
CIP

Printed in the United States of America

The paper used in this publication meets the minimum requirements of
American National Standard for Information Sciences
Permanence of Paper for Printed Library Materials,
ANSI Z 39.48-1984.

∞

BM (c) 10   9   8   7   6   5   4   3   2   1
BM (p) 10   9   8   7   6   5   4   3   2   1

To Janet

Contents

List of Tables, Figures, and Maps

Tables

Figures

Maps

Acknowledgments

This is a book written on, and in, a period of transition. While Russia was changing dramatically in the 1990s, so were the sources available to study it. During the course of the decade, the familiar touch and smell of Russian books and newsprint began to give way to purely visual images on a computer screen. Sitting in a small Florida town thousands of miles from Russia, one could read the transcripts of press conferences conducted only a short time earlier in the Kremlin. This technological revolution may increase a researcher's sense of independence, but it does not diminish his debts to the many individuals and institutions that serve as partners in the intellectual enterprise.

Despite the rise of electronic research, librarians remain indispensable "search engines" for all of us. For their generous help, I would like to thank librarians at the Institute of State and Law and the Russian State Library in Moscow, the Library of Congress, and the duPont-Ball Library of Stetson University. The National Council for Eurasian and East European Research (NCEEER) funded travel and a respite from teaching in the first half of 1995, which allowed me to begin research for the book in earnest. I am especially grateful for the support and counsel of NCEEER's former president, Vlad Toumanoff. Stetson University provided me a sabbatical leave in the second half of 1995, and its Russian Studies Program facilitated contacts with Russian and Western specialists in the field, whether through travel grants to Russia or through a regular speakers' series here in Florida. I also wish to acknowledge the assistance of the International Research and Exchanges Board (IREX), which funded a three-week research trip to Moscow and Riazan, and the Kennan Institute for Advanced Russian Studies, which hosted me for a month in Washington, DC.

No matter how well Westerners know Moscow, they remain dependent at times on their Russian friends and colleagues for assistance. Igor Filippov, Mark Slavin, Liudmila Diachenko, and Mikhail Guboglo were delightful companions as well as resourceful *tolchaki* ("fixers" in the positive sense of the word). I am also grateful to the many Russian scholars and officials who agreed to be interviewed for this book, including two survivors of the presidency and the academy, Valerii Savitskii and Aleksandr M. Yakovlev. With the emergence in Russia of a freer press and more stimulating academic publications, Western research is increasingly indebted to Russian journalism and scholarship for information and analysis. This project is no exception. Especially helpful to me was the work of two correspondents whose beats included the Russian presidency, Denis Babichenko, of *Segodnia*, and Irina Savvateeva, of *Izvestia*. They were among several journalists who graciously agreed to reverse roles and sit for interviews.

In this country, Ed Kline, perhaps the only person to move from retailing to Russian studies, was an early and astute reader of the manuscript and a constant source of encouragement. Tim Colton, Gary Maris, and Pat Willerton also read the manuscript in its entirety and offered valuable suggestions for revision. Todd Foglesong, Tom Remington, Mike Urban, George Breslauer, Archie Brown, Sergei Porshakov, Peter Reddaway, Darrell Slider, and Peter Solomon read one or more chapters and enriched the book with their expertise and commentary. I am indebted to Bruce Bradford for producing the maps of Moscow, to Stephanie Friese for research assistance at the inception of the project, and to Susan Bradford for always making work in the Russian Studies Center a little easier for me. I am grateful also to students at Stetson who tried out the "beta" version of this book and to audiences at the Kennan Institute, the State Department, Emory University, Kansas University, and the University of Wisconsin for their reactions to my ideas about the Russian presidency. To Patricia Kolb, my editor at M.E. Sharpe, and Bob Sharlet, the general editor of the series, The New Russian Political System, my thanks for using patience and prodding at just the right moments.

Finally, a word of appreciation to my family, who have lived with this book longer than they care to remember. They tolerated my absence, whether it was for weeks in Russia and Central Asia or for hours in our "computer room." They also provided their own distinct forms of support—Sarah and Charlotte, my daughters, by regularly asking me when the book was going to be finished, and Janet Martinez, my wife, by helping me to meet deadlines when she had so many of her own. It is to Janet that the book is dedicated.

PRESIDENTIAL POWER IN RUSSIA

1

Introduction

In the spring of 1991, a concert in the Great Hall of the Moscow Conservatory honored the late physicist and human rights activist Andrei Sakharov. The event brought to the stage eminent Russian musicians who rarely performed in Moscow: Mstislav Rostropovich, Sviatoslav Richter, and Vladimir Spivakov. Among the many dignitaries in the audience were Mikhail Gorbachev, perched to the side of the stage in the tsar's box, and Boris Yeltsin, sitting in the stalls.[1] Despite Gorbachev's rank as Soviet president and his visibility in the loge, it was the insurgent politician, Boris Yeltsin, who attracted the attention of the crowd that evening. During the intermission, while Gorbachev and his wife, Raisa, retreated to the privacy of an anteroom, Boris Yeltsin strode back to the public entrance hall, where he greeted a pressing throng of well-wishers. It was only three weeks before Russia's first democratic presidential elections, and candidate Yeltsin radiated an energy, charm, and resolve that would see him through to victory in June and to defeat of a right-wing coup attempt in August. With the collapse of the USSR—and Gorbachev's humiliating abdication of the Soviet presidency—in December 1991, Boris Yeltsin took the final step in his journey from rebel to ruler, joining the long line of princes, tsars, and general secretaries who have governed Russia.

Writing about these events almost eight years later, in the first days of 1999, it is difficult to conjure up the image of a vibrant and confident Boris Yeltsin, on whom so many hopes were placed, and misplaced. Having survived two violent constitutional crises, hyperinflation, a war of secession, a bruising reelection campaign, continuing budget shortfalls, major heart surgery, and mounting insults by politicians and public alike, the Russian president cut an almost pathetic figure midway through his second term. Even a high-ranking official in Yeltsin's own administration volunteered in July 1998 that the president "has accumulated such a burden of tiredness, both physical and psychological," that he should not run for a third term—an idea Yeltsin continued to toy with until the fall of 1998.[2]

But whenever, and however, Boris Yeltsin departs the political stage, he will leave a formidable legacy. On Yeltsin's watch, Russia destroyed the last vestiges of Communist Party rule, dismantled a centuries-old empire, joined the Council of Europe, enacted a market-oriented code of civil law, and began to recast relations between the citizen and the state and the capital and the provinces. Not since the French Revolution—or at least the Bolshevik Revolution of 1917—has a country experienced so much political change in a single decade. Our judgments about presidential leadership in Russia in the 1990s will surely be colored by whether the Yeltsin years represent a prelude to a deepening democracy or a new authoritarianism. Thus, how we view the role of the Russian presidency in this era of transition depends not only on our own politics but on Russia's future.

Like the French Revolution, Russia's protracted and painful transition from the ancien regime is generating a vast literature of reportage, reminiscence, and analysis. In the Western scholarly literature on Russian politics, studies of changes in society initially took center stage. This orientation in academic research and writing flowed in part from the desire to apply the sophisticated tools of social science analysis, especially public opinion polling, to a previously closed society. Where Western survey research in the Soviet era had been limited to emigrant populations from the 1940s and 1970s,[3] each unrepresentative of broader Soviet society in its own way, at the very end of the 1980s political scientists began to question large samples of citizens in Russia about their political attitudes, values, and beliefs.[4] In addition, the nine Russia-wide elections or referendums held between 1989 and 1996 provided scholars with rich—and even, by Western standards, unprecedented—sources of information on political behavior.[5] These attitudinal surveys and electoral studies revealed a complex, and in many ways deeply divided, society. On some issues, the new data merely confirmed what every Russian understood intuitively: a member of the Moscow intelligentsia thinks and acts differently in politics than a peasant in Orel province. But on other questions, Western social science research challenged the received wisdom, most notably on the democratic potential of the Russian population.[6]

Alongside studies of political attitudes and behavior, there has appeared a burgeoning literature on social groups and parties in Russia.[7] Throughout most of Soviet history, group membership had been limited to organizations sanctioned and controlled by the Communist Party. But by the end of the 1980s, Gorbachev's more tolerant approach to private associations gave birth to a spate of new "informal organizations," which began to mobilize citizens behind various ethnic, environmental, and political causes. This rise of social activism seemed to many Western scholars to signal the emergence in Russia of a civil society, that dense network of voluntary associations that instills habits of political trust and cooperation in citizens and serves as an institutional shield protecting individuals from the power of the state.[8] However, public interest in associational activities seemed to wane at the beginning of the 1990s, the very time when a more liberal legal and political environment was taking root.[9] Behind this "demobilization" of Russian society lay a disillusionment and exhaustion with politics as a remedy for societal ills. For many Russians, the excitement of participating in a political revolution hypertrophied into cynicism and despair once they experienced the immediate fruits of change: political instability, social deviance, and economic collapse. Ironically, as the formal impediments to associational activity fell in Russia, everyday life erected new, and in many ways more imposing, barriers. Members of the intelligentsia who had made a comfortable living in the Soviet era were forced by the early 1990s to take on additional jobs to make ends meet. Put simply, as a result of worsening economic conditions, Russians no longer had as much time for politics. Many began to withdraw into themselves and their families.

Despite the emphasis of the scholarly literature on citizens and groups, it is the state that merits the most intense scrutiny at this stage of Russian political development. The society-centered orientation of Western—and especially American—writing derives not only from methodological preferences and the torrent of new data on political participation in Russia but from the prevailing liberal model of politics, in which the state is seen as a product of social forces. To understand the state, the argument goes, one must first understand its progenitor, society. Open virtually any textbook on American government and one finds—after a nod in the direction of culture and history—a series of chapters devoted to such topics as parties, interest groups, public opinion, and the media. Only after this introduction to "society" does one encounter the core institutions of state—presidency, Congress, and courts. Whatever the value of this approach in American politics, it is inappropriate for Russia, where there has been no mythology—such as Lockean contract theory—or procedural regime to bind the state to society. Indeed, the Russian state has historically exercised a degree of autonomy from, and dominance over, society that clearly distinguishes it from its Western counterparts. Despite the introduction in recent years of a relatively open press and competitive elections, politics in Russia remains overwhelmingly state-centered. Robert C. Tucker's description of the origins of "dual Russia" still seems fresh at the end of the twentieth century:

> Far from developing as a dependent political "superstructure" over a social-economic "base," the Russian state organism took shape as an autonomous force acting to create or recreate its own social base, to shape and reshape the institutional pattern of society, in a series of revolutions from above.[10]

The dominant role of the state is evident in the politics of change.[11] Unlike the transition from authoritarianism in the Philippines, where "people power" pushed Ferdinand Marcos off the historical stage, the major impetus for the reform of Soviet politics came from Mikhail Gorbachev and a small group of supporters within the Communist Party.[12] Likewise, in the 1990s, President Yeltsin and his westernizing advisors have imposed a package of economic reforms on a largely unsuspecting, and unsympathetic, population. These episodes are but the latest in a series of revolutions from above that have transformed Russia during the last four centuries. Although Russia has adopted certain democratic institutions, its state is not yet accountable to a vibrant and demanding society.

Thus, for all it weaknesses and divisions, the state remains by far the most important story in Russian politics.[13] And within the state, there is no more dominant institution than the presidency, which serves as the engine of reform, the nerve center of political communications, the chief patron for positions in the executive and judicial branches, and a symbol, however flawed, of Russian national unity. Yet the Russian presidency has been the subject of little sustained analysis by scholars.[14] This book represents a first attempt to assess the role of the presidency in Russia's difficult transition from Communist rule.[15]

Although Boris Yeltsin looms large in the study, this is not a biography of the first Russian president but an analysis of political relations within the presidency and between the presidency and the other leading institutions of state: Government, parliament, courts, and regional authorities. Whether one speaks of the White House or the Kremlin, the presidency is far more than a single individual. In the Russian case, it is a collection of several thousand officials with diverse political views, expertise, interests, and bases of loyalty to the president. Given its size and its direct involvement in the full range of domestic and foreign policies, the Russian presidency operates as a state within a state, as the hub around which political decisionmaking revolves.

As Chapter 2 points out, the presidency is a new institution in Russian history, having appeared in the Soviet Union in March 1990 and in the Russian Federation, in slightly revised form, a year later. But the exercise of presidential power preserves many traditional patterns of authority in Russia. The most obvious is the division between a Government, or Council of Ministers, charged with the everyday management of the state bureaucracy, especially in economic affairs, and a political institution that stands above it as the "leading and guiding force" in politics.[16] In prerevolutionary Russia, this institution was the tsar and his personal chancelleries; in the Soviet era, it was the general secretary, the Politburo, and the Central Committee apparatus of the Communist Party; and in present-day Russia it is the president and his extensive administrative apparatus. As part of his offensive against the Communist Party in 1991, Yeltsin and his entourage sought to regather in the presidency many of the powers that the party had wielded in the old regime. Partly out of habit, partly in response to an immediate need to impose discipline on autonomy-seeking ministries and regions, Yeltsin revived in the presidency many of the structures and functions of the Communist Party Central Committee, without of course reviving the party's ideological or political monopoly. Where Lenin sent political commissars to the provinces to ensure Bolshevik rule among wavering or hostile local authorities, Yeltsin appointed his own presidential representatives in the country's eighty-nine subject territories to serve as his watchdogs.

One of the paradoxes of the Russian transition has been the use of traditional patterns of political authority by Gorbachev and Yeltsin to undo the traditional bases of economic and social relations. Frustrated by an uncooperative parliament, for example, the Russian president has sought, unsuccessfully, to introduce a free market in land by decree, a tactic smacking of authoritarian *diktat* in the eyes of Yeltsin's opponents.[17] When is a democratically elected president justified in ignoring, or circumventing, existing laws and the constitution in order to advance the cause of economic and social reform? This question, made all the more acute by the Russian population's hostility to many westernizing reforms, has dogged Yeltsin and his domestic and foreign supporters throughout his presidency. In contrast to the view proffered by many Western governments, the Russian transition is not a simple morality play: its leaders at times use illiberal means to achieve liberal ends.

Among the many continuities with the old order is institutional redundancy. As we noted above, the large bureaucracies surrounding the tsar, the general secretary, and now the president all duplicate a perfectly reasonable executive management team already in place in the Government and headed by a prime minister. But the duplication does not stop at the apex of Russian institutional arrangements. Yeltsin has permitted the development in the presidency of several competing power centers with overlapping responsibilities. Moreover, he has sanctioned the establishment of new, reform-oriented state committees whose jurisdictional lines cross those of long-standing, and politically stodgy, ministries. In the Communist regime, the proliferation of "checking mechanisms" was an essential ingredient of party rule. However, in the more open and competitive environment of post-Soviet politics, it has heightened administrative inefficiency and political conflict.[18]

A central assumption of this book is that how decisions are made tells us much about what decisions are made. Although a country's rules of governing—its institutional design—are themselves products of numerous factors, such as the cultural legacy, the interests and tactics of key elites, and the circumstances under which the rules of the political game were crafted, once in place institutional arrangements become a relatively autonomous force that makes certain political outcomes more likely than others.[19] To provide a stark example, if Russian electoral rules had provided for indirect, rather than direct, presidential elections, Boris Yeltsin would not have won the presidency in 1996.[20] Thus, all other things being equal, a shift in how citizens choose their leaders would have set Russia on a very different political course.

Rules matter in decision making by state officials as well as citizens. The provisions in the 1993 constitution granting the Russian president the power to veto legislation altered fundamentally the relationship between executive and legislative authority. Just as in the United States, the threat of a presidential veto in Russia encourages parliament to consider the interests of the president when it writes laws. Unless it can muster a two-thirds majority to override a presidential veto, parliament legislates in vain if it ignores the perspective of the presidency. Even the informal rules governing the adoption of decisions within the executive may play a key role in shaping policies. Continuing a tradition begun in the tsarist era and maintained by the Soviets, the Russian president and prime minister circulate draft decrees, directives, and other important documents along a lengthy chain of executive officials. Each bureaucrat must apply a stamp of approval, known as a visa, before the proposal can go forward to the next official in the chain. This laborious procedure allows officials to subvert policy initiatives by withholding the visa, sitting on the proposal, or even losing the document. Although an impatient and wilful leader may "fast-track" some decrees, or override the veto of a subordinate, the visa routine represents an inheritance that—in the absence of party discipline—devolves considerable authority onto second-tier officials in the presidency and Government.

In addition to institutional design, cultural legacies and economic relations influence how presidential power is wielded in Russia. To be sure, no culture is immutable, but deeply entrenched patterns of thought and behavior tend to change slowly and reluctantly. It is no surprise, then, that habits acquired in Soviet political and administrative practice should continue to make themselves felt under post-Communist rule, especially in light of the experience that most current Russian officials gained in the Soviet party and/or state bureaucracy.[21] An obvious cultural vestige in Russia is the personalization of authority. Where the Weberian model of bureaucracy calls for loyalty to an office, and the rules that surround it, Russian and Soviet administrative cultures have encouraged fealty to bosses. As we shall see, Yeltsin could not always count on unthinking loyalty from his own subordinates, but in general state employees in Russia seek patrons rather than mentors. The result is less a hierarchical network of offices than an intricate web of "family circles." In such an environment, it is exceedingly difficult to inculcate in officials a sense of *raison d'état*; the temptation is to "privatize" state power and wealth for one's own benefit. Working for the good of the clan rather than the good of the cause contributes to a fragmentation of power that is a central feature of contemporary Russian politics.

The painful transition toward a market-oriented economy has also had its effects on the exercise of presidential power in Russia. The concentration of capital in the hands of a few oligarchs—"the smart and the lucky but hardly ever the best," to borrow Chinua Achebe's description of the postcolonial Nigerian elite—has created private economic empires that command the attention of the president and the loyalties of some prominent state officials. It was, after all, a small group of bankers and industrialists who came forward in early 1996 to fill the coffers of Yeltsin's reelection campaign at a time when some observers were dismissing the president as a serious candidate. For most Russians, however, the economic policies of the Yeltsin era have lowered job security and living standards. Yeltsin has turned this economic vulnerability to his advantage by making leading state officials, including higher court judges and parliamentary deputies, dependent on a department of the presidency for the provision of scarce goods, such as apartments, country homes, vacations, and transportation. Because most state employees are unable to live on their meager wages alone, the presidency is able to use the disbursement of in-kind benefits as a lever of influence. Although there have been many reasons for the reluctance of the parliament to pass a no-confidence vote against the prime minister, one is the fear of having to stand for new elections. Risking a parliamentary seat, and all the perquisites, prestige, and goods that come with it, is an especially daunting prospect for middle-aged deputies with modest abilities, who would fare poorly on the private labor market. At least for some segments of the power elite, economic vulnerability invites political caution, an attitude that has proved useful to the presidency.

Having begun this introduction by referring to Yeltsin the politician, it is appropriate to conclude by recognizing that whatever the institutional, cultural, or economic context, individuals make political decisions, and individuals differ in their outlooks, ambitions, and leadership styles. To understand the course of Russian political development during the last decade, one must also consider, therefore, what political scientists call elite tactics—the important decisions taken by key politicians, especially Boris Yeltsin. The implications of individual decision making for Russian politics become apparent if one considers two personnel appointments made by Yeltsin at the end of the Soviet era. From among a large pool of candidates, Yeltsin chose Ruslan Khasbulatov to succeed him as leader of the Russian parliament and Aleksandr Rutskoi to serve as his vice presidential running mate in the June 1991 presidential election. These two "allies" abandoned the president's camp in 1992 and led the armed opposition to Yeltsin in the fall of 1993. Although Yeltsin's reform-oriented policies were bound to generate resistance from powerful forces in the Russian state and society, the militant and uncompromising character of that opposition owes something to the elite tactics of the very individuals whom Boris Yeltsin propelled to power.[22] Poor judgment in personnel decisions exacts a heavy toll in politics, especially at moments of regime transition.

Perhaps the most striking feature of Russian political leadership is the range of strategies and tactics represented. In Russia the choice is not between Tweedledum and Tweedledee but between politicians with radically different views of private property, elections, and the mutual obligations of the citizen and the state. There is, to borrow a phrase from the Alabama populist George Wallace, far more than a dime's worth of difference between Russian politicians. The absence of a consensus on fundamental political values raises the stakes in Russian politics to a level unimaginable in Western countries. The loss of a legislative battle may represent a historic defeat for the proponents of reform or tradition. Moreover, the loss of an election could bring to power an elite that will not only reverse existing policies but imprison the incumbents who introduced them. Elections in the West are associated with a change of administration; in Russia they may well bring a change of regime. The Communist speaker of the lower house in Russia, Gennadii Seleznev, has promised to abandon presidentialism in favor of a parliamentary republic if the anti-Yeltsin forces come to power.[23] As we suggested earlier, at certain moments in the last decade, the recognition of the high stakes involved in Russian politics has encouraged some citizens and elites to compromise on lesser principles in order to salvage higher ones. Concerned about the fate of a free press if a Communist were elected president, leading journalists in Moscow abandoned any pretense of journalistic objectivity to promote the candidacy of Boris Yeltsin during the 1996 presidential elections.

To argue, as this book does, that the presidency represents the best entry point for exploring contemporary Russian politics is not to claim that there is a presidential dictatorship or even a superpresidential order in Russia. Notwithstanding the formidable constitutional prerogatives accorded to the president, the alarmist comments about presidential power contained in the speeches and articles of some opposition politicians and publicists, and the occasional puffing of Yeltsin himself, the Russian presidency faces potent constraints on its authority from parliament, the bureaucracy, and the regions. It has neither the stable popular support essential to mature democratic rule nor the administrative discipline found in efficient authoritarian regimes. Lacking a loyal majority party or an iron fist, the presidency must cajole, compromise, and construct temporary coalitions to advance reform initiatives and manage the regular crises associated with transition-era politics. But while governing Russia with the formal and informal powers at its disposal, the presidency also seeks to acquire new levers of influence over political decision making. Its successes and failures in these two ventures—governing a country and building an institution of state—are the central concerns of this work.

2

The Making of the Russian Presidency

Presidencies—like parties—are relative newcomers to politics. Once introduced in the American constitution of 1789, however, this executive post spread rapidly to other continents. With the collapse of monarchies and empires during the last two hundred years, the presidency has emerged as the industry standard for republican heads of state, whatever the particular powers of their office. By the last quarter of the twentieth century, two-thirds of the world's two hundred states had presidencies. One of the exceptions was the Soviet Union.

If Russia's monarchical tradition ensured the absence of a presidency in the prerevolutionary era, the Communists' aversion to Western imports prevented its adoption throughout most of the twentieth century. Especially in the first two decades after the October Revolution of 1917, Bolshevik authorities explicitly rejected both the political inheritance of the old regime and the institutional models of the West. Traditional ministries became commissariats, and the legislature—a mere "talking shop," in Lenin's phrase—gave way to soviet parliamentarism, where executive and legislative functions were supposed to be fused in a single institution.[1] Just as the new Communist order promised to overcome the tensions between city and country and between mental and manual labor, so a soviet parliament was supposed to transcend the traditional distinctions between executive and legislative authority. Political practice, of course, proved otherwise. By the mid-1920s, a chief executive had emerged in the Soviet Union.

However, it was not a president or prime minister but the general secretary of the Communist Party, a novelty in political history.

The insistence on institutional exceptionalism began to fade, however, in the latter half of the 1930s, when Stalin launched a broad-based retreat from the utopian ideals of the revolution. During the framing of the 1936 constitution, the idea of a Soviet presidency was broached for the first time. The proposal envisioned the direct election of the USSR's formal head of state, who was chair of the national parliament, the Supreme Soviet. Stalin quickly dismissed the idea, however, as "undesirable," no doubt recognizing that a state leader with a direct national mandate, even one gained through controlled elections, would be a formidable rival for the general secretary.[2]

Calls for a Soviet presidency resurfaced in the early 1960s, again in connection with the drafting of a new constitution. This time the proposal came from aides close to Khrushchev, among them Fedor Burlatskii, who argued that the general secretary should combine his party post with the state office of president. But as he was already doubling as prime minister, the highest-ranking state official of the day, General Secretary Khrushchev saw little need to create a competing executive office at the apex of the Soviet state.[3]

During the two decades that separated the ouster of Khrushchev from the death of Konstantin Chernenko, the idea of a Soviet presidency remained alive among a small circle of advisors in the Communist Party, whose understanding of Western political systems far exceeded that of their bosses. Shortly after Mikhail Gorbachev succeeded Chernenko in March 1985, he received a memorandum from two of his closest advisors, Vadim Medvedev and Georgii Shakhnazarov, who set out the establishment of a presidency as one option in a package of political reforms.[4] In the summer of 1988, in discussions preceding the pathbreaking Nineteenth Communist Party Conference, Fedor Burlatskii—now a Gorbachev confidant—revived his proposal to create the office of president in the USSR. The conference itself laid the groundwork for a national presidency by calling for a single, directly elected governor to supersede the separate posts of party and state leader in each region. Then in early 1989 several opponents of Communist rule, including the human rights activist Andrei Sakharov, proposed the introduction of a presidency as a way of limiting the power of the Communist Party.[5]

Through at least October 1989, however, Gorbachev resisted attempts to establish a Soviet presidency. He remained committed to refining, rather than overturning, institutional arrangements in Moscow, aware that, in Soviet conditions, the creation of a presidency would be viewed by many as the first step toward a personal dictatorship.[6] Yet in March 1990 Gorbachev convinced the Soviet Congress of People's Deputies to amend the constitution and install him as the country's first president. What led to this dramatic turnaround? Put simply, Gorbachev recognized that existing instruments of rule limited his ability to address the country's mounting crises. Following a Politburo meeting in February 1988, at which Nina Andreeva's conservative manifesto was discussed, Gorbachev had confided to one of his aides: "Now I finally realize with whom I'm dealing. With these people one won't make perestroika."[7] Disillusioned with the Communist Party as a vehicle of reform, the general secretary had begun shifting power to state institutions at the end of 1988. Constitutional amendments introduced at that time led to the country's first competitive elections in March 1989 and the transformation of the moribund Soviet parliament into a lively, two-tiered legislature, consisting of a Congress of People's Deputies and a smaller Supreme Soviet—the "working parliament," which was elected by the Congress.[8]

With the opening session of the new Congress of People's Deputies in May 1989, the general secretary transferred his primary base of operations to the legislature, where he assumed the post of chair. At this point, as Georgii Shakhnazarov observed, Gorbachev began to spend more time in the Kremlin (parliamentary and Government headquarters) than on Old Square (party headquarters).[9] But the parliament proved little more cooperative, and vastly more time-consuming, than the party. In his new post, Gorbachev had to formulate policy, manage a growing parliamentary bureaucracy, and direct floor debate, all the while maintaining his Communist Party office. It was an unworkable amalgam. Prime Minister Nikolai Ryzhkov estimated that parliamentary duties occupied a third of his ministers' time.[10] Parliament also began to insist on direct involvement in the implementation of policy, that is, it sought to revive the original idea of soviet parliamentarism.[11] Moreover, an essential component of efficient parliamentarism in any country, a loyal and stable legislative majority, was missing. It was often unclear which faction presented the greater liability to Gorbachev: the conservative Communist majority, procedurally sycophantic but hostile to substantive change, or the vocal and independent-minded minority, which continually criticized the pace and depth of reforms.[12]

Frustrated in his role as speaker, Gorbachev authorized the design of a new political architecture barely six months into the life of the parliament. In his words, "[W]e are initiating new things in the economy and in politics. But without an executive mechanism we cannot achieve these initiatives. If there is no balance, we'll remain at the initial stage of meetings. . . . I think the main source of this acceleration is a strong executive mechanism."[13] Gorbachev understood, then, that the Soviet Union required a strong executive counterweight to a resurgent parliament and to an obstructionist party apparatus. The goal was to create for the leader a more dignified and powerful constitutional office distinct from the legislature, and in so doing to disarm the democratic opposition, which itself had proposed the establishment of a presidency in the spring of 1989.[14] But Gorbachev had little knowledge of, or interest in, the intricacies of institutional design. Responsibility for framing the Soviet presidency fell, therefore, to a small team of advisors who prepared the working drafts on the new institution.

The first phase in the creation of a presidency, which lasted throughout much of December 1989 and January 1990, was not a mere technical exercise but a deeply political struggle among Gorbachev's aides and associates over the future structure of power in the Soviet Union. Not all agreed even with the idea of a presidency. Anatolii Lukianov, a protege of Gorbachev since their law school days, sought unsuccessfully to defend his own creation, the Congress of People's Deputies, against an institution—the presidency—that he regarded as alien to the collegial traditions of Russia and the Soviet Union.[15]

Once the necessary political and legal documents had been prepared by his advisors, Gorbachev sought the Politburo's approval for the establishment of the presidency on 19 January 1990. During this "stormy" Politburo session, Yegor Ligachev, the party's second secretary, dared to oppose outright the plan for a presidency. Ligachev argued vigorously that a Soviet presidency would undermine the already declining role of the Communist Party and its Politburo.[16] Habits of loyalty died hard, however, and the force of logic wielded by Ligachev was no match for the personal authority of the general secretary. Party rule was falling victim to party discipline.

With the approval of the Politburo, the proposal for the creation of a Soviet presidency moved into its first public forum, the Supreme Soviet, which adopted a resolution in support of the institution on 7 February. In the two weeks that followed, the shape of the Soviet presidency was debated and refined in a series of meetings that brought together Gorbachev, his aides and associates, and some of the most active and progressive members of the Supreme Soviet, including Anatolii Sobchak, Sergei Stankevich, and Andrei Sakharov.[17] Bearing the concessions needed to gain the support of the parliament and the leaders of the country's fifteen republics, the Law on Instituting the Post of President was adopted overwhelmingly by the Congress of People's Deputies on 6 March 1990. Ten days later, against only token opposition, the Congress elected Mikhail Gorbachev the first president of the Soviet Union.[18] He took the oath of office on 28 May 1990.

In little more than three months, amid deliberations that were often hurried and haphazard, the Soviet political elite had altered fundamentally the country's institutional arrangements. To understand what was at stake in this exercise, one needs only to review the institutional choices made by those in power. The first, and most momentous, decision was to select a semipresidential model of government. Semipresidentialism represented a compromise between an American-style presidency, favored by several of Gorbachev's closest advisors, and soviet parliamentarism, defended by Anatolii Lukianov. Modeled on French institutional arrangements, it retained both a prime minister and a president.[19]

Semipresidentialism had numerous advantages for Gorbachev personally and for a regime in transition from one-party rule.[20] Like parliamentarism, semipresidentialism separates the posts of head of state (president) and head of government (prime minister). But unlike parliamentarism, where the head of state is a mere figurehead, semipresidentialism grants the president broad powers. With its dual executive, semipresidentialism elevated the Soviet president above the unpleasant business of managing a vast and inefficient bureaucracy, which was left to the prime minister. In semipresidentialism, the prime minister and not the president becomes the whipping boy for popular discontent. Removed from daily politics, the president could aspire to the majesty of an "enlightened monarch."[21] A Soviet presidency seemed to promise a new source of legitimacy for a regime with a failing ideology and institutions.

Semipresidentialism was also the least disruptive alternative to the existing institutional order. A parliament and a Government, headed by a prime minister, were already in place. The new arrangements required only the addition of a small presidential bureaucracy. With the decline of Communist rule, the presidency was a logical successor to the party's Central Committee apparatus. Indeed, at the end of the Soviet era, according to Georgii Shakhnazarov, the presidency "gradually began to take over the Central Committee apparatus."[22] A less charitable observer, Prime Minister Valentin Pavlov, called the apparatuses of the presidency and the Central Committee "Siamese twins."[23]

If officials outside of Gorbachev's immediate entourage had little direct influence on the selection of semipresidentialism as the model of government, many were involved in the institutional choices that gave Soviet semipresidentialism its distinctive shape. There were defining choices to be made in four areas: the powers of the presidency vis-à-vis the legislature; the relations of president and prime minister; the method of electing the president; and the role of presidencies in the country's fifteen constituent republics. The debate over executive-legislative relations centered on the future of the Congress of People's Deputies. The Congress functioned in some respects like a constituent assembly, which assumes control of the state temporarily in a time of crisis in order to lay the constitutional foundations of a new political order. But in the Soviet Union, this outsized institution—in terms of both membership and authority—possessed a permanent mandate. It was at once an arbiter of constitutional issues, an electoral college for the Supreme Soviet, and the highest legislative assembly, whose laws could not be challenged.

Sharing the political stage with the Congress of People's Deputies would limit severely the authority of a Soviet president. But Gorbachev refused to heed the advice of aides who sought to restrict the powers of the Congress, or to abolish the institution altogether. In many semipresidential systems, for example, the president has the power to dissolve the parliament under certain conditions. The deputies' fear of dissolution can, at crucial moments, afford the executive important leverage over a recalcitrant parliament. But in Soviet semipresidentialism, the fate of the Supreme Soviet was in the hands of the Congress. The president could only propose to the Congress that it dissolve the Supreme Soviet, a policy that Gorbachev believed would discourage the rise of an authoritarian executive.[24] The legislation on the presidency also kept in place the potentially powerful chairmanship of the Congress, a post assumed by the champion of soviet parliamentarism, Anatolii Lukianov. By retaining a Congress of People's Deputies with its full array of powers, Gorbachev and the Soviet elite created an institutional regime that invited executive-legislative stalemate in the USSR and, through inheritance, in post-Soviet Russia.

Perhaps the greatest danger posed by semipresidentialism in any country is a divided executive.[25] Although the president enjoys a fixed term of office, the prime minister serves at the pleasure of the parliament. The potential arises, therefore, for the parliament to insist on a prime minister with political views unlike those of the president. When this occurs, the president and prime minister are forced to "cohabit," to use the French term, an awkward arrangement that leads inevitably to tensions over the distribution of power between the two executive leaders. Success in managing these tensions depends on the personalities of the leaders and the broader circumstances as well as the correlation of political forces in the country. Although working papers prepared for Gorbachev and his staff alerted them to the problems of cohabitation under French semipresidentialism, the Soviet leader appears to have given little thought to the politics of a dual executive, apparently assuming that he would retain indefinitely the support of the parliament, and hence the prime minister.[26]

On the question of intraexecutive relations generally, Gorbachev seemed content with legislative provisions that ensured his right to propose the appointment and resignation of the prime minister to the parliament, to consult with the prime minister on the appointment of members of the Government, and to annul Government directives. From discussions with deputies in the weeks before the creation of the presidency, it is clear that Gorbachev expected the prime minister to function much as he had throughout the Soviet era, that is, to oversee the economy and, in Gorbachev's own words, to stay out of "politics."[27] This view failed to recognize, however, that the invigoration of parliament had raised the profile, and the potential power, of the prime minister. Moreover, it betrayed a naive belief that economic management, and public administration generally, could be reduced to a technical task.

The lack of precision and coherence in the new institutional arrangements reflected, in part, the political constraints within which Gorbachev and his aides operated. Redesigning institutions on the march naturally prompted resistance from those forces in the party, the parliament, and the republics that felt threatened by a strong presidency. Constitutional ambiguity and compromise helped to allay these fears. But the Soviet Union's new and confusing political system was also a product of Gorbachev's leadership style.[28] For Gorbachev, governing was less about carefully crafted organizations and rules than creating solutions through negotiation. He saw the president operating above the fray of daily politics and administration in a realm that transcended the traditional branches of government. He remarked to deputies in the weeks before becoming president that he would be a mediator between the executive and the legislature.[29] Traditional lines of authority meant little to him. Rather than disciplining the prime minister and his Government directly, Gorbachev proposed to do so through the Congress. His was the approach of an international statesman who sought compromise and not a chief executive officer who gave orders.

On some institutional questions, of course, Gorbachev had clear preferences. One of these was electoral rules. Few subjects excited more intense debate, both within Gorbachev's entourage and among the country's elite, than the method of electing the Soviet president. The choice was between some form of direct election by the population and indirect election by the Congress of People's Deputies.[30] Each option presented obvious risks and rewards to Gorbachev. Indirect election ensured Gorbachev's ascent to the presidency and a rapid, peaceful transition to the new institutional regime. But it also deprived the president of a popular mandate, and in so doing promised to solidify the authority of the Congress of People's Deputies, which would serve as electoral college for both parliament and president. Unwilling to risk personal defeat or the strains that a competitive election campaign would place on the nation,[31] Gorbachev insisted that the Congress select the first Soviet president, with subsequent presidential elections to be decided by direct popular vote.[32] The Congress agreed.

Virtually every political decision made in the last two years of Soviet rule was viewed through the prism of deteriorating relations between the center and the fifteen republics. The creation of a Soviet presidency was no exception. As pressures mounted in 1989 and 1990 for greater cultural, linguistic, and political autonomy, the authority of central party institutions declined, especially in the Baltic republics of Estonia, Latvia, and Lithuania. By shifting his political base to a state presidency, Gorbachev distanced himself from an increasingly discredited central party apparatus. Moreover, as president rather than the leader of a collegial Politburo, he acquired greater freedom of maneuver in his dealings with leaders of the republics. He appeared to believe that his diplomatic skills, used with such success in the international arena, offered the best hope for resolving the growing conflict between center and periphery in Soviet politics. But in case the politics of negotiation failed, the law on the presidency gave Gorbachev the authority to introduce a state of emergency or direct presidential rule in the republics "in the interests of safeguarding the security of citizens of the USSR."[33]

To overcome the objections of some republican leaders to the establishment of a presidency, Gorbachev agreed to grant them membership in a new body, the Federation Council, which would review policies on interethnic and interrepublican relations. But the more fateful concession was the extension of the semipresidential model to republican governments. In the last half of 1990, in a "demonstration effect" encouraged by Moscow, the fifteen Soviet republics hurriedly adopted the institutional arrangements crafted and introduced in the center.[34] Few understood at the time the dangers this concession posed to the integrity of the Union.[35] Newly established republican presidencies quickly became important symbols of nascent political communities, especially in cases where the local leader was willing to challenge the center. And just as in the center, presidents in many republics began to decouple themselves from the Communist Party, which had served to integrate the diverse peoples and territories of the Soviet Union. If before 1990 republican leaders—the Communist Party first secretaries—made their careers by proving their loyalty to Moscow, after the introduction of semipresidentialism they ensured their political future by appealing to republican interests. Unlike the Communist Party of old, the fledgling Soviet presidency had neither the administrative nor ideological authority to impose its will on the republics. There was no longer, therefore, a vertical command structure capable of ensuring the loyalty of local leaders.[36]

The introduction of direct elections for republican presidents in 1991 further undermined Moscow's authority. If the center still retained some ability to influence the actions of republican deputies, who had voted for presidents in the indirect elections of 1990, it carried little weight with ordinary voters. Indeed, in many republics the successful candidates for president ran against the center. The most dramatic example of this was in Ukraine, where all six presidential candidates urged voters to cast their ballots for Ukrainian independence in a referendum held on 1 December 1991, the same day as presidential balloting.[37]

To understand the collapse of the USSR, then, one must not stop at the traditional contextual explanations, such as a lagging economy, a crisis of identity and belief, and a more demanding population.[38] The institutional choices made at the end of the Soviet era recast the structure of incentives in ways that rewarded those favoring disintegration. Although there was much in Russian and Soviet history—and in the demands of the moment—to recommend semipresidentialism, there were other options that would have produced very different political outcomes, especially over the short term. It was the will of a small group of men to create a presidency constrained by a mammoth Congress and then to introduce presidencies in the republics, decisions that had momentous consequences for the Soviet Union and the world. Established in part to save the Union, the institution of the presidency contributed mightily to the USSR's demise.

The Gorbachev Presidency

The history of the Soviet presidency was brief and crisis-ridden. After only a few months in the office, Gorbachev realized that the presidency—like his former post of Congress chairman—lacked the powers needed to govern in an era of transition. He turned again, therefore, to the Congress to revise the institutional rules, this time receiving the right as president to introduce laws on economic reform, subject only to a vaguely defined legislative oversight. This shift of legislative authority came in the fall of 1990, at a time when the prime minister, Nikolai Ryzhkov, believed that the country had become ungovernable. The economic half measures of the late 1980s had broken the old system without creating a new one. In these conditions, Ryzhkov later lamented, it was impossible even to form a budget.[39] To overcome this financial impasse, Gorbachev considered using his newly granted powers to introduce one of several competing economic reform packages—such as the "five hundred days" program of economists Grigorii Yavlinskii and Stanislav Shatalin. But to the chagrin of many, especially the radical reformers, Gorbachev refused to commit himself and the country to a clear vision of the economic future.

Shortly after this shift of powers from the legislature to the president, Gorbachev realigned executive politics in a bid to strengthen the presidency further. When replacing Ryzhkov with Valentin Pavlov, the finance minister, in December 1990, he made the new prime minister head of a presidential Cabinet of Ministers, which succeeded the Council of Ministers, or Government, a mainstay of Russian institutional life since 1861. To the uninitiated, this measure may seem little more than a change in nomenclature. But the intention was to reduce the autonomy and visibility of the prime minister, as well as his apparatus, thereby shifting Soviet politics in the direction of American-style presidentialism.[40] There is no evidence, however, that the formal attachment of the Cabinet of Ministers to the presidency reduced the size of the Government or facilitated presidential control of the prime minister or the social and economic ministers who labored under him. On the contrary, Prime Minister Pavlov proved to be one of the least loyal members of the Soviet executive in 1991. After failing in an attempt to convince the Congress to expand the powers of the prime minister's office in June, he joined the conspiracy in August that sought to oust Gorbachev from the presidency and restore the traditional rules of Soviet politics.

The tensions between president and prime minister sprang from a division of executive labor inherent in semipresidentialism and in Soviet institutional traditions. In both the French model and earlier Soviet and Russian experience, the prime minister assumed day-to-day responsibility for social and economic management while the president, or general secretary or tsar before him, played the leading role in matters of national security. This pattern rewarded Gorbachev's passion for foreign affairs and his aversion to budgets. Under these institutional arrangements Gorbachev was free to reach strategic compromises, whether with foreign dignitaries or with the miners and other groups within the USSR. It then fell to the prime minister to make good on the often exaggerated promises of a president or general secretary.[41]

In important respects, then, the Soviet president functioned much as the general secretary had in the old institutional regime. The widely held view that "the party rules but does not govern" never accurately captured the separation of executive responsibilities that had characterized the Soviet political system. On a wide range of issues, from defense and foreign affairs to the media and agriculture, the general secretary and the Communist Party—not the prime minister and the Government—governed directly. Although formally members of the Government, the heads of such institutions as the KGB, the defense ministry, and the foreign ministry answered directly, and exclusively, to the general secretary and the party.[42] In this sense, the introduction of semipresidentialism merely transferred to the president the executive functions of the general secretary. That the prime minister's relations with the president never matched those with the general secretary reflected the decline of a shared ideology among the ruling elite, the contentiousness of the policies of perestroika, and the abandonment of collegial forums such as the Politburo, where the prime minister had been able to remain abreast of developments throughout the executive even if he did not always influence them.

Consolidating the power of the presidency required the building of an apparatus as well as redefining relations with the prime minister and parliament. At first, a number of Gorbachev's aides in the general secretary's office doubled as presidential advisors. Valerii Boldin, for example, was chief of staff to Gorbachev in both his roles as general secretary and as president, maintaining offices in the Kremlin and Old Square. But Gorbachev gradually created a separate presidential staff in the Kremlin, having removed the prime minister and his apparatus from the governing fortress under the pretext of office renovation.[43]

The institutional presidency under Gorbachev was, at best, a work in progress. Although he received carefully prepared plans from aides for the organization of the Soviet presidency, Gorbachev preferred to improvise—creating, merging, renaming, or abolishing offices as the mood and the political moment dictated. Initially, he viewed the Presidential Council, selected to represent diverse voices in the bureaucracy and society, as a substitute for the Politburo. But he quickly tired of the frankness of its members and allowed it to pass into oblivion after three or four sessions.[44] The presidency also contained a Security Council and a Federation Council, though they too met infrequently and had little influence on the shaping of presidential policy.

If there was a clearly discernible pattern in the development of a Soviet presidential bureaucracy, it was the extensive borrowing of personnel and methods of operation from the apparatus of the Communist Party Central

Committee. That Gorbachev recruited most of his presidential staff from among loyal and respected party workers should come as little surprise. While the Central Committee apparatus hired plenty of party hacks, who began quietly "migrating" to the presidency, it also employed some of the brightest and most politically astute personnel available in the Soviet Union.[45] What was less predictable was Gorbachev's willingness to replicate party practices in the presidency. In some cases, this represented little more than a continuation of long-standing political rituals. As one aide observed, the meetings of the Presidential Council were eerily similar to those of the Politburo: Gorbachev in the same seat, in the same room, with many of the same people, and with the same refreshments served at familiar intervals.[46] But more important was Gorbachev's decision to establish a large presidential bureaucracy that would oversee, and in many instances duplicate, the prime minister's apparatus.

Unlike in France, where the president maintains a staff of only a few dozen personal advisors, in the Soviet Union the president insisted on a fully developed executive management team of his own. Just as the party had departments that shadowed and supervised Government ministries, so the Soviet presidency began to create its own offices with responsibility for overseeing each major policy area. By August 1991, a growing presidential bureaucracy of four hundred persons operated alongside a Government apparatus of some two thousand persons.[47] Instead of reforming existing institutions and governing through them, he was creating parallel bodies designed to check the behavior of an ill-disciplined bureaucracy.

The development of the presidential apparatus, however, was glacially slow and largely rudderless, owing to the press of events and Gorbachev's inattention to administrative detail. His foreign policy advisor, A.S. Cherniaev, complained that Gorbachev spent more time preparing his inaugural speech than attending to the demands of the institutional transition.[48] Rather than building institutions, Gorbachev was increasingly dedicated to hammering out agreements with other members of the ruling elite, most notably the leaders of republics. By the end of 1990, he was less concerned with perfecting state institutions than with salvaging the state itself. The goal was to lead a process of negotiation between elites that would produce pacts capable of sustaining a viable center in Soviet politics. Such extraconstitutional agreements might then give rise to new formal rules and institutional arrangements. It was an approach common to regimes making the transition from authoritarian rule.[49]

The most important negotiations surrounded the struggle between the center and republics, which dominated politics in the twilight of Soviet rule. The logical forum for such discussions was the Federation Council, a presidential institution that brought together the leaders of the Union and the republics. But the desire for secrecy, informality, and a politically neutral site, away from Gorbachev's Kremlin, led to the convening of a series of meetings outside of formal institutional structures and outside of the capital, at Novo-Ogarevo, a government retreat on the outskirts of Moscow. Here, in the spring and summer of 1991, the presidents of the Union and the republics crafted agreements that promised to grant broad political and economic autonomy to the republics. Operating from a position of increasing weakness, Gorbachev reluctantly—and often angrily—acceded to republican demands, which would have been resisted a year earlier, before the unsuccessful use of troops in Lithuania (January 1991) and the direct election of Boris Yeltsin as the president of the Russian republic (June 1991).

The Novo-Ogarevo meetings produced a draft Union Treaty and several informal side agreements, among which was Gorbachev's commitment to replace the unpopular prime minister, Valentin Pavlov.[50] It was a pact that promised to revolutionize center-periphery relations and to revise yet again Soviet institutional arrangements. But on 19 August 1991, the day before the scheduled signing of the Union Treaty, leading members of the Communist Party and Soviet Government staged a coup designed to scuttle the Novo-Ogarevo agreements and to restore the old regime. Several of the coup plotters would later claim that Gorbachev backed away at the last minute from preparations for the introduction of emergency rule, leaving them to twist in the wind. Gorbachev had indeed been actively considering emergency rule as an alternative to a "pacted" settlement with republican leaders. But whatever the extent of Gorbachev's involvement in the putsch and its preparations, the failure of the coup on its third day benefited the republics—and most prominently the defender of the Russian White House, President Yeltsin—at the expense of the Union and Gorbachev. After three days of house arrest on the island of Foros, Gorbachev returned to a different country, where central leaders had lost the support of broad sectors of the bureaucracy and society.[51]

In the wake of the coup, Gorbachev fought desperately—some would say pathetically—to shore up the authority of the center. But efforts to revive the Novo-Ogarevo process inspired little interest among republican leaders, many of whom were vigorously encouraging the defection of central ministerial personnel to republican governments. During the fall of 1991, while this extraconstitutional transfer of governing authority continued unabated, Yeltsin and other republican presidents remained publicly committed to retaining a Soviet state in some form. They even envisioned a role for Gorbachev as the president of a new, if less powerful, Union. However, at a meeting on 7–8 December 1991 at Belovezhskaia Pushcha, near Minsk, Belarus, the leaders of the three Slavic republics put an end to the USSR, and to Gorbachev's presidency, by seceding from the Soviet Union and joining together in a loose confederation, known as the Commonwealth of Independent States. Most of the other republics quickly followed suit, though some, like the Baltic republics, declared their complete independence. By the end of December 1991, there was no longer a Soviet Union to govern.

The Presidency in the First Russian Republic[52]

The primary heir of the Soviet political and military inheritance was the Russian Federation, a republic that covered three-quarters of the territory of the USSR and contained 146 million of its 285 million people. When Gorbachev relinquished control of the ultimate symbol of state sovereignty, the nuclear black box, on 25 December 1991, it was the Russian president, Boris Yeltsin, who assumed command of the vast majority of the Soviet Union's strategic rocket forces and other military assets. Russia also took control of the Soviet Union's embassies abroad, the bulk of the Communist Party's extensive real estate and financial holdings, and the imposing state buildings in Moscow, such as the Kremlin. In a final indignity for the Soviet president, Yeltsin moved into Gorbachev's Kremlin office before the latter removed his belongings.

The history of the Russian presidency does not begin, however, with the transfer of the remains of Soviet central authority from Gorbachev to Yeltsin. The presidency of the Russian Federation was a political offshoot of the Soviet presidency. While similar in most respects to its progenitor, the Russian system had two distinguishing features: a vice president and different electoral rules. In the first, indirect elections for the Russian presidency, held in May 1990, the republican parliament required three rounds of voting before choosing Boris Yeltsin by the slimmest of margins. But indirect elections quickly gave way to direct, popular elections for the presidency.[53] In June 1991, riding a rising popular tide of anti-Communism, Yeltsin won direct election as president in a landslide, capturing over 60 percent of the vote in a six-man field.

For Yeltsin, the timing of the Russian presidential election was fortuitous. Coming only two months before the August coup, it provided him with a mantle of popular legitimacy that discouraged the coup plotters

Changing Locations: Russian State Institutions, 1991-1999

Location*	1991	1992	1999
1. Kremlin	USSR Presidency USSR Parliament Communist Party Politburo	Russian Presidency	Russian Presidency
2. Old Square	Communist Party Apparatus	Russian Presidential Apparatus Russian Government	Russian Presidential Apparatus
3. Ilinka St.	Communist Party Apparatus	Russian Presidential Apparatus	Russian Presidential Apparatus
4. White House	Russian Presidency Russian Government Russian Parliament	Russian Parliament	Russian Government
5. Okhotnyi Riad	Gosplan	Ministry of Economics	State Duma
6. Bolshaia Dmitrovka St.	USSR Government	Press House	Federation Council
7. Ilinka St.	USSR Peoples Control Comm.	Russian Constitutional Court	Russian Constitutional Court
8. Povarskaia St.	USSR Supreme Court	Russian Supreme Court	Russian Supreme Court
9. Ilinka St.	Russian Supreme Court	Russian Supreme Court	Russian Supreme Court

*Location numbers refer to building and/or street locations in Map 2.1.

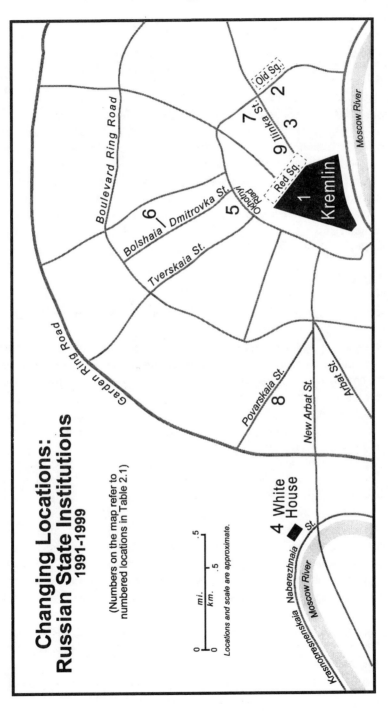

Changing Locations:
Russian State Institutions
1991-1999

(Numbers on the map refer to
numbered locations in Table 2.1)

Locations and scale are approximate.

from using force to subdue him and the defenders of the White House. The coup plotters' sensitivity to public opinion was readily apparent in lame attempts to cloak their actions in constitutional garb. As the coup unraveled, it was not only Yeltsin's actions but his more recent, and direct, popular mandate that allowed him to eclipse Gorbachev as the country's most powerful leader. In subsequent battles with the Russian parliament, Yeltsin again benefited from electoral timing. Elected more than a year after the parliament, Yeltsin could claim a mandate that was fresher and less tainted by the oddities of Soviet-era electoral practices.

The Russian president emerged from the August coup with enormous popularity but with little governing authority and only a skeletal staff. By the first months of 1992, the story was reversed. As economic, law enforcement, and ultimately military power shifted from the Union to the republics, Yeltsin acquired the instruments of rule from the dying Soviet state. If before the August coup Yeltsin's power lay primarily in his status as leader of the Russian nation, it now rested on a firmer institutional base. An independent Russian state was in the making.

Much like Gorbachev before him, Yeltsin received from parliament in November 1991 extraordinary lawmaking authority in order to introduce rapid economic reform. Moreover, in an attempt to prevent the centrifugal forces unleashed at the center from pulling apart the Russian Federation itself, he began to appoint personal commissars—and in most instances the governors themselves—in the country's eighty-nine regions. Finally, Yeltsin expanded dramatically his own institutional resources. The small staff of personal advisors working for the president at the time of the August coup grew quickly into a substantial presidential apparatus.

But as Yeltsin was expanding his powers as leader of state, he was losing the support of the nation. Growing popular disillusionment with the Russian president centered not on the accumulation of power itself but on how that power was being used, especially in economic affairs. In October 1991, Gennadii Burbulis, Yeltsin's closest policy advisor, had solicited economic reform proposals from the country's leading economists. The winner of this competition was a team of young economists led by Yegor Gaidar, who proposed a rapid, and painful, transition to a market economy, akin to the shock therapy applied with success in Poland. In December 1991, Yeltsin invested Gaidar—the new deputy prime minister—with the responsibility for introducing economic reform. Burbulis became "the de facto head of the Council of Ministers" and served as an intermediary between Gaidar and the president.[54] Formally, however, Yeltsin assumed the post of head of Government himself, aware that Gaidar's controversial policies and

Burbulis' limited political skills would expose them to a no-confidence vote in the parliament.[55] The deputies would be far less likely to challenge a democratically elected president.

The tasks facing Yeltsin and his Government at the beginning of 1992 were monumental. In the words of Ernest Gellner, few countries have sought simultaneously

> to dismantle an Empire, to operate an economic miracle, to transform a moral and economic climate, to turn a gulag state into a nightwatchman, to settle old national border and other disputes, and to revive a culture.[56]

On this ambitious agenda, it was the economic reforms of Yegor Gaidar that proved most unsettling to the population and parliament. Although the financial policies of the late Gorbachev era, taken together with the economic dislocations caused by the splintering of a single Soviet "economic space," contributed mightily to the twin crises of inflation and output in 1992, Gaidar's decisions to lift government subsidies and rapidly privatize commerce served as lightning rods for national discontent. At times, Gaidar's own political tactics complicated his policy initiatives. By continually referring to itself as a kamikaze Government, Gaidar and his associates limited their authority and longevity in office. As Anders Aslund observed, "[O]fficials and state enterprise managers treated the Gaidar team as a temporary phenomenon and consequently refused to adjust."[57]

The April 1992 session of the Congress of People's Deputies marked the first watershed in post-Soviet politics in Russia. It was here that Yeltsin lost a stable ruling majority in parliament. Studies of voting behavior in the Russian parliament reveal that the corps of deputies was divided at the beginning of 1992 into three roughly equal contingents: committed reformists, committed Communists, and a swing bloc without firm ideological loyalties.[58] It was this "centrist" group that altered the balance of power irrevocably in April 1992 by abandoning Yeltsin and joining the opposition.

The reasons for the parliamentary realignment lay partly in the changing agenda of Russian politics. Many deputies who supported Yeltsin over issues of statehood at the end of 1991 were unprepared to embrace the president's program of radical economic reform in 1992, especially given its destabilizing and stratifying effects on Russian society. But far more than policy disagreements were at stake in the widening gap between executive and legislative institutions in Russia. Politics was at bottom a matter of who governed, or, to put it in the less delicate language of early Soviet history, of who would devour whom (*kto kogo*).[59]

Just as the last two years of Soviet rule had witnessed a struggle for power between levels of government—the so-called war of laws between the Union and the republics—the first two years of the post-Soviet era saw a struggle between branches of government. In each case, the adversaries seemed to be driven by a Manichean instinct, a will to complete power, that would not be satisfied until it crushed its opposition. Underlying the institutional conflict were personal rivalries of brutal intensity. Commenting on the struggle for power in the late Soviet era, Gennadii Yanaev, the colorless Soviet vice president and coconspirator in the August 1991 coup, observed, "[T]he animal hatred between Gorbachev and Yeltsin, this was the subjective factor that played an evil trick on the nation, this is what eventually led to the disintegration of the country."[60] New nemeses for Yeltsin appeared almost immediately after the breakup of the Union in Aleksandr Rutskoi, the vice president, and Ruslan Khasbulatov, the speaker of parliament, both of whom, as we noted earlier, owed their political careers to the Russian president.[61]

Faced with an increasingly hostile parliament, Yeltsin made important concessions to the traditional forces in Russian politics during the last half of 1992. He scaled back Gaidar's radical economic program and reoriented his personnel policy. Brash young intellectuals—a group Rutskoi called "the boys in pink shorts"—were no longer in favor with the president. In their stead Yeltsin began to promote an older generation of Soviet-era officials, who were supposed to replace reformist zeal with administrative competence, and in so doing, to enhance the Government's support in parliament and the nation. "I was forced," Yeltsin remarked, "to bring in some energetic plant directors."[62]

Making policy concessions was easier for the president, however, than yielding decision-making authority to the legislature. In November 1992, the president was due to hand back responsibility for economic legislation to parliament, which had granted Yeltsin extraordinary powers in this sector for one year. As a means of retaining his prerogatives in the economy, Yeltsin insisted on the postponement of the December 1992 session of the Congress of the People's Deputies. The parliamentary leadership refused, plunging Russia into its first constitutional crisis of the post-Soviet era. In Ruslan Khasbulatov's estimation, this conflict between president and parliament "threatened the very existence of the state."[63]

With no constitutional means available to resolve the stalemate—neither president nor parliament could legally order the other about—Russia's leaders again sought a negotiated settlement of the crisis. Discussions between Yeltsin and Khasbulatov occurred in mid-December under the chairmanship of the head of the Constitutional Court, Valerii Zorkin. Each side made major concessions. The speaker consented to the holding of a referendum in April 1993 that would allow the nation to decide whether the presidency or parliament should be the dominant institution. For his part, Yeltsin agreed to select a new prime minister from among the three candidates who enjoyed the broadest support in the Congress. Following the Congress's straw poll and meetings with party leaders and regional governors, Yeltsin agreed to replace his unpopular acting prime minister, Gaidar, with a new prime minister, Viktor Chernomyrdin.[64] Chernomyrdin was a cautious manager with familiar and reassuring credentials for many conservative and centrist deputies—a technical education and three decades of experience in the Soviet natural gas industry.[65]

The four months separating the December accord from the April referendum was a period of guerrilla warfare in Russian politics, to borrow John Lowenhardt's apt phrase.[66] In mid-February, Yeltsin advanced a supplemental pact that would have committed both sides to respect a new demarcation of political authority and to refrain from actions that would "upset the balance of power."[67] However, parliament was in no mood for further compromise with the president. At an emergency session on 10 March, the Congress of People's Deputies reneged temporarily on its commitment to a referendum and called for constitutional amendments, adopted provisionally in December 1992, to come into effect immediately. These amendments would have weakened considerably the powers of the president. In response to this move by the Congress, Yeltsin issued a decree on 20 March that invested the president with extraordinary governing authority.[68]

This hastily prepared and controversial decree was a clear miscalculation on Yeltsin's part. Besides the predictably harsh reaction of Khasbulatov and Zorkin, there was vigorous dissent within the executive itself. Firmly opposed to the decree were Yurii Skokov, the chair of the president's Security Council, and Aleksandr Rutskoi, the vice president.[69] Rutskoi's refusal to give his visa to the decree brought to a head the long-simmering feud between the president and vice president. Rutskoi was now firmly in the camp of the parliamentary opposition, which viewed Yeltsin as a usurper.[70] When Sergei Filatov, the head of the Executive Office of the President, greeted Rutskoi, the vice president responded: "I won't shake your hand, you scum." According to Rutskoi, the following day Filatov reduced the vice presidential staff to six persons.[71]

Although the president removed the most contentious provisions from the decree before its publication, the stage was set for a decisive showdown between legislative and executive authority. Yeltsin believed that there was no longer a middle ground: the choice was now between a figurehead president or a newly constituted, and much weakened, parliament.[72] And the president had no intention of allowing his office to be transformed from an efficient institution to a dignified one by a parliament which, in Yeltsin's view was, like assemblies everywhere, "beset by sloth and scandal."[73]

When the on-again, off-again referendum on presidential and parliamentary authority finally took place on 25 April 1993, the voters gave Yeltsin the edge. Emboldened by what he interpreted as a renewed popular mandate—"essentially . . . a second presidential election two years after the first"—Yeltsin advanced a draft constitution that was designed to reduce considerably the powers of parliament.[74] To use the language of Adam Przeworski, the Russian president was attempting to adopt a new set of rules that would "fortify transitory political advantage."[75] But facing broad-based resistance to this draft, Yeltsin tried another tack, summoning a constitutional convention as a means of forcing through a draft constitution favorable to the presidency. The constitutional convention, however, faced enormous obstacles, including its size and diversity (seven hundred delegates drawn from the country's major regions and political forces) and the range and intensity of contested issues. Executive-legislative relations exercised passions less, for example, than the division of authority between Moscow and the regions. And besides drafting a constitution, the convention was responsible for proposing a method for its enactment, since the existing constitution was silent on this question.[76]

While representatives of president and parliament fought for advantage in the constitutional debates, each side was using its existing institutional resources to strengthen its hold on the fledgling Russian state.[77] The parliamentary arsenal included several executive-style agencies, most notably the Central Bank and the Procuracy. The parliamentary leadership used the Procuracy, which investigated and prosecuted criminal cases, to harass and undermine the authority of executive officials close to the president. Among those subjected to politically inspired criminal investigations were Mikhail Poltoranin, the head of the committee on information, and Vladimir Shumeiko, a deputy prime minister and close confidant of Yeltsin.[78] For its part, the Central Bank pursued an easy-money policy, which undercut attempts by the executive, and especially its Ministry of Finance, to battle skyrocketing inflation.

Had parliament's encroachment on executive authority been limited to its use of agencies such as the Procuracy and Central Bank, Yeltsin might have grudgingly tolerated the legislature's forays into what the president regarded as his domain. But the designs of parliament's leaders were more ambitious. They sought to restore the original concept of soviet parliamentarism, which called for executive and legislative functions to be combined in a single body. This strategy brought the parliament into direct competition with the presidency and Government for the loyalty of the ministries and regions, the building blocks of Russian state power. To enlist the ministries and regions as its allies, the parliament sought to outbid the presidency with promises of more generous financing and greater autonomy. According to the justice minister, Nikolai Fedorov, such tactics were part of the parliament's efforts "to create a parallel center of executive power."[79]

The ultimate weapon in the arsenal of the parliament was impeachment of the president, first broached by the opposition at the end of March 1993. As conflict between legislature and executive deepened through 1993, and the antipresidential bloc approached the two-thirds majority needed to impeach, Yeltsin's constitutional removal from office seemed a distinct possibility. According to the head of Yeltsin's Executive Office, Sergei Filatov, the president and his advisors were convinced that the parliamentary leadership would seek impeachment during the November–December 1993 parliamentary session.[80] For the president, the resolution to this conundrum was to dissolve the parliament on 21 September and hold new legislative elections and a constitutional referendum in mid-December. It was a bold, dangerous, and unconstitutional move.

The transition from the First to the Second Russian Republic did not follow the presidential script. Rather than accede to the president's demands, a rump of the parliament barricaded itself in the White House, the twenty-story legislative complex on the banks of the Moscow River that had served as the symbol of resistance to the Communist regime in the August 1991 coup. The legislators remaining in the building then voted to impeach Yeltsin and to install Vice President Aleksandr Rutskoi as the new president.

During the next fortnight, the standoff escalated toward civil war, as each side sought to present itself as the sole bearer of political legitimacy in the country. While delegates from the presidency and parliament talked with representatives of the Russian Orthodox patriarch in a well-publicized attempt to defuse the constitutional crisis, both sides were preparing for a violent conflict. As a former general with extensive contacts in the armed forces, Aleksandr Rutskoi mobilized disgruntled army and security personnel to the side of parliament. By the beginning of October, the White House contained an impressive cache of arms as well as an odd assortment of soldiers of political fortune.[81]

On 3 October, forces loyal to Rutskoi and the parliament launched an attack on the Moscow mayor's office, next door to the White House. Another contingent laid siege to the headquarters of Russian television, in the northern part of the capital. At this point, the loyalty of regular army troops to Yeltsin was in doubt. Armed units ordered into the capital had stopped at the beltway around the city, and even the crack Alpha force hesitated to carry out the orders of the president to attack. Its commanders reportedly wanted the Constitutional Court to confirm the legality of Yeltsin's actions. To tip the balance in its favor, each side had summoned the general population onto the streets of the capital. Only after the fervent, almost desperate, late-night personal pleas of the president to military leaders—and the felling of a member of the special forces by a sniper from the White House—did the wavering troops side with Yeltsin. Just before dawn on 4 October, tank crews loyal to Yeltsin took up positions on a bridge facing the White House and fired shells into the upper floors of the legislative building, setting fire to the abandoned offices of the parliamentary leadership.[82]

When the smoke cleared, Yeltsin appeared to have won a decisive victory over his opponents. The leaders of the parliamentary opposition were imprisoned, the members of the constitutional court—whose chairman backed the parliament—were sent on extended holiday, and the heads of Russia's regions were put on notice that Yeltsin would meet challenges to presidential power with force. Governing unencumbered by formal institutional opposition in the last three months of 1993, Yeltsin backed away from a promise of early presidential elections, revised the structure of the new legislature and the rules for parliamentary elections, and issued a draft constitution designed to elevate the president to a virtually impregnable position in Russian politics. Yeltsin's vision of the Second Russian Republic accorded with what Guillermo O'Donnell has called "delegative democracy," which rests

> on the premiss that whoever wins election to the presidency is thereby entitled to govern as he or she sees fit, constrained only by the hard facts of existing power relations and by a constitutionally limited term in office.[83]

David Remnick reported that two years into the new regime, all of the president's aides

> admitted that the illusion of a smooth and swift transfer from a communist dictatorship to a free-market democracy is gone. . . . Now the talk is of a transitional regime of "enlightened authoritarianism" or "guided democracy" or some such hybrid that makes no secret of the need for a prolonged concentration of power in the presidency.[84]

The Presidency in the Second Russian Republic

Yeltsin's extraconstitutional dissolution of parliament enabled him to advance two ballot initiatives for 12 December 1993, both designed to enhance presidential authority. The first, elections to a new parliament, was expected to produce a workable legislative majority for the president. Pollsters close to the presidency believed that the mood of the country, together with the electoral rules that the president himself had dictated, would permit the party of reform, Russia's Choice, to form the core, if not an outright majority, in the successor parliament.[85]

On 12 December, voters also cast ballots for a new constitution. Last-minute changes to this document dramatically strengthened presidential power at the expense of the parliament.[86] Gone was the Congress of People's Deputies, the most formidable constraint on presidential authority in the First Russian Republic. In its place was a more traditional, bicameral legislature, known as the Federal Assembly, comprised of a lower chamber, the Duma, and an upper house, the Federation Council, many of whose members were regional executive officials serving at the pleasure of Yeltsin. With a bicameral legislature, the parliament no longer spoke with a single voice. And even if both chambers were hostile to the executive, the constitution granted the president broad reserve powers that he could use to rule around the parliament.

Under the new constitution, which passed by a slim and still-disputed majority, the formal structure of Russian government remained semipresidential. A directly elected president shared executive responsibility with a prime minister, who needed the support, or more accurately the forbearance, of the parliament. But the rules governing the generation and accountability of the Government reduced to a minimum the parliament's ability to limit executive authority. According to the prime minister's chief of staff, the Government exercised executive power "independently [*samostoiatel'no*], subordinate to the president but not to the parliament, with whom it works in parallel."[87] Individual ministers were not subject to confirmation, recall, or sanction by the legislature, though they or their emissaries did appear occasionally at parliamentary question time.[88]

Although parliament retained the formal right to reject a president's appointee to the office of prime minister, or to express no confidence in a sitting Government, it could do so only under the most unappealing conditions. According to article 111.4 of the constitution, a president could insist on his candidate for prime minister through three successive rejections by the Duma, after which the president installed an interim prime minister, dissolved the parliament, and called new elections within four months. Moreover, article 117.3 granted the president the option of ignoring the Duma's first vote of no confidence in the Government. In the event a second no-confidence motion passed within three months, the president could opt to dissolve the Duma rather than sacrifice his prime minister. As the

Figure 2.1 **Leading Institutions of the Russian State** (1993 Constitution)

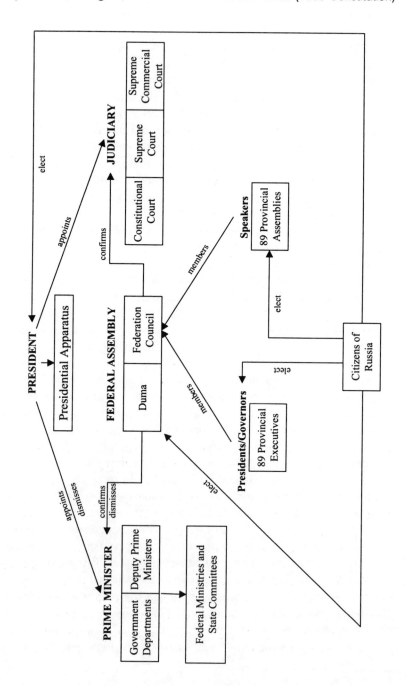

previous chapter pointed out, given the uncertainties of Russian politics and the dim job prospects for most unemployed politicians, few deputies would readily sacrifice their mandate to stand for reelection—witness the results of no-confidence votes in the spring of 1998.

The new institutional arrangements placed the president as well as the prime minister beyond the reach of all but the most united parliaments. To impeach the president, the State Duma first had to bring charges of high treason or other grave crimes against the president. These charges had to be supported by two-thirds of the deputies on the basis of a written opinion of a special Duma commission. As Vladimir Lysenko has noted, the president's power to dissolve the lower chamber—and keep in place the more malleable upper house, the Federation Council—"forestalls any attempt by the State Duma to raise first the question of impeaching the president."[89] Should the Duma bring charges, the Supreme Court had to issue a finding that the elements of a crime were present, and the Constitutional Court had to confirm that the Duma had respected the appropriate procedures in the bringing of the charges. It then fell to the Federation Council to convict the president by a two-thirds majority vote, taken no later than three months after the Duma's. In the event impeachment proceedings reached this final stage, the members of the Federation Council, many dependent at this time on the president for their executive posts, would be most unlikely to remove the president.

Given the broad powers and protections afforded the president, it is tempting to conclude that Yeltsin ruled without effective opposition in the last half of his first term, that is, from January 1994 through August 1996. Indeed, the constitution of the Second Russian Republic held that the president stood above all three branches—Government, parliament, and courts. Like the Communist Party in the old regime, the president was to "determine the basic objectives of the internal and foreign policy of the state" and "ensure the coordinated functioning and interaction of the institutions of state."[90] But these superpresidential arrangements did not in themselves ensure the implementation of the president's will in the daily affairs of state. Despite the obvious institutional advantages enjoyed by Yeltsin, political decisions resulted from a complex interplay of forces, among which were the vigor and skill of presidential leadership, the pressures of organized economic interests, and shifting divisions in the parliament, Government, and even the presidential apparatus itself. In short, neither the state nor society complied readily with the commands of the president.[91]

The limits of presidential authority became painfully evident to Yeltsin within weeks of the December 1993 parliamentary elections, which returned a Duma with an antipresidential majority. On 23 February 1994, the Duma voted to give amnesty to officials serving prison time for the August 1991 coup attempt as well as persons in jail awaiting trial for resisting the dissolution of parliament in the fall of 1993.[92] This measure represented more than a defeat on a matter of policy; it marked the rehabilitation and political revival of Yeltsin's personal enemies.

Stunned by what he considered to be a provocative and unconstitutional act, the president immediately ordered the procurator general, Aleksandr Kazannik, to block the release of his adversaries. To the astonishment of Yeltsin, who had recently appointed Kazannik to his post—under the new constitution, the Procuracy was subordinate to the president rather than the parliament—the procurator general acceded to the wishes of parliament and then resigned his office. It was clear that there was insufficient support in other law enforcement institutions, such as the Ministry of Internal Affairs (MVD), to reverse Kazannik's action. After several days of angry public statements and private discussions of his options with advisors, the president backed down.[93] In this episode, at least, Yeltsin exhibited an essential trait of a democratic politician, the willingness to accept defeat.[94]

Despite this inauspicious beginning, relations between president and parliament were not especially confrontational during the truncated, two-year first term of the Federal Assembly (January 1994–December 1995).[95] Several factors contributed to the more restrained political environment. First, the events of the fall alerted both sides to the costs of intransigence. The specter of a civil war seemed to push all parties away from the brink. In this sense, Russia was learning democracy. Second, the provisions of the 1993 constitution imposed a higher threshold of parliamentary consensus before collective action became attractive. Unable to effectively challenge the president on most matters, the Duma adopted a posture as the "conscience of the nation."[96]

Furthermore, contrary to the expectations of many, the speaker of the Duma in 1994 and 1995, the Communist-turned-Agrarian Ivan Rybkin, studiously avoided public conflict with the presidency.[97] Known in some circles as "Mr. Social Accord," Rybkin proved at least as cooperative as Vladimir Shumeiko, the chair of the Federation Council, who had been a close protege of Yeltsin before his move from the presidency to parliament in January 1994.[98] Because of a still-fragmented party system and the remnants of apparatus dominance in the legislature, the parliamentary leaders were able to resolve many disputes with the executive through private negotiations.[99] Unlike their predecessor, Ruslan Khasbulatov, Rybkin and Shumeiko were steady and discreet, if not always agreeable, in their dealings with the president.

For his part, the president attempted to anticipate and defuse potential conflict with the parliament by creating several new agencies in the presidency whose primary task was liaison with the legislature.[100] It was an effort to institutionalize what had been to that point haphazard relations between president and parliament. Rather than establish a presidential party or even a presidential coalition in parliament, the president introduced a kind of entente cordiale with virtually all forces in the legislature.[101] As part of this strategy, he sought to co-opt the heads of the two chambers of parliament by appointing them in 1994 to several key presidential structures, including the Security Council and the Council on Cadres Policy (*Sovet po kadrovoi politike*).[102] The advantages of this strategy for the president became evident after the beginning of the Chechen war, in December 1994, when, as fellow members of the Security Council, the leaders of parliament became mired in the Chechen debacle along with the executive.

The president's ability to restrain the parliament also rested on the more mundane grounds of financial dependence. Because the presidency's administrator of affairs (*upravliaiushchii delami*) distributed goods such as housing, telephones, and vacation packages to legislative as well as executive personnel, Yeltsin was able to use "dacha politics" to influence individual deputies.[103] An indication of parliament's frustrations with these arrangements came at the beginning of 1996, when the new Duma speaker, Gennadii Seleznev, insisted that responsibility for the maintenance of parliament and its deputies should be transferred from the president's administrator of affairs to the finance ministry. When deputies and their staffs failed to receive their pay in January 1996, many had assumed that the delay reflected presidential displeasure with the new, more conservative parliament.[104]

Electoral timing also restrained executive-legislative conflict. As new presidential elections approached, the opposition occasionally denied itself parliamentary victories in order to position itself for an assumption of executive power in the future. With the country in crisis and a presidential election scheduled for June 1996, the anti-Yeltsin majority in parliament preferred to remain in opposition during the presidential campaign. The strategy of the conservative parliamentary majority was to restrict Yeltsin's freedom of maneuver without assuming governing responsibility. Thus, when a vote of no confidence was held in October 1994, the result was what might be termed a "maximum losing coalition"—enough votes to distance the legislature from the executive and temporarily destabilize politics but not enough to force an early parliamentary election or to provoke a constitutional crisis.[105] For Yeltsin's opponents, there was nothing better than "a discredited Government hanging around the neck of the president."[106]

But in explaining the parliament's relative quiescence in the second half of Yeltsin's first term, perhaps no single factor was more important than the president's repeated concessions to legislative sentiment on personnel matters. Although the president stood behind his prime minister, Viktor Chernomyrdin, he was willing to sacrifice other prominent executive officials at critical junctures in order to placate a parliament that was hostile to zealous reformers. In the wake of the parliamentary elections of December 1993, Yeltsin removed from office several leading proponents of market reform, including Boris Fedorov, the minister of finance, and Yegor Gaidar, who had returned to the Government in the fall of 1993 to assume the post of first deputy prime minister. An even more far-reaching purge of the liberal wing of the executive came at the beginning of 1996, immediately following the December 1995 parliamentary elections. Among those removed from office were the long-serving—and long-suffering—foreign minister, Andrei Kozyrev, the head of the Executive Office of the President, Sergei Filatov, and the deputy prime minister and privatization tsar, Anatolii Chubais. With the ouster of Chubais, no vigorous advocate for radical economic reform remained in a leading Government post at the end of Yeltsin's first term.

If parliamentary pressure did not bring down the Government, it did at least remake it. When compared to those ousted from office, the new appointees were generally older, more closely tied to traditional Soviet institutions, and more suspicious of reform, qualities that served to blunt—at least for a time—parliamentary criticism of the executive. Typical of the change of guard was the appointment in January 1996 of Evgenii Primakov, a veteran of the Soviet security services, to replace Foreign Minister Kozyrev, who had pursued a decidedly westernizing line in Russian diplomacy. In abandoning his erstwhile allies, Yeltsin employed a time-honored tactic of chief executives: attempting to deflect criticism of their own leadership onto subordinates.

Yeltsin's willingness to accede to parliamentary and societal pressure for personnel changes was in part a logical, democratic response to growing evidence of a shift to the right in Russian public opinion. As the presidential election approached, Yeltsin sought to distance himself from the increasingly unpopular democratic and internationalist positions that had defined the early years of his presidency. This move toward Russia's political center was made easier by the president's own uncertainties about the country's reformist course. What animated Yeltsin in politics was not a deeply held commitment to democratic reform but an instinct for power and a fierce hatred of the Communist order. Thus, to prevent a resurgence of the Communists—this time through democratic means—Yeltsin was prepared to alter the pace and direction of change.

There was more than an electoral calculus at work, however, in the president's concessions to parliament and society. Had Yeltsin presided over a united, loyal, and efficient executive, he could have governed with fewer accomodations. But that was not the case. Deep divisions within the Russian executive weakened the president's hand and allowed regional and parliamentary leaders to play one part of the executive against the other. Thus, although the Russian president enjoyed vast formal powers, he lacked an essential ingredient of modern government—executive discipline, or what the British call collective responsibility. In Russia, unlike in Western democracies, the ministries at times were not agents of the president or prime minister but semi-independent fiefdoms that controlled vital national resources, from arms to energy supplies. Gaidar argued that "our ministries consider themselves first representatives of their own sphere of activity in the highest leadership of the country, and the interests of these spheres is very sharply divided."[107] For reasons that will become clearer in the chapters that follow, Yeltsin was never able to impose discipline on this unwieldy coalition of ministers. The absence of loyal executive agencies prepared to implement the president's will forced Yeltsin into frequent concessions and other political maneuvers to maintain his authority.

Unable to discipline the Government and its ministries through the normal mechanisms of patronage, law, and convention, Yeltsin—like Gorbachev—resorted to a technique of executive leadership with a long Russian pedigree: institutional redundancy. Where tsars in late imperial Russia had established their own chancelleries as a means of overseeing the work of state, the Communist Party created a vast Central Committee apparatus to monitor and direct the Council of Ministers in the Soviet era. Yeltsin was now forming his own inner bureaucracy, this time to shadow executive institutions inherited from the Communist regime. The institutional presidency, which grew to several thousand officials by the mid-1990s, duplicated a staff of some eleven hundred officials attached to the prime minister and his deputies.[108] It was institutional redundancy on a massive scale.

The formation of a presidential leviathan in Russia was more, however, than a calculated response to an ill-disciplined state administration. It also represented a part-socialist, part-feudal commitment to the full employment of the army of officials who were made redundant by the collapse of the USSR. At the beginning of the 1990s, personnel from the Soviet Government and the Communist Party leapt from sinking institutions to those still afloat. Many settled into the larger and more politically comfortable ministries, but a significant number clambered to safety on presidential structures.[109] Just as monarchical power revealed itself in earlier centuries in the grandeur of its entourage, so bureaucratic power expressed itself in an ability to hire more people and provide them with office space, telephones, cars, and staffs.[110] In Russia, as in the Soviet Union before it, the number of persons in one's retinue remained an important measure of authority. Thus, the extraordinary growth of the presidency represented a search for symbolic legitimacy as well as a normal human response to the pleas of supplicants desperate for work and its perquisites.[111]

By Yeltsin's second term, the institutional resources of the presidency were staggering in their scale and complexity. But like the formal powers of the office, in many respects they offered the mere illusion of political strength. Rather than enhancing the discipline of the executive, the president's own bureaucracy often undermined it through intrigue and self-destructive competition.[112] The size and political diversity of the presidential apparatus, the lack of clear jurisdictional boundaries, and the inattention of Yeltsin himself to problems of state administration created the conditions for a bureaucratic free-for-all within the presidency and between presidential and Government structures.[113] At no time was this more apparent than in the run-up to the June 1996 presidential election, when the presidential bureaucracy was deeply, and publicly, divided over whether an election should take place at all.[114] As one insider observed, there was as yet no clearly developed "technology of decision making" within the presidency.[115] By the end of 1998, when Yeltsin's health became ever more frail, the president seemed incapable of controlling even his own staff. Institutional redundancy was reaching its logical extreme, where "the position of the presidential apparatus no longer reflects the position of the president."[116]

3

The Institutional Presidency

Whether in Russia, the United States, or France, the presidency evokes three images: a leader, a set of formal and informal powers, and an administration assigned to shape and oversee the implementation of presidential programs. This third dimension—the institutional presidency—has attracted little attention from students of mature democracies, most of whom regard presidential staffs as faithful agents of the leader and therefore unworthy of study as political actors in their own right.[1] Whatever the validity of this approach in stable democracies, it is inappropriate for states in transition, such as Russia. There, the structure, personnel, and internal dynamics of the presidency may have a decisive effect on the use and distribution of power throughout the political system.

Turf battles, of course, are the stuff of bureaucratic politics in all states— witness the conflict in the Nixon administration between Henry Kissinger, the national security advisor, and Herb Klein, the president's communications chief. Out of the capital for a few days, Klein returned to the White House to find that a portion of his office had been appropriated—as a bathroom—by Kissinger.[2] But in Russia conflict within the presidency has not been limited to the usual jockeying for personal and political advantage by lieutenants. Officials in the Kremlin have squared off over the most fundamental issues of state, such as the relationship between executive and legislative authority and the pace and direction of economic reform.

Even more disturbing than the lack of a basic policy consensus has been the absence of even a minimal political etiquette within the presidency. Executive institutions cannot function properly without a measure of discipline and discretion, two of the finer cultural points of politics that enable the grand constitutional mechanisms to function. When disagreements arise within the Russian presidency, officials have been all too ready to pursue their own narrow agenda by mobilizing the press or interested political and economic elites. By dividing the Kremlin against itself, the president's men have diminished the authority and efficacy of the president and the presidency as actors in Russian politics.

The culture of discretion and loyalty among Russian officials, which had been a hallmark of the Communist regime, seemed to vanish with the old order. During the Yeltsin presidency, many aides insisted on an autonomy unthinkable in the Western, never mind the Communist, political tradition. It is easy to forget that democratic politics in the West presupposes more than individual freedom and government accountability. There must also be a strong, efficient, and cohesive executive. Russia has yet to construct such an executive. The current crisis in Russia, then, has its roots in the inadequacies of fledgling state institutions as well as in the strains generated by an ambitious policy agenda and an unfavorable political and economic environment. Weak states always rest on weak institutions.

One of the many ironies of Russian politics in transition is that state institutions have grown at once larger and weaker. One might have imagined that a shift in property ownership from public to private hands and a scaling back of the ideological and repressive machinery—all on a smaller territory—would have reduced considerably the scale and costs of government. But not so in Russia. Spending on the state bureaucracy increased from 0.23 percent of GDP in 1992 to 0.58 percent in 1994. Although approximately two-thirds of that expansion came in regional and local government, the uncontrolled growth of the state has been most visible, and troubling, in the Russian presidency.[3]

This chapter assesses the rise of a presidential leviathan by offering a brief historical survey of the institution and then a more detailed analysis of its several functional divisions during Yeltsin's first term. Personnel come and go, offices are created, renamed, merged, and at times abolished, but amid this organizational change the Russian presidency retained certain basic features. These include a corps of policy assistants, an administrative support staff, the Executive Office of the President, a security apparatus, presidential committees, and what might be termed "near-presidential" structures. These divisions form the subject of separate sections below, which explore the number and backgrounds of officials, the work they perform, and their sources of authority. The chapter concludes with observations about electoral politics and the state of the presidency in Yeltsin's second term.

The Development of a Presidential Apparatus in Yeltsin's First Term

Among the many crises experienced by Russia at its inception in late 1991, none was more pressing than the crisis of administration. Who would coordinate the vast state bureaucracy in the center and the provinces? The Communist Party, the "central nervous system" of the old regime, had collapsed without an heir apparent.[4] The absence of a strong center allowed the heads of ministries and regions to expand their own domains at the expense of the state. It was a pattern familiar to students of Russian history. "At the first sign of weaker authority," Gaidar observed, "the appointed governor starts to behave like an independent prince."[5]

The first and most important task of the Yeltsin administration was to contain the centrifugal forces unleashed by the fall of Communism and to build a new Russian state. To do this it was necessary to substitute a new "vertical" for the Communist Party, an institution that could hold together increasingly diverse and demanding segments of the state and society.[6] In Yeltsin's view, the presidency was to be the centerpiece of this new administrative structure, and the president the personification of state authority. "To put it bluntly," Yeltsin remarked, "somebody had to be the boss in the country."[7]

The Russian presidency began its development, then, as a functional substitute for the Communist Party Central Committee. But the replication of certain party offices and practices within the presidency also followed from the migration of Central Committee *apparatchiki* into presidential structures. Officials socialized for decades in a Communist administrative environment could not be expected to function like British civil servants overnight, especially when alternative methods of public administration were as yet undeveloped. Ironically, it was Communists and other conservatives who complained most bitterly about the parallels between party and presidency. But the case for institutional continuity has its limits. Although a number of presidential structures did shadow or duplicate Government agencies in ways that recalled party supervision under the old regime, the presidency operated in a very different political environment: there was no longer a single ideology, iron discipline, the cult of the general secretary, or what T. H. Rigby has called a mono-organizational society. That institutional redundancy was a shared characteristic of Soviet and post-Soviet politics does not signify the congruence of party and presidential rule.

If the first goal of the Yeltsin presidency was maintaining the integrity of the Russian state, the second was the construction of a new economic order. Both projects encouraged Yeltsin and his entourage to arrogate for themselves extraordinary powers and institutional resources. Yeltsin faced a classic dilemma of collective action when he launched economic reform at the end of 1991. With little support for the policy in the nation, and even less in the parliament and the ministerial bureaucracies, the president could not carry through the reforms using traditional democratic means. He insisted, therefore, on the acquisition of special powers, first for one year, beginning in the fall of 1991, and then on a permanent basis, with the adoption of the December 1993 constitution. Critics, including disingenous Communists, accused the president of employing neo-Bolshevik methods of rule. But the state forcing change on a recalcitrant nation was a Russian, and not just a Communist, tradition. In earlier centuries, Russian tsars had led revolutions from above. It was now the turn of a president.

As an agent of reform, however, the Russian presidency under Yeltsin exhibited numerous weaknesses. Perhaps the most important of these was the schism within the presidential apparatus between the friends and foes of radical change. On one wing of the presidency was a group of young, reform-minded policy advisors who favored a clean break with the old regime. The central figure in this camp was Gennadii Burbulis, a renegade ideologist from the higher party school in Yeltsin's hometown of Sverdlovsk (now Ekaterinburg). Although he had not known Yeltsin during his Sverdlovsk days, Burbulis rose quickly in the summer and fall of 1991 to become the president's closest policy advisor. He was the chief architect of radical reform and a patron for many like-minded younger officials in the executive, such as Yegor Gaidar, Andrei Kozyrev, and Sergei Shakhrai. Where Gaidar assumed responsibility for the transformation of the economy, and Kozyrev did the same for foreign policy, Shakhrai oversaw the reform of the legal system.

Set against this group of highly placed westernizing experts were traditionally minded presidential officials with more intimate ties to Yeltsin and to the old party and state machinery. Many lived in the same apartment building with Yeltsin in the Krylatskoe section of Moscow.[8] If the reformists dominated policy positions in the early Yeltsin presidency, the traditionalists occupied security portfolios and key administrative posts, which governed access to the president and shaped the flow of internal communications. Yurii Petrov, the president's first chief of staff, was one such offi-

cial. Petrov had worked under Yeltsin in the Sverdlovsk region and succeeded him as first secretary of the regional party organization when Yeltsin
was called to Moscow in 1985. Six years later, Petrov followed his patron
to the capital, where he acquired a reputation as an old-style party bureaucrat intent on limiting the influence of radical reformers on the president.[9]
Oleg Lobov was another Yeltsin protege from Sverdlovsk and an influential traditionalist in the presidency. The two first met on a trip to Scandinavia
in the late 1960s, and in the early 1970s Lobov served as Yeltsin's deputy
in the construction department of the Sverdlovsk regional party organization.[10] Although Lobov nurtured a public persona as a committed democrat
in the early Yeltsin presidency, he soon abandoned this mask. In his work
as minister of economics and then as chair of the presidential Security
Council, Lobov revealed his reluctance to dismantle important elements of
the old order.[11]

Because the president was continually tinkering with the mixture of radicals and conservatives in his entourage, the relations between the two camps
were in constant flux. Although presidential advisors were not constitutional officers, and therefore were not subject to interpellation or removal
by the parliament, Yeltsin used personnel changes in the presidency as a
means of currying favor with blocs of deputies and important regional and
economic elites. Like Government ministers, presidential officials could
be sacrificed at critical junctures to enhance the authority of the president
among select constituencies. At some moments, such as the beginning of
1993, Yeltsin would lean to the side of reform, dismissing Petrov as chief
of staff and appointing Filatov to the post of head of the Executive Office
of the President. On other occasions, the president purged radical reformers from key posts, whether Burbulis or Yurii Boldyrev, the head of the
president's Monitoring Administration.[12]

Amid the frequent reshuffling of cadres in the first two years of post-
Communist Russia, the reform-oriented forces in the presidential apparatus generally enjoyed greater influence than their rivals in shaping state
policy. But by the end of 1993, the balance of power in the presidency had
begun to shift decisively in favor of the traditionalists.[13] Several factors lay
behind this realignment, including the squeamishness of some liberals about
the use of force and extraconstitutional measures in politics. In his decisions to attack the parliament in October 1993 and to launch the war in
Chechnia in December 1994, the president relied heavily on the advice of
traditionalists in his administration. The head of the Executive Office of
the President, and the apparatus' leading democrat, Sergei Filatov, remained
"blissfully ignorant" of the plans to dissolve the parliament until the eve of

presidential action.[14] And Yurii Baturin, the president's national security advisor, was excluded from the Security Council meetings that mounted the war in Chechnia. Baturin had written position papers that warned the president of the serious military and political complications that would follow the outbreak of hostilities in Chechnia.[15]

The ascendance of the traditionalists in the presidency was of course part of a broader shift to the left in Russian politics, if by *left* one means that part of the political spectrum that is hostile to reform. The results of the parliamentary elections of December 1993 and December 1995, and a constant stream of public opinion polls, alerted Yeltsin to the growing gap between the conservative sentiment of the country and the radical views of one wing of his own administration. They also drove an increasingly embattled and disillusioned president into an ever tighter circle of advisors, some of whom were fierce loyalists but political neophytes. Yeltsin took refuge, for example, in his relationship with his personal security chief, General Aleksandr Korzhakov, and his tennis coach—and head of the president's committee on sports—Shamil Tarpishchev. Although these officials had no fixed ideological loyalties, they were clearly not committed to a democratic vision of Russia's future.

The temporary decline of the reformist wing of the presidency after 1993 was also due to the dearth of political skills among the radicals themselves. Most of the reformists in the presidency had risen to their high posts quickly from technocratic backgrounds, where public speaking, coalition building, and administrative competence were not highly prized. Many lacked an attractive public persona as well an ability to work constructively with officials who did not share their views. Alongside moderate reformists such as Sergei Filatov were numerous radicals whose uncompromising style made enemies everywhere, enemies who then encouraged the president to marginalize or dismiss the radicals.

The most prominent example of this hapless political type was Gennadii Burbulis. Possessing a high-pitched voice and an arrogant manner, Burbulis put together an impressive team of reformers in the presidency and Government. But he was ill-suited to the tasks of public political life. The combination of driving ambition and a tendency to alienate parliament and the public led eventually to his dismissal from the Kremlin staff.[16] Another archetype of the revolutionary ascetic was Sergei Pashin. As head of the presidency's Department for Court Reform, Pashin led the struggle to modernize and democratize the Russian judiciary, which had served as little more than an extension of the executive in the Soviet era. Perhaps his best-known achievement was the implementation of the law on the jury, which sought to revive an institution that had played an important role in Russian justice in the decades leading up to the Bolshevik revolution. Twenty-nine years old at the time of his appointment to a presidential post in 1992, Pashin showed little patience in working with legal officials and law scholars, even those who had been the leading advocates of legal reform in the late Soviet era. His tirades against senior judges and august legal scholars divided the reformist camp while uniting the opposition to radical change in the legal system. An increasingly isolated figure, Pashin lost his position in the presidency in the summer of 1995,[17] and then a judgeship in Moscow in 1998, allegedly for unprofessional behavior on the bench.[18]

Some observers view the undulations in the intrapresidential struggle as part of a grand strategy designed by Yeltsin to give the diverse constituencies in the country a sense that their interests were represented in the presidency, and also to keep his lieutenants off guard and thus incapable of coalescing against him. According to one Russian commentator, Yeltsin replaced divide and rule with "promote, dismiss, and rule."[19] It was a pattern of leadership that recalled the Stalin years, when the general secretary continually rotated factions in the Politburo in order to prevent any single group or individual from consolidating power. If this analysis is correct, then the politics of the presidential apparatus is merely an extension of the leadership style of Yeltsin. The president worked as puppeteer, pulling the strings of subordinates to advance his own, clearly defined agenda.

It would be a mistake, however, to portray Yeltsin as an ever guileful and engaged politician who carefully manipulated relations among subordinates. Indeed, his leadership at most points was anything but cunning and energetic. He tended to appoint a motley group of officials and then allow them to work with little supervision or direction. Even the highest-ranking staff members in the presidency had little personal contact with Yeltsin, perhaps a welcome pattern of behavior given the president's often abusive tone with subordinates.[20] According to Aleksandr Korzhakov, Yeltsin's security chief, the president so resented having to deal with paperwork that he occasionally vented his frustration at those who disturbed him with such matters. When the leader of the Executive Office of the President, Sergei Filatov, came into the president's office once with a stack of papers, Yeltsin remarked: "Put half of the papers away." In response to Filatov's query as to which papers he should set aside, Yeltsin responded: "It doesn't matter" (*da liubuiu*).[21] If Korzhakov's memoirs can be believed, by the mid-1990s Yeltsin had ceased watching television or reading newspapers, and was therefore increasingly isolated from the society that he was governing.[22]

Whatever conclusions one may reach about Yeltsin's contributions to the development of democracy in Russia, as the leader of the presidency, he exhibited an authoritarian personality and a remarkable disinterest in the everyday running of the state. With the exception of a few moments of high political drama—the coup of August 1991, the parliamentary assault of October 1993, and the last weeks of the 1996 presidential election campaign—Yeltsin was an extraordinarily passive president. His leadership style was far closer to that of Reagan than Stalin. In favoring a hands-off approach to management, Yeltsin accorded his aides and advisors wide latitude in the operation of the presidential apparatus.[23] The limitations and idiosyncrisies of Russia's first president clearly retarded the development of the presidency as an institution.

Rather than actively controlling the bureaucracy, Yeltsin tended to react to the supplications of officials in the presidency, the Government, and beyond. It was a style of rule associated more with traditional monarchs than modern chief executives.[24] Whether through established or back-channel lines of communications, the president received a steady stream of requests for favors: tax breaks from factory managers, decrees on crime fighting from law enforcement organs, and an expansion of office staff and responsibilities from presidential aides. Yeltsin's generosity in granting such requests deepened the country's financial crisis, undermined the integrity of the laws, and encouraged unhealthy rivalry within the presidential administration. Instead of a presidency with a clear division of labor between offices, Yeltsin permitted the development of competing centers of presidential power, each with pretensions to expertise and influence on a wide range of policy. Thus, not only did presidential structures duplicate the functions of Government, they duplicated each other. Institutional redundancy extended to the presidential administration itself.

Administrative Support Staff

Within the president's immediate support staff in the Kremlin were several personal aides, the Chancellery, and the business office. The Chancellery, a Russian institution since tsarist times, managed the flow of paper into and out of the president's office. By the mid-1990s, it employed twenty-two persons, who processed approximately 2,500–3,000 documents a day. Before reaching the president's desk, many of these documents traversed innumerable bureaus in the executive branch, receiving the required visa in each office. In most cases, the last office to issue a visa to a document before it entered the Chancellery was the secretariat of the Executive Office of the President. Highly classified materials, however, passed through the First Section of the president's administrator of affairs before reaching the Chancellery.

According to the chief of the Chancellery, Valerii Semenchenko, a former head of the Letters Department of the Moscow City Party Committee under Viktor Grishin, incoming documents and outgoing presidential assignments sit in a special order on the president's desk. Once the president signs or acknowledges the documents—Yeltsin's custom was to place a simple check mark to signify approval, an exclamation point to note disagreement—they return to the Chancellery and then back to the Executive Office. In the case of presidential decrees, the Executive Office's Administration of Business Correspondence issued each a number and date of issuance before it received the official stamp of the Chancellery of the President, formalizing its status as law.[25]

The Kremlin business office, known as the Administration of Affairs, has no parallel in Western public administration.[26] Overseeing the expenditure of roughly half of the budget for the presidency, 5 trillion rubles in 1994, the Administration of Affairs used these funds in part to pay salaries. President Yeltsin, for example, received his pay—26 million rubles in 1995, or approximately $5,000—from the Administration of Affairs.[27] The Administration of Affairs maintained for official use more than three hundred buildings and three thousand cars in Moscow.[28] It oversaw the reconstruction of the White House after the violent confrontations of October 1993. And it carried out most of the mundane tasks associated with day-to-day life in the Kremlin. In the words of the administrator of affairs, Pavel Borodin, "we put flowers and mineral water on meeting tables, and if protocol calls for it, stronger stuff."[29]

But it was also the responsibility of this business office to create "appropriate living conditions for officials." For top-ranking Russian officials, the Administration of Affairs made clothing and footwear, provided medical services, and built apartments. Yeltsin's health, for example, was overseen by a special medical division attached to the Administration of Affairs. Despite moves toward a market economy, officials of state continued to rely primarily on the goods and services provided by the Administration of Affairs rather than on their salaries. Just like the old *nomenklatura* class in the Soviet era, the Russian political elite lived off the state in a very immediate sense. Unable to afford a comfortable life on their salaries alone, members of the presidential apparatus, parliament, Government, and the courts depended on the presidency's business office to supply the accoutrements of modern life. In an astute political move, Yeltsin centralized in the presidency the distribution of scarce housing, summer cottages (dachas), cars, and telephones. Whether a leading official got one of the 20 dachas with a chef and security, one of the 150 year-round dachas without these amenities, or one of the 200 summer-season dachas could depend as much on his or her standing with the president as rank in office.[30] Dacha politics was therefore a potent weapon in the president's arsenal.

In many respects the Administration of Affairs was not a business office but a business empire. It brought under one roof several business offices inherited from the old regime, those attached to the Communist Party Central Committee, the USSR and Russian Supreme Soviets, and the USSR and Russian Councils of Ministers. These offices not only disbursed funds but maintained a network of factories throughout the country—a testament to the old regime's obsession with economic autarky and to the ambition of the last administrator of affairs for the Central Committee, Nikolai Kruchina. In a secret internal memorandum of the Central Committee's Administration of Affairs in 1990, Kruchina advised the Communist Party to create its own firms and companies, which would form part of an invisible party economy.[31] A year later, in the wake of the August 1991 coup, Kruchina committed suicide, apparently fearful that his dealings as administrator of affairs would prompt criminal prosecution. Whatever Yeltsin's and Borodin's attitudes were toward Kruchina and his office, they did not hesitate to accept the legacy of the old order. In addition to its responsibilities in the capital, where it employed a staff of 350, the Administration of Affairs ran seventy-five factories throughout the country by the mid-1990s.[32] It also operated a network of state-owned hotels and dachas, in Russia and the near abroad, which were rented out at times on a private basis. In all, more than thirty thousand persons worked in the various divisions of the Administration of Affairs in the mid-1990s.[33]

The Administration of Affairs in the presidency was an example of a widespread phenomenon in post-Communist Russia: a state institution engaged in private business. In the budgetary crises of the 1990s, locating a supplemental source of revenue was for some state organizations a matter of survival. At the most modest level, this meant that the Institute of Linguistics in Moscow let its basement to a Chinese restaurant, for which it received not only highly subsidized meals for its members but also rent payments that covered the salaries of scholars and staff. Most ministries and agencies—and even many individual bureaus—established extrabudgetary funds to enhance their revenues and therefore their independence from bureaucratic superiors. Such funds protected institutions from regular shortfalls in the central budget and enabled them to outbid their competitors for personnel. Income flowed directly to the agency and not through the state treasury.[34] This bureaucratic practice was also widespread in China, where the armed forces maintained a vast business empire of its own.[35]

The business operations of Yeltsin's Administration of Affairs offered the presidency a measure of security from attempts by the parliament to limit its expenditures. In addition, it created a slush fund that could be used by Yeltsin and Borodin to advance institutional or personal interests outside of public scrutiny. Hard evidence on such activity is understandably difficult to obtain, but it is clear that the president at times accorded special tax and export privileges to factories owned by the Administration of Affairs.[36]

Pavel Borodin followed an unorthodox route to his post as administrator of affairs. He was the rare non-Muscovite in Yeltsin's first term who did not have ties to the president's home region of Sverdlovsk. Born in the Siberian republic of Tuva, he worked as a carpenter and mechanic before receiving training in economics. After completing his higher education, Borodin moved to Yakutsk, where he was a member of parliament and mayor of the city at the end of the Soviet era. Yeltsin discovered Borodin in Yakutsk in early 1990, while on a tour of Siberia. Borodin's organizational skills on a harsh winter day in Yakutsk—it was 57 degrees below zero—so impressed Yeltsin that he brought the mayor to Moscow two years later to serve as the first head of the precursor to the Administration of Affairs, the Main Socio-Production Administration in the Executive Office of the President.[37] In January 1994, this business office became an independent agency answering directly to the president—an indication of Borodin's rising authority. At the end of Yeltsin's first term, only four other officers in the presidential bureaucracy—the leader of the Executive Office, the chief presidential counselor, the head of the Security Council, and the head of the Security Guard—enjoyed a similar state service rank, B-101.[38]

Like many other high-ranking officials in the Russian presidency, and very much unlike business officers in most Western countries, Borodin could not resist the temptation to combine political and administrative careers.[39] He allowed his name to be put forward by the Duma speaker, Ivan Rybkin, as the number four candidate on Rybkin's party list for the December 1995 parliamentary elections. In the event, Rybkin's party failed to receive the 5 percent of the votes necessary for party list representation in the Duma. Borodin was left to realize his political ambitions within the presidency.

The other financial powerhouse in the Yeltsin presidency was the Center for Presidential Programs, headed by Nikolai Malyshev. The five trillion rubles allocated to the presidency in the 1994 budget was divided almost equally between the Administration of Affairs and the Center for Presidential Programs. Where Borodin's office spent its money on the presidency itself, Malyshev's center distributed its funds among outside applicants from the state and private sector. In some cases, the Center for Presidential Programs financed regularly scheduled events, such as holiday celebrations in Moscow, or competitions, such as book prizes. In 1995, the center for the first time began to invest some of its funds in newly privatized enterprises.[40] But it also held money in reserve to respond to natural disasters or other catastrophes not foreseen by the annual federal budget.[41] Although formally a part of the Executive Office of the President, the Center for Presidential Programs answered directly to the president.[42]

Presidential Counselors

By the middle of the 1990s, four divisions of the presidency had broad, and often overlapping, policy interests. These were the Counselors' Service (*Sluzhba pomoshchnikov*), the Executive Office of the President (*Administratsiia prezidenta*), the Security Council (*Sovet besopasnosti*), and the Kremlin Security Guard (*Sluzhba okhrany*). The smallest, though most strategically positioned of these, was the Counselors' Service. Located in the Kremlin, in close proximity to the president's office, the ten-odd members of the Counselors' Service worked as Yeltsin's personal policy staff. Headed after 1992 by Viktor Iliushin, the president's chief counselor (*pervyi pomoshchnik*), the service included advisors in each of the major policy areas, much like the *conseillers techniques* who assist the French president. Each advisor had his own personal staff of several professional assistants, known as *konsultanty* or *referenty,* terms also used for staff specialists in the old Communist Party apparatus.[43]

Although the chief counselor presided over regular meetings of the Counselors' Service and exercised broad supervision over its members, it would be a mistake to regard him as the president's chief policy advisor or as the commander of a tightly knit team of policy counselors. The Counselors' Service was not a neat institutional pyramid, with information always flowing to the president through the chief counselor. In many instances, Iliushin did summarize, filter, or merely pass on information to the president from the diverse sectoral advisors. But in other cases, policy advisors communicated directly with the president, either in person or by memorandum. Although all advisors had direct telephone lines to Yeltsin's office for matters

Figure 3.1 **The Russian Presidency** (May 1994)

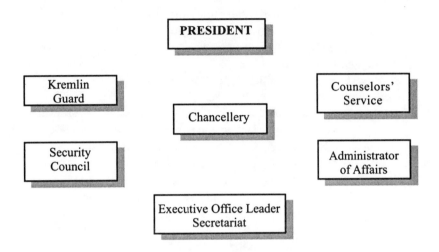

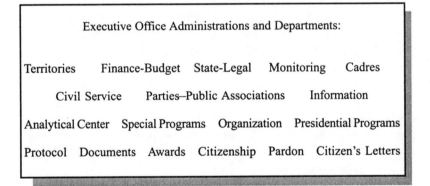

of great urgency, only a few enjoyed more than occasional access to the president. In general, the more important the sector and the more experienced the advisor, the more likely he was to be in direct contact with the president. Where Mikhail Krasnov, the young counselor on legal affairs, had only rare meetings with Yeltsin, Georgii Satarov, the political counselor, and Aleksandr Livshits, the economics counselor, saw the president more frequently, though still sparingly.

Among the members of the Counselors' Service, only Iliushin met with the president daily. After absorbing about two dozen reports that arrived on his desk early each weekday morning, Iliushin reported to the president at 9:00 A.M. He was usually the last person to examine documents before they moved to the president's desk for his review or signature. He also recommended new members of the Counselors' Service to the president. This unparallelled access and responsibility reflected not only Iliushin's position in the apparatus but his long personal service to the president. After an early career in the Young Communist League, the Komsomol, Iliushin worked for fifteen years as Yeltsin's personal assistant in Sverdlovsk before following him to Moscow. When Gorbachev unceremoniously removed Yeltsin as head of the Moscow party organization in early 1988, Iliushin also spent time in the political wilderness, more precisely in Afghanistan, advising the local Communist Party.[44] During the critical moments of the Yeltsin presidency, such as the August coup, the Belovezhskaia Pushcha accords, and the dissolution of parliament, Iliushin was at Yeltsin's side, helping him to craft key presidential speeches and decrees. Despite his title as chief policy counselor, Iliushin served as de facto chief of staff in Yeltsin's first term.[45]

The other members of the Counselors' Service rose to their positions based on policy expertise rather than personal ties to the president. Indeed, Yurii Baturin, the counselor for national security affairs, assumed his post in spite of his earlier association with Mikhail Gorbachev. After initial hesitation, Yeltsin put aside his reservations and appointed Baturin, who, with degrees in physics, law, and journalism, brought a wide circle of talents to the presidency.[46] Like Baturin, who came to the presidency from the Institute of State and Law, most other advisors had held posts in Moscow in policy-oriented institutes or think tanks before their appointment. Krasnov followed Baturin, his academic supervisor, from the Institute of State and Law. From 1993 to 1995, while Baturin held both the law and national security portfolios in the Counselors' Service, Krasnov worked as a *referent* for his patron. When a separate post of counselor for legal affairs was created, Krasnov ascended to this position with the support of Baturin and

Iliushin.[47] Previously an economics professor in the Institute of World Economy, Aleksandr Livshits began his service in the presidency in the Group of Experts, an analytical division of the Executive Office of the President. After rising to the chairmanship of this body, he transferred in November 1994 to the Counselors' Service, where he became Yeltsin's counselor on economics.[48] Before his appointment to the Kremlin staff, the president's political counselor, Georgii Satarov, had worked as a political science professor, the director of Moscow's Public and Political Center, and a television journalist on the popular public affairs show *Itogi*.[49]

The major task of the presidential counselors was to filter the deluge of information and requests directed to the president from other state institutions, whether in Moscow or the provinces. In the words of Mikhail Krasnov, Yeltsin expected his counselors "to decide which questions required the immediate attention of the president."[50] But if the gatekeeper function was the most time-consuming for the counselors, it was by no means their sole responsibility. They offered analyses of current issues in their respective fields and reviewed—and in some cases helped to draft—legislative proposals and presidential speeches. Early each year, Satarov, Livshits, and other counselors devoted considerable time to preparing the president's State of the Union address, required under the 1993 constitution.[51] By 1998, this exercise was costing the presidency a staggering $3.5 million, much of which went for the hiring of outside consultants and food, lodging, and entertainment for drafting groups who prepared the document at state dachas in the environs of Moscow.[52]

Depending on sector and personality, some counselors also served as spokesman and public representative for the president in their area of expertise. Where Dmitrii Riurikov, the president's foreign affairs counselor, shunned the public eye, other advisors, most notably Satarov and Livshits, actively courted the press. At times, however, it was not altogether clear whose position the counselor was espousing, his own or the president's. This independent streak was especially evident in the behavior of Satarov and Livshits. Queried by a reporter about the widely held perspective that relations in the presidency were chaotic, Satarov agreed with his interlocutor. Yeltsin had not yet introduced an effective "technology of decision making," he lamented.[53] For his part, Livshits confided to an interviewer the limits of Yeltsin's competence in economics. In Livshits' words, Yeltsin "doesn't know a lot [about the economy] and tries to help everyone. . . . [B]ut some people need to be imprisoned rather than helped."[54]

The political orientation of the Counselors' Service was, at best, cautiously reformist. Reflecting the tone set by its head, Viktor Iliushin, most counselors avoided taking resolutely conservative or radical positions on matters of policy. The philosophical tenor of this division of the presidency also owes something to the period of its formation. Most of the members serving at the end of the first term of the Yeltsin presidency had been recruited during the early part of 1994, by which time revolutionary romanticism had passed. This "middle generation" of officials appeared more interested in the accommodation of competing interests than in aggressively advancing their own agenda.

The political moderation of the Counselors' Service did not diminish its institutional ambitions within the presidency. Beginning in the late summer of 1993, Viktor Iliushin launched an assault on his major rival in the presidency, Sergei Filatov, the head of the Executive Office of the Presidency, which dwarfed the Counselors' Service in size. Iliushin sought to eliminate the duplication between their two divisions by merging their operations into a single institution, with himself at the apex of the new pyramid and his counselors in charge of all offices within their area of policy competence. As part of this campaign, there appeared a highly critical article on Filatov in February 1994 in the influential Moscow newspaper *Izvestia.* Only after a protracted bureaucratic struggle was Filatov able to beat back Iliushin's initiative and maintain the integrity of the Executive Office of the President.[55]

The Executive Office of the President

If the Counselors' Service has counterparts in most presidential or semipresidential systems, the Executive Office of the President is an institution unique to Russia. Officially established in early 1993, the Executive Office sought to bring under one organizational roof a disparate group of presidential agencies, ranging from the State-Legal Administration and Monitoring Administration to the analytical centers of the president. But at least during Yeltsin's first term, the Executive Office never succeeded in establishing clear vertical lines of authority or horizontal lines of jurisdiction between offices. Its many subdivisions enjoyed different degrees of autonomy and access to the president. In part a hierarchical bureaucracy, in part a loose confederation of offices, the Executive Office of the President defies traditional categories of organizational analysis.

Two features of the Executive Office are undisputed, however. The first is its mammoth size and complexity. From a small set of presidential agencies, the Executive Office developed into an institution with forty-three bureaus and two thousand professional staff members, most of whom worked on Old Square in the former headquarters of the Communist Party Central Committee, only a few hundred yards from the Kremlin.[56] In a purely presidential system, such as that of the United States, a presidential apparatus of this size would appear large, though unremarkable. The current White House staff in Washington, for example, includes more than fifteen hundred officials. But in the United States, there is not a separate executive leader—the prime minister—with his own extensive apparatus. The more fitting comparison, then, is France, where the Élysée Palace— home to the president—employs fewer than a hundred officials.

The unchecked growth of the Executive Office in the early 1990s attracted numerous critics in other divisions of the presidency and at both poles of the Russian political spectrum. At one point, a parliamentary committee explicitly attacked the duplication of offices within the presidency and the executive.[57] Bending to this pressure, Yeltsin ordered a reduction in the size of the institution at the end of 1993. However, the head of the Executive Office, Sergei Filatov, blunted this initiative by scaling back positions that had no occupants, an old Soviet administrative maneuver. Only on the eve of the 1996 presidential elections, with the removal of Filatov, did a serious downsizing begin, affecting an estimated one-quarter of the personnel in the Executive Office of the President.

The second undisputed feature of the Executive Office was its structural similarity to the Communist Party Central Committee. The Central Committee had maintained approximately twenty sectoral departments (*otdely*) to oversee state institutions in areas as diverse as law, economics, and the media; the Executive Office had similar subdivisions, the larger ones known as administrations (*upravleniia*), the smaller ones departments. Although the presidential administrations and departments did not command the same attention and respect in the state bureaucracy as their Central Committee predecessors, they performed many of the same functions. The various subdivisions of the Executive Office of the President supervised and in some cases duplicated the work of Government ministries and committees. According to one observer, the Executive Office was involved in creating "an ideology of reform, in developing an economic strategy, in monitoring the implementation of presidential decisions, and in cadres policy."[58]

Among the leading political institutions in the transition from Communism—presidency, Government, judiciary, and parliament—it was the most reform-oriented, the presidency, that began to revive instruments of rule associated with the Communist Party. How does one explain this seeming paradox? Both party and presidency shared a belief in the inertness and backwardness of the state and society and therefore the legitimacy of

Table 3.1

Leading Members of the President's Staff (May 1994)

Leader of Executive Office	*Filatov, S.A.*	Counselors' Service	*Iliushin, V.V. (Chair)*
			Baturin, Iu.M.
			Korabel'shchikov, A.I.
Deputy Leaders	*Krasavchenko, S.N.*		*Riurikov, D.B.*
			Satarov, G.A.
	Volkov, V.V.		*Sukhanov, L.E.*
Heads of Administrations:			*Kostikov, V.V*
			Livshits, A.L.
			Il'in, A.L.
State-Legal (GPU)	*Orekhov, R.G.*		*Pikhoia, L.G.*
Monitoring	*Zaitsev, V.Ia.*		
		Advisors	*Tarpishchev, Sh.A.*
Finance-Budget	*Moskovskii, I.D.*		
		Chancellery	*Semenchenko, V.P.*
Civil Service	*Kurbatov, A.M.*		
		Administration of Affairs	*Borodin, P.P.*
Organizational	*Chernov, V.A.*		
Territorial	*Medvedev, N.P.*	Kremlin Security	*Korzhakov, A.V.*
Information Systems	*Filippov, P.S.*	Security Council	*Lobov, O.I.*
Citizenship	*Mikitaev, A.K.*	Protocol	*Shevchenko, V.N.*
Pardons	*Ivanushkin, E.A.*	Press Service	*Krasikov, A.A.*
Documentation	*Matveenko, V.A.*	Presidential Programs	*Malyshev, N.G.**
Personnel	*Rumiantsev, D.D.*		
		Special Programs	*Frolov, V.A.*
Parties and Movements	*Shchegortsov, V.A.*		
Analytical Service	*Yasin, E.G.*		
State Awards	*Belova, V.A.*		

Source: Spisok telefonov rabotnikov Administratsii Prezidenta Rossiiskoi Federatsii (Moscow: May 1994).
*Also served as advisor

imposing change from above. Reform in the Russian political tradition was viewed as a general moral imperative and not as one possible outcome of democratic political procedures. In a word, substantive justice meant more than procedural justice. For this reason, the Executive Office of the President was willing to borrow what it regarded as effective techniques of administration from the Communist Party.

Directing the Executive Office during much of Yeltsin's first term was Sergei Filatov, a prominent reformer who, in the words of one conservative critic, advanced "abstract market ideas."[59] Filatov had first attracted Yeltsin's attention in the late Gorbachev era, when the two served together in the Russian parliament. When Yeltsin departed the parliament for the presidency in June 1991, he left behind Filatov as a deputy speaker. Increasingly marginalized in the first year of the post-Soviet era by the conservative speaker Ruslan Khasbulatov, Filatov—like many other reformist deputies—found refuge in the presidency, becoming head of the newly formed Executive Office in January 1993.

At its founding, the Executive Office included within its bounds virtually all presidential agencies except the Counselors' Service and the Security Council. Maintaining the unity of an institution of this size and complexity challenged Filatov throughout his tenure. In some cases he lost the battle, either through offices breaking away to attain independent status within the presidency, such as the financially powerful business office (*upravlaiiushchii delami*), or through their circumvention of Filatov's authority on important administrative or public policy issues. In general, the offices carrying the label "administrations" operated with greater autonomy than the "departments," which tended to be either subvisions of administrations or discrete offices concerned with support services rather than with policy matters.

At the apex of the Executive Office was a secretariat, which housed Filatov's personal apparatus and his deputies. In all, approximately a hundred officials worked on this central staff of the Executive Office of the President. The formal powers of the leader of the Executive Office enabled Filatov to appoint the heads of departments and the deputy heads of administrations and to recommend to the president candidates for heads of administrations. The leader of the Executive Office also confirmed the budget and staffing levels for each office as well as hiring and firing lower-level personnel within the administrations and departments. However, the formal titles and powers of officials were not always reliable measures of their authority. Much depended on political ambition, skills, and connections, especially with the central leader, in this case the president. Although

Filatov exercised considerable influence within the presidency and beyond, his contacts with Yeltsin were never frequent or intimate enough to allow him to realize the full potential of his office. With weak ties to the president and limited control over important administrations within the Executive Office itself, Filatov remained largely a symbol of democratic aspirations in the Yeltsin presidency rather than an efficient administrator directing the engine of reform.

Immediately subordinate to Filatov and his secretariat were several offices with responsibility for providing administrative support to the Executive Office or to the president himself. These included agencies such as the Administration for Business Correspondence and the General Department. Formed in March 1993, the General Department employed fourteen officials who coordinated schedules and assignments within the Executive Office and between presidential agencies and their Government counterparts. The department bore the same name and performed some of the same functions as an office in the old Central Committee apparatus. But according to the head of the General Department in the presidency, Valerii Chernov—a Komsomol activist from St. Petersburg whose previous job was in the State Standards Committee—the two offices were not comparable. "Our people don't lead [*rukovodiat*]," he argued, "they just monitor."[60]

As products of the Communist regime, officials in the presidency understood well the central role of patronage in politics. The question was how to develop in a democratizing state what the party had called a cadres policy. To ensure the selection and promotion of loyal and competent personnel in the Russian executive, Yeltsin authorized the creation of a Cadres Administration within the Executive Office of the President. Headed initially by Dmitrii Rumiantsev, this office provided technical support, such as maintaining files on eligible personnel, to a newly created Council on Cadres Policy. This small council, chaired through much of Yeltsin's first term by Filatov and Shumeiko, included leading figures from the presidency, Government, and parliament. According to the deputy leader of the Executive Office, Viacheslav Volkov, the task of the council was to revive the positive elements of the old *nomenklatura* system, which had guaranteed a large pool of trained personnel for key political and administrative posts in the Soviet era.[61]

The Council on Cadres Policy, working in tandem with the Cadres Administration, began to form a "reserve" of personnel, to develop policies for periodic performance reviews, and to prepare draft legislation on the civil service. In the mid-1990s the Council on Cadres Policy was still developing mechanisms for the selection and promotion of personnel.[62] In specialized fields, for example, separate subcommittees of the Council on Cadres Policy operated with considerably autonomy. The Commission on Higher Military Ranks (*Komissiia po vysshim voinskim dolzhnostiam*) reviewed appointments and promotions in the armed forces, while a commission on judicial cadres worked in conjunction with leading judges to make regular recommendations to the president for appointments to the bench. These commissions at times encountered serious resistance from other state institutions, with regional and republican governments asserting their own appointment privileges in the local judiciary and the armed forces objecting to certain promotions and dismissals emanating from the presidency.[63]

Although the president received information from all segments of the Executive Office, several subdivisions of the presidency were concerned exclusively with its collection, storage, or dissemination. This sector was to the 1990s what the chemical industry was to the Khrushchev era—the key to greater efficiency, or so the leadership believed. If information was power in all political eras, it was touted as a virtual panacea for problems at the end of the twentieth century. Among the more traditional information-related subdivisions of the presidency were the library and the archives. Inheriting the library resources of the Communist Party's Central Committee, the Secretariat of the USSR Supreme Soviet, and the Soviet Council of Ministers, the Russian presidency possessed one of the largest collection of books and periodicals in the country, some two million volumes. Presidential librarians not only maintained the collection, including over seventy-five newspapers and a thousand current periodicals, but produced regular digests and analyses of the foreign and domestic press for executive officials. Besides members of the executive, justices and staff of the Constitutional Court were among the users of the presidential library.[64]

The Russian presidency also became the guardian for the vast, and politically sensitive, archives of the Communist Party general secretary. The past can stir controversy in any country, but especially in Russia, where the Communist Party's insistence on a single historical orthodoxy required it to keep much of the workings of state from public view. Among the holdings in the presidential archive were fifty folders containing the complete records of Politburo meetings.[65] If in the early 1990s Yeltsin approved the transfer of large sections of the presidential archives to *Rosarkhiv,* the main state depository, which was open to the public, he began to adopt a less liberal approach to the archives later in his first term. Archival information was more than a curiosity; it was a potential weapon in the hands of the political leadership, which could selectively reveal its treasures to serve its own ends. On the eve of the presidential election of 1996, for example,

Yeltsin released new information from the archives designed to undermine support for the Russian Communist Party of Gennadii Ziuganov, Yeltsin's most serious opponent in the presidential race.[66] Georgii Satarov, the president's political counselor, had pressed for the declassification of these documents as a key element in the anti-Communist campaign strategy of the president.[67]

The Russian presidency also supported two important publishing ventures as a means of influencing the flow of information to the nation. The Executive Office owned and operated one of the country's leading newspapers, *Rossiiskie vesti*, which was published in Moscow and eleven other cities. Although the paper at times published material mildly critical of the president, its mission was clearly to enhance support for the president and his program. On the eve of the first round of the presidential elections, *Rossiiskie vesti* led with the banner headline "Vote for Boris Yeltsin."[68] Outside of the Executive Office, the presidency also operated its own publishing house, Legal Literature, which had also been a state-owned enterprise in the Soviet era. As the publishers of official digests, in addition to legal treatises, Legal Literature was somewhat akin to the Government Printing Office in the United States.

Numerous presidential bureaus had responsibility for the collection and dissemination of current information. Some of these were in the Executive Office, such as the Information Support Administration, the successor to two smaller offices, the Urgent Information Service (*Sluzhba operativnoi informatsii*) and the Department of Information Resources (*Otdel po informatsionnym resursam*). But in this, as in many other sectors, the Executive Office was in competition with other presidential structures. Until 1995, daily liaison with the media was the responsibility of the press service, headed by Anatolii Krasikov, and the office of the press secretary, Viacheslav Kostikov, the latter a member of the Counselors' Service. With the dismissal of Krasikov and Kostikov in May 1995, the two offices were combined into a single Federal Press Service, employing a staff of seventeen persons, within the Executive Office of the President.[69] The new head of the Federal Press Service was Sergei Medvedev, a respected television journalist who moved to the presidency from his post as anchor of the nightly news.

For a time, an even more serious rival to the authority of Filatov in the information arena was Mikhail Poltoranin, the head of the Federal Information Center and a close confidant of the president. After the August coup, when he had been at Yeltsin's side at the White House, Poltoranin worked closely with Gaidar and Burbulis in the launching of radical economic reform. Occupying the post of minister of the press in the Russian Government, Poltoranin attracted the wrath of the increasingly conservative parliament in early 1992. In April, Yeltsin removed him from the Government to deflect parliamentary criticism, but then immediately appointed him to head the new Federal Information Service in the presidency. Poltoranin sought to transform his office into a research and planning division of the presidency—an analytical center, in the language of the new Russian bureaucracy. From this post, he made numerous unsuccessful forays into policy issues, including a memorable attempt to negotiate a settlement with the Japanese over the Kurile Islands.[70] The Federal Information Service did not survive Poltoranin's unceremonious departure from the presidency in late 1993. Like many others who had stood with Yeltsin at the fall of the old order, Poltoranin became an implacable critic of the president by the mid-1990s.[71]

In the struggle for political advantage in the presidency, access to information was not enough. One also needed specialists who could synthesize and analyze information and then link it to specific policy proposals. This was the role of the analytical centers, which drew heavily on experts in fields such as economics and public opinion research. During Yeltsin's first term, these brain trusts sprung up throughout the presidential apparatus, including in the Executive Office of the President. At the beginning of 1994, three analytical centers coexisted in the Executive Office: the Group of Experts, headed by the economist—and future presidential counselor— Aleksandr Livshits; an Expert-Analytical Council, which brought together outside specialists for periodic seminars; and the Analytical Center for Socioeconomic Policy, headed by Petr Filippov. In May 1994, the three separate bureaus were intregrated into a new Analytical Service, led by the economist—and future minister of economics—Yevgenii Yasin. According to Yasin, there was a rough division of labor within this new institution, with the officials inherited from Group of Experts focusing on current problems and speechwriting while those from the old Expert-Analytical Council and Analytical Center for Socioeconomic Policy engaged in strategic planning.[72] Much of the information from this newly expanded Analytical Service flowed to Filatov through yet another addition to the Executive Office, the Administration on Information Support, to which Petr Filippov had ascended as head.[73]

The Analytical Service was not the only major employer of economists in the Executive Office of the President. A separate Finance-Budget Administration reviewed the country's annual budgets and oversaw the work of numerous Government agencies, most notably the Ministry of Finance.

The first head of the Finance-Budget Administration, Igor Moskovskii, had previously been head of a similarly named department in the Government.[74] Vladimir Panskov, a deputy to Moskovskii in the presidential administration, became minister of finance in 1994. And Evgenii Yasin, the economist in charge of the Analytical Service, shifted to the Government at approximately the same time to become minister of economics. As we shall argue in Chapter 5, the contacts between economic officials in the presidential and Government apparatuses were closer and more fruitful than those between other policy specialists in the executive.

There were two subdivisions of the Executive Office of the President with explicitly political profiles. The first was the awkwardly titled Administration for Cooperation with Political Parties, Public Organizations, and Factions and Deputies of the Chambers of the Federal Assembly. Created in August 1994, this administration combined into a single organization two existing presidential departments. Headed by Andrei Loginov, the new office sought to expand the social base of support for the president among the growing number of parties and associations that emerged in post-Communist Russia. Indeed, the original departments emerged in early 1993 as part of a plan to establish a single presidential bloc of parties in the parliament.[75] Although this effort was later abandoned, the office continued to cultivate parliamentary factions and selected groups in Russian society, carrying out the charge to "provide information to the president about political forces in parliament and society and to portray presidential policy to the latter in a favorable light."[76] Among the groups most actively recruited to the side of the president were the Cossacks, traditional defenders of Russian tsars and Russian borderlands.[77]

The Administration for Cooperation with Political Parties is an excellent example of how lines of authority within the presidency often disregard normal organizational patterns. Although a part of the Executive Office, and subordinate to Filatov on housekeeping matters, this administration took its direction from the president's political counselor, Georgii Satarov. Set out explicitly in the presidential decree forming the administration, this exception to the normal rules undoubtedly reflected the ongoing struggle for bureaucratic preeminence between the Executive Office and the Counselors' Service.[78]

The second overtly political subdivision of the Executive Office was the Administration for Work with Territories, the presidential office for liaison with the country's eighty-nine subject territories. The administration was led in Yeltsin's first term by Nikolai Medvedev, who had previously served as the head of a parliamentary committee on nationalities and the structure of the Russian state. A comparatively small bureau, with fewer than twenty full-time specialists, the Administration for Work with Territories prepared analyses of trends in regional affairs and responded to socioeconomic issues arising in Russia's territories.[79] The administration also served as an intermediary between the president and local authorities, especially the president's personal representatives in each of the subject territories.[80]

The Administration for Work with Territories was one of several state institutions involved in the endless negotiations between center and periphery over the nature of Russian federalism. Because Russia, unlike the United States, pursued a policy of asymmetrical federalism, where some territories enjoyed special legal—and not just financial—privileges, it was not possible to develop a single presidential stance on relations between center and periphery.[81] The primary sources of this asymmetrical federalism—a policy championed by Nikolai Medvedev—lay in the extraordinary ethnic and cultural diversity of Russia, which created different political demands in Tatarstan and Chechnia than in the historically Russian regions of Orel or Tambov.[82] Relations between Moscow and the ethnic republics occupied much of the energies of the Administration for Work with Territories, several of whose members had backgrounds as ethnologists. This concern with the interface between ethnic politics and federalism mirrored that in the Government's own Ministry of Nationalities, and at one point the minister protested loudly that the president's staff was duplicating functions performed in the Government.[83]

Much of the activity of the Executive Office was devoted to legal affairs, broadly defined. Even in the Administration for Citizen Relations, whose ninety-nine employees were responsible for processing the torrent of correspondence received from the public, a large proportion of the letters concerned current criminal cases or the behavior of law enforcement organs.[84] According to Mikhail Mironov, the head of the administration, formerly known as the Letters Department, President Yeltsin received approximately a thousand pieces of mail a day in early 1994, with criticism of law enforcement personnel second only to attacks on state policies.[85] Sergei Filatov noted that the same year every fourth letter of complaint concerned a court decision.[86] Those most likely to write to the president were pensioners, whose correspondence accounted for 72 percent of the letters reviewed by the Executive Office during 1994.[87]

Citizens also brought their complaints to the presidency in person, continuing a tradition with roots in the tsarist and Communist periods. With little faith in the courts as a source of remedies, the people of Russia turned directly to the leader in search of justice. On a side street near Old Square, opposite the Constitutional Court, the Reception Bureau (*priemnaia*) of the president greeted a steady stream of supplicants. Together with a similar office in the Government, the Reception Bureau in 1994 saw thirty-three thousand Russians, who came from all parts of the country to place their requests before the president.[88]

On some matters, the president was indeed the final legal authority and the logical target of petitions. Like chief executives in most states, the president possessed the power of the pardon, which he used liberally. Recommendations for pardons came to the president from a Pardons Commission inside the Executive Office of the President. Comprised primarily of leading intellectuals, a group believed to represent the least corruptible segment of Russian society, the Pardons Commission met periodically to review voluminous files on prisoners seeking pardons or commutation of sentences.[89] Assisting the commission in its work was a full-time support staff in the Executive Office's Department of Pardons (*Otdel po voprosam pomilovaniia*), which was headed by Yevgenii Ivanushkin.

There was also a separate Citizenship Department in the Executive Office, led by Abdulakh Mikitaev, which reviewed the large number of requests for Russian Federation citizenship. These requests came from ethnic Russians living beyond the borders of the Russian Federation at the time of the collapse of the Soviet Union—over twenty million found themselves outside of their ancestral homeland in 1992—as well as non-Russians in the near abroad who saw the Russian Federation as a political and economic haven. Russia's citizenship law, unlike those in many other Soviet successor states, did not seek to limit the influx of persons from other former republics or to render stateless persons who had migrated to the country in the Soviet era.[90]

As important as the bureaus above were for the lives of individuals, as institutions of state they paled in comparison to the two largest legal departments in Executive Office, the State-Legal Administration and the Monitoring Administration. The State-Legal Administration was created on 7 December 1991, to advise the Russian president on legal matters and to facilitate the establishment of a "single legal space" in Russia.[91] The latter function seemed especially urgent at the end of 1991, when, in the wake of the war of laws between Soviet central authority and the republics, Russia was beginning to assert legal and political hegemony over its more than fourscore subject territories. The fledgling state in Moscow sought to ensure that it would win the second round in the war of laws, this one between Russia and its provinces.

The origins of the State-Legal Administration also lie in the political ambitions of its founder and "ideologist," Sergei Shakhrai.[92] No other sub-division of the Executive Office has been so closely associated with a major political figure. Shakhrai transformed a small personal staff of legal advisors into an institution that could rival established ministries. Although Shakhrai departed the State-Legal Administration in mid-1992, its organization, functions, and personnel continued to bear his mark. In many respects, the profile of the State-Legal Administration was similar to that of a Central Committee office of the same name, known before the Gorbachev era as the Administrative Organs Department. They both monitored the legal ministries and oversaw certain personnel and doctrinal matters in the armed forces. But as we shall see in subsequent chapters, Yeltsin's State-Legal Administration had greater influence on policy than its party counterpart. It was a key gatekeeper in the legislative process, whether shepherding executive bills through parliament, advising the president on the appropriate response to legislative vetoes, or drafting and reviewing decrees for the president's signature. In this role, the State-Legal Administration worked at times in cooperation with the president's counselor for legal affairs, Mikhail Krasnov, and at times in competition. The State-Legal Administration, or more precisely its Department for Court Reform, was also the prime mover behind the radical reform of the Russian court system in the early 1990s. With its expansive legal and political jurisdiction and as many as two hundred officials on staff, the State-Legal Administration was arguably the most prominent and influential bureau in the Executive Office during Filatov's tenure.

Located in the same building as the State-Legal Administration, between the Kremlin and Old Square, was the Monitoring Administration. With a staffing level of 230 officials, the Monitoring Administration was the largest subdivision of the Executive Office of the President. Like many other presidential structures, it also replicated functions that had been carried out by a Communist Party organ, in this case the Party Control Committee. The Monitoring Administration even occupied the same physical premises as its party predecessor. Among the many administrations and departments within the Executive Office of the President, the Monitoring Administration was one of the most autonomous. While it continued to work closely with Filatov, after the spring of 1994 the Monitoring Administration answered directly to the president through the remainder of Yeltsin's first term.[93]

Perhaps the closest Western equivalent of the Monitoring Administration would be a national inspector general's office, which continually reviews the adherence of officials and agencies to the law. Because Russia still lacks many basic elements of a developed legal system, such as smoothly functioning administrative courts and respect for legal norms among officials, it relies instead on cruder methods to encourage central and local bureaucrats to implement the laws and policies enacted by president and parliament. One of these is the checking mechanism, of which the Monitoring Administration is the leading example. Where the Bolsheviks sought to impose order on an ill-disciplined state bureaucracy by creating a host of checking mechanisms, from the Workers' and Peasants' Inspectorate to the Party Control Committee, the Yeltsin administration attempted to use the Monitoring Administration as an instrument in the establishment of an effective executive "vertical." To carry out its charge, the Monitoring Administration conducts periodic on-site inspections of state institutions, from central ministries to local agencies; reviews complaints about bureaucratic malfeasance from citizens and businesses; and compiles information from in-house inspectors in federal agencies. Like other subdivisions of the presidency, however, the Monitoring Administration does not have enforcement powers of its own. On the basis of its inspections and analyses, it submits recommendations for action to the president, the leader of the Executive Office, or appropriate law enforcement bodies.[94]

The Security Apparatus

One of the striking features of the Russian presidency in Yeltsin's first term was the virtual absence of officials with portfolios in foreign affairs. Besides the office of Dmitrii Riurikov, the president's foreign policy counselor, a small part of the Security Council, and a Protocol Administration in the Executive Office, whose staff of twenty organizes overseas travel and the reception of foreign dignitaries, the subdivisions of the presidency throughout most of Yeltsin's first term were focused on domestic affairs.[95] In this sense, the Russian presidency was fundamentally different from the Communist Party, whose Central Committee had four separate bureaus with foreign interests: the International Department, the International Information Department, the Cadres Abroad Department, and the Ruling Parties Department.

But if the foreign policy staff of the Russian president was meager in Yeltsin's first term, the same could not be said of the domestic security bureaucracy. As a land-based, multiethnic empire, Russia had always maintained an expansive internal security apparatus to ensure order among its diverse, and often newly acquired, populations. While the image of Russians under arms is most frequently associated with foreign conflicts—the Napoleonic wars, World War II, and the Cold War—there has been no shortage of domestic wars, whether against peasants in the Pugachev rebellion of the eighteenth century and the collectivization of the 1930s or with non-Russian populations, such as the Poles in the 1860s or the Chechens in the 1990s. At a time of political crisis and resurgent nationalism, Boris Yeltsin sanctioned the creation within the presidency of a network of agencies concerned with internal security.[96]

Perhaps the most secretive security agency in the presidency was FAPSI, the Federal Agency for the Protection of Government Communications. FAPSI was in charge of information security, ranging from the black box for nuclear weapons and domestic wiretaps to the encryption of bank transfers.[97] All leading state officials used a telephone system—the *vertushka*—designed and maintained by FAPSI. As in the Soviet era, the number of telephones on a desk was a rough measure of an official's standing, and it was not unusual for a high-ranking Kremlin aide to have ten telephones. Where ordinary phones could be dialed to reach a variety of internal or external lines, phones in the *vertushka* were connected directly to a single superior or subordinate. Which of the two secure telephone networks— ATS-1 or ATS-2—an official used was also an indicator of political status, and apparently a matter for FAPSI to decide in consultation with the highest-ranking presidential aides.

In a country where the expression "That's not a conversation for the telephone" has not lost its resonance among those in power, FAPSI naturally aroused suspicion. Many believed that it fed surveillance information to political allies as a means of influencing the intraelite struggle. Two democratically oriented leaders, Sergei Filatov and Ramazan Abdulatipov, complained that their home phones were bugged by FAPSI, and a leading Russian journalist asserted that while the more visible power institutions, such as the Ministry of Internal Affairs, sought court permission for wiretaps in criminal cases, FAPSI violated the new antiwiretap law in the name of national security.[98] According to the Kremlin press secretary, Viacheslav Kostikov, all the presidential counselors believed that their phones were bugged, and therefore they exchanged written notes among themselves when they did not want the "big ears" of the security services to overhear them.[99]

The origins of FAPSI lie in the breakup of the Committee on State Security, the KGB, in the wake of the August 1991 coup. The Twelfth Section of the KGB was reborn as FAPSI, an agency that migrated first to the Council of Ministers before finding a home in the more powerful presidency. The total number of officials working in the agency is not known, though it employs at least three hundred scholars working in technical fields such as encryption. Like almost all presidential institutions, FAPSI has been reluctant to limit its activity to its primary mission of government communications. Under the leadership of General A. Starovoitov, FAPSI maintained a vast database in its Main Administration for Information Resources and it recruited a large number of armed personnel.[100]

Although the role of FAPSI in Kremlin politics remains murky, it is clear that the agency allied at times with other presidential security officials in order to limit the influence of the Executive Office of the President and its head, Sergei Filatov. In a series of complicated bureaucratic maneuvers in 1994 and 1995, Filatov and Starovoitov struggled for supremacy in the field of information security. In the opening gambit, FAPSI wrestled from the Executive Office of the President its Administration of Information Resources, absorbing its buildings, technology, and four hundred officials. But several months later, apparently under pressure from Filatov, Yeltsin sanctioned yet another bureaucratic reorganization, this time reducing the control of FAPSI over information resources. In the spring of 1995, Filatov sought to reclaim more power in this sector by creating a new Administration for Information and Documentation Support in the Executive Office, an office that asserted the right to review all proposals by FAPSI regarding the introduction of new technology.[101]

FAPSI's closest political allies in the presidency were the Main Security Administration (*Glavnoe upravlenie okhrany,* or GUO) of General Mikhail Barsukov and the Security Guard of General Aleksandr Korzhakov. Like FAPSI, the GUO was an offshoot of the KGB, more specifically its Ninth Administration.[102] With forty-four thousand personnel, the Main Security Administration was primarily responsible for protecting state buildings and leading state officials.[103] Among its troops were the elite Alpha and Vympel units, which played key roles in the events of August 1991 and October 1993. But the GUO's interests were not limited to Moscow or even to matters of security. It also managed an array of former Communist Party compounds and nature preserves that had served as vacation spots for high-ranking Communist officials, among which were two hunting parks in the Black Sea resort of Sochi.[104] Like all Russian state institutions, it was loath to part with its inheritance; its far-flung holdings were a matter of institutional pride and a potential source of income at a time of budgetary austerity. In 1994, Barsukov approached the president's business office with a request for several billion rubles to maintain rare wildlife on its properties and an additional billion rubles to introduce new species there![105]

During Yeltsin's first term, no subdivision of the Russian presidency was more controversial than General Korzhakov's Security Guard (*Sluzhba okhrany*). The Security Guard was not a relic from the old regime but an institution created especially for Korzhakov, a former KGB officer who served as Yeltsin's personal bodyguard in the Gorbachev era. Korzhakov risked his career in 1988 by staying with Yeltsin when the latter lost his post as Moscow party chief; he then risked his life in August 1991 by standing with Yeltsin during the abortive coup attempt. By all accounts, he was Yeltsin's most intimate and trusted associate during the first term. Yeltsin rewarded Korzhakov's loyalty by granting him wide latitude in the development of his Kremlin security detachment, which grew to some fifteen hundred personnel, including not just armed troops but personal aides such as the presidential photographer and cook.[106] In the summer of 1995, Korzhakov brought the Main Security Administration of Barsukov under his supervision.[107]

Korzhakov was unwilling to limit his interests to security matters. The Weberian ideal of clearly defined offices, jurisdictions, and careers had no place in the Russian presidency—everyone was interested in everything, whatever their current post or past training. Thus, Korzhakov, the former bodyguard, created an analytical center within the Security Guard to advise him on the full range of the country's political and economic affairs. The research center, employing from sixty to a hundred persons, was led by another veteran of the KGB, General Georgii Rogozin, who had worked for part of his career in military counterintelligence. Dubbed a modern-day Rasputin by one Russian journalist, Rogozin sought to apply his interest in parapsychology and the abnormal to the Yeltsin presidency. He ensured, for example, that the president's bed was aligned on a north-south axis.[108] On some weighty policy issues, Korzhakov took matters into his own hands, apparently without consulting the president. In November 1995, after Korzhakov and Moscow mayor Yurii Luzhkov had sparred over the boundaries of presidential and mayoral authority in the capital, Korzhakov dispatched an armed unit to the headquarters of the powerful MOST company in an attempt to intimidate its chairman, Vladimir Gusinskii, and his political patron, Luzhkov. Gusinskii and Luzhkov shared the same office building as well as broad political and economic interests. At the same time, Korzhakov was pressuring the prime minister, Viktor Chernomyrdin, to alter Government policy on the use of oil pipelines in order to favor Russian companies over Western investors.[109] Though Korzhakov's widely publicized lobbying on the pipeline issue led to his lampooning in the liberal press, it met with the approval of conservative figures such as Aleksandr Sterligov, the head of the Russian National Community.[110]

In the presidency and the nation at large, Korzhakov acquired the reputation of an eminence grise by the middle of Yeltsin's first term. In a poll conducted at the beginning of 1995, Korzhakov was regarded as the fifth most influential person in the country.[111] According to one report, he gained the right to review virtually every major presidential decision, including personnel appointments.[112] He also contributed to the revival of an atmosphere of secrecy and suspicion in the apparatus. Analysts with academic backgrounds in the presidency complained that information had become so secretive that they were reduced to using only open sources.[113] Even high-ranking officials in the presidency became more careful in their utterances. As the keeper of the Kremlin gates, Korzhakov could also limit access to the presidential staff. His men denied entrance, for example, to an *Izvestia* journalist who had an arranged an interview with Sergei Filatov. The journalist, it seems, had written an article critical of Korzhakov's action in the MOST case.[114]

In April 1996, as the presidential balloting approached, Korzhakov became one of the first officials in the Kremlin to call openly for the postponement of the elections. Aware that Yeltsin's defeat would bring an end to his political career and perhaps to his own freedom—several opposition leaders had called for criminal prosecutions of leading officials in the Yeltsin administration—Korzhakov began to search with his allies for extraconstitutional ways of maintaining his patron in office. This contingency planning ended abruptly, however, after the first round of the election, in June 1996, when Yeltsin sacrificed Korzhakov in order to install fellow presidential candidate General Aleksandr Lebed as the head of the Security Council.

The Security Council was the most prominent division of the presidency concerned with national security. Formed in June 1992 with a staff of only ten persons, the Security Council expanded quickly to a staff of eighty and then doubled in size during the next two years.[115] Besides the full-time staff, more than three hundred persons performed contract work for the agency by mid-1995.[116] Headquartered on Ilinka Street, which runs between Red Square and Old Square, the Security Council occupies three floors of a heavily guarded building—three checkpoints must be cleared before entering.[117] As the only section of the presidency mentioned in the 1993 constitution, the Security Council was in theory accountable to the parliament and Constitutional Court as well as to the president. But in practice it answered directly and exclusively to the president, who served as its chair.

Like the National Security Council in the United States, Russia's Security Council had two identities: a permanent support staff that assisted the president, and a collection of senior political figures—a cabinet of sorts—that gathered to discuss policy.[118] As a cabinet, the Security Council consisted of several permanent members with formal voting rights—the

Table 3.2

Security Council Membership (15 December 1998)

President of the Russian Federation*	Yeltsin, B.N. (Chair)
Leader, Executive Office of the President	Bordiuzha N.N.
Secretary, Security Council*	Bordiuzha, N.N.
General Director, Federal Agency for Government Communications (FAPSI)	Sherstiuk, V.P.
Prime Minister*	Primakov, E.M.
First Deputy Prime Minister	Gustov, V.A.
First Deputy Prime Minister	Masliukov, Iu.D.
Minister of Foreign Affairs*	Ivanov, I.S.
Minister of Internal Affairs (MVD)	Stepashin, S.V.
Director, Federal Security Service (FSB)*	Putin, V.V.
Minister of Defense*	Sergeev, I.D.
Minister of Emergency Situations	Shoigu, S.K.
Minister of Finance	Zadornov, M.M.
Minister of Atomic Energy	Adamov, E.O.
Minister of Justice	Krasheninnikov, P.V.
Leader, Federal Protection Service (FSO)	Krapivin, Iu.V.
Director, Federal Border Guards	Totskii, K.V.
Director, Foreign Intelligence Service (SVR)	Trubnikov, V.I.
President, Russian Academy of Sciences	Osipov, Iu.S.

*Offices that come with permanent membership on the Security Council.

president, the prime minister, the secretary of the Security Council, and the speakers of both houses of parliament—and numerous members with a consultative voice, including the ministers of interior, defense, finance, justice, and atomic energy and the heads of the various offshoots of the KGB, such as the border troops, the Federal Security Service (FSB), and the foreign intelligence and counterintelligence services. Other officials, such as Viktor Iliushin and the president's counselor on national security affairs, Yurii Baturin, were regular visitors to the meetings, which were usually held monthly, with a single major item on the agenda.[119] There were also a dozen specialized Security Council commissions that drew members from throughout the executive branch. With profiles as diverse as information and economic security, the commissions worked with widely varying degrees of intensity. Some met as infrequently as every six months.

Especially in their formative stages, institutions bear the unmistakable imprint of their leaders, who help to define their jurisdiction, to forge a pattern of relations with subordinates and superiors, and to establish the institution's culture and method of internal operation. Because the Security Council had very different secretaries during the Yeltsin presidency, it resists generalizations that extend much beyond its structure and formal mission. The first leader of the Security Council, Yurii Skokov, was an inscrutable middle-aged manager from the military-industrial complex, with conservative views and wide-ranging political ambitions. Skokov sought to create a Security Council staff that would serve as an intermediary between the president and the so-called power ministries in the Government, such as defense and internal affairs. He wanted the Security Council staff to supervise the operations of the power ministries and not just to advise the president on policy matters. One plan for achieving this involved transferring the General Staff from the Ministry of Defense to the Security Council.[120] In essence, Skokov was reviving Sergei Shakhrai's bold attempt in early 1992 to create a superministry of security. That effort failed when the Constitutional Court ruled the initiative unconstitutional. But Skokov's designs were not limited to the security field. In a controversial—and apparently hurriedly prepared—presidential decree issued in early July 1992, the Security Council received broad powers to impose its decisions on all federal and local agencies. These newly won powers prompted some commentators to view Skokov's Security Council as a Politburo in the making.[121]

That the Security Council did not develop into a new Politburo owes much to its many enemies in Moscow. In the words of one journalist, "[T]here are quite a few people who want to abolish the Security Council entirely or scrap the post of secretary—such ideas have been put forward a number of times by [Defense Minister Andrei] Grachev, [Foreign Minister Andrei] Kozyrev, and [Internal Affairs Minister Viktor] Yerin, not to mention . . . [privatization tsar Anatolii] Chubais and Gaidar."[122] Skokov's plans for the Security Council met with fierce and effective resistance from the power ministries, which were jealous of their autonomy and direct access to the president, and from the parliament, which feared any shift of decision-making authority from the Government to presidential institutions. Unlike Government ministries, presidential structures operated outside the scrutiny of parliament.[123] Skokov had adversaries within the presidency as well, most notably Sergei Filatov, who as head of the Executive Office sought to contain the development of the Security Council, in which he had been denied membership. In his struggle with Skokov, Filatov succeeded in transferring some of the Security Council's functions to the Executive Office of the President in early 1993.[124]

Various institutions targeted by Skokov restricted the power of the Security Council by denying it full and fresh information on their areas of competence. A Security Council staff member revealed that Skokov received no materials from the Foreign Ministry, and very little from the Ministry of Internal Affairs. He was forced to rely instead on information collected by FAPSI and the intelligence services, which limited his ability to develop policy positions in key areas.[125] Although the Security Council had its own permanent staff, it also housed personnel seconded from Government ministries, especially the Defense Ministry. This rotation of cadres through the Security Council—a practice common to Western presidencies as well as the Communist Party Central Committee—was apparently designed to bring expertise to the Security Council and to enhance the coordination of policy among different security agencies. But these seconded officials may also have served as informants for their primary institutions, thus limiting further the autonomy and influence of the Security Council and its secretary.[126]

Frustrated in his designs for the Security Council and in his bid to succeed Gaidar as prime minister, Skokov began to distance himself from Yeltsin. On 10 May 1993, he lost his post as secretary of the Security Council and began a gradual political march toward the opposition, creating short-lived alliances and institutions in the quest for a new political base. He remained for a time at the edge of Yeltsin's entourage, and in early 1994 was appointed cochair—with Filatov—of a new Council on Cadres Policy, yet another example of Yeltsin's strategy of balancing the competing wings of his presidency. However, Skokov would later break completely with the president and form his own party, the Congress of Russian Communities, a peculiar mix of factory managers and nationalists. Despite attracting General Aleksandr Lebed to his ticket for the parliamentary elections of December 1995, Skokov was unable to win any party-list seats in the Duma, thus joining the growing list of renegades from the president who were resigned to the political wilderness. Yeltsin admitted, only partly in jest, that some of his former allies had formed their own political party, the "party of the offended" (*partiia obizhennykh*).[127]

After an unsuccessful attempt to install General Yevgenii Shaposhnikov as Skokov's successor, Yeltsin settled on Oleg Lobov as the new secretary of the Security Council. Lobov assumed the position in September 1993, on the heels of his dismissal from the Ministry of Economics. As economics minister, Lobov had incurred the wrath of reformers by calling for an increase in state control of the economy. Unlike Skokov, who casted about endlessly for bureaucratic alliances, Lobov—as Yeltsin's longtime protege—

seemed content to remain dependent on the president alone.[128] But while Lobov remained personally loyal to the president, the same could not always be said of the Security Council itself. According to one source, "[T]he president thinks that the Security Council is primarily Lobov, 'his man.' But it is a collection of the most diverse politicians, seasoned, shrewd and calculating, who have their own interests and goals."[129]

Under Lobov's leadership, the Security Council concentrated its energies almost exclusively on domestic affairs. To be sure, the Security Council did have a Strategic Security Department, headed by for a time by the deputy secretary, and professional diplomat, Yurii Nazarkin.[130] The Security Council also assumed responsibility for outfitting the president's situation room in the mid-1990s.[131] At times the Security Council played a modest role in international affairs, receiving the Cuban ambassador or discussing the procedures for the ratification of the SALT II treaty. The minister of foreign affairs, Andrei Kozyrev, was a member of the body after January 1994, an appointment Kozyrev must have accepted with ambivalence—at one Security Council meeting, the defense minister, Pavel Grachev, bluntly criticized the foreign minister and demanded his resignation.[132] But following Skokov's unsuccessful forays into foreign policy, the Security Council remained on the periphery of Russian foreign-policy making. In the words of an observer, "[T]he belatedly established-foreign policy structure in the Security Council all but collapsed" after Skokov left office.[133]

In his first year as secretary of the Security Council, Lobov focused on issues of economic security, such as trade and industrial policy and what he suspected was criminal manipulation of the ruble by currency speculators in October 1994.[134] Five months earlier, in June 1994, Yeltsin had placed Lobov in charge of a broad-based effort to reduce crime and corruption, an initiative that appears to have originated in the Ministry of Internal Affairs. This ministry stood to benefit most directly from presidential decrees that expanded dramatically the prerogatives of the police at the expense of criminal suspects. Yeltsin's crime-fighting decrees also revived other policies associated with the old regime. Within two months of the issuance of the decree, for example, all color copiers in the country were to be registered with the Ministry of Internal Affairs.[135] Like many campaigns in the Soviet and post-Soviet eras, the fight against crime and corruption advanced narrow institutional interests rather than sound public policy. A year earlier, there had been a serious attempt by the young head of the president's Monitoring Administration, Yurii Boldyrev, to attack official corruption. Yeltsin removed Boldyrev, however, before his investigations could lead to criminal charges against leading officials.[136]

The development of the Security Council under Lobov took a decisive turn in December 1994, when it became the primary forum for decision making on the conflict in Chechnia. Until that point, the Security Council had been an institution in search of a mission, dabbling in security issues as diverse as the brain drain of Russian scientists, defense conversion, the declining health of the Russian population, and relations with the former Soviet republics—the so-called near abroad. The war in Chechnia gave it a definite reason for being, though the decision to send in troops on a massive scale did not enjoy the full support of the Security Council. Indeed, the justice minister, Yurii Kalmykov, a native of the Caucasus, resigned over the Chechen war. He complained that several Security Council members, including himself, Vladimir Shumeiko, and the head of the foreign intelligence services, Yevgenii Primakov, favored alternatives to the military option. But Yeltsin allowed discussion of the matter only after a vote on the use of force had been taken at the fateful Security Council meeting.[137]

Responsible for launching and overseeing the hostilities in Chechnia, the Security Council became Russia's war cabinet, and in August 1995, Yeltsin designated Lobov as the president's representative in Chechnia. The fate of the Security Council, and of Lobov personally, was now tied inextricably to the conflict in the Caucasus. Despite the assurances of Defense Minister Pavel Grachev that Russian troops would regain control of the breakaway republic in a matter of days, the war dragged on with no resolution. The failure of the military option in Chechnia—taken together with brazen hostage taking by Chechen guerrillas in neighboring regions— undermined the authority of the Russian army and the Russian president. The image of Yeltsin as war leader suffered immeasurable damage during the hostage crisis in Budennovsk, in October 1995, when it fell to the prime minister, Viktor Chernomyrdin, to negotiate the release of a large number of Russian civilians held by Chechen fighters. The war also exacerbated the already tense relations between members of the executive apparatus. In an outburst on Russian television, General Korzhakov noted that "Grachev dragged Yeltsin into the Chechen mess, and a man of integrity in Grachev's shoes would have shot himself."[138]

With over thirty thousand deaths by the beginning of 1996, the Chechen war threatened to scuttle the president's reelection efforts. Recognizing at last the unpopularity of the war, Yeltsin committed himself in February 1996 to ending the conflict before the elections. It was a difficult promise to keep. Yeltsin maneuvered the Chechen leader into signing a cease-fire in Moscow in May, but the Russian president was unable—or unwilling— to restrain Russian forces on the ground, who seemed intent on presenting the president with a military victory in Chechnia before the elections. In the usual dissonance characterizing Russian public life, media accounts of the war's end competed with stories about continuing hostitilies in the region. But in one brilliant tactical stroke made between the first and second rounds of the presidential elections, Yeltsin calmed public fears about Chechnia. On 18 June 1996, he replaced Oleg Lobov—whose political authority and health had declined in the preceding months—with General Aleksandr Lebed, the Moldovan and Afghan war hero and presidential candidate, who had garnered a surprising 15 percent of the vote in the first round. At the head of the Security Council was now a respected general who promised to end the Chechen war and to fight corruption aggressively. It was a measure of Lebed's bargaining power with Yeltsin that he also replaced Yurii Baturin as the president's counselor for national security affairs.[139] Baturin's office in the Counselors' Service had long competed with the secretary of the Security Council for the president's attention in security matters.[140]

Presidential Representatives, Committees, and "Near-Presidential" Structures

One of the peculiar features of the Russian state is the institution of the personal representative (*predstavitel'*) of the president. The original representatives—appointed in the second half of 1991—operated in the country's regions as the eyes of the president in provincial politics. When Marshal Yevgenii Shaposhnikov lost his position as head of the armed forces of the Commonwealth of Independent States, Yeltsin found work for him as his personal representative to Russia's main arms supply company, *Rosvooruzhenie.* Presidential representatives to the parliament and the Constitutional Court were added in 1994 and 1995,[141] and in 1998, Anatolii Chubais served for a time as presidential representative to international financial institutions.[142] Supported by a staff of less than ten persons, each representative was charged with advancing the presidential program in his particular region or institution. The representative in the Constitutional Court, for example, defended the president's interests during oral arguments before the court, advised the president on the constitutionality of the drafts of presidential decrees, and formulated requests for review (*zaposy*) for the Constitutional Court.[143] As important as these offices appear, they were in almost every case duplicating tasks already performed by Government ministries or other presidential agencies. The institution of the personal representative of the president was yet another example of institutional redundancy.

The presence of these representatives "in" (*v*) nonpresidential structures illustrates that the Russian presidency refused to respect the idea of a separation of powers. Much like the tsar or other traditional monarchs, the president stood above Government, parliament, courts, and the regions and sent his emissaries to them. In June 1998, for example, Yeltsin met in the Kremlin with the chief justice of the Constitutional Court, Marat Baglai, with whom he spoke about issues pending before the court.[144] In the case of parliament, the presidential representative to the Duma literally stood above the legislature in a loge at the back of the chamber, from where he could participate in debates. Thus, to identify the presidency as a "branch" of government, or to conflate the Government (*pravitel'stvo*) and presidency into a single executive branch, is to misunderstand the conceptual underpinnings of the Russian state in the post-Communist era. Yeltsin sought to rule above the state as well as above parties.

The presidential bureaucracy also contained a number of commissions that operated with boards of luminaries supported by small permanent staffs. Besides the Council on Cadres Policy and the Council on Pardons, which carried out important administrative functions, the presidency had numerous advisory commissions touching virtually every area of Russian life. The most general of these was the Presidential Council, a think tank dominated by progressive officials and scholars. Like Gorbachev before him, Yeltsin seemed to have turned to this institution for advice only rarely. It operated in relative obscurity for almost all of Yeltsin's first term, until several of its twenty-eight members resigned to protest the Chechen war at the beginning of the presidential election campaign.[145] It ceased operations shortly thereafter. Other advisory bodies included the Commission on Relations with Religious Groups; the Commission on Women, the Family, and Demography, whose first chair, Yekaterina Lakhova, later became a parliamentary deputy and head of the Women of Russia party; and the Commission for Physical Culture and Sport, chaired by Yeltsin's tennis coach, Shamil Tarpishchev. Reportedly, Tarpishchev exploited his personal contacts with the president to enrich himself and numerous colleagues in the sporting world, traditionally one of the most corrupt sectors of Russian society. With Tarpishchev's assistance, the National Sports Foundation received "a national monopoly over the tax-free import of spirits and tobacco into Russia," ostensibly as a means of financing the training of Russian sportsmen.[146]

For Yeltsin, perhaps the most troubling commission was that on human rights. Headed by the human rights activist Sergei Kovalev, this commission moved to the presidency from the parliament in the fall of 1993, in the wake of the legislature's dissolution. The change of venue did not restrain

Kovalev's criticisms of what he perceived to be violations of human rights. He became a relentless critic of presidential crime-fighting decrees and of the war in Chechnia,[147] and resigned his post as head of the Commission on Human Rights at the beginning of 1996,[148] by which time the responsibilities for human rights monitoring were being shifted from the presidency to an ombudsman's office affiliated with parliament. The first human rights ombudsman operating under full statutory authority was Oleg Mironov, a Communist lawyer approved by the Duma in May 1998.[149]

At the outer edges of the presidency lay a number of institutions that had migrated from the Government after the collapse of the Soviet Union. Many of these "near-presidential" institutions served as technical advisory bodies. Attached to the presidency (*pri Prezidente*), for example, were the Committee on Information Systems Policy, the Committee on Chemical and Biological Weapons, and the State Technological Commission. Employing over three hundred officials, these three organizations had little in common with the core policy and administrative support offices of the presidency.[150] But they stood as testimony to the unfettered growth of the Russian presidency during Yeltsin's first term.

One of the more unusual appendages of the presidency was the Judicial Chamber for Informational Disputes, a mediation tribunal that heard cases concerning the press and broadcast media. Created in December 1993 in response to complaints about media behavior in the parliamentary election campaign, the Judicial Chamber had eight members—half lawyers, half journalists—who heard a steady stream of cases brought by reporters denied access to information and provincial officials indignant over their treatment by the media. With only social sanctions at its disposal, the Judicial Chamber adjudicated disputes in that difficult space between "law and decency."[151] Reading the almost 150 decisions issued by the chamber in its first three years of existence, one finds a serious attempt to establish an etiquette of relations between the fourth estate and the state. At times, the chamber's decisions exhibited courage as well as finesse. In a January 1995 decree, it demanded that the Main Security Administration, headed by Mikhail Barsukov, restore a Kremlin press pass to a Russian journalist who had been stripped of her privileges for writing an article critical of the Kremlin Security Guard. Barsukov complied.[152]

The Presidency and Electoral Politics

As Yeltsin's first term drew to a close, the presidential apparatus began to devote less energy to wielding power and more to retaining it, an understandable shift in focus given the dismal showing of the president in the polls. To satisfy the formal requirements of the electoral law, the president formed an independent reelection committee. But this committee was little more than an extension of the presidential offices located in the Kremlin and on Old Square. As in the earlier parliamentary elections, executive institutions mobilized their considerable resources to support the candidate of the "party of power." Thus, challengers for the presidency in 1996 found themselves running against the Russian state and not just Boris Yeltsin. To ensure that Yeltsin collected qualifying signatures more quickly than any of his rivals, the deputy prime minister and presidential campaign chief, Oleg Soskovets, turned to the minister of railways, Gennadii Matveev, who quickly organized railway workers behind the effort.[153] Furthermore, as the leader of a state that had created and nurtured a powerful group of financial oligarchs, who got rich by exploiting artificially low prices on property, capital, and natural resources in the transition from Communism, Yeltsin received a much-needed infusion of cash into his campaign from wealthy bankers.

Nowhere was the power of incumbency more evident than in the media's role in the election. To ensure the support of the broadcast media, Yeltsin installed a loyal client as head of the largest television network, ORT. He then coopted the director of the more independently minded network, NTV, Igor Malashenko, by appointing him as one of the twelve members of the president's reelection committee. Fearful of the threat that a Communist victory would pose to press freedoms, prominent Russian journalists in Moscow joined what was in effect a media campaign to promote Yeltsin and ignore or smear his opponents. In the selection and presentation of stories—even in the tone of the delivery on radio and TV—Russian journalists came to the aid of the president.[154]

Although Yeltsin, with rare exceptions, enjoyed the support of the national media outlets based in Moscow, he was less popular among journalists in conservative regions, especially those in the so-called Red Belt south of the capital. To combat the opposition press in these areas, the presidential apparatus formed the Agency of the Regional Press, which sought to leapfrog the hostile regional authorities by making direct contact with journalists working on local newspapers. By accrediting these small-town journalists to the presidential apparatus and offering them exclusive interviews with the country's leading politicians, the president's apparatus was taking the political fight to the Communist heartland. In the official explanation proffered by the Executive Office of the President, the agency was formed "to help the media come closer to an adequate reflection of Russian reality."[155]

During the election campaign, the presidency's own newspaper, *Rossiiskie vesti,* suddenly exhibited unusual interest in the views of its readers and other Russian citizens. There were weekly articles analyzing letters received by the presidential apparatus.[156] Front-page insets, entitled "Ask the President, Tell the President," invited readers to contact Yeltsin with their concerns, and many of those writing in response found their names listed under this rubric in subsequent issues. During the spring of 1996, page after page of *Rossiiskie vesti* was devoted to persons honored with various presidential awards. By publicly recognizing as many of the country's one hundred million voters as possible before the election, Yeltsin sought to convince the electorate of his concern for their welfare.

Yeltsin's largesse during the election campaign was not restricted to the symbols of state. Through a series of decrees, the Russian president raided the treasury to pay wage arrears to workers, to raise payments to those on state assistance, to reward regional governments loyal to the president, and to reimburse the oldest members of Russian society for losses in their inflation-ravaged savings accounts. Businesses benefited, too, from the politics of generosity. During the electoral campaign, they were often able to reduce or forgo tax payments to the state, thus contributing to a volatile financial mixture—rising expenditures and declining revenues.[157]

Besides being an instrument in Yeltsin's campaign, the presidential apparatus was also an issue. To blunt criticism of his large and controversial apparatus, Yeltsin launched a reform of the presidency at the end of 1995. At stake were the institution's size, structure, and personnel. The liberal leader of the Executive Office of the President, Sergei Filatov, lost his position to Nikolai Yegorov, a nationalist and former collective farm chairman from south Russia whose views had more in common with the old regime than with the democratic wing of the presidency.[158] Yegorov implemented the long-delayed reduction in the staff of the Executive Office—removing approximately one-quarter of its two thousand personnel—and oversaw the introduction of a major reorganization of the institution in January 1996.

Under these reforms, a diverse assortment of presidential structures found new homes in six main administrations, whose heads—as deputy leaders of the Executive Office—answered directly to Yegorov. Only the Monitoring Administration and the State-Legal Administration remained untouched—merely adding the designation "Main" to their title. The other four main administrations gathered under their wings the remaining subdivisions of the Executive Office. Thus, the Main Administration on Domestic and Foreign Policy embraced the Administration for Work with Territories, the Administration for Cooperation with Political Parties, and the newly created Administration for Foreign Policy. The Main Administration on Constitutional Guarantees of Citizens' Rights took in the offices concerned with such areas as letters from citizens, pardons, awards, and women and the family. The Main Program-Analytical Administration consolidated under one roof the various analytical centers and information-oriented departments as well as the Center for Presidential Programs. And the Main Administration on Civil Service and Personnel brought together the two existing administrations with responsibilities in this area.[159] The restructuring of the presidency also expanded slightly the authority of Viktor Iliushin, Yeltsin's chief counselor, by bringing the press secretary, the chief of protocol, and the Chancellery under his wing.[160]

Although the downsizing and reorganization of the presidency appeared to have served Yeltsin well during the campaign, the removal of Filatov remained a point of controversy among reform-minded Russians.[161] With leading liberals such as Filatov, Chubais, and Kozyrev out of the Russian executive by the beginning of 1996, Yeltsin was exposed to an electoral challenge from the right—the more westernizing pole of the Russian political spectrum—by the young economist Grigorii Yavlinsky. To blunt Yavlinsky's presidential bid and to mobilize democratic forces behind his own campaign, Yeltsin began to lean in a reformist direction again in personnel policy. In March 1996, he appointed Filatov to serve as the head of the All-Russian Movement for Public Support of the First Russian President, an offshoot of the presidential election committee. And barely two months after signing Chubais' dismissal notice, which contained gratuitous language about his "failure to carry out a number of presidential assignments," Yeltsin recruited Chubais to work in the inner circles of his reelection campaign.[162]

Having limited the defections of reform-oriented voters by these nods to the democratic camp, Yeltsin sought next to heighten his support among the disillusioned center and wavering Communist and nationalist segments of the Russian electorate. He did this by directing funds and media attention to the presidential campaign of Aleksandr Lebed, who took votes from the Communist candidate, Gennadii Ziuganov, and thereby ensured Yeltsin a modest lead over Ziuganov—35 percent to 32 percent—at the end of the first round of the presidential elections. As we noted earlier, while Yeltsin and Ziuganov were preparing to face off in the second and decisive round of presidential voting, the president appointed Lebed as secretary of the Security Council, hoping to attract a significant share of the 15 percent of the voters who had voted for Lebed in the first round. Despite suffering a mild heart attack in the final days of the campaign, a fact well hidden from the Russian public, Yeltsin emerged victorious against Ziuganov in the 3 July contest by a margin of 54 percent to 40 percent.[163]

While Yeltsin was completing a physically debilitating campaign, Lebed began his tenure as secretary of the Security Council in dramatic fashion. The day after his appointment, amid a bitter fight for supremacy by several of Yeltsin's lieutenants, Lebed helped to force the removal from office of a powerful troika associated with presidential security and the military-industrial complex: Aleksandr Korzhakov, Mikhail Barsukov, and Oleg Soskovets, the first deputy prime minister.[164] The dismissal of this formidable conservative alliance brought another shift in the balance of power within the presidency. In early July 1996, reformist forces in the presidency again seemed to be in the ascendant. Personnel changes proved once more to be a potent weapon in the presidential arsenal, this time directed toward the nation and not political and economic elites.

The recruitment of a strong figure like General Lebed appeared to hold the promise of what Max Weber called a rationalization of authority, if not in the executive writ large then at least in its security-related offices. Within limits, this concentration of authority is an essential ingredient of a modern state, effacing the institutional redundancy and competition among suzerains that is characteristic of a feudal order. Exploiting a moment of crisis, Lebed—the soft authoritarian—sought to attack official corruption and to eliminate all effective competition to the Security Council from within the presidency, whether from Baturin in the Counselors' Service or Korzhakov and Barsukov in Yeltsin's armed security detachments.[165] But as Chapter 5 illustrates, by attacking deeply entrenched bureaucratic interests throughout the executive branch and exhibiting a vigorous leadership style that contrasted with that of a president in failing health, Lebed ensured his early removal from office.

Within weeks of Lebed's appointment came another personnel decision that roiled the Russian political elite. Yeltsin replaced Nikolai Yegorov, the leader of his Executive Office, with Anatolii Chubais, the country's most prominent and effective advocate of radical economic change. Western governments chose to view this move as a sign that the Russian president—now unfettered by electoral concerns—was returning the country to the reform course. But the appointment of Chubais appeared tied as much to concerns about power as policy. Unlike Yegorov, a figure who rose to national politics "by accident"—to use the Russian phrase—Chubais was a formidable player in Russian bureaucratic politics who could serve as an effective counterweight to the ambitions of General Lebed. In this role, Chubais shared the stage with Viktor Chernomyrdin, the Russian prime minister, who began sparring with Lebed within days after the latter's appointment to the presidency. According to Gennadii Burbulis, at the beginning of his second term, Yeltsin had created "a dynamically tense complex of power where each person is capable of something important but none has the independence to act alone."[166]

The Institutional Presidency in Yeltsin's Second Term

Chubais wasted no time in dismantling Yegorov's institutional changes and in creating a new structure for the presidential apparatus that maximized his personal authority. The new institutional arrangements were in place by early October 1996, when an ailing President Yeltsin—only weeks from major heart surgery—signed a decree giving Chubais control over all key presidential structures, including the Counselors' Service.[167] It was a reform, in Filatov's view, that "Boris Nikolaevich . . . should have taken a long time ago."[168] The old parallel centers of power in the presidency gave way to a more streamlined chain of command, with Chubais the sole leader on all communications and policy issues, save national security. In administering the newly reformed presidency, Chubais worked through a first deputy and six deputy leaders of the Executive Office, each of whom was accountable for a particular policy realm. Although two of these seven officials were holdovers from the first term—Semenchenko in the Chancellery and Orekhov in the State-Legal Administration—the remainder were new recruits with reformist pedigrees and close personal ties to Chubais.[169] Like Chubais, the first deputy leader of the Executive Office of the President, Aleksandr Kazakov, had worked in the State Committee on Property. The new deputy leader responsible for relations with parties and civic associations, Maxim Boika, also had considerable experience in state privatization efforts. And three other deputy leaders, Yurii Yarov, Aleksei Kudrin, and Yevgenii Savostianov, hailed from Chubais' hometown of St. Petersburg. Savostioanov, a general whose portfolio in the presidency included personnel policy and appointments, had emerged from the ranks of democratic activists in August 1991 to assume responsibility for the reform of the Moscow office of the KGB.[170] He was one of a large number of presidential officials during Yeltsin's second term who had experience in the security services.

For the first time in post-Soviet politics, a young and politically cohesive team of officials was leading the presidential administration. The Chubais era in the presidency did not last long, however. In March 1997, Yeltsin returned Chubais to the Government as first deputy premier in

Table 3.3

Leading Members of the President's Staff (April 1997)

Office Leader of the Executive	*Yumashev, V.B.*	Counselors' Service	*Korabel'shchikov, A.I.*
			Krasnov, M.A.
			Kuzyk, B.N.
First Deputy Leaders	*Kazakov, A.*		*Prikhod'ka, S.E.*
	Yarov, Iu.F		*Satarov, G.A.*
			Sukhanov, L.E.
Deputy Leaders	*Boiko, M.V*		*Shaposhnikov, E.I.*
	Savost'ianov, E.V.		
Heads of Administrations:		Advisors	*Volkov, V.V.*
			Krasavchenko, S.N.
			Malyshev, N.G.
State-Legal (GPU) †	*Orekhov, R.G.**		*Pain, E.A.*
Monitoring †	*Putin, V.V.**	Chancellery	*Semenchenko, V.P.**
Economic	*Livshits, A.Ia.**	Administration of Affairs	*Borodin, P.P.*
Cossack Forces †	*Semenov, A.P.*		
		Security Council	*Rybkin, I.P.*
Administrative-Technical	*Vasiagin, V.P.*	Defense Council	*Baturin, Iu.M.*
Organizational	*Chernov, V.A.*	Protection Service	*Krapivin, Iu.V.*
Territorial	*Samoilov, S.N.*	Protocol	*Shevchenko, V.N.‡*
Pardons	*Ivanushkin, E.A.*	Press Secretary	*Yastrzhembskii, S.V.**
Documentation	*Shustitskii, Iu.S.*	Press Service	*Gromov, A.A.*
Personnel	*Romanov, V.I.*	Presidential Programs	*Grigor'ev, B.A.*
Personnel Policy	*Matsko, S.V.*		
		Special Programs †	*Frolov, V.A.*
Parties and Groups	*Loginov, A.V.*		
State Awards	*Sivova, N.A.*		
Regional-level Representatives	*Fedorov, A.Iu.*		
Work with Citizens	*Mironov, M.A.*		
Work with Society	*Margelov, M.V.*		

Source: Spisok telefonov rabotnikov Administratsii Prezidenta Rossiiskoi Federatsii (Moscow: April 1997).
*Also served as deputy leaders
†Designates Main Administrations
‡Also served as counselor

Table 3.4

Leading Members of the President's Staff (May 1998)

Leader of the Executive Office	*Yumashev, V.B.*	Counselor's Service	*Korabel'shchikov, A.I. Prikhod'ka, S.E. Shaposhnikov, E.I.*
First Deputy Leaders	*Yarov, Iu.F. Putin, V.V.*	Advisors	*D'iachenko, T.B. Krasavchenko, S.N. Pain, E.A.*
Deputy Leaders	*Komissar, M.V. Livshits, A.Ia. Shabdurasulova, I.V. Savost'ianov, E.V. Ogarev, A.V.*	Chancellery	*Semenchenko, V.P.**
Heads of Administrations:	*Yastrzhembskii, S.V.*	Administration of Affairs	*Borodin, P.P.*
State-Legal (GPU)†	*Orekhov, R.G.**	Security Council	*Kokoshin, A.A.*
Monitoring†	*Samoilov, S.N.*	Protocol	*Semenov, I.N.*
Internal Policy	*Loginov, A.V.*	Press Service	*Gromov, A.A.*
Foreign Policy	*Manzhosin, A.L.*	Presidential Programs	*Grigor'ev, B.A.*
Economic	*Danilov-Danil'ian, A.V.*	Special Programs†	*Frolov, V.A.*
Cossack Forces†	*Semenov, A.P.*	Regional-level Representatives	*Fedorov, A.Iu.*
Administrative-Technical	*Vasiagin, V.P.*		
Organizational	*Chernov, V.A.*	Federal-level Representatives	*Yanik, A.A.*
Territorial	*Samoilov, S.N.*	Work with Citizens	*Mironov, M.A.*
Pardons	*Mitiukov, M.A.*	Work with Society	*Molchanov, D.V.*
Citizenship	*Shumov, V.G.*		
Documentation	*Shustitskii, Iu.S.*		
Personnel	*Romanov, V.I.*		
Personnel Policy	*Matsko, S.V.*		
State Awards	*Sivova, N.A.*		
Local Government	*Mints, B.I.*		

Source: Spisok telefonov Administratsii Prezidenta Rossiiskoi Federatsii (Moscow: May 1998).
*Also served as deputy leaders
†Designates Main Administrations

charge of economic reform. As Chubais and several of his presidential associates made the move from the Kremlin and Old Square to the White House, some Government officials were moving in the opposite direction along New Arbat Street to take up positions in the presidency. Among those returning to the presidency was Aleksandr Livshits, who left his post as finance minister and deputy premier to reprise his role as the leading economist in the presidency, this time as head of a new Economics Administration in the Executive Office rather than as presidential counselor. This circulation of elites between presidency and Government recalled a similar practice in the Soviet era, when senior officials moved back and forth between posts in the party's Central Committee apparatus and the Government.

It was clearly in Anatolii Chubais' interest to cede his leadership post in the presidency to a client of less political ambition and prominence. In this regard, Yeltsin's appointment of the thirty-nine-year-old journalist Valentin Yumashev to lead the Executive Office did not disappoint. Even more than a year after taking up the post of leader of the Executive Office of the President, Yumashev ranked only twelfth among leading Russian politicians in the eyes of expert observers, whereas Chubais placed second, behind only Yeltsin.[171] A graduate of the journalism faculty of Moscow State University, Yumashev had worked as a correspondent for the Soviet youth newspaper *Komsomol'skaia pravda* before moving to the glossy newsmagazine *Ogonek,* where he rose to the directorship of the magazine's publishing house in 1995.[172] This position brought him into the network of Boris Berezovskii, *Ogonek*'s owner and a financial oligarch who cultivated high-ranking officials, including Anatolii Chubais.[173] In the spring of 1996, Chubais had recruited Yumashev to work in Yeltsin's reelection campaign, and shortly after the election, he went to work for the president as an advisor on relations with the press. But Yumashev owed his meteoric rise to power as much to Yeltsin and his family as to Chubais and Berezovskii. From 1989 through 1994, while ghostwriting the president's two autobiographies, Yumashev spent long hours with Yeltsin and his clan.[174] During this period, he developed close relations not only with the president but with his younger daughter, Tatiana Diachenko, who emerged as a pivotal figure in the presidency in Yeltsin's second term. Like Korzhakov, Diachenko was a political amateur who could make or break careers.[175]

Despite his impeccable contacts, Yumashev was in some respects an unlikely choice for the job of leader of the Executive Office. A journalistic outsider eavesdropping on the world of Russian officialdom, he lacked management experience and the habits of bureaucratic life. A person who by his own admission felt uncomfortable in a tie, Yumashev was said by some to be incapable of showing up for work on time.[176] Not surprisingly, Yumashev continued Chubais' initiatives designed to consolidate the position of the Executive Office vis-à-vis other presidential structures. The most notable successes in this campaign came with the virtual elimination of the Counselors' Service in 1997 and 1998. When the chief of the Counselors' Service, Viktor Iliushin, departed for a high Government post in the summer of 1996, responsibility for the president's scheduling and appointments began to shift to the Executive Office, and more specifically its first deputy leader. In several waves between March 1997 and June 1998, the president removed virtually all of his counselors without replacing them. Several personal advisors to Yeltsin—who worked in the Kremlin outside the reach of the Executive Office—also departed in this period. Among the counselors ousted were such prominent figures as Georgii Satarov, Yurii Baturin, Lev Sukhanov, and Mikhail Krasnov.

While dismantling the Counselors' Service, Yumashev was expanding the number of officials who bore the title of deputy leader of the Executive Office of the President. Again, parallels with the Communist Party Central Committee spring to mind. By redistributing the responsibilities of the presidential counselors among new or existing deputy leaders of the Executive Office, Yumashev was replicating the organizational framework of the old Central Committee, where party secretaries—like the current deputy leaders—exercised supervision over one or more subordinate departments. And just as in the Communist regime, some deputy leaders were themselves heads of a prominent policy- or support-oriented department while others supervised the work of several departments in their area of competence. For example, deputy leaders Ruslan Orekhov and Valerii Semenchenko served, respectively, as heads of the State-Legal Administration and the Chancellery, while Mikhail Komissar, the deputy leader for media relations, worked with a small office staff to oversee the departments in his policy domain.

Facilitating the effective closure of the Counselors' Service, as well as the merger of other presidential structures, was a campaign in the first half of 1998 to reduce the size of the state bureaucracy, including the presidency and Government. Pressure to reduce spending on state administration came from international donors, such as the IMF, and Russian labor unions, most notably the miners'. Playing the zero-sum game of budgetary politics, representatives of miners picketing outside the White House insisted that savings from reductions in force in state administration be used to save jobs—and pay wage arrears—to workers in the increasingly uncompetitive coal pits. Although reliable figures on cutbacks in the presidency are difficult to obtain, it appears that Yumashev oversaw the removal of something less than two hundred persons from the presidency.[177]

For high-ranking casualties of this downsizing, such as presidential counselors, Yeltsin softened the blow by creating new positions for them in near-presidential structures. For example, Georgii Satarov became the head of a political think tank, INDEM, which was funded from the business office of Pavel Borodin. Satarov then hired Mikhail Krasnov and other unemployed veterans of the Kremlin or Old Square.[178] When Nikolai Yegorov was fired in July 1996 from the post of leader of the Executive Office, Yeltsin reportedly told him upon departure: "Choose which position in the Government you like."[179] Whereas democracy and the market offer "institutionalized uncertainty," in Adam Przeworski's phrase, the Russian and Soviet tradition tended to circulate elites rather than abandon them to their fate—an approach that is at once more humane and more likely to discourage the rise of an opposition. But if the security of the old *nomenklatura* system survived the collapse of Communism in at least modified form, it did not extend to the rank and file. Some lower-level personnel who lost their jobs in the presidency had to turn instead to the courts for reinstatement or other remedies.[180]

Although the institutional presidency under Yumashev differed only modestly in its structure from the Chubais inheritance, a significant evolution had occurred in the complexion of the presidential staff and in the role of the institution in executive politics.[181] While a few pure policy specialists remained in leadership posts in the presidency, by the summer of 1998 half of the leaders in the Executive Office had backgrounds and current portfolios in the field of information and communications. As a result, image making rather than policy formulation or analysis occupied center stage in the presidency in the Yumashev era. Besides the leader of the Executive Office himself, officials devoted to selling the president included Mikhail Komissar, a deputy leader for media relations who had worked in Radio Moscow World Service "before forming Russia's first non-governmental news service, Interfax, in 1989"; Sergei Yastrzhembskii, an international lawyer, diplomat, and publicist who worked as deputy leader and presidential press secretary; Igor Shabdurasulov, another deputy leader who joined the presidency after serving as press spokesman for Prime Minister Viktor Chernomyrdin; and Tatiana Diachenko, who served her father in the capacity of presidential "image advisor" (*sovetnik po imidzhu*).[182]

The departure of Chubais from the presidency in March 1997—and the appointment of a radical reform cabinet under Prime Minister Sergei Kirienko a year later—sharpened the division of labor between the presi-

Figure 3.2 **The Russian Presidency Staffing Levels** (May 1998)

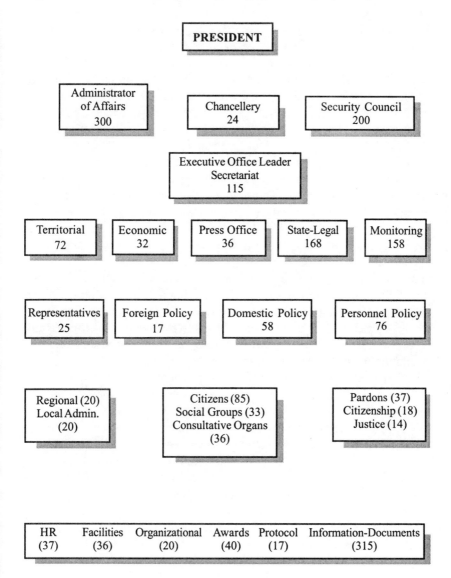

dency and the Government. Although considerable duplication of functions continued, the presidency began to retreat to the more narrowly political role that it had always claimed for itself publicly, entrusting the technocratic tasks associated with economic reform and management to the Government. If marketing an aging president—and his boyish selection for prime minister—represented the most urgent and challenging assignment for the Executive Office in the middle of Yeltsin's second term, another vital task was neutralizing parliamentary threats to executive prerogatives while gaining parliamentary cooperation for legislative initiatives. The presidential personnel responsible for regular liaison with the opposition-minded parliament remained little changed under Yumashev. Two former officials of the State-Legal Administration, Aleksandr Kotenkov and Anatolii Sliva, served as presidential representatives in the Duma and Federation Council, respectively, while Andrei Loginov, the head of the Administration for Domestic Policy, exercised immediate supervision over the presidency's relations with parliamentary parties. As the stakes rose in executive-legislative negotiations, whether over an important law or the confirmation of a prime minister, Yumashev, Borodin, and even the president himself became involved in efforts to mobilize a temporary winning coalition in parliament. In contrast to Yeltsin's first years in office, when the presidency tended to wait until "the smell of powder was in the air" before seeking the support of parliamentary parties, in the second term the institution maintained closer relations with party factions.[183]

Besides running political interference for the president with parliament and the nation, the presidential administration under Yumashev became more deeply involved in relations with Russia's eighty-nine regions and the local governments that operated beneath them. As we shall see in Chapter 7, the first gubernatorial elections in Russia, held in late 1996, accorded regional leaders a political base and job security lacking in the early years of post-Communist rule, when governors were subject to appointment and removal by the president. Recognizing the dangers that democratization in the regions posed for Moscow's control of the provinces, the presidency actively supported its regional political allies in their electoral contests. The results, however, were disappointing. In the summer of 1997, confronting a regional landscape with governors at once more hostile and powerful, the president launched an effort to heighten the authority of presidential representatives in the regions, who could serve as a counterweight to this ambitious new class of provincial elites. Supervising the work of these emissaries was a special division of the presidency, the Administration for the Coordination of the Activity of Presidential

Representatives in the Regions, headed by Anton Fedorov.

Security affairs also remained a central concern of the presidency, though in Yeltsin's second term the Security Council adopted a lower public profile and a less ambitious agenda. The routinization of the operations of this branch of the presidency owed much to its unassuming secretaries in Yeltsin's second term, Ivan Rybkin (October 1996–March 1998), and Andrei Kokoshin (March–September 1998). The conciliatory speaker of the lower house of parliament from 1994 to 1996, Rybkin was content to manage an existing bureaucracy rather than seek to expand its powers, as had earlier leaders such as Yurii Skokov and Aleksandr Lebed. Rybkin's successor, Andrei Kokoshin, had served as the first civilian First Deputy Minister of Defense and was a scholar with an in-depth knowledge of Soviet strategic thinking but, in the words of the respected military correspondent Pavel Felgengauer, "little political clout."[184] The institution remained, nonetheless, an important forum for shaping presidential policy on issues such as military reform, military doctrine, economic and technology security, and relations with Chechnia and other troublesome regions in the North Caucasus. For a time at the beginning of Yeltsin's second term, its authority was undermined by the formation of two competing organs in the presidency, a Defense Council and a State Military Inspectorate. But these new elements of Russia's "byzantine military-bureaucratic chain of command" were collapsed into the Security Council in 1998.[185]

In the realm of foreign affairs, the presidency strengthened its staff considerably during Yeltsin's second term. The aging counselor for foreign affairs, Dmitrii Riurikov, was replaced in April 1997 by a forty-year-old diplomat, Sergei Prikhod'ka, who had worked in the Foreign Ministry after his graduation from Moscow's prestigious Institute of International Relations in 1980. In late 1996, the Executive Office of the President created a separate Foreign Policy Administration, headed by Aleksandr Manzhosin. Even some presidential officials with primary responsibilities in domestic affairs brought considerable international expertise to their posts. For example, Mikhail Margelov, the thirty-three-year-old head of the Administration for Relations with Society, began his career as a translator in the International Department of the Central Committee and as a teacher of Arabic in the higher school of the KGB before working in American consulting firms in the early 1990s.[186]

But it was Yeltsin's press secretary, Sergei Yastrzhembskii, who assumed the most visible role in foreign affairs in the presidency during the first two years of Yeltsin's second term. An official who had experience in both the Central Committee's International Department and the Foreign Ministry, having served as director of the ministry's press service from 1992 to 1993 and as Russian ambassador to Slovakia from 1993 to 1996, Yastrzhembskii not only communicated the president's positions on world affairs but organized his foreign trips and assisted him in the formulation of foreign policy.[187] Rumored to be a possible successor to the foreign minister, Yevgenii Primakov, Yastrzhembskii paid for his prominence in the fall of 1998, when Primakov ascended to the post of prime minister and helped to oust Yastrzhembskii from the presidency.

Conclusion

The development of the institutional presidency took another dramatic turn in early December 1998, when an enfeebled Boris Yeltsin traveled from his hospital bed to the Kremlin to fire Yumashev and several of his assistants.[188] The new leader of the Executive Office of the President was Nikolai Bordiuzha, a little-known military officer who, just months before, had risen to the post of secretary of the Security Council from the directorship of the Border Guards. Whereas Chubais' accession to the leadership of the Executive Office had signaled the recruitment of economic reform specialists to the presidency, and Yumashev's appointment brought image makers aboard, Bordiuzha's selection seemed to mark what might be called a militarization of the presidency, with experience in the armed forces or security services increasingly common among the leadership of the presidential apparatus. Responding to mounting attacks on his rule by nationalists, Communists, and democrats as well as an increasing insubordination in his own ranks, Yeltsin was turning for administrative support to a group schooled in loyalty and discipline.[189] To confront what he claimed what was the most pressing threat to Russia's stability, political extremism, Yeltsin directed Bordiuzha to combine his secretaryship of the Security Council with his new role as leader of the Executive Office of the President. In the words of the presidential press secretary, placing these posts in the hands of one man would "enhance the supervision of the structures of power, which is one of the most important tasks of the moment."[190]

During Yeltsin's second term, the presidential apparatus under Chubais, Yumashev, and Bordiuzha became a slightly less expansive, untidy, ambitious, and conflicted institution. But the fundamental pathologies of the institutional presidency remained: overlapping or blurred lines of jurisdiction between offices, a lack of accountability for its operations to parliament or the nation, and the absence of an ideology, a policy program, or a president that could unite a large and diverse staff behind common tasks, a problem made more acute by the declining health of the leader. Yeltsin was not content to elevate the presidency above the other institutions of state; he all too frequently insisted on elevating himself above the operation of the presidency. Into this leadership vacuum flowed the competing ambitions of the scores of presidential officials chronicled in this chapter.

Revolutions are not self-executing. As Lenin understood all too well, they depend on organization, discipline, and ideas, none of which marked presidential leadership under Yeltsin. It is one of the ironies of Yeltsin's presidency that he forgot the lessons of the earlier revolution while retaining, in diluted form, some of the institutional features of Communist rule.

4

President and Prime Minister

All institutional arrangements are inherently unstable in periods of political transition. But if no institutional design can inoculate a country against the pains of giving birth to a new order, some may mitigate—or exacerbate—the strains associated with rapid political and economic change. Russia's model of government, semipresidentialism, seems especially prone to create a structure of incentives that impedes the establishment of a governing consensus and administrative discipline. As a hybrid of presidential and parliamentary systems, it is subject to the tensions found in both these classic forms of government. Where presidentialism pits a popularly elected executive against a popularly elected legislature—producing "dual democratic legitimacies," in Juan Linz's phrase—parliamentarism sets legislative faction against legislative faction. Besides bearing these two traditional axes of institutional conflict, semipresidentialism creates for itself a third, that between two executive leaders, president and prime minister. This relationship is subject to special strains when the president lacks a supporting majority in parliament, because it is the parliament that traditionally expresses confidence in a prime minister.

An antidote to the politics of the dual executive would seem to lie in the establishment of a clear division of labor between president and prime minister. But the shifting fortunes of president and prime minister among bureaucrats, deputies, and citizens tend to upset attempts to maintain fixed roles for the two powerful executive leaders. History has moved instead toward other equilibria. One of the most imaginative of these is found in Fifth Republic France, which supports two very different forms of relations between president and prime minister. Rather than attempt to rule around a hostile parliament through reserved powers or the plebiscite, the French president has deferred to the parliamentary majority and retreated into a less visible and influential role in domestic affairs when the opposition controls the legislature.[1] During these periods of "cohabitation," the prime minister assumes the central role in executive leadership. Thus, semipresidentialism in France has developed "a safety valve that avoids the clash and crises of two popularly elected legitimacies by permitting the political system to function now as a presidential system, now as a parliamentary system."[2] But attempts to reconcile conflicts between president and prime minister have rarely been as subtle or successful as in France. In Weimar Germany, arguably the first political system to experiment with semipresidentialism, a prime minister—Chancellor Hitler—overcame the politics of the dual executive by assuming the presidency himself when the incumbent, General von Hindenburg, died in office in 1934. Hitler soon eliminated the presidency, however, to take on the loftier title of Führer.

In post-Communist Russia, Boris Yeltsin has sought to reduce the tensions inherent in the dual executive arrangements by dramatically limiting the prime minister's dependence on parliament as a source of political authority, and thereby increasing his dependence on the presidency. Although under the 1993 constitution the Russian parliament could in theory still deny a president his choice for prime minister or remove a sitting prime minister from office, it first had to overcome formidable institutional and political hurdles.[3] In practical terms, the prime minister has been the president's man rather than the parliament's. Russia has therefore addressed the dual-executive dilemma by emasculating one of the fundamental elements of semipresidentialism, the accountability of the prime minister and his Government to the legislature. These institutional arrangements appear to ensure that in Russia's version of this hybrid model of government, presidential—and not parliamentary—features predominate.

According to Russian law, the president has the power to countermand any directive issued by the prime minister.[4] Indeed, at least until the spring of 1998, when Yeltsin began to loosen somewhat presidential oversight of the Government, the presidency reviewed all decisions made by the Government, much as the Communist Party had done in the Soviet era. An official with extensive executive and parliamentary experience in the Yeltsin years, Aleksandr Shokhin, explained that

> all draft decisions of the Government, even those signed by the Chairman of the Government [the prime minister], had to be sent to the Kremlin for

clearance. As a rule, this was a list of Government decisions readied for signing. The President would go through the list and mark those which he wanted to study in greater detail. Then draft decisions would be sent to the President. It is hard for me to say who actually read them, the President himself or the corresponding structures in the presidential administration. In any case, various remarks were made. And it was only after initialling by, say, an assistant to the President, an aide, a deputy chief of staff, of the President himself [that] the decisions were made public.[5]

Given the formal constraints on parliamentary authority and the patronage and supervisory powers of the presidency, one might have expected the prime minister and his Government to serve as faithful agents of the president. It is the president, after all, who hires and fires the prime minister and makes the major decisions of state. But relations between president and prime minister, and between presidency and Government, have been marked at times by intense competition and even conflict. Even during periods of relative harmony, the two bureaucratic machines—presidency and Government—have rarely worked in tandem. Put simply, Boris Yeltsin could not rely on the Government and its ministries to carry out his directives. In 1994, for example, of the 296 presidential "assignments" (*porucheniia*) issued to the Russian Government, only a little over half (156) had been fully implemented by the country's ministries and executive agencies.[6] For its part, the Government could not rely on Yeltsin to provide firm, consistent leadership.

Perhaps the most serious breakdown in interexecutive relations occurred in the summer of 1995, when Chechen rebels seized a hospital and a thousand hostages in the city of Budennovsk, deep in Russian territory. After an abortive assault on the hospital by Russian special forces, President Yeltsin seemed to distance himself from the crisis, leaving the prime minister to negotiate with the rebels. The medium for the negotiations was live television, apparently chosen by the prime minister less as an instrument of self-promotion than of self-protection—the president could not feign ignorance of the prime minister's tactics as he had with those of the special forces.

> For two days the president and prime minister behaved as if the other did not exist at all. Not even once did they utter the familiar chant "The president and I agreed" or "The prime minister and I decided . . ." Roughly speaking, for two days the two top officials in Russia did not see each other.

The Budennovsk crisis offered "a glimpse of two states in one country: the Russia where there is a president, and the Russia where there is a prime minister."[7]

The assertion of a Yeltsin aide that "[t]he President sets the course and the Government carries it out" is therefore a tidy and enticing, but wholly misleading, description of the division of labor within the Russian executive.[8] Rather than rule through the Government, Yeltsin has at times ruled around it, in part as a means of minimizing resistance to presidential initiatives. At other moments, notably under the prime ministership of Yevgenii Primakov, the president has ceded considerable authority to the Government, due to his own ill health, an economic crisis, and an aggessively opposition-minded parliament. To appreciate the limits that other executive institutions have imposed on presidential authority, it is essential to understand the vast apparatus of Government and ministries operating under the prime minister.

What Is the Government?

Unlike Americans, who associate the word *government* exclusively with what political scientists call the state, those schooled in the parliamentary tradition have a second, and narrower, meaning for the term in their political repertoire. *Government* as a proper noun refers to the ensemble of ministers who direct the country's leading executive agencies under the guidance of the prime minister and his staff.[9] Russia has had a Government in this sense since 1802, though it has at times borne different formal titles, such as the Council of Ministers or Cabinet of Ministers.[10] Unlike the presidential bureaucracy, whose authority rests on the president's popular election, the Russian Government derives its constitutional legitimacy from the parliament, to which it is at least formally accountable. To ensure the separation of executive and legislative power, Russian law does not permit members of the Government to hold legislative seats, whether in the national parliament or local assemblies.[11]

The current Russian Government differs from its European counterparts by its imposing size as well as its greater autonomy from parliament. Rather than a modest historic home, such as 10 Downing Street, or even a small palace, such as Matignon, the headquarters of the Russian Government since 1994 has been the White House, a modern skyscraper on the banks of the Moscow River. The Russian White House boasts four thousand separate telephone lines and a million square feet of office space—with a little less than a thousand on the fifth floor devoted to the prime minister's personal office.[12] Where the British prime minister and German chancellor govern with a support staff of no more than a hundred officials each, the Russian prime minister oversees a Government bureaucracy with approximately a thousand professional staff employees. In this, as in so many areas of institutional life, continuity rather than change has characterized the transition from Communist rule. Although the number of ministries and state committees in Russia has declined from its high of over one hundred in the late Soviet period to thirty-three in the streamlined Kirienko Government in 1998, there has been no corresponding reduction in the scale or complexity of the bureaucracy operating between the prime minister and the "federal organs of executive power," the formal term for the central ministries and state committees. This Government bureaucracy represents a maze of offices and personnel with obvious parallels to the presidency— and to the apparatus of the old Communist Party Central Committee.

Periodic reductions in the number of ministries have had all the earmarks of the bureaucratic shell games of the Soviet era. Under pressure to scale back a swollen Government bureaucracy, Soviet officials traditionally responded with two measures designed to maintain the status quo while offering the appearance of reform. First, they stripped some bureaucracies of their ministerial title and transferred them to the jurisdiction of other, larger ministries, where they acquired the status of a separate department or administration. These mergers were often no more than legal fictions, with little if any impact on the scale or operation of the erstwhile ministries. Having been "eliminated" in an administrative reorganization, these bureaucracies would regain their ministerial status several years later when the fervor of a downsizing campaign had waned. Avoiding the firing of officials during these campaigns required similar ingenuity on the part of the Government's leaders. Anticipating possible reductions in force, ministries always maintained formal staffing levels that were significantly higher than the number of officials they were authorized to employ. This gap between positions and personnel meant that ministries were perennially understaffed, or *nedokomplektovany,* to use the Russian bureaucratese. Thus, ministries could significantly reduce their staffing levels without actually firing anyone.

Post-Communist Russia appears equally enamored of this bureaucratic sleight of hand. When Yeltsin ordered a substantial "reduction in the number of ministries" and at least a 20 percent decrease in the number of Government personnel, officials were able to satisfy the formal requirements of the president's directive without a painful reduction of offices or personnel.[13] As Stanislav Shatalin and Stanislav Assekritov noted, "The Ministry of Economics and the Ministry of Finance were combined [in 1992], but no sooner had they changed the signboards than they were split up again. There was the same picture with the Foreign Ministry and the Ministry of

Foreign Economic Relations."[14] The December 1993 constitution brought further changes in Russia's institutional design that eroded parliament's ability to shape policy on executive personnel and organization—one of the primary functions of assemblies in democratic regimes. Indeed, Russian law now grants the Government itself the right "to confirm the staffing levels and salaries in federal and regional executive agencies."[15]

Perhaps the most remarkable feature of the Russian Government is its fragmented power. All parliamentary and semiparliamentary systems, of course, are subject to divisions in the cabinet. Depending on the correlation of forces in parliament and its parties, cabinet ministers may serve as potent checks on the freedom of maneuver of the prime minister, especially in coalition governments. But something quite different goes on in Russia. There the members of the Government limit the authority of the prime minister not by political interventions during cabinet meetings but by carving out for themselves a broad measure of autonomy in their own administrative portfolios. In Russia, a minister is more likely to influence policy through bureaucratic intrigue—by sabotaging the drafting or implementation of an initiative—than through cabinet debates. Thus, unlike Western executives, with their traditions of party discipline and collective responsibility, the Russian Government is an unwieldy coalition of ministers, most of whom are devoted first and foremost to their own institutional interests.

With surprising regularity, ministerial officials oppose openly the policies of the president and prime minister. Responding in early 1998 to several egregious cases of ministerial insubordination, President Yeltsin ordered the prime minister, Viktor Chernomyrdin, "to investigate the scandalous cases of officials lobbying for their own departmental interests against those of the state." In one instance, a deputy minister of defense encouraged the upper house of parliament to approve without delay a bill expanding privileges for servicemen, only minutes after the presidential representative in the Federation Council had argued against it. In another case, the deputy minister of agriculture supported a parliamentary bill on land reform that was a competitor to that offered by the president and prime minister.[16]

What explains this "ministerial feudalism," where members of the Government behave at times like independent princes in their own domains?[17] Besides the lack of a clearly defined political line imposed from above, an important factor has been the absence of a legal culture, which would inculcate in ministers an obligation to adhere strictly to norms emanating from above.[18] Traditionally, bureaucratic discipline in Russia rested not on legal foundations but on patron-client relations and on concerns for political or personal survival. The Communist regime had ensured a measure of bureaucratic loyalty by employing a mixture of crude but nonetheless effective methods, including purges, political indoctrination, and internal and external oversight of ministerial behavior. The collapse of the Communist Party either eliminated or markedly weakened these control mechanisms, and the new regime was unable to put in place effective replacements at the very time when a political and economic revolution alienated officials in many ministries. The result was a campaign of ministerial disobedience in the face of radical reforms.

Why didn't the new Russian leadership simply rely on the "cadres weapon," to use the Soviet term for a personnel shake-up? Put another way, why didn't the Russian prime minister select a group of loyal ministers and thereby eliminate the competing centers of power in the Government? For one, the president never granted the prime minister such political flexibility. Yeltsin preferred instead to allow leading members of the executive to negotiate with him, and at times with each other, over key appointments. When the president reshuffled the cabinet in March 1997, Prime Minister Chernomyrdin fought off attempts by more reformist politicians to remove his ally, Vladimir Babichev, from the influential post of head of the Government Secretariat. But he was forced to accept the appointment of Anatolii Chubais's client, Sergei Vasiliev, as Babichev's deputy. This intraoffice coalition ensured that Vasil'ev would be "breathing down the neck of Babichev."[19] Such political compromises over administrative positions help to explain the inefficiencies and byzantine intrigue that permeated the Russian bureaucracy.

There were several other impediments to the formation of a cohesive team of Government officials, not the least of which was the dearth of officials who were both professionally qualified and politically committed to the president. In this sense, Russian leaders in the early 1990s faced the conundrum encountered by the Bolsheviks in the first years of Soviet power, when officials were either Red or expert but not both. Further narrowing the patronage options—and lessening executive discipline—was the Russian and Soviet tradition of promoting ministers from within the organization, or at least from within one sector of the economy or society. Unlike in Western Europe, where senior party leaders often moved through several different ministerial portfolios in their career, in Russia ministers tended to be promoted from below. This promotion from below is one of the reasons that ministers behaved like independent princes even though they were personally vulnerable to removal. As Sergei Porshakov has observed, the "positive side of this is that [ministers] accumulate considerable professional experience. On the negative side, few [ministers] are able to think globally, in the interests of the whole executive system."[20]

Furthermore, ministers were often selected to appease certain constituencies, whether the president, parliament, or regional or economic elites. Where the president insisted on having his own allies in the newly formed Government committees overseeing economic reform, he was willing to accept more conservative figures—including some desired by parliament—in traditional portfolios such as agriculture. According to Yeltsin's press secretary, the selection of the Communist Aleksandr Nazarchuk as agricultural minister in late 1994 represented "a concession to the Agrarian-Communist lobby [in the parliament]" that was necessary "to lower political tension, to avoid a Government crisis and worsening relations between the president and deputies."[21] In approving the appointment of some ministers, Yeltsin also acceded to the demands of powerful social and economic elites that had worked closely with particular branch ministries in the Soviet era. Thus, to have appointed a minister of the timber industry who had no experience in, or support from, lumbering concerns and regions would have invited protests from prominent constituents as well as insubordination from lower-level officials in the ministry.

The permanent staff of the ministries were themselves potent interest groups with which the president and prime minister had to contend. As Yeltsin and Gaidar discovered in the early months of post-Communist Russia, appointing politically loyal but inexperienced officials to ministerial positions did not ensure presidential control of the executive. Writing in the spring of 1992, a prominent Russian economist complained that

> [t]he ministers in the present Government—amateurs at the apparatus game—are cut off from real life by this apparatus: they tell each other about the importance of the decisions they make, but unbeknown to them these decisions never get beyond the office, and there is no one to blame for this. Accountability is spread around like watery porridge.[22]

Whereas in mature democracies political parties serve as the primary mediating institutions between the state and society, ministries have performed that function in Russia in wake of Communism's demise. Forming a Government in Russia has therefore been a very different enterprise than in the West. Because mollifying important sectoral elites, such as the industrialists, is often more important than satisfying parliamentary parties and factions, the prime minister will include in the Government some ministers who exhibit little loyalty to parliament, prime minister, or president. These are functional representatives, whose base of support and legitimacy lie in the country and not in the formal institutions of state. As extensions of powerful social and economic interests that predate the new Russian state, such ministers have been able to flout Western conventions of collective responsibility, which would impose discipline on a fractious Russian executive.

The lack of discipline in the Government may also be due to the shortage of authoritative, institutionalized forums for airing and resolving the competing claims of ministers. What regularized deliberation there is appears to come in the weekly meetings of the presidium—or inner circle—of the Government, an institution of between eight and fifteen members that is as secretive as its Soviet counterpart.[23] There are, to be sure, quarterly plenary sessions attended by the heads of all Government agencies and chaired at times by the president.[24] But these gatherings are often little more than political theater, staged to shore up the image of the president or prime minister or to announce the latest Government initiatives. They are not forums that encourage a broad exchange of ideas and information. Deprived of such an outlet, politics retreats to the back room, where it breeds distrust among ministers and between the state and society.

An indication of the tenor of Government meetings emerges from the sessions in the spring of 1994, when a frustrated prime minister railed against ministers for their failure to adhere to Government directives as well as for their truancy at earlier meetings. "We aren't playing games," Chernomyrdin warned, "we're running a country."[25] It was not the voice of a senior colleague urging consensus and discipline but the tone of a headmaster upbraiding his unruly charges—in this case, for public consumption. Using a well-worn instrument inherited from the Soviet Union's culture of blame,[26] the prime minister handed out reprimands (*vygovory*) to several ministers—the kind of punishment normally reserved in the West for children and military recruits.[27] Members of the Government not turning up for meetings were instructed to bring a note of excuse.[28] At the beginning of 1997, Chernomyrdin issued reprimands to the ministers of finance and economics for failing to make up the vast wage arrears owed the country's workers—a thinly veiled attempt to shift the blame for Government policy onto subordinates.[29] Such measures represent "the quintessence of Russia's political culture, with its marked penchant for personifying blunders and failures."[30]

To understand the pathologies of the Russian executive, one must also appreciate the culture of isolation among its leadership. As Mikhail Gorbachev explained in his memoirs, it was particularly lonely at the top of Soviet politics because of the ban on fraternization among the senior leadership.[31] This vestige of the Soviet era leaves the current Russian political elite with few formal or informal venues for consensus building. To be sure, the British prime minister has at times looked askance at social contacts between members of the cabinet, but at least there is the opportunity in Britain for substantive debate at regular parliamentary and cabinet meetings.

The very organization of the Government has also complicated efforts to rein in the ministries. Unlike the British prime minister, the Russian premier does not directly oversee the ministries. Beneath his personal secretariat of some twenty-five officials are two sizable bureaucracies that mediate the prime minister's contacts with the federal organs of executive power.[32] The first contains a host of first deputy and deputy prime ministers, each of whom is responsible for a particular group of ministries, and therefore a distinct slice of political, economic, or social affairs. This group of Government leaders is subject to a clearly established pecking order, so that in the absence of the prime minister or a deputy a temporary replacement is elevated immediately.[33] In their role in the Government bureaucracy, the deputy prime ministers parallel the deputy leaders in the Executive Office of the President, and before them the secretaries of the Communist Party's Central Committee. And just as with secretaries in the party and deputy leaders in the presidency, there are some "pure" deputy prime ministers who oversee a number of ministers in their policy area, while other deputy prime ministers have their own ministerial portfolio. In the latter years of the Chernomyrdin Government, for example, Anatolii Kulikov was at one and the same time minister of internal affairs and deputy prime minister.

The loyalties of the deputy prime ministers vary widely, since their selection—and the breadth of their responsibilities—depends on not only the prime minister but the president and, to a lesser extent, parliamentary, regional, and economic elites. As first deputy prime minister for economic reform from 1993 to 1995, and then again from 1997 to 1998, Anatolii Chubais looked to the president and not the prime minister for approval of his actions. The same could be said of Viktor Iliushin, who moved from the presidency to the Government to become first deputy prime minister for social and cultural affairs after Chubais' appointment to the presidential apparatus in the summer of 1996. Many individual ministers were also reticent to follow the prime minister's lead. Upon his appointment as economics minister in late 1994, Yevgenii Yasin remarked, "My duty of course is to support my prime minister, but I will do so with some reservations."[34] For his part, Aleksandr Nazarchuk, a deputy prime minister in charge of agriculture, exhibited less loyalty to the prime minister than to the ministries under his tutelage. Commenting on the new group of first deputy and deputy prime ministers

Figure 4.1 **The Russian Government** (May 1998)

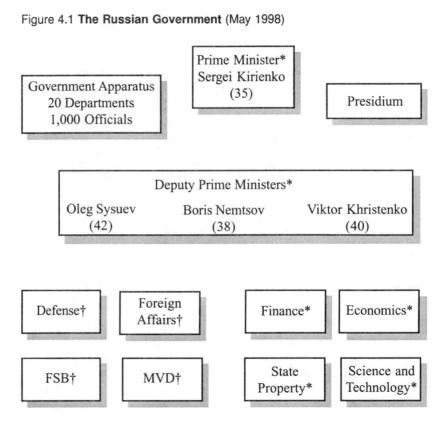

Government Apparatus
20 Departments
1,000 Officials

Prime Minister*
Sergei Kirienko
(35)

Presidium

Deputy Prime Ministers*

| Oleg Sysuev (42) | Boris Nemtsov (38) | Viktor Khristenko (40) |

Defense†

Foreign Affairs†

Finance*

Economics*

FSB†

MVD†

State Property*

Science and Technology*

Approximately 60 Other Ministries,
State Committees,
and Agencies

*Represented on Presidium
† Agencies under direct presidential control

appointed in August 1996, a Russian journalist observed that only one—Oleg Davidov, a specialist in foreign trade—was a close ally of Chernomyrdin. "With this kind of mandate," he continued, "what can one expect of the prime minister, no matter how brilliant he is?"[35]

Despite the presence in the Government of reformers such as Chubais, the proliferation of deputy prime ministers has tended to complicate attempts to mobilize the ministries behind a new economic and political course. Greater bureaucratic complexity and fragmentation has played into the hands of conservative forces by increasing the number of policy choke points at which one can erect roadblocks to change. In the phrase of the former minister of finance Boris Fedorov, "the more deputy premiers, the fewer reforms."[36] In the early part of Yeltsin's second term, the Government had nine first deputy or deputy prime ministers—a group almost as big as an entire cabinet of ministers in some countries.

By themselves, the offices of the first deputy and deputy prime ministers are modest in scale. No more than fifteen support personnel work in each. But parallel to the offices of the deputy prime ministers is another thick layer of bureaucracy, which bears a striking resemblance to the Executive Office of the President. This is the Government Secretariat (*Apparat Pravitel'stva*), whose head enjoyed the rank of deputy prime minister at the beginnning of Yeltsin's second term.[37] The core of the Government Secretariat is more than twenty departments employing an average of forty officials each and an equally large technical and support staff.[38] Many of these departments—legal affairs, civil service, relations with regions, and relations with the parliament and public organizations—have titles and responsibilities that mirror those of administrations in the presidency. Only in economic affairs, the traditional core of the Government's activity, has there been significant divergence between the two bureaucracies, with the Government Secretariat maintaining departments in such specialized sectors as transport and communications, investment and construction, and the defense industry. These departments continue the long-standing Soviet tradition of Government supervision of the economy according to the "branch principle."

The structure of the Government Secretariat may suggest that these departments operate solely as instruments of the deputy prime ministers, who use them to monitor and control the ministries within their portfolio. The reality, however, is more complex. Politics within the Government pulls the departments in three different directions. The departments answer lesss to the deputy prime ministers than to the head of the Government Secretariat, a kind of permanent secretary and political protege of the prime minister, among whose many duties is the preparation of the agenda for the meetings of the Government and its presidium.[39] From the beginning of 1993 through the fall of 1995, the leader of the Government Secretariat was Vladimir Kvasov, who had worked for more than a decade as Chernomyrdin's assistant in the gas industry.[40] According to *Izvestia*'s economics correspondent, Irina Savvateeva, Kvasov was the White House's eminence grise, controlling the flow of visitors and papers to the prime minister and exercising considerable influence on personnel decisions.[41] Kvasov's replacement, Vladimir Stepanovich Babichev, also had strong personal ties to the prime minister, having worked in the gas industry in the southern Russian region of Astrakhan.[42] Besides serving as a chief of staff to Chernomyrdin, Babichev worked as the coordinator of the "party of power," Our Home Is Russia, which is the electoral arm of the Russian executive. Babichev had arrived in his post with experience in party organization, having been appointed in the fall of 1990 to transform the Communist Party faction in the USSR Supreme Soviet into an effective parliamentary party.[43] The tug-of-war for control of the Government departments created serious tensions at times between Kvasov or Babichev, on the one hand, and the remaining first deputy and deputy prime ministers, on the other.[44] According to Aleksandr Bekker, "Babichev regulated the flow of documents as he saw fit. It is said that a mere look from him was enough to cause a document to be shelved."[45]

There is also a third set of suitors who seek to lure the departments into their corner, the ministries themselves. Rather than serving as loyal subordinates of the prime minister or his deputies, the departments in the Government Secretariat may act as advocates within the White House for the ministries under their tutelage. This tendency to "go native"—to borrow a phrase from American public administration—is found in varying degrees in all organizations, though it is especially pronounced in Russia, where departmental and ministerial interests have long coincided. But the departments could also conspire with ministerial officials behind the backs of the ministers. At times,

> White House staffers played games with the staffs of various ministers, making arrangements such as "Let's not show this document to your minister." On the other hand, when the spirit moved them, bureaucrats would see to it that a resolution on, say, foreign trade privileges or tax breaks for the South Podunk Economic Zone was whisked right through to signing.[46]

The discussion thus far has focused on offices in the White House, which is home to the prime minister, first deputy and deputy prime ministers, and the Government Secretariat. While the heads of the ministries and state committees come to the White House for cabinet sessions or for other meetings with the central Government administration, most of their time is spent in their own headquarters, which are scattered throughout Moscow, usually in large and imposing buildings inherited from the Soviet era. Excluding the main branches of the armed forces, by the mid-1990s the federal organs of executive power employed almost 1 million administrative personnel, about 40,000 of whom worked in the capital.[47] In 1995, the Federal Security Service alone had a staff of 77,640 personnel, a figure that did not include the many persons working in its research, medical, and support divisions.[48] It is such ministerial bureaucracies—the building blocks of state power—that form the core of the Russian executive. It is also these ministries that remain at the center of the political struggle in Russia among president, prime minister, parliament, and the regions.

As noted earlier, the steady expansion of the executive bureaucracy in Moscow and the provinces has occurred alongside a marked decline in the state's ability to raise revenues and to govern. From 1994 to 1995, at a time of rising budget deficits, the total number of civil servants in federal and regional agencies increased by 6 percent.[49] Although the marketizing reforms of the early 1990s eliminated the raison d'être of many executive agencies charged with administering state enterprises, some continued to expand apace. In the first months after the collapse of the USSR, the Moscow apparatus of the Ministry of Agriculture had reportedly grown to two thousand staff, two and a half times the size of the Soviet Ministry of Agriculture.[50] In some cases, old-line bureaucrats moved into newly created state institutions responsible for relations with an expanding private economy. Boris Yeltsin's chief of staff, Yurii Petrov, a former regional secretary of the Communist Party, left the Kremlin in 1992 to head a newly created State Investment Fund, which was charged with investing $100 million in public funds in promising business ventures. In the first three years after the collapse of Communism, the Russian Government created sixty such agencies to assist small and midsized businesses. Whether these executive agencies served to stimulate the growth of fledgling businesses remains a point of contention. The Society of Merchants and Industrialists offered to pay a million rubles to any business that could document the receipt of assistance from these agencies. According to the society, no businesses came forward to make a claim.[51]

Like executive departments in all countries, Russia's ministries are not created equal. Whether because of their functions or their leaders, certain ministries have assumed a more prominent role than others in the making

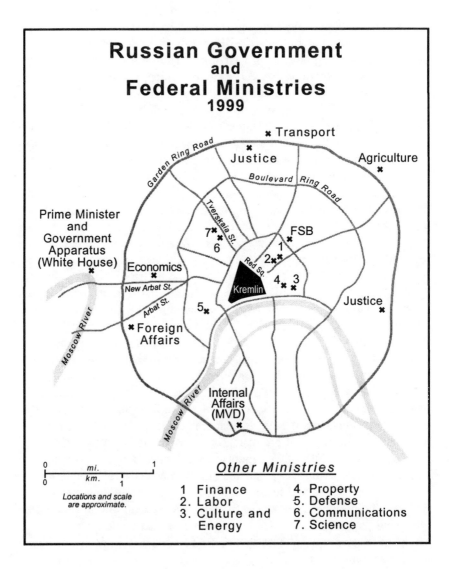

Russian Government
and
Federal Ministries
1999

✗ Transport

Justice

Agriculture ✗

Garden Ring Road

Boulevard Ring Road

Prime Minister
and
Government
Apparatus
(White House)
✗

Tverskaia St.

7✗
✗
6

FSB
✗
1
✗

Economics

2✗
✗

Red Sq.

New Arbat St.

4✗ 3
✗ ✗

Kremlin

Arbat St.

5✗

Justice
✗

✗ Foreign
Affairs

Moscow River

Internal
Affairs
(MVD)
✗

Moscow River

| 0 | mi. | 1 |

| 0 | km. | 1 |

Locations and scale
are approximate.

Other Ministries

1 Finance
2. Labor
3. Culture and
   Energy

4. Property
5. Defense
6. Communications
7. Science

Table 4.1

The Federal Organs of Executive Power (September 1998)

The Government of the Russian Federation

Federal Ministries

Agriculture and Farm Production
Antimonopoly Policy and the Support of
 Enterpreneurship
Atomic Energy
Commonwealth of Independent States
 Affairs
Culture
Defense*
Economics
Emergency Situations*
Energy
Finance
Foreign Affairs (MID)*
General and Professional Education
Health
Internal Affairs (MVD)*
Justice
Labor and Social Development
Nationalities Policy
Natural Resources
Railways
Regional Policy
Science and Technology
State Property
Transport

State Committees

Cinematography
Communications and Information Systems
Construction, Architecture, and
 Housing Policy
Customs
Environmental Preservation
Fishing
Land
Physical Culture and Tourism Press
Standards and Meteorology
State Reserves
Statistics

Federal Commissions

Stocks and Bonds
Energetics

Federal Services

Archives
Aviation
Bankruptcy and Financial Recovery
Borders*
Counterintelligence*
Currency and Export Control
Forestry
Geodetics and Cartography
Highways
Hydrometeorology and Environ-
 mental Monitoring
Migration
Protection (FSO)*
Railway Troops*
Security (FSB)*
Tax
Tax Policy
Television and Radio

Agencies

Government Communications
 (FAPSI)*
Patents and Trademarks
Space

Inspectorates

Atomic and Radiation Security
Mining and Industry

Source: Sobranie zakonodatel'stva, no. 39 (1998), st. 4886. Established by presidential decree of 22 September 1998.
 *Executive institutions that answer directly to the president and not the prime minister.

and implementation of state policy. In the first rank are the foreign, defense, and internal security ministries. Unlike the other federal organs of state power, these power ministries answer directly to the president rather than to the prime minister. Although these ministries remain accountable to the Government on budgetary questions, on policy and operational matters they act as "presidential ministers," to use Yegor Gaidar's phrase. Indeed, it was only when Yeltsin went in for surgery in November 1996 that he relinquished control of the power ministries, and the nuclear button, to his prime minister—and then for less than twenty-four hours. This special relationship between the presidency and one sector of the federal organs of state power—formalized in a presidential decree of 17 January 1994—serves as a reminder that the ranking politician in any state will wish to exercise immediate control of the means of legitimate violence.[52]

Among the executive agencies operating in the prime minister's traditional bailiwicks of economic and social affairs, the Ministry of Finance is arguably the most influential. Evidence of the political weight of the Finance Ministry comes not only from the pay of its personnel, which is more than twice that of officials in the Ministry of Agriculture, but also from its share of the state budget.[53] Security-related agencies aside, the Ministry of Finance receives more than five times as much as its nearest competitor.[54] And even though much of this money is earmarked for disbursement to other institutions, discretion in how and when the funds are transferred gives the Ministry of Finance enormous leverage with other state institutions in Moscow and throughout the country. In addition, proposals for new projects—and therefore new expenditures—have to first pass muster with the Ministry of Finance. This power to open or close the state purse places the Finance Ministry near the epicenter of executive politics.

Like the Ministry of Economics, which took over the offices and personnel of the old State Planning Committee (Gosplan), the Ministry of Finance has the entire economy within its field of vision. Not so the branch ministries, such as agriculture, which focus on a single sector of the economy. If the branch ministries have been the most resistant to change, the most "dedicated reformist bodies" have been what one might call thematic state committees, created at the beginning of the 1990s to introduce elements of a market economy in Russia.[55] These include the State Committee—now Ministry—on Property (Goskomimushchestvo), which was the original political base of Anatolii Chubais; the State Committee for Antimonopoly Policy; the Federal Administration for Insolvency Matters; the State Committee on Nonpayments; and the Federal Energy Committee. Whatever success these institutions have enjoyed as instruments of eco-

Table 4.2

Leading Members of Russian Governments in Yeltsin's First Term

	15 June 1992	15 January 1994
Prime Minister	Gaidar, E.T.*	Chernomyrdin, V.S.
First Deputy Prime Ministers	None	Shumeiko, V.F.
		Lobov, O.I.
		Soskovets, O.N.
Deputy Prime Ministers	Shokhin, A.N.	Fedorov, B.G.
	Poltoranin, M.N.	Chubais, A.B.
	Makharadze, V.A.	Shakhrai, S.M.
	Khizha, G.S.	Shokhin. A.N.
	Chernomyrdin, V.S.	Yarov, Iu.F.
	Chubais, A.B.	Zaveriukha, A.Kh.
	Shumeiko, V.F.	
	Saltykov, B.G.	
Agriculture	Khlystun, V.N.	Khlystun, V.N.
Atomic Energy	Mikhailov, V.N.	Mikhailov, V.N.
Culture	Sidorov, E.Iu.	Sidorov, E.Iu.
Defense	Grachev, P.S.	Grachev, P.S.
Economics	Nechaev, A.A.	Gaidar, E.T.*
Finance	Barchuk, V.V.	Fedorov, B.G.
Foreign Affairs	Kozyrev, A.V.	Kozyrev, A.V.
Health	Vorob´ev, A.I.	Nechaev, E.A.
Internal Affairs (MVD)	Yerin, V.F.	Yerin, V.F.
Justice	Fedorov, N.V.	Kalmykov, Iu.Kh.
State Property	Chubais, A.B.	Chubais, A.B.
Transport	Yefimov, V.B.	Yefimov, V.B.

*Acting

nomic change may be attributed in large measure to their political proximity to the presidency and their progressive personnel. As new and relatively small agencies, these state committees were able to fill their ranks with officials sympathetic to a new economic course.[56] In contrast, the reformist contingent in the Ministries of Finance and Economics was restricted to a small group at the top of each apparatus. Beneath them worked officials with largely unreconstructed views.[57]

Table 4.3

Leading Members of Russian Governments in Yeltsin's Second Term

	15 April 1997	15 May 1998	15 January 1999
Prime Minister	Chernomyrdin, V.S.	Kirienko, S.V.	Primakov, E.M.
First Deputy Prime Ministers	Nemtsov, B.E. Chubais, A.B.	None	Masliukov, Iu.D. Gustov, V.A.
Deputy Prime Ministers	Bulgak, V.B. Kokh, A.P. Kulikov, A.S. Serov, V.M., Sysuev, O.N., Urinson, Ia.M.,	Nemtsov, B.E. Sysuev, O.N. Khristenko, V.B.	Bulgak, V.B. Kulik, G.V. Matvienko, V.L.
Agriculture	Khlystun, V.N.	Semenov, V.A.	Semenov, V.A.
Atomic Energy	Mikhailov, V.N.	Adamov, E.O.	Adamov, E.O.
Culture	Sidorov, E.Iu.	Dementeva, N.L.	Yegorov, V.K.
Defense	Rodionov, I.N.	Sergeev, I.D.	Sergeev, I.D.
Economics	Urinson, Ia.M.	Urinson, Ia.M.	Shapoval'iants, A.G.
Emergency Situations	Shoigu, S.K.	Shoigu, S.K.	Shoigu, S.K.
Finance	Chubais, A.B.	Zadornov, M.M.	Zadornov, M.M.
Foreign Affairs	Primakov, E.M.	Primakov, E.M.	Ivanov, I.S.
Health	Dmitrieva, T.B.	Rutkovskii, O.V.	Starodubov, V.I.
Internal Affairs (MVD)	Kulikov, A.S.	Stepashin, S.V.	Stepashin, S.V.
Justice	Stepashin, S.V. P.V.	Krasheninnikov, P.V.	Krasheninnikov, P.V.
State Property	Kokh, A.R.	Gazizullin, F.R.	Gazizullin, F.R.
Transport	Tsakh, N.P.	Frank, S.O.	Frank, S.O.

Besides an array of ministries and other executive agencies, the Russian executive also boasts a network of councils and interministerial commissions that operate under the auspices of the Government, and usually under the chairmanship of first deputy or deputy prime ministers.[58] In the middle of 1995, there were twenty-eight such institutions, ranging from commissions on economic reform and agrarian policy to the Government's news service—ITAR-TASS—and academic think tanks. A few of these bodies carried out important administrative duties, such as the Russian Fund for Federal Property, which was created to sell state property to the private sector. Most of these institutions, however, were designed to enhance cooperation among executive agencies or provide expertise in specialized fields. Unlike in France, however, where the president and prime minister often use interministerial councils or commissions as important policy-making forums, senior Russian leaders have shown little direct interest in the work of interagency organizations. When they wish to forge new policies, they tend to rely instead on more informal brainstorming sessions at state dachas on the outskirts of Moscow.

These brainstorming sessions merit serious attention as a policy-making forum in the USSR and in post-Communist Russia. Because of the paucity of cabinetlike institutions in Moscow that could air and resolve the competing claims of state institutions, policy debates have at times migrated to other, more efficient, venues during moments of political crisis or policy transition. Following Yeltsin's reelection in July 1996, for example, two working groups met at the Government retreat in Volynskoe—Stalin's former dacha—to draft urgent financial stabilization measures as well as a proposal to reform the structure of the Government itself. These sessions were merely the latest confirmation of Volynskoe's long-standing role as a center for dispute resolution and policy innovation. Volynskoe's advantages lay in its informal atmosphere and in the deadlines imposed on the negotiations. But these brainstorming sessions have had one serious, and often fatal, disadvantage: the top leaders stayed home and sent their representatives. Thus, the results of these summits of underlings did not bind the country's leadership. The proposals crafted at Volynskoe and other retreats were sure to attract the attention, but not necessarily the support, of the president, prime minister, and heads of the federal organs of state power.[59]

Reforming the Civil Service

Behind the complex executive edifice described above works an army of Russian civil servants. Due to the exodus of "national cadres" to their respective republics and the migration of ambitious and highly qualified officials to rewarding jobs in the private sector, the new Russian state was able to replace approximately half of this bureaucratic army during 1992 and 1993.[60] The result was a civil service divided between remnants of the old order and fresh recruits who at times lacked the professional qualifications and experience necessary for their posts. In a disparaging reference to this "enrollment" of personnel in the early Yeltsin years, the head of the Russian Civil Service Academy observed that "quite a number of rally-type activists found their way into the service on the crest of this wave."[61] In Yeltsin's own words, a part of this group—which included former journalists, deputies, and leaders of social movements—"ceded to the temptations of power."[62]

During his first term, the Russian president and his associates recognized the need for fundamental reform of the civil service. According to Sergei Filatov:

> [W]e don't have a careful and well worked out system of recruitment and assessment of qualifications of state workers. Because hiring and firing are not institutionalized, this area is subject to the most naked political efforts of groups of influence to have their way on cadres questions, often in opposition to interests of the president and Government. These groups of influence are not at all interested in professional qualities. It's sufficient to have their man in office.[63]

Distancing Russia from its Communist past required, therefore, adjustments in the methods of training, selection, promotion, and operation of these officials. Again to quote Yeltsin: "Any [policy] changes are doomed to failure if the staff of the service is not reformed at the same time."[64]

But two factors delayed the reform of the Russian bureaucracy until the very end of 1993. The first was a concern for the stability of the fledgling Russian state. According to the Russian president:

> After August 1991, at a critical juncture for Russian statehood, we consciously refrained from personnel reshuffles. This is precisely why the state did not go over the brink into anarchy and chaos.[65]

Second, in 1992 and 1993, a struggle for control of the bureaucracy among the presidency, Government, and parliament prevented the development of new legislation on the civil service. During this period, attempts to draft laws governing the bureaucracy failed, as each institution insisted on provisions that would work to its own advantage.[66]

Immediately following the enactment of the December 1993 constitution, which transformed the presidency into the central institution in the Russian state, Yeltsin issued an expansive decree setting out the contours of a new federal civil service.[67] It would be another year, however, before the appearance of presidential directives that mandated the implementation of civil service reform, and still longer before changes began to take hold in the Russian bureaucracy.[68] Here, as in so many areas of Russian life, the president's resolve did not match the powerful institutional resistance from within the Government. As one observer remarked, Yeltsin's decree on the civil service launched "a struggle between the presidential apparatus and the head of the Government for control of the Council of Ministers."[69]

The politics of civil service reform in Russia engaged many distinct sets of interests: those of the presidency, the Government apparatus and the various ministries, the parliament, rank-and-file civil servants, and scholars of law and administration. Many in the last camp sought to bring Russian officialdom closer to Weberian principles of modern public administration, with its emphases on professionalism in training and career advancement, political independence and neutrality of officials, and clear jurisdictional boundaries between offices.[70] For their part, civil servants—especially those in the middle and lower ranks—appeared less concerned about their autonomy from politics than with job perquisites and security. In the transition economy, state officials found themselves less well remunerated than private-sector professionals but also less subject to the wage arrears and layoffs that affected other public-sector employees.

For the presidency, civil service reform represented an opportunity to recruit and train a new generation of officials who would follow the lead of the head of state. As an office standing above the Government, parliament, and judiciary—and as the self-styled engine of reform during the transition from Communism—the Russian presidency viewed itself as the country's primary institutional patron, much like the Communist Party. The head of the presidential administration, Sergei Filatov, described the Russian civil service as "an extremely important instrument of state that has a special role in the strategy and tactics of reform."[71] Implicit in these remarks was the belief that that this particular lever of authority belonged in the hands of the presidency. The official in charge of cadres policy in the presidency later made this point explicitly when he referred to the Russian civil service as "an extension of presidential power."[72]

The presidency sought to professionalize and centralize control over Russian officialdom through four related reforms. In a decree of 6 June 1994, Yeltsin created a new Academy of Civil Service, which assumed primary responsibility for developing a discipline of public administration in Russia and of training—and retraining—the country's bureaucrats.[73] An appendage of the presidency, the Academy of Civil Service drew together a vast network of regional training institutes that had served in the Soviet era as "higher party schools."[74] Just as under the old regime, bureaucrats spent from two weeks to several months in these centers "raising their qualifications." Although the training centers were still dominated by instructors inherited from the higher party schools, their curriculum had been infused with concepts drawn from both Western organizational theory and the new Russian constitution.[75]

Standardizing civil service rules across branches and institutions was a centerpiece of bureaucratic reform in post-Communist Russia. Russia had inherited from the Soviet Union an intricate system of civil service rankings that allowed institutions to maintain differential pay scales and service grades. Obviously, the more powerful and better-funded agencies benefited from this decentralized approach to personnel issues. Referring to the discrepancies in wages across agencies, Yeltsin asked:

> Why is it that in some state departments allowances are several times higher than in others, and for the same work? Whose purpose does this serve? I am sure it is not the majority of civil servants. It is time to tackle this extremely neglected problem.[76]

In a decree of 11 January 1995, Yeltsin introduced a unified civil service ranking that embraced personnel in the presidency, Government and ministers, parliament, and judiciary.[77] One finds echoes here of the Table of Ranks, which organized the prerevolutionary Russian service classes into a rigid hierarchy.[78] The fourteen grades in the current Russian civil service belong to one of five service categories: higher, main, leading, senior, or junior. Where the president sets the qualifications needed for admission to the top two categories, the prime minister, or his designated agent, establishes the qualifications for the bottom three. Because the two highest groups contain all key leadership posts in the bureaucracy, the president is the preeminent figure in shaping the profile of Russian officialdom.

Perhaps the most important distinction in the new civil service rankings is between political appointees, who serve at the pleasure of their immediate superiors, and career civil servants, who receive contracts for up to five years after completing a three- to six-month probationary period. Whereas the president's personal staff and the heads of institutions immediately accountable to the head of state form part of the first group—known in Russian as "category B"—subordinate personnel in presidential departments, from deputy heads on down, are considered permanent civil servants, part of "category V."[79] Likewise, in the Government, those officials subject to dismissal by presidential, prime ministerial, or ministerial decree may be distinguished from career officials. The precise number of officials comprising this political class is not known. But in comparative terms, Russia clearly falls between Great Britain, where a change of Government exposes only a hundred-odd executive officials to removal, and the United States, where a new administration can fill approximately three thousand top federal executive posts with its own loyalists. Such at least are the provisions contained in current Russian legislation. But the test of the country's ability to separate political and administrative posts—and therefore to insulate permanent civil servants against undue political pressure—will come only with the first change of leadership in the post-Communist era. Consolidating democracy requires not just the transfer of power from one ruling group to another but the willingness of the new ruling group to respect the independence of the country's permanent administrative class.

One of the more contentious elements of civil service reform concerns the prohibitions imposed on bureaucrats that do not extend to the general population. Under new legislation, Russian civil servants may not strike, engage in private business, or receive outside remuneration, save that associated with teaching, research, or creative activity. Reacting against the Communist Party's penetration of the Soviet bureaucracy, the Yeltsin leadership has also insisted on a formal ban on party organizations in the civil service.[80] It should be noted, however, that this provision has not prevented leading executive officials from mobilizing subordinates in the bureaucracy behind their own—or their allies'—campaigns during national and regional elections. Thus, the ban seems to be applied to all parties except the "party of power," which at the national level is Our Home Is Russia, the party of the prime minister, Viktor Chernomyrdin.

In the formal perquisites of office, Russian civil servants appear in some respects to rival their West European counterparts. Although the pay itself is modest by private sector standards, the benefits are generous: a paid annual leave of a month for beginning officials, free medical care, and an indexed pension equal to 80 percent of salary at the time of retirement.[81] Whether a fledgling state in the grip of an economic crisis can afford the provisions found in mature democracies remains in doubt. On the other hand, to deny civil servants a comfortable living invites them to use their public positions for private gain. Dissatisfied with their meager pay, and unchecked by either esprit de corps or effective law enforcement, Russian bureaucrats have in fact extracted bribes on a massive scale from businesses and ordinary citizens alike.[82] Such corrupt practices not only raised the transaction costs of doing business but undermined the integrity of state administration. Rather than faithfully carrying out orders from above, officials at times took their cues instead from the demands of society's most insistent and prosperous members.

As we noted earlier, to centralize and standardize policy on the civil service, Yeltsin created a new office in the presidency in March 1996, the Main Administration for Civil Service and Personnel Issues, later renamed the Administration for Personnel Policy.[83] Much like its Communist Party predecessors, this presidential agency was empowered to develop a list of eligible candidates for posts to be filled by the president, including those at the summit of the armed forces and the diplomatic service and throughout the judiciary. But for all its prominence in personnel matters, the presidency did not monopolize decision making in this arena. For one, the Administration for Personnel Policy was a support arm of the interbranch Council on Civil Service, a successor to the Council on Cadres Policy. It is this council that made the formal recommendations for appointments to the president. The Council on Civil Service drew its twenty-four members in equal numbers from the four institutional pillars of the Russian state: six each from the presidency, the Government, the parliament (three from each chamber), and the judiciary (two from each of the three supreme courts).[84] Moreover, responsibility for the appointment of civil servants remained, for the most part, in the hands of the institutions in which the officials worked.

The considerable formal authority amassed by the president in the personnel field should not be confused, therefore, with more traditional, and effective, forms of patronage power. The president may hire and fire a small circle of executive officials—and shape broader policy on the civil service writ large—but he does not yet have mechanisms of control in place that would ensure the loyalty of Russian officialdom.[85] In this sense, he lacks traditional, charismatic, or rational-legal authority. It is still possible, as one observer recently lamented, for a person to work in the state apparatus and complain openly that the president is destroying the country—less a testament to Russia's newfound freedom than to a kind of bureaucratic anarchy.[86] President Yeltsin finds himself, therefore, in the quandary of the ordinary citizen in Soviet times. When the citizen asks if he has the right to do something, the official answers yes. But when he inquires if he can use that right, the response is no.[87]

More than five years into the post-Communist era, the Russian political leadership had not succeeded in developing a civil service that accepted its "constitutional role of carrying out the will of elected governments."[88] In this respect, the Russian bureaucracy operated as an extreme version of the

Continental administrative model, in which officials maintain "an aloof, even suspicious, attitude toward party politics."[89] As Ferrel Heady has observed, in Continental bureaucracies, state officials believe that, "possessing a bit of sovereignty," they are entitled to the "respectful attention" of the citizenry. In such systems, "the bureaucrat is considered a public official rather than a public servant."[90] It is, however, in developing societies, and not Continental Europe, that one finds the closest parallels to Russian officialdom. In their reluctance to accept "the universality of rules" and to elevate civic and legal loyalty above personal and parochial interests, Russian bureaucrats have returned to a premodern culture of administration, with its emphases on bartering and negotiation rather than the application of fixed and impersonal rules.[91]

Conclusion

The size, fragmentation, and arcane procedures of the Russian bureaucracy make the Government one of the most inscrutable and inefficient elements of the new Russian political system. In mocking tribute to the complexity of Russian officialdom, a Moscow journalist remarked that there are now three perennial questions troubling the Russian nation. Besides "Who is to blame?" and "What is to be done?" Russians puzzle over "What is the Government?"[92] Fedor Burlatskii made a similar point more forcefully and prosaically: "Never mind those pipe dreams about building a legal state or a welfare state, we need to revive a Government."[93]

In *Political Order in Changing Societies,* written thirty years ago, Samuel Huntington observed that, for all their ideological differences, the political systems of the Soviet Union and the West were alike in vital respects. "These governments command the loyalties of their citizens and have the capacity to tax resources, to conscript manpower, and to innovate and execute policy. If the [Soviet] Politburo, the [British] Cabinet, or the [American] President makes a decision, the probability is high that it will be implemented through the government machinery."[94] The same could not said of the Russian Government, or the Russian state, by the mid-1990s.

Russia's political decay was evident to Yeltsin, but the Russian president proved unwilling, or unable, to support projects that could have reversed this trend. Following his election to a second term in July 1996, Yeltsin committed himself rhetorically to the establishment of a "strong government." To achieve this goal, a working group under the direction of the minister of economics, Yevgenii Yasin, advanced a radical plan to "transform the Government into a compact team in the style of European cabinets of ministers." This proposal envisioned a Government composed of only twenty to twenty-five members, where the ministers would be—in the Western tradition—purely political figures recruited from outside the ministries and appointed by the president. Working immediately under each minister would be a "minister of state," a specialist appointed from within the ministry by the prime minister. Such a system would have balanced the need for political control from above with the requirement for expertise from below.[95]

A bold challenge to deeply entrenched bureaucratic interests, this initiative encountered fierce resistance from high-ranking executive officials, including First Deputy Prime Minister Oleg Soskovets, and Oleg Lobov, secretary of the president's own Security Council and former minister of economics. A team of specialists linked to Soskovets proposed an alternative reform of the Government, which "maintain[ed] continuity with the old Council of Ministers by making 'cosmetic repairs' to the current Government." In the event, the president and prime minister rejected the "extreme" and "romantic" proposal of the Ministry of Economics in favor of an incremental reform of the existing structure of Government.[96] Only with the formation of the Kirienko Government in the spring of 1998 did one see a serious—if short-lived—attempt to introduce elements of the Yasin plan.[97]

Besides the peculiar structure of the Russian executive, the absence of a well-developed patronage system has also complicated the governance of Russia. To harness bureaucratic power in the absence of a mature legal culture among officials, political leaders must rely on a spoils system as an instrument of control. To Russia's detriment, however, Boris Yeltsin never put a team of officials atop the Russian bureaucracy that possessed the loyalty and cohesion essential to govern a complex modern state, save the stillborn Government of Kirienko. As Fred Riggs observed in the 1960s in regard to new states,

> without firm political guidance bureaucrats have weak incentives to provide good service, whatever their formal, pre-entry training and professional qualifications. . . . They tend to use these effective controls to safeguard their expedient bureaucratic interests—tenure, seniority rights, fringe benefits, tolerance of poor performance, the right to violate official norms—rather than to advance the achievement of program goals. Hence the career, merit bureaucracy in a developing country not only fails to accomplish the administrative goals set for it but also stands in the way of political development.[98]

This failure leads "to a lack of balance between political policy-making institutions and bureaucratic policy-implementing structures. The relative weakness of political organs means that the political function tends to be appropriated, in considerable measure, by bureaucrats. Intra-bureaucratic struggles become a primary focus of politics."[99] Such was the case in Yeltsin's Russia.

5

The Politics of the Dual Executive

Policy Making on War and Peace, Finance, and Legal Affairs

Approaching Russian politics through the prism of institutions highlights the powerful effect of rules and organizations on political behavior. But it can also obscure the impact of more changeable features of the political landscape. Although intraexecutive tensions follow inexorably from the institutional arrangements of semipresidentialism, the politics of the dual executive can assume various forms, depending on the particular mix of issues, circumstances, and personalities. Thus, answering the question "Who governs in Russia?" invites another set of questions, among the most important of which is "On what issue?" To understand the varieties of Russian executive politics, this chapter examines policy making in three fields: national security, finance, and judicial reform.

National Security and the Chechen War

Policy making and implementation in the field of national security have defied the traditional rules of political engagement between Government and presidency. As we noted earlier, the power ministries form a distinct part of the Government that operates under the direct tutelage of the president. Although the prime minister may help to shape budgetary policy in the national security sector—an especially contentious issue in an era of military downsizing—he lies outside of the chain of command. Only in Yeltsin's second term, during the Primakov Government, does one find a prime minister who sought to play a more prominent role in national security issues in light of his own personal background in foreign affairs and intelligence and the illness of the president.

Minimizing the role of the prime minister on questions of national security does not eliminate bureaucratic politics between the presidency and the security ministries or between the ministries themselves. A case in point is foreign affairs. Andrei Kozyrev, the Russian foreign minister from 1991 to 1995, waged an ongoing battle with the Security Council and other presidential structures to prevent them from interfering in the work of the Ministry of Foreign Affairs. In September 1992, for example, influential members of the Security Council convinced Yeltsin to reject the advice of the foreign ministry and postpone a scheduled trip to Japan—a decision that caused a diplomatic furor. In his memoirs, Kozyrev accused the Security Council under Yurii Skokov of seeking to transform itself into a coordinating agency akin to the Communist Party's General Department.[1] Such an institution would have eroded the influence and access of individual ministers—including the foreign minister—and undermined the reformist line in national security policy.

That the Security Council did not emerge as a more powerful counterweight to the Foreign Ministry may appear surprising given the relative weakness of Kozyrev. Like most foreign ministers in the early years of Soviet power, Kozyrev was a specialist in diplomacy with little expertise or influence in Kremlin politics. Furthermore, he acquired a reputation as an ally of the West at a time when growing numbers of Russians were souring on the westernizing currents that had been unleashed by Gorbachev. But Security Council leaders had their own vulnerabilities. The president's Security Council tended to attract the most conservative elements from the military and the secret police, including Vice President Aleksandr Rutskoi, who sought to use the institution in the early 1990s as a staging point from which to challenge Yeltsin's authority. The presence of such discredited forces undermined the efforts of the Security Council to interpose itself between the president and the foreign minister.[2] Thus, both Kozyrev and his more experienced and weighty successor as foreign minister, Evgenii Primakov, managed to retain direct access to the president. In the making and implementation of Russian foreign policy in the Yeltsin years, there was arguably less institutional redundancy than in the Soviet era—or, for that matter, in the recent American politics.[3]

Within the Russian presidency, it was not only the Security Council that competed with the foreign ministry for influence in international affairs. On occasion, officials in the president's Executive Office intervened directly in international affairs. While leading an advance team to Japan in 1992 to prepare for the Russian president's visit, Yeltsin's chief of staff, Yurii Petrov, allowed himself to be drawn into substantive negotiations with his Japanese hosts. Presidential aides could also be a source of scorching criticism of the foreign minister. An outspoken political advisor to Yeltsin, Andrik Migranian, characterized Kozyrev as globetrotting "like a madman from Vancouver to Cape Town to Casablanca, raising huge clouds of dust. . . . [The result was] hectic but fruitless activity, improvisation, incompetence."[4] Ironically, the foreign ministry appears to have had little conflict with the one person in the Kremlin whose portfolio targeted international relations exclusively, Dmitrii Riurikov, the presidential counselor for foreign affairs.

The same could not be said of General Pavel Grachev, the minister of defense. In numerous episodes during Yeltsin's first term, Grachev displayed an unwillingness to respect the foreign policy line advanced by Kozyrev. As Scott Parrish has argued, "Grachev and the Defense Ministry . . . pursue[d] a quasi-independent line of policy with little regard for the Foreign Ministry—most conspicuously on the issue of NATO expansion," but also on Chinese nuclear testing and Russia's claims to the Kurile Islands.[5] Conflicts between ministers of foreign affairs and defense are, of course, commonplace in modern states. But what is remarkable about the Russian case is the frequency and publicity of these disputes, which can be attributed, like so much else in Russian politics, to a failure of presidential leadership. In the field of foreign affairs, then, the major axis of institutional conflict was not between the foreign ministry and the presidential apparatus but between the foreign ministry and other members of the Government, especially the defense ministry.

On issues of domestic security, intraexecutive politics was even more complicated and turbulent, owing to the larger number of actors and the greater range and urgency of the issues. Because the immediate threats to Russian statehood after 1991 originated within the country and not overseas, and because the power ministries were themselves instruments in the struggle for power in Moscow and between Moscow and the provinces, much was at stake in the management of domestic security policy. As Chapter 3 illustrates, throughout Yeltsin's first term, the president's Security Council attempted to establish itself as an intermediary in the chain of command between the president and the Government's domestic security agencies. But at no point was the Security Council more assertive toward the power ministries than in the late summer of 1996, when the lack of military success in the Chechen conflict, and the appointment of General Lebed to head the Security Council, challenged existing institutional relations in the field of domestic security.

Of all the issues facing the domestic security sector, the most visible and divisive was waging war and peace in Chechnia. Sensitive to the unpopularity of the Chechen conflict, Yeltsin had distanced himself from the prosecution of the war and even the negotiation of the peace. As the president's health deteriorated in the second half of 1996, his neglect of the Chechen conflict became even more pronounced. Presidential disengagement from the Chechen crisis allowed the ministers of defense and internal affairs wide latitude in the conduct of the hostilities. But this lack of presidential leadership led inevitably to sharp conflicts between the two ministries over military strategy and tactics. Uncertainties about the precise lines of authority resulted not only in endless bureaucratic intrigue in Moscow but also in occasional tensions between defense and internal affairs units on the ground in Chechnia. Even the prime minister, whose traditional writ did not run to military operations, became deeply involved in the Budennovsk hostage drama and then in the tortuous debates over peacemaking in Chechnia.

The injection of General Lebed into this already volatile mixture of institutions and personalities proved explosive. On assuming office in June 1996, Lebed moved quickly to consolidate his role as security tsar, not only in the presidency but throughout the Russian executive. A purge of his competitors began in late June with the removal of Yurii Baturin as Yeltsin's counselor for national security affairs. Lebed immediately stepped in to fill this position, and thus to occupy both of the Kremlin's policy-oriented posts in national security. He turned next to the two leading operational institutions in security affairs in the presidency, the Kremlin Guard and the Main Security Administration. Working with Anatolii Chubais, Yeltsin's new chief of staff, Lebed engineered the dismissal of their leaders, Generals Korzhakov and Barsukov.

Having eliminated his adversaries in the presidency, Lebed demanded personnel changes in the Government's power ministries. On 18 June, Yeltsin acceded to Lebed's request for the removal of General Andrei Grachev, who, like Korzhakov, had been a fierce Yeltsin loyalist since the late Soviet era. Grachev's eventual replacement was a Lebed ally, General Igor Rodionov, whose distinguished career was overshadowed in the minds of some by his involvement in the repression of Georgian nationalist demonstrations in Tbilisi in 1989.[6] At this point, Lebed appeared to be on his way to achieving his broader strategy of replenishing the higher ranks of the armed forces with his own clients. As one Russian journalist observed, recent revisions in the Security Council's charter had invited Lebed "to create his own 'party' in Army circles."[7]

Lebed encountered fierce bureaucratic resistance, however, in his attempts to remake security institutions in his image. His most unyielding opponent was the head of the Ministry of Internal Affairs, General Anatolii Kulikov, but even Rodionov refused Lebed's requests to purge leading officers serving under him.[8] The security bureaucracies—and the Russian executive writ large—closed ranks to defend themselves against Lebed's advance.[9] Responding to pressures from worried lieutenants and to his own misgivings about Lebed's political aspirations, Yeltsin moved to limit the powers of his Security Council chief. The instrument was once again institutional redundancy. On 26 July 1996, Yeltsin formed a new security organization in the presidency, the Defense Council, whose functional profile clearly overlapped that of the Lebed's Security Council. Although Lebed secured a place among the Defense Council's eighteen members, he failed to occupy the post of chair or deputy chair, which the president reserved for himself and the prime minister. This institutional reform brought Lebed two other indignities. Among the members of the Defense Council was the chief of the presidential staff, Anatolii Chubais, an economist with no experience in the security field but with broad political ambitions of his own. And directing the Defense Council's fifty-person staff was Yurii Baturin, whom Lebed had removed as a rival in the presidency only a month earlier. Although it was not clear how much power, if any, the president intended to invest in the Defense Council, the mere existence of parallel institutions and the ensuing jurisdictional ambiguity undermined the authority of the Security Council and its leader.[10]

The formation of the Defense Council was a tactical defeat for Lebed, but the larger battle for control of security policy and operations continued. That Lebed still retained a healthy measure of presidential confidence was illustrated by Yeltsin's assignment of the Chechen portfolio to his Security Council chief in mid-August 1996.[11] Instructed to bring the Chechen conflict to an end, Lebed threw himself into negotiations with the Chechen rebels with his usual energy and resolve. Overcoming the political—and at times physical—obstructions to peace talks raised by Russian military and civilian leaders, Lebed signed a peace treaty with the Chechen rebel leader, Zelimkhan Yanderbiev, in late September in the northern Caucasus city of Khasaviurt.[12]

The treaty created a political firestorm in Moscow, where Russian nationalists allied with Lebed's bureaucratic enemies to denounce treaty provisions that anticipated the staged secession of Chechnia from the Russian Federation. Whether for political or health reasons, Yeltsin remained on the sidelines in this debate. His silence enabled the accord's opponents to launch a vigorous and highly publicized campaign against Lebed's peacemaking efforts. Speaking to a sympathetic Russian parliament, General Kulikov characterized the treaty negotiated by Lebed as "a national betrayal." Raising the specter of a Russia encircled by hostile regimes, Kulikov argued that Lebed had "capitulated to forces that are seeking the systematic elimination of the Russian state."[13]

In this dispute Kulikov was fighting for his job as well as the territorial integrity of the Russian Federation. To consolidate his grip over security policy and operations, Lebed had demanded in mid-August that Yeltsin fire the head of the Ministry of Internal Affairs (MVD), whose troops had played a leading role in the fighting in Chechnia.[14] But the removal of Kulikov clearly would have upset the traditional balance of personalities and institutions around the president by granting a virtual monopoly of authority on security matters to Lebed, who had little respect for the low-intensity warfare that normally characterized Russian bureaucratic politics. Lebed's preferred method of engagement was the full frontal assault. When Yeltsin refused to remove Kulikov, Lebed attempted to impose his authority and policies on the head of the MVD. But Kulikov refused to subordinate himself to the Security Council chief. Responding to orders from Lebed to cease hostilities in Chechnia, Kulikov remarked that he answered only to Yeltsin. "I have a president," he insisted.[15]

The Lebed-Kulikov feud took a dramatic and dangerous turn in mid-October, when the minister of internal affairs publicly accused his rival of plotting a coup against the president, this at a time when Yeltsin was on the eve of heart surgery. According to Kulikov, in a "maniacal drive for power," Lebed was conspiring with Chechen rebels and "criminal structures" to overthrow Russia's constitutional order. The final stage in the preparations for the coup, in Kulikov's view, was the formation of a "Russian Legion," fifty thousand crack troops to be drawn from various uniformed services and subordinated directly to Lebed. Waving about documents during a press conference that purported to prove Lebed's involvement in this conspiracy, Kulikov claimed that the Security Council chief had on numerous occasions tried to involve him in the plot, justifying it on the grounds of the president's "incapacity" to hold office. To reward Kulikov for his participation, Lebed was prepared—in the words of the minister of internal affairs—to allow the police "to shoot criminals on the spot." Lebed's response to these accusations was characteristically sharp and terse: "For the first time in my life, I'm planning to sue someone—Anatolii Kulikov," though he would sue for honor and not Kulikov's money, which he alleged came from bribe taking.[16] With the fate of a nation at stake, executive politics had degenerated into a schoolyard brawl.

Kulikov represented the angry, public face of the anti-Lebed coalition that had been forming in the Russian executive for weeks. At the beginning of October, it had convinced the president to strip Lebed of one his most important powers: the review of appointments in the armed forces. With the formation of yet another institution in the presidency, the Commission on Higher Military Ranks and Positions, Yeltsin transferred the military appointment portfolio from Lebed to Baturin, the Commission's newly appointed chair. "In a minute," one retired general remarked, "Lebed became nothing to the whole Army. Now all of them will line up to see Baturin and will fight for the right to kiss his ass."[17] As if this reform were not a sufficient affront to Lebed, the president appeared on national television to criticize his Security Council chief for his inability to work harmoniously with other officials.[18]

The denouement to this extraordinary struggle within the Russian executive came in mid-October, when Yeltsin removed Lebed from his post. By all accounts, the dismissal was not a rejection of the Khasaviurt treaty but a sign of the president's disillusionment with Lebed's political style and ambition. A few days before his firing, Lebed had made an unlikely alliance with his former adversary in the presidency, General Korzhakov, who was now running for the parliamentary seat in Tula that had been vacated by Lebed. After years of faithful service to the president, Korzhakov had turned on his former patron with a vengeance, attacking the political role of Yeltsin's daughter and threatening to offer evidence of corruption in the president's entourage.[19] Whether it was this act of disloyalty or some other issue or interlocutor that prompted Yeltsin to abandon his Security Council chief, this personnel decision returned the making and implementation of security policy to the state of affairs that had existed prior to the presidential elections.[20]

With the failure of Lebed's attempt to rationalize authority in the security field, the politics of the Russian executive began to descend again into the ministerial feudalism that suited so many bureaucratic and economic interests in post-Communist Russia. But there quickly emerged from within the presidency other figures intent on coordinating and reforming the Government's uniformed services, notably Anatolii Chubais and Yurii Baturin. On the very eve of Yeltsin's heart operation, Chubais convinced the president to sign a decree that created a State Military Inspectorate. A subdivision of the presidency headed by Chubais, this inspectorate was authorized to supervise all service personnel in uniform—something that the ministry of defense had been trying to establish for itself ever since the collapse of the Soviet Union.[21] It was the latest, and in many ways the most ambitious, attempt of the presidential apparatus to create an efficient civilian apparatus of control over Russia's power ministries.[22] Like most developing states with strong presidencies, Russia entrusted the management of the power ministries to men in uniform.[23]

The difficult task of downsizing the armed forces fell to Yurii Baturin, an assignment that brought him into direct and bitter conflict with the power ministers, and especially Rodionov, whose troops had suffered most from wage arrears and underfunding.[24] Along with the fiscal conservatives in the finance ministry, Baturin and other presidential officials viewed downsizing as a means of reducing funding for the military and thereby containing a ballooning budget deficit. The minister of defense thought otherwise. He agreed to reduce his forces, but only if they received additional funding, which was needed, he argued, to make the transition to a more professional and better-equipped fighting force.[25] To press their claims, the power ministers painted an alarming picture of the state of the armed services, even the elite strategic rocket forces, which controlled nuclear weapons. In another example of the Russian executive publicly divided against itself, Baturin dismissed Rodionov's warning of "a possible command breakdown" in the strategic forces, noting that these troops were in fact "in good shape." Rodionov responded by calling, indirectly, for Baturin's dismissal.[26]

It was in fact Rodionov who would lose his post in the spring of 1997 when Yeltsin accepted the "civilians'" model of military reform, apparently frustrated by the refusal of some leaders of the uniformed services to reduce manpower, especially in the bloated senior officers corps.[27] Immediately after dismissing Rodionov and the chief of the General Staff, Viktor Samsonov, the Russian president formed two new commissions in the Defense Council, one on military organization (*voennoe stroitel'stvo*), headed by Chernomyrdin, the other on the financing of military reform, chaired by Chubais. The establishment of these oversight bodies brought a reduction in the financial and personnel autonomy of all uniformed services, from the border troops and the internal security troops of the MVD to the regular armed forces. "In one day, the Defense Ministry lost not only discretionary spending power over money received from the Finance Ministry but also control over 'internal' sources of financing," a euphemism for income from quasi-legal business ventures that had supplemented state assignations.[28] With its bureaucratic defenses being stripped away, the uniformed services were vulnerable to efforts by Baturin, Chubais, and other executive officials to reduce and reorganize the Russian armed forces.

Creating a new, post–Cold War military in Russia required changes in mission, organization, and personnel. From a troop strength of 2.8 million in 1992, the Russian military declined to 1.7 million persons in 1996 on the way to a planned force of 1.2 million by the end of the 1990s. But Russia was not so much scaling back as building down, to borrow a term from the politics of nuclear disarmament. Troop reduction came at a hefty price. Demobilized forces required severance pay and new civilian housing while the recruits for the professional—that is, nonconscripted—army that Yeltsin envisioned for the country would need better pay and conditions.[29] Thus, even if a leaner and more modern Russian army could live on the budget of its bloated predecessor, making the transition was itself an expensive and therefore politically difficult proposition, given the budgetary crises.[30] Finding additional funding for reform was especially problematic at a time when pay in the military was falling further behind the civilian sector and when wage arrears of three months or more were common. Conscious of the rise of political opposition within the armed forces, linked in part to deteriorating living and working conditions, Yeltsin approved a significant pay increase for military personnel in April 1997.[31]

With the assistance of a new and more reform-oriented defense minister, Igor Sergeev, Russia made considerable progress in the streamlining of its military organizations in Yeltsin's second term. Here, as in the executive writ large, institutional redundancy had been rampant. By the summer of 1998, Sergeev had been able to reduce the number of military districts as well as merge whole service branches. Separate organizations for air defense and the regular air force had been collapsed into a single unit. Similarly, three organizations responsible for nuclear and space warfare merged.[32] Finally, Russia began to address the proliferation of sizable armed units within the many power ministries that dotted the executive landscape. In late 1997, the MVD transferred its internal security forces to the regular army. According to Sergeev, such controversial reforms were essential to save a demoralized Russian military: "Either we keep an army which is falling apart and a navy which is sinking, or we take extremely unpopular measures to optimise and reduce the armed forces."[33]

Leadership Responses to Financial Crises

Removing the Chechen war from the forefront of Russian politics refocused attention on the serious financial crisis that had been building in the country for years. By 1996, the Russian budget was in shambles. Taken together with a decline in economic output and unsustainable spending on defense and other state services, massive tax evasion by enterprises large and small had produced a catastrophic shortfall in state revenues. The earlier expedient of printing money to close the deficit was no longer available to a Russian Government that had committed itself to a policy of low inflation, in part to satisfy requirements for a $10.5 billion loan from the IMF. As the 1996 fiscal year progressed, the official budget passed by the Duma ceased to function as an effective guideline for public expenditures. Faced with an annual deficit approaching 40 percent, the Government simply halted or curtailed spending on many state programs in midyear. What had been a more or less open and democratic struggle over the official budget now turned into a no-holds-barred back-room battle for disbursements among executive officials, parliamentary leaders, and regional elites, each pressuring president and prime minister for a share of scarce treasury receipts.[34]

Russia's inability to perform one of the essential tasks of the modern state—filling the treasury—invited bureaucratic and popular responses that weakened presidential authority. State organizations in Russia sought to insulate themselves from the vagaries of federal budgetary politics by establishing sources of revenue that were independent of the state treasury. These so-called extrabudgetary funds (*vnebiudzhetnye fondy*) built on the long-standing Soviet tradition of economic autarchy. But instead of creating "hidden reserves" in the form of hoarded material and personnel *wealth,* post-Communist institutions in Russia sought a steady stream of *income* to broaden their economic and political autonomy. For example, the republic of Sakha retained 20 percent of the diamonds mined in the region for its own use, but rather than directing the proceeds into the republican treasury, it channeled them into various extrabudgetary funds, which remained outside the scrutiny of the public and federal authorities.[35]

For many of the country's eighty-nine regions and republics, the financial crisis in the center validated their attempts to expand their own taxing power and hence their fiscal and political autonomy. Aware of the restive mood outside of the capital, the Government did not renege on the payment of what amounted to block grants to subsidized regions, though they often delayed these disbursements. And all regions and republics suffered from the sequestration of funds that had been earmarked for local institutions and individual citizens. It was a "new federalism"—to use the American term for the recent shift in financial responsibility from federal to state governments—but one spawned as much by a fiscal emergency as a rejection of a potent national government.

For many ordinary Russians, the fiscal crisis of the mid-1990s had dire consequences. Winter food supplies arrived perilously late in the most vulnerable northern districts. Numerous cities strapped for cash introduced power blackouts to conserve energy. In Vladivostok, the city's residents went without electricity in May 1997 for up to twenty-three hours a day. On Sakhalin Island, the local media reported that children had begun a hunger strike in the spring of 1998 to protest the nonpayment of wages and benefits to their parents.[36] And in a period when many large, privatized enterprises withheld pay from their workers for months at a time, the Government was also grossly delinquent in making payments to pensioners as well as its own employees. Independent from the state budget in much the same way as the United States' Social Security trust fund, the Russian Pension Fund owed retirees more than 16 trillion rubles (about $3 billion) by the end of 1996.[37] According to President Yeltsin, "more than half of the country's citizens suffer from delays in the payment of wages and pensions; the noose of non-payments is paralyzing the economy."[38]

With their household economies in crisis, many Russians turned to moonlighting in one or more jobs to supplement the sporadic payments and basic social services offered by their employer of record. Those in government service often resorted to bribe taking from businesses seeking licenses or other state "goods." A sense of social injustice fed this illegal activity. For example, officials in the Ministry of Fuel and Energy asked themselves, "Why should our top personnel make less than charwomen in Gazprom?" the prosperous natural gas company that they regulated.[39] Ordinary Russians also extracted a form of credit from the state by refusing to pay rent and utilities on time. One-third of all Muscovites in 1996 were at least three months behind on their rent payments, and one-tenth had effectively ceased paying rent at all.[40]

Where the lucky or enterprising found a shelter, or *krysha,* to protect them from the fallout of a command economy in transition, most remained vulnerable to its painful and unpredictable course. The widespread feeling of economic insecurity strengthened the hand of opposition parties, most notably the Communists and Liberal Democrats, who attributed Russia's economic crisis and national humiliation to the policies of President Yeltsin. Although the opposition failed to unseat Yeltsin in the 1996 presidential election, it retained the preponderance of seats in the Duma, whose responsibility for budgetary and tax laws limited the president's freedom of maneuver in economic affairs. Indeed, the reluctance of the parliament to scale back expenditures or to modernize the tax code contributed significantly to the country's financial crisis.

The Russian experience illustrates that democratic politics can be a potent barrier to fundamental economic reform. When societies move from a command economy to a market economy, their citizens are asked to sacrifice living standards and job security in exchange for the promise of a future economic revival.[41] Such bargains are hard for even the most persuasive and engaged politicians to strike, never mind leaders such as Boris Yeltsin, who had limited knowledge of, and a wavering commitment to, a market economy. One finds the political roots of Russia's financial crisis, therefore, in Yeltsin's own indecisiveness, in popular resistance to the costs of transforming the economy, and in the ability of bureaucratic and business elites to protect their interests at the expense of the state's.

By encouraging the fragmentation and privatization of political power, bureaucratic and business elites impeded the development of a coherent and effective economic policy in post-Communist Russia. Assessing Russia's political and economic transition, Mancur Olson lamented the absence of an essential ingredient of the postwar economic miracles in Germany and Japan: the destruction of entrenched lobbies and cartels.[42] Where foreign occupation swept away institutional barriers to economic reform in Germany and Japan, the collapse of Communism had the opposite effect in Russia: it gave new life to sectoral and regional structures that had been tamed by the oversight, socialization, and patronage policies of the Communist Party.

Temporarily disoriented by the August coup and its aftermath, the old interest networks quickly regathered their forces and, with new sectoral lobbies such as the banks, began to extract from the state far-reaching political and economic concessions. Seeking what economists call "rents," that is, superprofits derived from protection against competition, well-connected Russian businesses carved out a privileged economy for themselves that was neither market nor Communist.[43] For example, the state electric monopoly reportedly had three hundred small subsidiaries that sold energy on the black market.[44]

Tax and customs privileges granted to firms and organizations with close ties to the political leadership served as a major source of hemorrhaging from the treasury. Even seemingly minor relief from customs duties at times produced enormous losses to the state. A case in point was the removal of customs duties on items imported by the Russian Sports Committee, which was responsible for preparing athletes for the 1996 Olympic games. Besides sports equipment, the committee imported alcohol—millions of bottles of it. The state thereby lost the lucrative tax on imported spirits as well as revenues from the consumption of domestically produced alcohol, whose sales were undermined by duty-free foreign liquor. In few sectors of the economy was so much at stake for the treasury as in the production and sale of alcoholic beverages, over which tsars and Soviets had maintained a monopoly for more than a century. If during that period the taxes and profits from alcohol accounted for between 30 and 50 percent of the state's revenues, that figure had fallen to less than 5 percent in the post-Communist era. Where the Soviet treasury had received 9 rubles for each half liter of vodka sold in 1990, the Russian treasury took in only 2 rubles, in constant prices, at the end of 1996.[45] Whether out of ignorance, "friendship," or political calculation, Boris Yeltsin issued many of the decrees that undermined fiscal discipline. A steady stream of supplicants—ministerial officials, regional politicians, and enterprise directors—approached the president in search of favors. Economics Minister Yevgenii Yasin complained that Yeltsin had "his favorite directors who can open any doors."[46]

For a time, Russia appeared to have a government that couldn't say no. With neither parliament nor president committed to budgetary austerity, the usual guardian of the national till, the finance minister, had little success in imposing fiscal discipline. In the spring of 1994, however, a mounting budget deficit strengthened the hand of those in the executive who opposed the granting of tax and customs relief. With the support of Yeltsin, a presidential advisor on the economy, Aleksandr Livshits, began to target the destructive power of lobbies in Russia's transition from a command economy. A central task of the presidency, Livshits argued, was to uphold a national economic policy against the special pleading of "forces in the Duma and . . . representives of certain sector[al] blocs."[47] Along with several other members of the presidential apparatus, Livshits inspired the presidential decrees of May 1994 and March 1995 that annulled scores of earlier directives granting special privileges in foreign trade to organizations and regions.[48] These directives had cost the state treasury an estimated 15 trillion rubles in lost revenues. For Livshits, the political and cultural significance of the new decrees exceeded their financial import. Such acts, he argued, "break traditions and stereotypes of thinking" about exchange relations between the center, on the one hand, and sectors and regions on the other. "Even if we can prevent large-scale leaks in the budget for just two to three months, we will succeed in inculcating order in the nation" (*priuchit' narod k poriadku*).[49]

But the storm of lobbying following these decrees was so intense that one Kremlin visitor commented to Livshits: "I'm surprised to find you alive."[50] On 1 June 1994, only a week after issuing the first decree, the president granted an exemption from the decree to the energy sector, known in Russian by its acronym, TEK (*toplivo-energicheskii kompleks*), which had received the vast majority of special licenses and quotas.[51] The exemption reportedly followed vigorous pressure by the Government,[52] whose leader, Viktor Chernomyrdin, was bound to the TEK by what one critic called "old-boy gas-industry friendship" (*muzhkaia gazpromovskaia druzhba*).[53] It is not surprising, then, that many of the TEK's most prominent companies, such as LUKoil, owed the largest tax bills to the state.[54]

Among the many regions seeking relief from the 1995 decree was Kaliningrad, which protested that the president's action, annulling a ten-year exemption on customs duties signed in 1993, would cost the territory three hundred billion rubles. Kaliningrad was one of eleven economic or administrative regions to have received favored status in foreign trade relations.[55] Again, the president and key ministers began to bend under the political pressure. In April 1995, Deputy Prime Minister Chubais promised Kaliningrad officials that the center would make good on their losses. Heightening the pressure from Kaliningrad was an alarming shift in the political loyalties of the local citizens. Whereas Russia's Choice—a party sympathetic to the president—had received a majority of the vote in the region in the 1993 parliamentary elections, the Communists and the Liberal Democrats enjoyed the greatest popular support in Kaliningrad by the middle of 1995, only a few months before the critical parliamentary elections of December.[56]

During the more than six months of parliamentary and presidential election campaigns—from the end of 1995 through the early summer of 1996—Yeltsin called off officials such as Livshits who sought to elevate *raison d'état* above private economic power. After a Government commission on nonpayments, headed by then First Deputy Prime Minister Anatolii Chubais, issued an edict instructing a large Siberian oil company to pay its substantial tax arrears, the local governor countered with a decree that postponed the obligation. Not wishing to alienate officials during the electoral campaign, Yeltsin refused to stand up to such maneuvers, and in so doing "crushed the nonpayments commission once and for all."[57] By the time of the presidential elections, according to one estimate, Yeltsin and Chernomyrdin had issued 155 "dispensation granting" decrees and resolutions.[58]

Using Russia's equivalent of an easy-money policy to attract votes, Yeltsin allowed enterprises to amass vast tax debts to the state, all the while drawing on reserves to ensure, at least temporarily, timely salary and pension payments. In April and May 1996, more than half the budget receipts from businesses were in the form of treasury tax credits, essentially IOUs to the state.[59] In the words of a leading Duma official:

The election of Boris Yeltsin came at a high price, literally speaking. There was a 47 percent drop in gold and foreign currency reserves, money was pumped out of the securities market at murderously high interest rates, and half of all budgetary receipts, including foreign loans, went toward the payment of wages, salaries, pensions, and essentially non-repayable loans to the regions.[60]

No sooner had the election season ended, however, than Yeltsin signaled a new campaign of fiscal responsibility. The change in official rhetoric was striking. The head of the State Tax Service, Vitalii Artiukhin, warned that "the election is over. The period of softness and leniency toward taxpayers has ended." Using language designed to appeal to his traditional constituents, the MVD chief, General Anatolii Kulikov, called tax evasion "robbery of the teachers, doctors, soldiers, and policemen standing at their posts."[61] The reliance on neo-Bolshevik symbols was also evident in the naming of a new organization devoted to combating tax delinquency, the Temporary Extraordinary Commission on Strengthening Tax and Budget Discipline. It bore the same acronym, VChK, as Lenin's secret police—the dreaded Vecheka.

The formation of the VChK in early October 1996 represented a bold attempt to fuse presidential and Government leadership of the economy. The presidency, of course, had long maintained its own economic affairs departments, which had functioned as independent sources of expertise for the president, as overseers of Government economic performance, and as a training ground for future Government economic officials, among them Aleksandr Livshits, Yevgenii Yasin, Vladimir Panskov, Sergei Ignatiev, and Aleksei Kudrin. In these respects, as we noted earlier, it replicated the role of the Communist Party in Soviet political economy.[62] But there was no precedent for a high-ranking interagency commission such as the VChK, which brought together the leading presidential and Government officials concerned with the economy. Although the formal mission of the VChK was limited, in Yeltsin's own words, "to oversee[ing] the work of the customs office and the tax service . . . and to keep[ing] strict watch on the proper expenditure of money from the budget," it was far more than the enforcer of fiscal discipline.[63] With its interlocking membership of top executive officials, and with responsibilities for issues as varied as macroeconomic policy and ministerial appointments, the VChK could claim to be "the real Russian Government," at least on the implementation of tax policy.[64] Once recovered from heart surgery in late 1996, Yeltsin further enhanced the status of the VChK by periodically presiding over its sessions.

The VChK was on one level a testament to the failure of existing institutional arrangements in Russian semipresidentialism. Before the formation of this commission, "the Government of Chernomyrdin, the Security Council and Aleksandr Lebed personally, and a third structure, the President's staff—that is Chubais, [were] all involved in trying to bring order to the economy, and they [were] getting in one another's way."[65] But the VChK was also an instrument in the intraexecutive struggle, which Chubais employed to expand his own role in economic decision making. Although President Yeltsin appointed Viktor Chernomyrdin to chair the new commission, he reserved almost half of the twenty-three seats on the VChK for allies of Chubais—the commission's deputy chair—or officials answering directly to the president.[66] As one commentator observed, where Chernomyrdin "served as the commission's political front . . . its real ideologist is Anatolii Chubais."[67] Much like Yegor Gaidar, another technocrat who aroused the opposition of public and parliament, Chubais had to rely on others to screen him from political assaults.

Predictably, Chubais' bid to streamline the structure of economic decision making alienated many Russian politicians. They resented the prominence of an unelected—and unelectable—*apparatchik,* who, they believed, had taken advantage of Yeltsin's mental state on the eve of his surgery to engineer this organizational reform. Moscow's mayor, Yurii Luzhkov, complained that "Chubais had [concentrated] in his own hands Government functions that had never been the prerogative of the President's Chief of Staff."[68] Several opposition members of the Duma filed a suit in the Constitutional Court to protest what they regarded as the illegal transfer of Government powers to the Executive Office of the President. Only the Government, of course, was subject to parliamentary oversight.[69]

The appearance of the VChK clearly elevated the authority of the presidential apparatus in economic decision making at the expense of the prime minister and his Government. Only three months before the establishment of the VChK, Chernomyrdin had created a Government commission with a similar mission and title—the Task Force for Implementing a Set of Urgent Measures for the Stabilization of the Country's Economic Situation. This body, which pressed into service leading Government ministers as well as two officials from the presidency—Aleksandr Livshits, Yeltsin's economic aide, and Ruslan Orekhov, the head of the State-Legal Department—faded into oblivion with the appearance of the higher-profile VChk.[70] Moreover, the presidency in this period claimed direct control of two Government agencies, the Tax Police and the State Tax Service. These institutions joined the Government's numerous security-related ministries and state committees that answered directly to the president—and not the prime minister—on operational matters.

In the view of reformers such as Chubais, the reduction of the prime minister's authority in economic decision making was a necessary but not sufficient condition for the resolution of the "payments crisis." Obstructing the fiscal discipline campaign were numerous features of the Russian political and economic landscape, including inefficient and corrupt law enforcement agencies, inadequate tax codes, massive capital flight, and the state's own dependency on private economic interests. For its part, the law enforcement community viewed the president, and executive leadership writ large, as fickle and unreliable patrons. In Ivanovo, for example, 340 of the city's tax inspectors signed an open letter revealing the low morale in their ranks. Because of budget cutbacks, it read,

> [o]ur main source of food has become bread and potatoes. Many of us haven't paid our rents for six months, and have no way to pay for child care or even for public transport to get us back and forth to work.[71]

In such conditions, state employees became easy prey for business interests that rely on bribes to minimize or avoid taxes. Those reluctant to accept "material stimuli" became the targets of violence and intimidation. In the first quarter of 1997, there were 111 reported attacks on the members of the Tax Police or their families. In the same period, the authorities uncovered nineteen attempts by criminal groups to infiltrate the Tax Police with their representatives.[72]

The tax laws themselves encouraged evasion because of the high, and in some instances confiscatory, rates on business activity. For many firms, to pay taxes at official rates was to invite bankruptcy. As a matter of policy, the state was relying on a small number of filers to pay taxes at exorbitant rates. Thus, Russian tax legislation penalized the minority of law-abiding individuals and enterprises as a means of making up a deficit generated by the delinquent and privileged. Furthermore, the anemic sanctions contained in the existing tax code did little to deter tax evaders. The head of the State Tax Service complained that "[a]n enterprise director can save tens of billions of rubles by not paying taxes. Yet all we can do is fine him an amount equal to a few times the minimal monthly wage." Moreover, "the new Criminal Code that went into effect on January 1 [1997] . . . does not treat failure to pay taxes as a criminal offense, regardless of the amount of the arrears or whether the defaulter had malicious intent."[73] And contrary to the practice in most modern economies, the Russian bankruptcy code makes the state tax authorities stand in line behind several other categories of creditors before their claims are met. This normative chaos served well the political opposition and economic lobbies, both of whom favored a weak state.

The goal of the VChK was not just to collect tax arrears but to reduce dramatically the number of "free riders" in the Russian economy. Free riding took numerous forms, from enterprises exploiting state-sanctioned tax privileges to businesses laundering money to avoid reporting requirements. A Duma expert estimated that the illegal economy accounted for as much as 40 percent of the country's GDP.[74] The search for legal and illegal means to avoid the state's tolls became a national obsession. Some companies, for example, paid salaries in preferential loans or high-interest-bearing accounts in order to reduce taxes for themselves and their employees. Others simply appropriated company, or public, funds for their own use. Tax agency officials estimated that "certifiable theft" accounted for more than half of the nonpayments. "In such cases, money received in payment for output goes into the personal accounts of enterprise executives or to subsidiary structures headed by the same people, rather than the enterprise's current account."[75]

One of the surest ways for Russians to avoid taxes—as well as the threat of inflation and confiscatory currency reform—was to export earnings to off-shore banks. In some cases, even state budgetary allocations found their way out of the country. In early 1997, the Federal Service for the Monitoring of Hard Currency revealed a scheme by which Ministry of Defense officials had diverted $4.2 million earmarked for feeding the troops into a bank account in Gibraltar.[76] While a few tens of billions of dollars flowed into Russia from 1991 to 1997 in the form of direct investment or loans from international agencies, such as the IMF, an amount at least equal to that was leaving the country for safe havens abroad.[77] Some estimates placed the level of capital flight as high as $250 billion for this period. Whatever the precise scale of the capital outflow, it represented a devastating loss for the treasury and for the fledgling capital market in Russia. Despite articles to the contrary in the American press, the real financial story in the 1990s was not Western investment in Russia but Russia's investment in the West.

It is easy, of course, to turn an analysis of Russia's financial crisis into a morality play, with a weak state cast as the victim of private greed. But the reality is more complex. To understand the Russian economic predicament in Yeltsin's second term, one must also consider the massive debt owed by the regions to federal authorities—approximately half of the total indebtedness—as well as the public burden borne by private economic enterprises.[78] In its own way, the state was deeply indebted to the private sector, especially the largest and oldest enterprises, some of which, under pressure from the political leadership, sold goods at subsidized levels to domestic consumers, retained unprofitable workers, underwrote local social services, and fulfilled state orders on undesirable terms. Many of these firms were among the seventy-three Russian companies that accounted for half of the tax arrears to the state.[79] With the knowledge—some would say at the instigation—of the state, many enterprises kept themselves afloat by extending credit to each other in the form of promissory notes, or *veksely.* According to one Russian analyst:

> We have gotten into a vicious circle. Enterprises are not paying taxes to the treasury because they are not being paid by major consumers of industrial services and energy—the Army, the Ministry of Internal Affairs, educational institutions, housing authorities, public utilities. The nonpayers have no money because they are maintained by the budget, which is not getting any taxes![80]

This mutual dependence of the state and private enterprises contributed to a conspiracy of half measures: campaigns of policy pronouncements without policy implementation. To vigorously pursue payment of all arrears owed the treasury and Pension Fund would have risked closing factories and throwing millions of people out of work. According to the head of the State Tax Service, "[T]he 77 trillion rubles' worth of uncollected taxes is money that is just not in the economy. We would destroy [economic] production if we tried to collect [all of] it."[81] The lack of political will in the fiscal discipline campaign did not represent, therefore, a mere deficit of personal leadership. It was also a by-product of a peculiar political economy, where many public and private authorities feared that a change in existing relations could lead to a social explosion or economic catastrophe.

In this public-private condominium, Chubais and other liberal reformers—no less than the traditionalists—operated with remarkable agility as representatives of both state institutions and business interests. Everyone understood that, unlike the Brezhnev era, the state no longer provided a reliable shelter. Thus, besides the personal support of the president, which could be withdrawn at any moment, Chubais enjoyed two other shelters, or *kryshi,* that enhanced his economic security and political authority. One was international economic agencies, which offered technical advice and financial support to Russia—and to Chubais personally. His close ties with the IMF provided Chubais with leverage in discussions with the president and prime minister over macroeconomic policy and the rationalization of economic decision making. On a more mundane level, his relationship with the United States Agency for International Development led to his employment as a well-paid consultant when Chubais lost his post in the Government in January 1996.[82] Chubais also enjoyed the patronage of a group of prominent Russian banks, which helped to fund Yeltsin's reelection effort—led by Chubais—in the spring of 1996. Chubais was not, therefore, a lonely public crusader isolated from the world of commerce. Like all prominent officials, he had his friends, patrons, and clients in the private sector, though they were concentrated in "new" fields such as finance rather than in the "old" world of smokestack industries and natural-energy monopolies.

Given the depth of the country's economic malaise and the lack of autonomy of the Russian state, it is not surprising that the VChK failed to resolve the "payments crisis." To be sure, the campaign launched by the VChK in October 1996 threatened tax delinquents with numerous sanctions, including bankruptcy and arrest. Peter Mostovoi, a Chubais client and head of the federal bankruptcy commission, prepared bankruptcy proceedings against twelve large enterprises in the oil and gas sector.[83] Addressing a conference of Russian bankers and businessmen, Chubais claimed that the state "would use ruthless measures against those evading taxes." He concluded his speech with the ominous words "Expect arrests."[84] And arrests there were. In the first quarter of 1997, the Tax Police initiated about 1,400 criminal cases, producing 117 convictions and treasury receipts of 17 trillion rubles, a figure five times higher than that realized a year earlier.[85] Some of this work was based on carefully targeted inspections by the presidential Monitoring Administration, which exposed widespread tax fraud in several prominent Russian organizations. On the basis of an inspection led by the Monitoring Administration, for example, the VChK closed down the Office of International Humanitarian and Technical Assistance, which had been importing duty-free cars, tobacco, and alcohol, reportedly at a loss of more than 1 trillion rubles to the treasury.[86] But despite such efforts, tax receipts for the first three months of 1997 represented only 56 percent of planned revenue, or a 100-trillion-ruble shortfall, disappointing figures even for an inflated budget.[87] Of the more than two and a half million businesses and legal entities in Russia, approximately one-third paid no, or only nominal, taxes.[88] Although almost three million citizens submitted personal income tax payments because of their status as high-wage earners (more than 1 million rubles monthly), self-employed, or employees of more than one company, none of the very rich was reportedly among this number.[89]

Taking advantage of VChK's failings, the conservative head of the MVD, Anatolii Kulikov, convinced the president to assign him and his ministry a more prominent role in the campaign for fiscal discipline. Said one source:

> [T]he vexation and fright that the state's top officials felt [regarding the shortfall in tax receipts] was given material form in the transfer of fiscal

powers to the country's "No. 1 policeman." "Go to it, Kulikov, old boy—save the treasury."[90]

After a forty-minute meeting with Yeltsin on 13 February 1997, Kulikov emerged to tell reporters that "the president gave me *carte blanche* to wage a tough struggle against economic crimes."[91] Appointed first deputy prime minister in the Government, while retaining his MVD portfolio, Kulikov acquired the authority to coordinate activities of the major executive agencies in the field of tax and customs, some of which had answered previously to the minister of finance. For the moment, at least, the "wandering center" of Russian politics seemed to shift away from Chubais and his camp and toward more traditional figures in the Russian executive.[92]

Within weeks, however, Yeltsin used the occasion of the annual State of the Union message to announce a new, and more radical, economic course for the nation. The issue was not just collecting more taxes but reducing expenditures by eliminating subsidies and downsizing the most costly state institution of all, the armed forces. Speaking amid a growing threat of strikes and civil unrest, Yeltsin also took up the cudgel against corrupt and incompetent officials and against insubordinate regional elites. There followed a spate of decrees designed to "cut out the roots of corruption" by introducing competitive bidding on state contracts and by requiring all officials to report their personal income and property.[93]

Immediately following his speech, entitled "Order in Government—Order in the Country," Yeltsin also launched a dramatic series of administrative reorganizations and personnel moves that decimated the ranks of traditionalist forces in the Government.[94] Leaving their posts were two inveterate opponents of economic reform, Aleksandr Zaveriukha and Oleg Lobov. The primary beneficiary of this reshuffle was Anatolii Chubais, who moved from the presidency in early March 1997 to become the first deputy prime minister, and in effect the chief minister for economic affairs. To avoid a repeat of his earlier Government experience, when conservative ministers and deputy prime ministers undermined his initiatives, Chubais insisted on bringing his own team to power. Among those joining the Government as deputy prime ministers in the economic sphere were Yakov Urinson and Alfred Kokh, both young reformers with political ties to Chubais. Another young Chubais client, Aleksandr Pochinok, became head of the State Tax Service. When Chubais failed in his effort to install yet another ally, Andrei Kudrin—the head of the Monitoring Administration—as the sixth minister of finance in the Chernomyrdin era, he assumed the portfolio himself and brought in Kudrin as his first deputy.

By the middle of March 1997, Chubais' men dominated the Government's key economic posts as well as the presidency. As Chapter 3 points out, Chubais had left behind a large group of loyalists in the Executive Office of the President, including Valentin Yumashev, who assumed his patron's post as head of the presidential apparatus. Although the move to the White House put greater physical distance between Chubais and Yeltsin, it did not diminish Chubais' access to the president. Indeed, Chubais' transfer to the White House represented a further fusing of presidency and Government, since the first deputy prime minister retained his presidential posts as chair of the Political Consultative Council and the Economic and Financial Reform Commission of the Defense Council.

The "second coming" of Chubais to the Government did not, however, sweep away all the personnel obstacles to radical economic reform in Russia. For one, Chernomyrdin remained a moderating force at the head of the cabinet, even if on some issues he had become a figurehead prime minister. Although personal relations between Chernomyrdin and his new first deputy prime minister were reportedly on solid footing in this period, the values and styles of the two leaders were quite different. As one journalist put it, "Chubais was the only liberal egghead that didn't cause Chernomyrdin psychological discomfort."[95] There were limits, therefore, to Chernomyrdin's willingness to accede to Chubais' initiatives or to shield him from his many enemies. Moreover, even though General Kulikov lost his title of first deputy prime minister as well as oversight of the tax and customs services, he retained a prominent role in the Government as MVD chief and one of four deputy prime ministers.[96] To reiterate a point made in the preceding chapter, despite pressure from Yeltsin and Chubais, Chernomyrdin refused to remove Vasilii Babichev, the head of the Government apparatus. As a kind of permanent secretary for the Government, Babichev was the consummate Russian bureaucrat, who used his influence over personnel decisions and administrative communications to thwart the designs of reformers. Unable to unseat Babichev, Chubais resorted to other tactics to limit his authority. He convinced Yeltsin to strip Babichev of his post as deputy prime minister and to appoint a Chubais ally, Sergei Vasiliev, as Babichev's deputy. As one observer remarked, "[S]ince the first deputy prime minister [Chubais] failed to achieve his objective in a frontal attack on Babichev, . . . he is now prepared to wage long-term positional warfare."[97]

The contours of the battlefield changed again on 17 March 1997, when the president appointed Boris Nemtsov to work alongside Chubais as the "second" first deputy prime minister. Thirty-seven years old and a physicist by training, Nemtsov had for the previous five years served as the governor of the Nizhnii Novgorod region. Known for his commitment to economic reform and his ability to attract Western capital for his experiments, Nemtsov assumed responsibility in the Government for the breakup of economic monopolies and the privatization and modernization of housing and communal services. Designed to eliminate subsidies that were costly for the treasury and the economy writ large—the housing sector alone was a 119-trillion-ruble drain annually on federal and local budgets—both assignments seemed politically suicidal for Nemtsov, one of Russia's most popular politicians.[98] The first challenged the privileges of the country's most powerful companies, including energy giants such as the Unified Electrical Service, the owner of Russia's national electric grid, and Gazprom, the natural gas monopoly for which Chernomyrdin had long served as patron.[99] The second threatened to undermine entitlements that had prevented a social explosion among ordinary Russians—cheap rent and meterless utilities.[100] Economically, Russia could no longer afford to maintain a massive housing subsidy, but politically it could not afford to eliminate it.[101] Into this dilemma waded Boris Nemtsov.[102]

Although Nemtsov's appointment reduced somewhat Chubais' influence over economic decision making, it also limited his exposure to elite and mass criticism. In many respects, the new personnel arrangements placed Chubais in an enviable position. Chernomyrdin continued to answer for the political work of the Government before the parliament and the nation, and as such was both "a lightning rod for the Duma majority and . . . the president's whipping boy."[103] Another ambitious politician, Boris Nemtsov, assumed responsibility for unpopular and long-delayed elements of economic reform, not only as first deputy prime minister but as minister of fuel and energy.[104] Buffered by these two leaders, Chubais was for a short time able to guide economic reform in relative calm.

By the middle of 1997, the Russian Government appeared to have come full circle from its radical origins in the early months of Yegor Gaidar's leadership in 1992.[105] At the top once again were economic leaders devoted to rapid and far-reaching reform. The radical reform team in the Government was further strengthened in April 1998 with the appointment of Sergei Kirienko as prime minister. For a few weeks at least, behind Kirienko stood a relatively engaged and energetic president who, while still aware of the advantages of political ambiguity and factional balance, appeared willing to commit his authority to the implementation, not simply the articulation, of a reform program.[106]

In the field of tax collection, the center of institutional gravity began to shift in the Kirienko era from the VChK to the State Tax Service, whose new head, Boris Fedorov, launched a high-profile campaign against the country's wealthiest individuals and corporations. With state revenues continuing to lag far behind expenditures, Fedorov complained that the "state has been too liberal toward its taxpayers[, h]aving allowed more than 5,000 enterprises to run tax debts of over 50 billion dollars."[107] His solution was the politics of intimidation: seize assets of indebted companies and hold them until tax payments are made. One such raid targeted the Moscow headquarters of Gazprom. After a tense and protracted battle of wills in the summer of 1998, Gazprom's chairman, Rem Viakhirev, grudgingly agreed to pay a hefty installment on the company's $2 billion tax bill.[108]

Just as six years earlier, the immediate costs of rapid economic change were bound to play into the hands of the president's opposition, who would press for yet another Government reshuffle, a rightward shift of the executive's "wandering center." Such a capitulation, however, threatened to destroy domestic and international confidence in Russia's ability to reform itself. As an IMF publication observed, "[A]lthough the current Government's economic program is more coherent than its predecessors, the political risks facing the team are substantially greater. If their policies prove unsuccessful, there is no telling what this might portend for the future of economic reform." With so much at stake, the IMF's director for Russia, Aleksei Mozhin, warned: "This is the team that has no right to fail."[109] These comments, made upon the return of Chubais to the Government in March 1997, applied with even more force to the reform team assembled under Kirienko in 1998.

Yet fail it did in August of that year when Yeltsin, on the heels of a ruble devaluation, sought to bring Chernomyrdin back as prime minister. When that effort failed, due to vigorous resistance from parliament, Yeltsin chose Yevgenii Primakov to serve as his new prime minister. Even more so than Chernomyrdin, Primakov arrived in his post with considerable goodwill in parliament, in large measure because he shared the legislative majority's aversion to radical economic reform. The pendulum in Russian politics had swung again. Both the more statist orientation of the prime minister and the heterodox complexion of his cabinet—a liberal finance minister, Mikhail Zadornov, had to work with a former leader of Soviet state planning, the first deputy prime minister, Yurii Masliukov—seemed to foreshadow an abandonment of the "market fundamentalism" that had characterized the policies of Anatolii Chubais and Yegor Gaidar.[110]

The Politics of Judicial Reform

While issues such as the Chechen war and budgetary politics were at the forefront of public debate, policy conflicts in many other fields raged behind the scenes, making only fleeting appearances in the national spotlight. One of the most important of these issues was legal reform, whose origins lay in the Gorbachev era. After decades of halting, incremental change, Soviet law seemed on the verge of a revolution in the late 1980s, when the ideological and institutional pillars of Soviet legal orthodoxy began to weaken in the face of a campaign for a law-based state (*pravovoe gosudarstvo*).[111] At the level of discourse, this campaign replaced the dominant view of the distinctiveness, and superiority, of Soviet law with an acceptance of what Eugene Kamenka and Alice Erh-Soon Tay have called the "heritability" of Western law. It was an ideological concession as sweeping in its implications for domestic affairs as the "new thinking" was for foreign policy. Philosophically at least, the way was open for the wholesale incorporation of Western legal ideas, such as the adversary principle and judicial independence, into Soviet law.[112]

Standing in the path of reform, however, was the institutional self-interest of the dominant agencies of Soviet law. Since the 1930s, a conservative alliance of institutions, including the Ministry of Internal Affairs (MVD), the Committee on State Security (KGB), the Procuracy, and the Communist Party's administrative organs departments, had fiercely defended the legal status quo. This permanent institutional majority—the equivalent of a cartel in the legal sphere—was committed to retaining the existing distribution of power among branches of the legal profession and between the individual and the state. But the campaign for a *pravovoe gosudarstvo* began to break down this alliance by mobilizing the central institutions of the Communist Party behind legal reform. Once the party emerged as the institutional patron of change, the collective responsibility characteristic of Soviet politics imposed a measure of discipline on state legal institutions. Equally important, the party's patronage brought out previously muted reformist voices within institutions such as the courts and the Procuracy. The variety of reform proposals also created new lines of institutional conflict that cut across the ruling conservative alliance. In short, a new configuration of institutional power was in the making.

But the collapse of the Soviet Union created conditions that, paradoxically, complicated attempts to establish a legal order, which, in the Western experience at least, had always served as a foundation for the development of democratic institutions. Could the impetus for legal change survive the growth in corruption and the corollary rise in public cynicism about law?[113] Could legal initiatives designed to restrain state power succeed in an era of state formation, when political leaders were tempted to adopt a nihilist attitude to law in order to act with dispatch and flexibility at moments of political crisis, which were inevitable in a transition regime? Finally, could legal reform survive the diffusion of political power that accompanied the collapse of Communism? The demise of the Communist Party as ruling institution left legal reform without an institutional patron, an uncomfortable, if not untenable, position for reform movements in Russian history. To fill this vacuum, legal reformists close to Yeltsin began to put in place a new engine of legal reform, this time in the Russian presidency. The driving force behind the revival of an institutional headquarters for legal change was Sergei Shakhrai, the first legal counselor to Yeltsin and a fellow defender of the White House during the dramatic days of August 1991. In December 1991, at Shakhrai's urging, Yeltsin formed within the presidency a State-Legal Administration (*Gosudarstvenno-Pravovoe Upravlenie,* or GPU) of some three hundred persons, which had responsibility for the oversight of law and legal institutions. One of the GPU's eight subdivisions, the Department for Court Reform and Court Procedure, had as its explicit mission the transformation of the Russian court system.

The head of the Department for Court Reform, Sergei Pashin, quickly emerged as the most visible, and controversial, advocate of change in the Russian judiciary. Only twenty-nine years old at the time of his appointment, Pashin was perhaps best known for his contributions to the Conception of Court Reform, an agenda for legal reform that was adopted by the Russian parliament in October 1991.[114] Where the GPU's Department of Court Reform replaced the party as institutional sponsor of legal change, the Conception of Court Reform served as a substitute for the conception of a *pravovoe gosudarstvo,* which, as Peter Solomon points out, "had disappeared from the rhetoric of politicians and legal reformers alike."[115] In advancing the Conception of Court Reform, Pashin sought to create a new "general line" on law, this time, however, with a more explicit statement of the measures to be taken in pursuit of reform. In his position as department head in the GPU, Pashin had Shakhrai's assurances that he would be able to carry out court reform "under the protection of the very highest spheres."[116]

Transforming the Soviet judical inheritance into an independent and professional court system was, however, an immensely complex and politically contested project. At issue were changes in the courts' staffing and method of selection, pay and work conditions, structure and administration, and criminal and civil procedure. Each issue piqued the interest, and opposition, of a different set of political and legal elites. On the question of who appoints judges, for example, many parliamentary and regional leaders resisted vigorously the initiatives of the presidency, which were designed to concentrate patronage power in the hands of Boris Yeltsin and his advisors. In the constitution of December 1993, the Russian president reserved for himself the power to appoint all federal judges without seeking the advice or consent of legislators. The only exceptions were justices on the country's highest courts—the Supreme Court, the Constitutional Court, and the Supreme Commercial (*Arbitrazh*) Court—who had to be approved by the Federation Council. In theory, then, President Yeltsin alone had the authority to select the more than fifteen thousand judges working in republic, regional, city, and district courts.[117] But because the presidency lacked the staff and expertise to identify and nominate judges across the length and breadth of the Russian Federation, it permitted judicial nominating commissions—panels of senior judges created in 1991—to continue to recommend candidates for the bench.[118] Beginning in early 1995, these recommendations passed through the presidency's Council on Judicial Cadres, which consisted of the leaders of Russia's courts and legal ministries, before reaching Yeltsin's desk.

Notwithstanding the wording of the constitution, executive leaders in some subject territories began to assume responsibility for appointing judges to vacancies on district, city, and in some cases even regional courts. This practice was particularly widespread in the ethnic republics, which enjoy a special—though as yet ambiguous—status in Russian federalism. When the leaders of the twenty republics were asked in 1994 whether they acknowledged that judges at all levels should be appointed by the president, "thirteen replied with a flat no, six gave evasive answers, and only the Ingush Republic agreed with the constitutional norm."[119] This resistance prompted President Yeltsin to issue a decree in November 1994 that warned local authorities against "investing judges with powers and elaborating normative acts on questions concerning the judiciary."[120] The decree had little impact, however, on patronage practice. More than two years later, in December 1996, then presidential chief of staff Anatolii Chubais complained to a conference of judges that in some subject territories judicial vacancies were still being filled by local authorities rather than the president, which he characterized as "extremely risky, extremely dangerous . . . violations of the constitutional powers of the president."[121]

During 1995 and 1996, the contestation of constitutional provisions on judicial selection was an important part of the struggle over a new Law on the Court System. This act was one of several "federal constitutional laws" envisioned by the 1993 constitution, each designed to supplement the broad wording of the country's basic law with detailed legislation. Because such laws in effect interpreted the constitution, their passage required a supermajority of two-thirds in the State Duma and three-quarters in the

Federation Council. This fine point of Russian institutional design complicated attempts by the presidency to push its draft of the Law on the Court System through parliament. Although a version of the law prepared by Sergei Pashin passed the Duma in July 1995, it failed to satisfy the concerns of Russia's powerful regions, whose representatives filled the upper chamber.[122] Only in December 1996, after revisions that limited presidential patronage power over the judiciary and eliminated the federal monopoly on Russian courts, did the Law on the Court System pass both houses of parliament and receive the president's signature.[123]

Although the president remained the central figure in judicial appointments, the Law on the Court System granted a voice in the selection of judges to legislative institutions, court chairmen, and judicial nominating commissions. For example, judges serving in republic, regional, and city courts were appointed "by the president on the basis of recommendations made by the chair of the Russian Supreme Court, which in turn were based on a review of a judicial nominating commission and the agreement of the legislature on the same administrative level as the court."[124] That no one fully understood what this convoluted wording would signify in practice allowed all sides to claim a political victory. But the very ambiguity that allowed the president's team to mobilize sufficient political support for the passage of the law invited further contestation of numerous issues relating to judicial selection, this time in the administrative rather than the legislative arena.

The law also authorized the country's eighty-nine republics and regions to create their own courts, which included justices of the peace (*mirovye sud'i*) to handle less serious criminal and civil cases and charter courts (*ustavnye sudy*) to act as constitutional courts of sorts in each subject territory. Given the tensions in Russian federalism, this devolution of judicial power raised the specter of a new "war of laws" between center and periphery in Russia. Although the law proclaimed that the sovereignty of federal law and the centralized financing of the judiciary would ensure "unity of the court system," its concessions to regional interests in fact contributed to new skirmishes over the division of legal authority between the federal Government and the subject territories.[125] Once again, by pursuing the politics of ambiguity in policy making, the presidency raised the stakes in the politics of implementation.

Where the most radical reform proposals emanated from the presidency, the most serious opposition to broad-based judicial reform was centered not in the parliament or the regions but in Government legal institutions, most notably the Ministry of Justice, the Procuracy, and the MVD.[126] Each institution had its own motives for limiting the scope of court reform.[127]

For its part, the Ministry of Justice feared losing its last levers of influence over judicial behavior. Through its logistical support, training programs, quantitative measurements of judicial competence, and recommendations for pay and promotions, the Ministry of Justice had long served as the primary patron of the courts. This patronage ensured a measure of judicial deference toward the ministry. Reformist proposals, however, envisioned a self-governing judiciary, wholly independent of the Ministry of Justice, with a separate Judicial Department, subordinate to the Supreme Court, to provide support services. For Justice officials, such changes called into question the very raison d'être of the Ministry.[128] They also threatened to reduce dramatically, or even eliminate, the funding channeled through the ministry for the courts, money that at times—according to some accounts—never reached the judiciary.[129] Furthermore, after losing most of its supervisory responsibilities over the defense bar at the end of the Soviet era, the ministry witnessed the encroachment of the State-Legal Administration on its traditional functions of legislative drafting and the gathering of legal information in the 1990s.[130] Two ministers of justice, Nikolai Fedorov and Yurii Kalmykov, left office in Yeltsin's first term protesting loudly the loss of their institutional prerogatives to the presidency. Their successor, Valentin Kovalev, a Communist, resisted even more vigorously—though with little more success—attempts to create a judiciary that was independent of the Ministry of Justice.

Judicial reform presented a more subtle, but no less far-reaching, threat to the Procuracy. As George Fletcher argued three decades ago, in the Russian tradition the courts and Procuracy are natural adversaries.[131] This institutional conflict was evident at the beginning of the 1990s when judges employed newly granted powers to challenge the arrest orders of procurators. The Procuracy responded with "shrieks, threats, and provocations" (*okriki, ugrozi i provokatsii*).[132] Through its oversight of legality, the Procuracy claims that it, even more than the courts, serves as the guarantor of justice in the Russian legal system. It refuses to be bound by the classical concepts of separate judicial and executive authority. In the deeply held view of Russian procurators, the Procuracy is an original Russian contribution to law that transcends traditional Western categories.[133] When the December 1993 constitution relegated the Procuracy to an article within the section on the judiciary, procurators cried foul.[134] An official in the Moscow regional procuracy argued that "the subordination of the Procuracy to the executive or judicial branch would destroy the emerging system of checks and balances and would heighten the danger of legal violations."[135] Procurators don't just prosecute crimes, they also review the validity of judicial and executive decisions. Procurators have opposed, therefore, any efforts to narrow their functions to prosecution alone, a change that would deny their role as guardian of legality and transform them into merely one "side" in an adversarial process. Yet without such a reform, the Russian judiciary seems destined to remain in the shadow of the larger, better-funded, and more prestigious Procuracy.[136]

The MVD's opposition to court reform reflected a preference for executive rather than judicial solutions to issues of law and order. Like law enforcement organs everywhere, the MVD views legal reform in terms of changes in policing rather than changes in judicial procedures. Indeed, for the MVD, the courts are viewed as impediments to law enforcement. In the words of the former minister of internal affairs, Viktor Yerin, "Crime is growing and becoming more brazen, but the judges frequently display liberalism, to put it mildly."[137] To maintain the dominance of executive over judicial power in the legal system, the MVD launched a campaign of intimidation against Russian judges in late 1993. An MVD inspection of the courts purported to reveal a widespread pattern of inappropriate pretrial release and acquittals in cases involving criminal gangs. On the basis of its statistical analyses, the MVD compiled a list of 111 unreliable judges, "whose verdicts give rise to considerable . . . doubts." Suspicious that judges were taking bribes in exchange for favorable verdicts, Yerin asked, in reference to the privileges enjoyed by judges, "[A]re not the categories of officials in our country who have legal guarantees of immunity too broad?"[138]

When the MVD places new law enforcement campaigns on the political agenda, they tend to crowd out initiatives designed to enhance the authority of the courts. Such was the case in May 1994, when the MVD convinced Yeltsin to sign a forty-page crime-fighting decree that openly violated the constitution and existing law.[139] Responding to liberal criticisms of the decree, the head of the Federal Counterintelligence Service (FSK), one of several successor institutions to the KGB, commented, "I'm all for the violation of human rights if the human is a bandit or criminal."[140] Whatever the nature of the political system, a liberalization of judicial policy is difficult to sustain in the midst of a campaign against crime and terrorism. It has been all the more difficult in Russia because of the proliferation of executive agencies responsible for security and the state's fear of disorder in the transition from Communism.

The judiciary is itself divided into several discrete court hierarchies. Besides a Supreme Court of general jurisdiction, there is a Supreme Commercial Court to hear business disputes and a Constitutional Court to interpret the country's basic law. Such a system may produce sound law—Germany, after all, has a similar judicial structure—but it has the potential to dilute the political influence of the judiciary.[141] In contrast to the 1980s, when Vladimir Terebilov served as the champion of the judiciary from his position as chief justice of the USSR Supreme Court, the Russian judiciary now has several leaders who have been unable to act in concert. Besides the chairs of the three highest courts, the president of a newly formed Council of Russian Judges can also claim to represent the interests of the judiciary. This splintering of judicial leadership has almost certainly weakened the courts' voice in the political arena.

Throughout the Soviet era, legal scholars were at the forefront of law reform, both as legal draftsmen and publicists. In this regard, the historical record is unbroken through the mid-1990s. But what is remarkable about the latest wave of reform is the depth of divisions among the advocates of legal change. Ranged against conservative in-house scholars from state legal institutions are two competing groups of reform-oriented jurists. These reformist groups are divided by generation, by their models of legal development (Continental versus Anglo-American), and by their approach to legal change, which recalls the split between geneticists and teleologists in the USSR of the late 1920s. Where the older generation of reformist scholars tend to work "from the achieved level," building incrementally on the Continental and Soviet traditions, their younger and brasher counterparts envision a series of great reforms in law to rival those of the 1860s.

Efforts in the last decade to reintroduce the jury trial to Russia illustrate vividly the divisions within the legal community and between presidency and Government. Imported from Western Europe in the 1860s, jury trials were among the most visible and controversial elements of the judicial reform introduced by Tsar Alexander II. Although they decided only a small portion of criminal cases, and then primarily in the largest cities, juries at times presented an unwelcome challenge to autocratic rule. Such was the case in the 1878 trial of Vera Zasulich, the revolutionary who was acquitted by a jury after killing the police commissioner in St. Petersburg. Loath to accept the unpredictability of jury verdicts, the Bolsheviks officially eliminated the institution in 1920, less than three years after coming to power. They settled instead on a three-person bench, consisting of a professional judge presiding over court proceedings and two lay assessors to assist in the deliberations. In the ensuing decades, the assessors acquired a reputation as "nodders" because of their sycophancy before professional judges, who in turn took their direction—in subtle and not so subtle form—from officials in the Communist Party, the Ministry of Justice, and higher courts.

The Gorbachev-era campaign for a law-based state opened the way for a revival of the jury trial in Russia. Some reformists expressed an almost romantic faith in the jury as "democratic conscience" of the nation and as counterweight to the conservative cartel of state legal institutions.[142] Introducing a popular check on criminal proceedings, they reasoned, would enhance the accountability and professionalism of the police, investigative personnel, and judges, who had long covered up each other's mistakes in their cozy, almost conspiratorial circle. It was one thing, however, to remove the stamp of heresy from the jury and something else again to introduce this complex and costly legal reform. Before the collapse of the Soviet Union, the proponents of jury reform managed only to receive the state's sanctification of their project in the USSR Fundamentals of Court Organization, enacted by the Soviet parliament in 1989, and in the Conception on Court Reform, passed by the parliament of the Russian republic in the fall of 1991.[143]

Having received the state's political blessing of jury reform in the late Soviet era, legal reformists turned to the more difficult task of passing detailed legislation in the opening months of Russia's transition regime. Spearheading the drive for a new law on the jury was Sergei Pashin, who, along with Boris Zolotukhin, a defense counsel and deputy chair of the parliament's committee on legislation, served as the primary draftsmen of the law. Pashin used the authority of the presidency to coordinate the preparation of the law on the jury and to convince—some would say bully—wavering officials to accept his version of jury reform. But fierce resistance to the use of the jury in Russian criminal proceedings forced Pashin and his allies to settle for a law that imposed severe restrictions on jury trials. Adopted in July 1993, near the height of legislative-executive conflict in Russia's First Republic, the law limited jury trials to criminal cases heard in regional-level courts, whose jurisdiction as trial courts included only the most serious crimes, such as premeditated murder.[144] More important, the enabling legislation accompanying the law on the jury mandated that juries be introduced immediately only in five regions, to be followed several months later by four additional regions.[145] These territories were distinguished by a relative absence of ethnic, political, and economic conflict and by support for jury reform among local political and legal elites. Seizing on the restricted geographical and jurisdictional reach of the juries, the opponents of the jury reform emphasized its "experimental" character, a concept that carried Soviet-era associations with radical—and usually unsuccessful—economic reforms.[146]

Given the opposition to the jury trial in virtually every quarter except Pashin's department in the presidency, it is surprising that the law on the jury passed in any form. The reform aroused antagonisms on institutional, financial, and philosophical grounds. Under the old system, officials in the MVD and the Procuracy had been able to forward unsubstantiated or ill-prepared cases to the courts, which either convicted defendants in spite of evidentiary flaws or returned the case to the MVD or Procuracy for "supplemental investigation," in effect giving the investigators another chance to put their house in order. Because the juries, unlike professional judges, were more inclined to acquit in such cases, they held investigative personnel to a much higher professional standard—a benefit for the justice system as a whole but a loss of flexibility and face for the state institutions in question.[147] Likewise, prosecutors no longer enjoyed a privileged position in the courtroom. In a jury system, they were, like defense counsel, merely one of the "sides" in an adversarial process, the outcome of which was in the hands of twelve laymen rather than a state official.

Aware of the indelicacy of opposing jury reform on narrow institutional grounds, the Government's legal agencies emphasized instead the high costs of reviving the Russian jury. At a time when many court buildings were in disrepair and judges were threatening to strike over inadequate pay, the opponents of jury reform argued that the country could ill afford the high costs of lay justice.[148] Among the added expenses associated with jury trials were new chambers to house the juries, new personnel to summon and manage jury pools, new training courses to prepare judges, prosecutors, and defense counsel, and handsome payments to the jurors themselves.[149] In order to attract jurors, and avoid a repetition of the growing boycott of the courts by poorly paid lay assessors, the law on the jury offered jurors a per diem equal to no less than half of the daily salary of judges, plus payment for travel, housing, and food. According to one estimate, the costs of remunerating jurors amounted "to more than it would cost to pay seven judges for each day of trial."[150] These expenditures caught the attention of the Ministry of Finance and other Government financial officials, who emerged as implacable opponents of the extension of the jury trial to additional regions of Russia. When the Finance Ministry placed barriers in the way of judicial reform, it was only the president himself who could remove them.[151]

Although the defense bar and the bench stood to benefit most from the reintroduction of juries, most rank-and-file judges and attorneys—known as "advocates" in Russian—were far from enthusiastic about the reform. Bar and bench support appeared to be concentrated among the leaders of the professions in Moscow and in the regions where the jury experiment was under way. For judges and advocates alike, jury trials threatened a professional routine that had remained little changed for decades. And for the advocates, there was little financial incentive to adapt to the new demands of jury cases. The payment schedule for court-appointed cases failed to compensate defense counsel for the added length and complexity of jury trials.

Finally, even some reform-oriented members of the Russian legal community objected to the jury reform as an irrelevant extravagance, uncritically borrowed from the Anglo-American world, where it was under attack.[152] In conflict here were two very different views of Russian criminal procedure. For Sergei Pashin and his allies, the jury trial was the opening wedge in what might be called the anglicization of the criminal process, which envisioned the equalization of defense and prosecution at the pretrial stage as well as at the trial itself. Rather than retaining the old Continental-style inquisitorial proceedings, in which the state assumed sole responsibility for the discovery of the facts, the Anglo-American school sought to make both prosecution and defense collectors of evidence before the trial.[153] The contest between the "sides" would therefore begin immediately after arrest and not, as in the Soviet era or in Continental systems, after an indictment based on an "objective" investigation of the crime by state legal officials. Understandably, such indictments carried greater weight at trial than those in Anglo-American systems and therefore made judicial adherence to the presumption of innocence more difficult. However, it appeared that for most Russian jurists, whatever their general attitude about legal reform, the movement toward the Anglo-American model represented an unwelcome assault on the laudable idea at the core of the inquisitorial system, that all state institutions should be seekers of the truth and not merely representatives of a "side." Viewed more narrowly, the jury trial also represented a potentially dangerous experiment with lay justice, which many older jurists associated with utopian moments in Soviet legal history. Although the jury had a prerevolutionary pedigree in Russia, subsequent attempts in the Soviet era to introduce amateurs in law invoked images of mob justice and legal nihilism rather than the "democratic conscience" of the nation.

That jury reform succeeded even on a limited scale is testimony to Pashin's aggressive use of presidential authority and his ability to attract foreign money and expertise to support his cause. Like Anatolii Chubais and Boris Nemtsov, Sergei Pashin developed close ties with American donors, especially the Ford Foundation and the American Bar Association, which enabled Pashin to finance the planning and initial implementation of jury reform. With Western seed money, the presidency's Department of Court Reform translated bench books to assist judges presiding in jury trials; it invited judges, prosecutors, and defense counsel to several Russian cities—and in a few cases overseas—to take part in mock jury trials and to attend lectures by leading Russian and Western specialists; and it outfitted some regional courtrooms with the latest furnishings and equipment. Even jurists suspicious of the value of the jury found it difficult to resist participation in a project that promised to enhance their knowledge and work environment.

But Pashin's unlimited ambition and brash style bred resentment among an ever-widening circle of political and legal elites. Like Aleksandr Lebed, Pashin found himself an increasingly isolated and vulnerable figure in Russian bureaucratic politics. In September 1995, a group of liberal jurists met in Moscow to announce the death of judicial reform in Russia. The fatal blow, in their view, was the elimination of the GPU's Department of Court Reform and the resignation of its head, Sergei Pashin. Olga Chaikovskaia, the conscience of the Russian legal community for more than three decades, warned of the "horrible" (*strashnye*) consequences that Pashin's departure would have for law reform in general.[154] Pashin himself was more circumspect in his assessment of the prospects for reform after the bureaucratic shakeup, though he admitted that "our work ha[s] been rejected." Speaking of the progress made in the 1990s in the field of judicial reform, he noted that "we cannot yet say that it is irreversible. The whole approach can go backward. I have some fears."[155]

It appears that the decisive pressure to undercut Pashin's authority and institutional resources came from senior officials in the presidency who resented Pashin's attempts to elevate the status of his department. Circumventing the established lines of bureaucratic authority in the presidency, Pashin made a direct, and successful, appeal to Yeltsin in March 1995 to officially designate his office as the "head agency" (*golovnoi otdel*) for judicial reform. In Pashin's own words, "[A]t a certain stage our work outgrew the confines of a 'department.' " The concession from the president provoked "furious resistance" from Pashin's immediate superior, Ruslan Orekhov, the head of the State-Legal Administration, who then raised the matter with Sergei Filatov, the leader of the Executive Office of the President. On April 21, while Pashin was on vacation, Filatov fired five of Pashin's eighteen subordinates and relabeled his office the Department of Criminal Law and Procedure.[156] The fate of law reform depended, therefore, on political relations within the presidency as well as between presidency and Government.

Can the Russian political system sustain judicial reform without an institutional patron akin to the Department of Court Reform? Russia's dramatic transition from Communism owes much to a small, and until recently dwindling, group of reform-minded officials. Linking their institutions to the authority of the president, these officials have maneuvered around the barricades protecting entrenched bureaucratic interests. Because there is still little demand for fundamental court reform in the population, in the state bureaucracies, and even in the judicial corps itself, the impetus for change will almost certainly continue to come from above, from the commanding heights of Russian politics. One may argue, of course, that, more than seven years into the post-Soviet era, judicial reform is self-sustaining. The basic laws necessary to support a new court system are already in place—save a hotly debated Code of Criminal Procedure. But Russian history illustrates that the decisive phase for law reform occurs after the normative foundations of a new legal order are in place. It is then that the conservative state bureaucracies seek their revenge on reformers by ignoring, delaying, or distorting the implementation of new laws. At times, such as in the 1970s, this revenge takes the form of a quiet erosion of provisions of reform legislation. At other times, such as in the 1880s, reactionary forces exploit a crisis of authority to mount a full-fledged counterreform, during which the philosophical underpinnings of reform procedures and institutions come under attack.

In the twilight of Yeltsin's rule and beyond, one can expect a vigorous struggle between the friends and foes of judicial reform as they seek to support—or obstruct—the implementation of new laws governing the courts. Where the passage of reform legislation requires only a momentary political victory, its faithful execution demands the continuing political hegemony of progressive forces or a respect for the spirit of the law among state officials and the public.[157] Russian reformists can rely on neither, at least over the short term. They must prepare themselves for a protracted battle to be fought step by step, issue by issue, over the expansion of the jury experiment, the deepening of the adversary system in criminal proceedings, and the extension of the courts' independence and authority.[158]

Conclusion

Since the groundbreaking work of Robert Dahl in the late 1950s, students of democratic politics have recognized that political relations within the state and between state and society assume different forms depending on the policy in dispute. This insight is no less applicable to Russia in transition. As one moves from higher-profile and higher-stakes issues such as national security and budgetary politics to the reform of the legal system, one finds a different set of actors, a different level of presidential engagement, and different decision making forums. Where new laws on the courts emerge after months of detailed discussion dominated by legal scholars and lesser officials in the presidency and Government, new policies on military reform and budgetary sequestration often follow intensive negotiations that involve the leading figures of state. Similarly, if neither the introduction of the jury trial nor military reform excites much public passion, revisions to the tax laws can create a national outcry. In August 1996, for example, intense public reaction led President Yeltsin to abandon an ill-conceived tax decree that would have imposed a surcharge on all bank transactions.[159]

But for all the distinctive features of politics in each policy field, there are patterns of behavior that recur across a broad range of issues. One such regularity in Russia is the role of the presidency as champion of reform. In all three case studies, a coterie of individuals within—or allied to—the presidency advanced reforms that challenged powerful interest networks in the Government, the Duma, and the regions. These conservative cartels sought, with varying degrees of success, to retain the status quo or, at a minimum, to dilute the proposed reforms. Thus, Lebed settled the Chechen war in the face of resistance from the armed forces and the nationalists. Baturin and Chubais launched a reform of the military against the wishes of the leadership of the power ministries. Livshits and Chubais pursued a campaign to introduce budgetary discipline against the opposition of regional and business interests and their allies in the Government and Duma. And Pashin helped to push through a reform of the courts over the objections of the law enforcement community.

In all political systems, of course, well-placed and ambitious men and women make things happen. But what is remarkable about contemporary Russian politics is the extent to which these individuals—acting as agents of the president—have imposed reform from above without first building a broad base of support in the bureaucracy and society. In this sense, the current transition from Communist rule mirrors earlier reform episodes in Russian history, which ultimately failed because the conservative cartels—unable to forestall the introduction of new laws and decrees—found ways to scuttle the implementation of state policy.[160] Such is the danger of reformism without democracy. As Guillermo O'Donnell observed:

> [I]nstitutionalized democracies are slow at making decisions. But once those decisions are made, they are relatively more likely to be implemented. In delegative democracies, in contrast, we witness a decision-making frenzy, what in Latin America we call *decretismo*. Because such hasty, unilateral executive orders are likely to offend important and politically mobilized interests, they are unlikely to be implemented.[161]

Another element of continuity with the Russian past is the role of the international environment in inspiring political and economic change. A lagging society compared to the rest of Europe, Russia has periodically imported ideas and institutions from the West, most notably during the reigns of Peter the Great and Alexander II. As the case studies illustrate, Russia has again borrowed heavily from the West in recent years, whether in the neoliberal economic reforms advanced by Chubais or the highly adversarial criminal procedure favored by Pashin. But whereas in previous centuries the West was merely a passive source of inspiration, it now offers incentives to encourage Russia to accept its political and economic imports, to join what Gorbachev called a "common European home." Thus, in exchange for adopting monetary and financial policies that they believe will help to stabilize and marketize the economy, the IMF and other Western financial institutions have extended large-scale loans to Russia. As an incentive for "responsible" political and economic behavior, the world's most advanced countries have offered to receive Russia as a member of the expanded G-7.[162] Likewise, the Council of Europe has agreed to grant Russia membership in this political wing of the European Community if it brings its political and legal systems into conformity with the council's basic principles. To appreciate the importance that such invitations can have on internal policy debates, one has only to read the transcripts of a session of the presidency's Council on Judicial Reform, which viewed the regulations of the Council of Europe as binding on Russian legal policy.[163] One may even argue that in making Government personnel decisions, especially in the economic sphere, Yeltsin was at times more attentive to the reaction of international financial institutions than to the Duma. It is perhaps no accident that Yeltsin's embrace of radical economic reform in March 1997 came immediately after an IMF mission departed from Moscow without extending expected credits.[164]

Given the role of international actors in encouraging Russian reforms—conceptually, politically, and financially—one may wish to characterize the Russian transition as a revolution from above and beyond. What reformists like Chubais and Pashin lacked in internal support they appeared to make up for in international assistance. This model of political change is disturbingly close to the compradorism found in Latin America, which brings together a narrow circle of domestic elites and their Western partners. Such an alliance, vulnerable even in smaller and less globally ambitious states, is highly unstable in a country such as Russia, where a resurgent nationalism feeds on the humiliation that has accompanied the country's loss of international prestige. To consolidate their positions, reformists must either broaden their domestic political base—presumably through the very success of their policies—or resort to authoritarian measures.

6

The Presidency and Parliament

Boris Yeltsin faced two different parliaments during his presidency. The composition and political ambitions of the first parliament betrayed its origins in the late Soviet era. An unwieldy two-tiered assembly modeled on the last USSR parliament, this legislature sought to make good on the Leninist slogan "All power to the soviets."[1] In its first year of existence, during which time the legislature selected the republic's chief executives—the chair of the Congress of People's Deputies and the prime minister—it faced no effective challenge to its authority within the Russian Republic. But when Boris Yeltsin gave up the chair of the Congress in June 1991 to become the first directly elected president in Russian history, he assumed the reins of a new institution that would not accept the legislature's claim to constitutional preeminence. Not only did the president—like parliament—enjoy the democratic legitimacy that comes with direct elections, he had a mandate that was fresher than that of the parliament, which had been elected in March 1990.

Competition between the president and parliament intensified in the waning months of 1991, as Yeltsin sought to substitute the presidency for the Communist Party as the guiding force in Russian politics. Within weeks after the Soviet Union collapsed, in April 1992, the Russian parliament—dominated by traditionalist politicians—attempted to halt Yeltsin's market-oriented economic reforms. On matters of power and policy, president and parliament remained at loggerheads until Yeltsin's extraconstitutional dissolution of the assembly in September 1993. The violent standoff that ensued resulted from the confluence of three features of Russian politics: the institutional design of semipresidentialism, which has no constitutional cure for executive-legislative stalemate; the different political verdicts rendered by the Russian population at the 1990 and 1991 elections, which pitted a reformist-oriented president against a conservative parliament; and the intransigence of the country's leaders. Yeltsin's own unwillingness to compromise was evident as early as April 1992, when he argued that

> [g]iven the current alignment of political forces, including in the parliament, ... the transition to a parliamentary form would simply be inadmissible. ... In the conditions of crisis such a policy would be equivalent to suicide. I, as president, will never agree to such an option. ... [I]n the current situation, for the next two-three years, one can only speak of a presidential republic.[2]

A presidential republic was what Yeltsin sought to introduce in December 1993, when he submitted a new constitution to the nation for its approval in a referendum. This constitution reduced the parliament to a supporting role in the political system of the Second Russian Republic. As we shall see below, the parliament retained enough authority to frustrate presidential ambition on occasion, but not enough to threaten the survival of the executive, which is a litmus test of legislative strength. After 1993, to bring down a Government in Russia was to invite the dissolution of parliament itself.

Critical to an understanding of the relations between president and parliament in Russia is the role of parties. Like the Fourth Republic in France, the First Russian Republic (December 1991–December 1993) lacked a stable legislative majority, which is the classic source of political strength in parliamentary and semipresidential systems. To make up for this absence of party support, the constitutional framers of both the Fifth French Republic and the Second Russian Republic invested the executive with exceptional powers, including decree making. The granting of such prerogatives provided the executive with little incentive to nurture the development of parties or parliament. Empowered to rule in the face of party and parliamentary resistance, the Russian executive saw little reason to bind its fate to deputies inspired by Communist nostalgia or "street demonstration" democracy. Moreover, as Matthew Soberg Shugart has observed, "the more poorly institutionalized the party system, the more opportunities the president has to exploit divisions among the parties and exercise influence."[3] The weakness of the party system has impeded, therefore, the integration of executive and legislative leadership, which is a feature of efficient democratic regimes.

This is not to say, however, that the presidency and Government in Russia could afford to ignore parties altogether. Although Yeltsin refused to sanction the creation of an explicitly presidential party, he tacitly encouraged the formation of Our Home Is Russia, a "party of power" led by Viktor Chernomyrdin and other prominent executive officials in Moscow and the provinces.[4] Furthermore, the leader of the presidency's Department for Relations with Parties and Social Organizations, Andrei Loginov, sought to generate support for the presidency among centrist and reformist deputies in the Duma.[5] In 1995, for example, he was actively involved in the attempt to establish a bloc of centrist deputies, Stable Russia (*Stabil'naia Rossiia*), which was generally sympathetic to the presidential program.[6] Loginov and others in the presidency, most notably Yeltsin's political counselor, Georgii Satarov, also worked to elect pro-presidential deputies during the 1993 and 1995 parliamentary campaigns, though with very limited success.

Elements of the parliament's own institutional design have further limited its ability to hold the executive accountable. Known formally as the Federal Assembly, the parliament in the Second Russian Republic is a bicameral legislature consisting of the 450–seat State Duma and the 178-seat Federation Council. The diffusion of legislative power across two chambers complicates parliamentary attempts to impose legislation on a veto-wielding president. Summoning the two-thirds majority needed to override the president in both houses is a formidable challenge, especially given the fractiousness of parties and the high rate of absenteeism by deputies. By the same token, these features of the legislature make it difficult for the executive to push its legislative agenda through parliament. However, this checking power of the Federal Assembly is tempered by the ability of a frustrated president to issue decrees that circumvent the traditional legislative process. Such was the case in April 1996, when Boris Yeltsin, in the midst of the presidential campaign, decreed a right to private ownership of land, which the parliament had refused to sanction despite repeated prodding from the president.[7]

The chambers' own internal structures and procedures—what in Russia is called the *reglament*—can also undermine its ability to restrain executive power. Unlike Western parliaments, the Russian Duma has at its apex a powerful "committee on committees," known as the Council of the Duma. For reasons explored in the work of Thomas Remington and Steven Smith, each party has equal representation on this body, which makes committee assignments and decides important housekeeping matters. These "egalitarian and consensual arrangements for [the Duma's] steering body" discour-

Figure 6.1 **The Russian Federal Assembly** (Parliament)

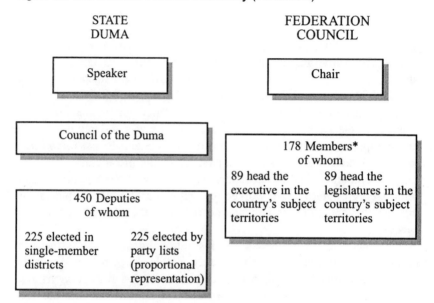

STATE DUMA

FEDERATION COUNCIL

Speaker

Chair

Council of the Duma

450 Deputies of whom

225 elected in single-member districts

225 elected by party lists (proportional representation)

178 Members* of whom

89 head the executive in the country's subject territories

89 head the legislatures in the country's subject territories

*The Republic of Chechnia has refused to seat its two members.

age the rise of discipline and cohesion in parliamentary behavior.[8] Compromise decisions made by the Council of the Duma contribute to a lack of coordination between party factions and legislative committees, which become—in Joel Ostrow's phrase—"parallel, autonomous channels of organization," yet another form of institutional redundancy. Intended to balance partisan interests, the procedure for distributing committee assignments may produce a committee whose chair, deputy chair, and rank-and-file majority represent three very different factions. And once ensconced on a committee, a deputy may find that his commitment to the "professional" work of the committee—as well as the perquisites of committee membership—outweighs his allegiance to the "political" activity of what are often weak party organizations. Furthermore, committees may be redundant. Denied what it felt to be adequate representation on the Duma's foreign affairs committee, the Liberal Democratic Party insisted on the creation of a parallel structure, the committee on geopolitics. These internal divisions in the parliament create "incentives for deputies to pursue strategies of sabotage and confrontation, rather than consensus-building and conflict management."[9]

Many observers also point to Russia's electoral rules as impediments to party, and parliamentary, development. Because the members of the Federation Council now occupy their seats by virtue of their positions as heads of the executive or legislative branches in the country's eighty-nine regions, they tend to eschew national party affiliations. As a result, the Federation Council lacks the partisan structures that one normally finds in democratic assemblies. In the Duma, on the other hand, there are active party factions, due in considerable measure to the use of proportional representation (PR) to fill half of the 450 seats.[10] Proportional representation elections, which award seats to parties in proportion to the share of the popular vote received, present voters with a choice between parties rather than individual politicians. Single-member-district voting, comparable to that used in American congressional elections, determines who will occupy the other 225 seats in the Duma. Where the campaign for PR seats is waged on the national level, treating the Russian Federation as if it were one large constituency, the race for single-member-district seats occurs in 225 different constituencies, each with its own demography and policy concerns. In such elections, the personality of the candidate, and his or her position in the local political economy, is often more important than party affiliation. Thus, less than half of the winning candidates in single-member-district seats stood under a party banner in the December 1995 elections, though many unaffiliated members did join factions once in the parliament in order to gain access to committee assignments and other benefits.

As a means of discouraging the representation of extreme parties, Russia's electoral rules require that parties contesting the PR seats receive at least 5 percent of the vote before any seats are awarded to them. In theory, the 5 percent threshold should have encouraged the merger of smaller parties into more competitive electoral blocs. Yet the experience of the 1993 and 1995 parliamentary elections illustrates what some in the West have labeled the irrational behavior of Russian parties.[11] In December 1995, forty-three different parties sought PR seats. The result: only five political parties, garnering barely 50 percent of the total popular vote, crossed the 5 percent threshold and achieved representation in the Duma. The other thirty-eight parties saw their votes redistributed to the four "winners," who thereby received twice the number of seats to which the popular vote would have otherwise entitled them.[12]

That most parties maintained their seemingly quixotic struggle is due to the absence of a culture of compromise and of viable career alternatives for party leaders. But it was also due to the nature of the PR campaign itself, which can be mounted from the capital with minimal funding. With a threshold of only 5 percent, the risks of such a campaign appeared minimal compared with the rewards. When asked about their performance in the 1993 elections, where they received 6 percent of the PR vote, a member of the Women of Russia party replied: "We won" (*my pobedili*).[13] The point was not that they had won the right to govern—such a thought seemed inappropriate anyway in an executive-dominated political system. Rather, they had won the visibility, the legitimacy, and the staff, offices, and other perquisites that come with parliamentary seats. Why lose their identity and "sovereignty" as a party just to join a larger group, when that group cannot offer seats on the front benches? Viewed in this light, perhaps the behavior of small Russian parties is not so irrational after all. It is yet another example of the scramble to carve out pockets of autonomy, whether in a region, an executive agency, or parliament.

For all of its weaknesses, however, the Federal Assembly still serves to check the freedom of executive action. Like all democratically elected assemblies, the Russian parliament rallies—and at times inflames—public opinion against the policies of presidency and Government. Absent a mature civil society, with its well-organized and influential associations, a parliamentary leader is one of the few public figures who can bring popular pressure to bear against the executive. Merely publicizing the Government's failures on such issues as pension payments and military hazing can at times embarrass the state into action. The parliament is therefore not only a lawmaking body but a political theater whose stage can be used to shame as well as inform. For example, the parliament expended considerable energy in 1997 attempting to discredit the president's chief economic advisor, Anatolii Chubais, by linking him to various financial improprieties.[14] The parliament has also passed an endless stream of nonbinding resolutions, many of which are designed to embarrass the president.[15]

On certain issues, most notably the budget and legal reform, the executive cannot govern without some measure of parliamentary consent. Although drafted by the Government, the annual Law on the Budget must pass the legislature. The protracted annual negotiations over budgetary allocations give the deputies opportunities to wrest concessions from the executive in exchange for passage. And although the budget may be revised by administrative action during the course of the fiscal year, it nonetheless establishes the basic parameters of state spending. The criminal justice system also operates on the basis of legal codes that only the parliament can exact. The introduction of an executive-sponsored reform of criminal arrest and detention has been delayed for several years while parliament debates provisions of the Criminal Procedure Code. Moreover, the 1993 constitution grants the parliament the right to issue amnesties for entire categories of criminals, a standard practice carried over from the Soviet era, when each anniversary of a revolutionary milestone was greeted by the early release of prisoners. As we observe in an earlier chapter, this prerogative was employed in dramatic and controversial fashion in February 1994, when the legislature freed anti-Yeltsin officials convicted—or awaiting trial—for their involvement in the 1991 August putsch and the armed insurrection of parliament in October 1993. There are few clearer examples of the use of political power, defined classically as the ability to force another party, in this case Yeltsin, to do something against its will.

The ultimate weapon in the legislative arsenal is the veto override. Achieving supermajorities in two highly fragmented chambers is a formidable task, but in a handful of cases during Yeltsin's second term, the parliament reversed the president's veto. In the spring of 1997, for example, the assembly overrode Yeltsin's veto of the Law on Trophy Art, which forbade the repatriation of art captured from the Nazis in World War II. In this case, the nationalist sentiments of the parliament triumphed over the desire of the president to avoid an awkward confrontation with his staunchest Western ally, the German chancellor, Helmut Kohl. However, although overriding a veto forces the president to sign a law it does not compel him to implement it. Just as some earlier American presidents have "impounded" funds allocated by Congress, so the Russian executive has at times refused to carry out legislative mandates.

Finally, whereas the president needs the support of the Duma for his selection of prime minister, he requires the consent of the Federation Council for appointments to many leading executive and legislative posts. On numerous occasions, the Federation Council has used its power of confirmation to thwart the cadres policy of the president. Besides the repeated rejection in 1993 of Yeltsin's nominee for procurator general, the upper house also turned back several candidates proposed for the Constitutional Court, including Valerii Savitskii, who had to settle for the post of presidential representative to the Court, which did not require parliamentary approval. As Peter Bachrach and Morton Baratz have illustrated in the American context, such sporadic presidential defeats represent only one face of parliamentary power.[16] The less visible—but no less important— face was the continual self-restraint that the potential for a confirmation denial imposed on the president and his advisors. The more interesting question, therefore, is not who was rejected by the Federation Council but who was not nominated—or even considered—by the president because of their unacceptability to the parliament.

Already reckoning with the opposition of the Federal Council to many of his appointments, Yeltsin reacted angrily to attempts by the Duma in 1996 and 1998 to amend the constitution in order to grant it the authority to confirm individual ministers and not just the prime minister. This proposal, successfully resisted by the president, would have altered fundamentally the complexion of the Government as well as relations between president and parliament. Given the political divide between Yeltsin and the dominant factions in parliament, such an amendment would almost certainly have led to a constitutional or governing crisis.

Ruling with the Parliament

To overcome parliamentary resistance to presidential leadership, Yeltsin employed diverse levers of influence, some grounded in formal powers, others in paraconstitutional practice. Perhaps most surprising is the frequency with which the Russian president conceded to the will of parliament on some issues in order to avoid debilitating confrontations. In the spring of 1994, for example, the Russian president agreed to sign the Law on the Status of Deputies, which granted the deputies unfettered access to Government officials and agencies and expanded their immunity from prosecution. In accepting this controversial bill, the president overruled most of his senior advisors in the presidency, including Sergei Filatov and the head of the State-Legal Administration.[17]

It was in the field of personnel policy, however, that the president made his most visible and significant concessions. Put simply, Yeltsin periodically defused the rising hostility of parliament and the nation by sacrificing unpopular ministers. Like a sated beast, following each sacrifice the parliament lost for a time the will to stalk the executive. Whereas noteworthy Government reshuffles occurred every few months through most of the Yeltsin presidency, the replacement of a prime minister took place only once in Yeltsin's first term, in December 1992, when Viktor Chernomyrdin replaced Yegor Gaidar. For Yeltsin, as for all leaders in semipresidential systems, the prime minister is usually held in reserve, to be sacrificed when all other means of fending off the parliament and the nation have been exhausted. An indication of the rapid erosion of presidential authority in 1998 was Yeltsin's dismissal of two prime ministers in less than six months, Chernomyrdin in March and Kirienko in August. As we noted earlier, when Yeltsin attempted to return Chernomyrdin to the prime ministership in late August, he was rebuffed twice by the parliament. Rather than risk a constitutional crisis or a new election by subjecting Chernomyrdin to a third and final confirmation vote, Yeltsin selected another candidate, Yevgenii Primakov, who enjoyed broad support in the Duma. This confrontation appeared to represent the beginning of a shift in the balance of power between presidency and parliament, and also between president and prime minister. It is premature, however, to conclude that the reshaping of institutional relations will outlive the financial crises and ill health that spawned it.

The president's concessions on personnel represented one strand in a complex web of relationships between the executive and legislature. In return for the support or forbearance of the parliament, deputies extracted—or the president proffered—a variety of "goods," some benefiting the parliament as a whole, others targeting individual leaders. We have already had occasion to mention several such exchanges, including apartments, transportation, and vacation packages allocated to deputies by the president's Administration of Affairs, and posts on the presidency's Security Council, granted to the leaders of the Duma and Federation Council. Whether designed to co-opt deputies more broadly or to enlist their temporary support for a bill before parliament, such measures have been instrumental in taming a legislature whose political instincts are decidedly antipresidential.[18]

Corruption in parliament has also weakened the resolve of deputies. Of course, private gain, or at least private sustenance, is a concern of politicians in all but the most revolutionary environments. But in Russia, as in many developing societies, corruption has assumed a particularly insidious and blatant form in the legislature. Among the 450 members of the Duma elected in December 1995, more than 30 were under criminal investigation by the prosecutor's office. Because criminals fearing prosecution could hide behind Russia's generous parliamentary immunity, which could only be revoked by a majority vote of the assembly, some outlaws sought refuge in a parliamentary seat. Criminal elements were especially numerous among the more than fifteen thousand persons registered as "aides" to parliamentarians. When a police investigator went to the Duma for a committee hearing on a draft of the Criminal Procedure Code, he

> found [himself] at something resembling a gathering of crime kingpins. [He] probably saw more old acquaintances in the Duma than . . . in the prisons cells at Butyrki![19]

In 1996 alone, twelve parliamentary aides were murdered—presumably because of their ties to the criminal world.[20]

The Duma attracted criminal elements in part because of the illicit trade in votes. According to a report in *Izvestia* in 1997, "making laws 'to order' has become a very stable and perhaps the most dependable way for deputies to augment their personal and party budgets." In passing the law on mineral rights, for example, several leading energy companies were reportedly among the businesses that "placed the order."[21] One could argue, of course, that business interests in the United States exercise similar power over individual members of the legislature through campaign donations and other forms of financial and political support. But not only is this activity less regulated and visible in Russia, it also enables the executive itself to use monetary rewards to generate a legislative majority. According to one source, in order to push through the 1997 budget, "circles close to the Government" channeled $27 million to the Communist and Liberal Democratic parties, two of the parliament's largest and most opposition-minded factions.[22] While functionally valuable as an antidote to executive-legislative gridlock, such criminality undermines the very foundations of representative and responsible government. It is no wonder that parliament is unable to halt the "bloating and corruption" in the executive.

The ability of the president to generate temporary majorities in a hostile parliament also rests on the deputies' lack of a will to power and their peculiar sense of functional dualism. Again to invoke Ostrow, deputies often view themselves as lawmaking professionals as well as partisan politicians. In the first role, deputies want to pass legislation, and the threat of a presidential veto encourages them to reach compromises with the executive in order to avoid stalemate. Recognizing the space for political accomodation that this incentive structure provides, the presidency has regularly employed three institutions to advance its legislative agenda. The first is the Domestic Policy Administration, which informs the president of the correlation of political forces in parliament while at the same time trying "to convince deputies of the advantages [*tselesoobraznost'*] of the legislative initiatives of the president."[23] The second institution is the presidential representatives to the Duma and Federation Council, who represent somewhat tepid versions of a Government whip in a parliamentary system. In the Russian case, this figure is part political operative, part legal official, someone who oversees the movement of a bill from its drafting in the executive—at which stage he advises the president on the parliament's likely reaction to the legislation—through its various committee hearings and the requisite three readings before the chambers.[24] In addition, for important bills, the leader of the Executive Office of the President also assigns a high-ranking Government official to "bulldog" the bill through the two houses. Whether presidential representative or minister designated ad hoc, these officials serve as important conduits of information between executive and legislative leaders. In cases where the legislation originates in the parliament rather than the executive, after a bill's first reading the presidential representative communicates to the legislature any changes in the law desired by the president. Suggestions for legislative revisions usually emanate from the president's State-Legal Administration, which carefully reviews all draft legislation.[25]

Despite the best efforts of the president's "pushers" (*tolkachi*), to borrow a term from Soviet political economy, attempts to pass legislation frequently reach an impasse, either because of divisions within or between the Duma and Federation Council or between president and parliament. But if a minimal consensus exists among executive and legislative officials on the need to adopt legislation, a conciliation commission (*soglasitel'naia komissiia*) may be created to forge a compromise bill. Drawing its members from the presidency, the Government, and the relevant parliamentary committees, this joint executive-legislative commission shunts the legislative process onto a siding, where a small group works intensively in closed sessions to find language that will accommodate the interests of all sides. If this multibranch roundtable reaches agreement, the revised bill returns to the parliament for further consideration.

Although passage of bills emanating from such conciliation commissions are by no means guaranteed, they usually carry with them the support of key parliamentary leaders. Conciliation commissions, therefore, are a means by which the executive can informally negotiate a solution to legislative stalemate. It is profoundly different, then, from the conference committee in the American Congress, which brings together key legislators to reconcile competing versions of Senate and House bills. Where the American conference committee is an integral part of Congress, the Russian multibranch conciliation commission is a constitutionally mandated body (article 85) that lies in the institutional interstices between executive and legislative power.[26]

Yeltsin has used the multibranch conciliation commission to forestall veto overrides as well as to break legislative logjams. Rather than send a rejected law back to parliament, and face an embarrassing defeat if the veto is overriden, the Russian president may ask for the establishment of a conciliation commission to review the law. The president is most likely to resort to this tactic if he anticipates that the veto will not be sustained on a law that threatens to seriously undermine his policies or authority. Such was the case in the summer of 1997, when a controversial law restricting the freedom of religion passed both houses by overwhelming majorities. Responding in part to the outrage of the international community, Yeltsin vetoed the legislation and almost immediately called for the summoning of a conciliation commission to devise wording that would impose fewer limitations on nonconformist faiths.[27]

The conciliation commission is only one of several institutions that serve as surrogates, or at least supplements, to parliament. In the summer of 1996, Boris Yeltsin created a Political Consultative Council that included leading officials from executive and legislative institutions. Where the conciliatory commissions reviewed specific bills, the Consultative Council discussed the broader course of Russian political and economic development. It offered another venue through which the president and his prime minister could work to co-opt key members of parliament and thereby transform the tenor of executive-legislative relations from confrontation to cooperation.[28] By early 1998, the Consultative Council had transmogrified into the Big Four, an informal committee uniting the president, prime minister, speaker of the Duma, and chairman of the Federation Council.

The idea of establishing alternatives to a recalcitrant parliament first surfaced in the early 1990s, when President Yeltsin created a Social Chamber (*obshchestvennaia palata*) comprised of representatives from the country's leading religious, ethnic, and civic associations. Although the Social Chamber never assumed an especially active or visible role in public affairs, its very existence threatened for a time the parliament's monopoly as the nation's assembly. It also provided the president with a ready-made alternative leg of legitimacy on which to stand in the event of a dissolution of parliament.[29] But when Yeltsin shut down the parliament in September 1993, he looked not to the Social Chamber but to regional elites for political support. In the first few days after the closing of parliament, Yeltsin considered creating a Council of the Federation, made up of leading provincial officials, to legitimate his rule during the interregnum. However, the relative popular quiescence that followed the military defeat of the parliamentary opposition apparently convinced the Russian president that he could rule alone until the introduction of a new constitution.

The concept of a pro-presidential assembly of regional elites found its way, however, into the 1993 constitution in the form of the upper house of the Federal Assembly, the Federation Council, sometimes referred to informally as the Senate. Believing the indirectly elected Federation Council to be a desirable counterweight to a directly elected Duma, the framers of the 1993 constitution made the upper house a permanent body, not subject to dissolution. Thus, Russia's institutional arrangements reduced the stakes of a Duma dissolution. Any future closure of the Duma would leave one-half of the assembly still in place.

Unlike in some parliamentary and semipresidential systems, Russia does not permit the president to dissolve a parliament on his own, even after a certain time period has elapsed following parliamentary elections. A constitutional dissolution of parliament may occur only as a result of the deputies' own actions. If the Duma rejects the president's nominee for prime minister thrice, the parliament is dissolved and new elections held.[30] The president may also dissolve the Duma if it expresses no confidence in the Government. If the Duma initiates the no-confidence motion, the president is empowered to dissolve parliament if a majority of the deputies vote against the Government twice within a three-month period. When the Government itself raises the question of parliamentary confidence in its work, the president may dissolve the Duma within a mere seven days after the motion of confidence fails.[31] In order to pressure the Duma into passing the 1998 budget, Prime Minister Chernomyrdin considered calling for a vote of no confidence in late 1997.[32]

Despite the fact that the deputies retain the ultimate decision regarding their fate, it would be a mistake to view dissolution politics as a one-sided parliamentary game. By appointing a prime minister who is unacceptable to deputies, the president can in effect force the Duma to seize the poison pen. Likewise, the prime minister at a moment of enormous unpopularity could provoke the Duma into dissolution by calling for a no-confidence vote. In this sense, the president is as much the master of the parliament's fate as the deputies. Indeed, the mere circulation of rumors that the executive plans to encourage a Duma dissolution—such as occurred in the summer of 1997—may serve to intimidate the deputies into a less confrontational posture.

Given their fear of the unknown in electoral politics, many Duma deputies have been reluctant to move beyond opposition of specific policies of the executive to a complete withdrawal of confidence in the prime minister and his Government. According to one observer:

> [W]hile [the Duma] periodically threatens the Government with a vote of no confidence, it is simultaneously afraid of its own radicalism. It doesn't want to end up being dissolved.[33]

Only twice in the Chernomyrdin era, in October 1994 and July 1995, did deputies advance a no-confidence motion in the Government, and only in the latter instance did the motion pass. That the Duma failed to follow this up with a second and decisive vote of no confidence reflected the unwillingness of deputies to risk their seats, and in many cases their livelihood, to contest elections whose outcome would not alter fundamentally the distribution of power between president and parliament.[34] Regardless of the results, the Duma would not be able to force a prime minister on the president, as in France. Indeed, a dramatically increased majority of opposition forces in parliament might encourage the president to reduce his cooperation with the assembly, or to close it altogether by unconstitutional means. Furthermore, because the constitution allows the president to rule for up to four months after a parliamentary dissolution, by forcing new elections the deputies would remove legislative oversight of the executive for a lengthy, and potentially crisis-ridden, period. Here again, the institutional design of Russian politics favors the president at the expense of parliament.

Ruling Around the Parliament

Through the use of institutions such as the presidential representative and the conciliation commissions, Yeltsin has shown a willingness to adhere to the logic of semipresidential rule on some issues. But impatience with parliamentary obstruction and delays leads the Russian president at times to invoke the rhetoric and methods of rule associated with authoritarian regimes. Frustrated with the parliament's refusal to accede to desperately needed budget cuts, Yeltsin rashly announced in July 1997 that he would no longer allow the Federal Assembly to make any important decisions:

> The Government should tackle 80 percent of issues on its own, without referring them to parliament. . . . In future only 20 percent of measures should be referred to parliament for approval.[35]

In the event, the president did not carry through on this threat. But he continued to remind the parliament of the lawmaking powers that he held in reserve. In the summer of 1998, amid a severe financial crisis, Yeltsin promised to enact a packet of anticrisis measures demanded by the IMF if the parliament failed to approve it. The politics of presidential engagement and cooperation with parliament represented, therefore, only one face of governing in Russia. The other, darker, side of Russian politics exhibited features familiar to students of autocracy, including the refusal of the supreme leader to be checked by other state institutions.

At least through the middle of Yeltsin's second term, the president and his legislative assistants adopted a generally harsh public tone toward the Duma while exhibiting moderation toward the Federation Council. For years, Yeltsin refused to make an appearance in the Duma, upset by what he considered to be its lack of respect toward the presidency. In April 1998, rather than present his nominee for prime minister in person, as is customary in many semipresidential systems, he instructed his representative,

Aleksandr Kotenkov, to introduce the nomination of Sergei Kirienko. This departure from protocol was all the more insulting because the majority of Duma members regarded Kotenkov with suspicion or disdain. Unlike his predecessor in the Duma, Aleksandr M. Yakovlev, or his counterpart in the Federation Council, Anatolii Sliva, Kotenkov was a brusque and undiplomatic lawyer whose attitude toward Duma deputies bordered at times on contempt. As Kirienko was forming his cabinet in the spring of 1998, party factions in the Duma were exerting pressure on the president and prime minister designate to include some of their leaders in the new Government. During these negotiations, Kotenkov damned the Duma with faint praise when he said that he knew "virtually all the deputies, and there are [some] really outstanding characters among them deserving to hold a ministerial post. But there are no more than ten such people."[36] In other words, from among the 450 members of the Duma, an organization that in most semipresidential systems would serve as the prime recruiting pool for the Government, Kotenkov regarded only 2 percent as qualified to become ministers. Kotenkov's careful scrutiny of Duma voting procedures also angered many deputies. On several occasions, he accused the Duma of counting the votes of deputies who were absent from the chamber—and even the country—during roll call. Such a challenge to the validity of the Duma's voting results led the president to reject the override of his veto on a conservative Land Code in 1997.[37]

To avoid parliamentary constraints, Yeltsin has relied heavily on presidential decrees as an instrument of direct rule. In so doing, he has employed the authority of a constitution that his team of advisors tailored to his needs. Article 90 empowers the Russian president to issue decrees (*ukazy*) and directives (*rasporiazheniia*) as long as they do not contradict other provisions of the constitution or parliamentary statutes (*zakony*). Given the paucity of new Russian laws, and the illegitimacy of much of the Soviet legal inheritance, Yeltsin enjoyed sweeping lawmaking authority, especially during his first term.[38] Thus, ruling around parliament by decree assumed a patina of respectability and legitimacy, even if some decrees appeared to encroach on existing parliamentary laws. Like numerous presidentialist regimes in Latin America, Russia sanctioned *decretismo* as a means of overcoming the legislative stalemate that plagues presidential and semipresidential regimes in transition.[39] In the view of Robert Orttung and Scott Parrish, Yeltsin enjoys "what are probably the strongest legislative powers of any elected president in the world."[40]

The scale of Yeltsin's decree-making activity has been staggering. Recall that the order to dissolve the parliament in September 1993 was the fourteen hundredth decree issued that year. The number of decrees signed annually continues to approach one thousand. To be sure, a relatively small percentage of these decrees possess what lawyers would call normative authority; that is, they rarely set down a permanent or general rule that binds the bureaucracy and society. Most affect a single institution, a single region, or even a single individual. Indeed, fully a third of the decrees issued by Yeltsin in 1996 merely announced the appointment— or in some cases, dismissal—of judges and high-ranking executive officials, such as ambassadors, ministers, and regional representatives. The president uses the more humble "directives" to hire and fire less exalted officials, those occupying posts at department head level and below in the presidency and at deputy minister level and below in the Government. Another sizable minority of the decrees issued in 1996, approximately one-quarter of the total, concerned the management of executive agencies or the supervision of national security affairs, two areas over which the Russian president has traditionally exercised hegemony. Presidential decrees, for example, launched the reorganization of the Ministry of Internal Affairs in the spring of 1996 and established a new passport regime later that same year.[41]

A recognition of the diverse uses to which presidential decrees are put in Russia administration should not obscure, however, their lawmaking role in matters that lie within the provenance of parliaments in most democratic regimes. A quarter of the decrees issued in 1996 addressed policy questions in areas as diverse as economics and finance, education, culture and science, and social security. One of the centerpieces of economic reform in Russia, the privatization of state property, was introduced almost exclusively through presidential decrees. Likewise, the decision to move to a convertible currency was made by decrees and not laws. Because parliamentary statutes were silent on these subjects, the president and his economic advisors could claim constitutional authority for these initiatives. Presidential decrees were filling in empty normative space.

In most cases where presidential decrees appeared to be at variance with existing statutes, the laws in question were legacies from the Soviet era. That did not mean, however, that the laws necessarily lacked legal force. Just as Soviet Russia accepted for a time part of the legal inheritance from the tsarist regime, numerous laws that had been adopted in the Soviet era were adapted to the changing political and economic environment through statutory revision. When Yeltsin issued his controversial decree to combat organized crime in May 1994, it violated provisions of the long-standing, and much-amended, Criminal Procedure Code.[42] Similarly, the president's decree privatizing peasant land in June 1996 not only contradicted existing statutes on real property, it directly flouted the will of a majority of the sitting parliament, which had pointedly refused to pass a new law on land with similar provisions. Thus, although Yeltsin may have preferred to rule with the parliament, he was prepared to rule around it if it repeatedly refused to accommodate his interests.

Besides competition from presidential decrees, parliamentary bills faced the threat of a presidential veto, which Yeltsin used with increasing frequency during his second term. In the summer of 1997, Duma speaker Gennadii Seleznev complained that the president's heavy reliance on the veto had led to a virtual "embargo on the legislative process." In Seleznev's view, such obstruction of the legislature's work amounted to "an abuse of constitutional authority." His harshest words, however, were reserved not for the president but his State-Legal Administration, whose "anonymous bureaucrats . . . write memos for the president that are critical of parliamentary statutes." Of particular concern to the speaker, and many members of parliament, were the conflicting signals received from the various centers of executive power. As Seleznev observed, in fourteen cases Yeltsin vetoed legislation that had been submitted to parliament by the Government. But it was naive—or disingenous—of the speaker to assume that "on the [president's] own team they'd be able to agree" on a legislative program. As we have seen in earlier chapters, institutional redundancy within the presidency and between presidency and Government impeded the development of cooperation and discipline within the executive itself, a fact well known to Seleznev and other deputies.[43]

Once enacted and signed into law, parliamentary statutes also faced neglect or distortion at the hands of executive officials responsible for implementing the law. In this regard, little had changed from the Soviet era: laws remained without effect until they had been "concretized" through the issuance of enabling acts by the Government and relevant ministries. It was therefore these substatutory acts, and not the laws themselves, that moved officialdom to action. How faithfully and quickly bureaucrats executed the laws depended on the directives, orders, and instructional letters that they received from ministers and other executive leaders. Without a well-developed system of administrative courts, a culture of legality and bureaucratic discipline, or a tradition of individual ministerial responsibility to parliament through interpellation or votes of confidence, the assembly has not been able to ensure the faithful execution of the laws by the presidency and the Government.[44]

Conclusion

The widely divergent assessments of Boris Yeltsin's political leadership—a democrat to some, a dictator to others—follow as much from the two faces of presidential power as from the polarization of Russian society. Those sympathetic to Yeltsin point to the constant give-and-take between president and parliament over legislation and patronage, a pattern of political exchange that is certainly familiar to students of American politics.[45] Each institution has formal and informal levers of influence that it uses to advance its interests. To be sure, the balance of constitutional power is tilted heavily in favor of the president, a result of his clan's dominance among the document's framers. But the parliamentary opposition has its own heavy weapons, including the ability to mobilize popular protests against executive action. Signaling its dissatisfaction with the policies of the president, the Communist Party began to organize massive strikes throughout the country in the summer of 1997, and in so doing sought to put pressure on the executive to moderate the second round of radical economic reform directed by Chubais and Nemtsov. Yeltsin's decision to abandon his young prime minister, Sergei Kirienko, after only five months in office must also be seen as a reaction to rising discontent among members of parliament as well as Russian oligarchs and foreign investors.

Those who view Yeltsin's presidency as a continuation of the autocratic tradition will emphasize instead the willingness of the president to rule around parliament at moments of crisis or frustration. Given the institutional design of the Second Russian Republic, Yeltsin doesn't have to suspend parliament; he may simply ignore it. Like the Dumas that sat under the last Russian tsar, Nicholas II, the current State Duma in Russia exerts influence but does not in any real sense share sovereignty with the chief executive. Despite its antipresidential majority, the parliament cannot force the hand of the executive.

The political opposition has chosen, therefore, to play two parallel games. On the field of rhetoric—in speeches, newspaper articles, and party programs—the Communists and nationalists portray Yeltsin and his advisors as the enemies of Russia. But behind the scenes, they continually negotiate with the presidency and Government over the allocation of jobs, funds, and the other "goods" of state. Without this kind of engagement, the opposition would have enjoyed few spoils of office.

Cooperation has had its limits, however. At least until the Primakov Government, the Communists and nationalists refused to be drawn into public actions that would blur the lines between Government and opposition. When Yeltsin included a Communist, Valentin Kovalev, in the cabinet in the fall of 1994, the Communist Party expelled him and thereby avoided the perception that it had joined the Government. It sought to avoid even partial responsibility for the actions of the executive.

In periods of crisis, such as Russia experienced in the 1990s, opposition to the ruling elite has been a politically comfortable and electorally advantageous position. For this reason, deputies were alarmed in the summer of 1996 when a little-understood provision of the budget law forced the parliament to approve the specific cuts to be made in the annual sequestration of funds. Previously, reducing expenditure had been the sole responsibility of the executive. Where parliament offered generous funding to institutions and programs at the beginning of the budget year, the executive was forced in the middle of the year to scale it back. Most deputies preferred to keep it that way.[46] Indeed, some analysts argue that the Duma intentionally passed deficit-ridden budgets to satisfy not only the struggling pensioners, soldiers, and students but prominent banking interests who stand to make handsome profits on the financing of the state deficit. In general, the higher the deficit, the higher the yield on state bonds held by the banks and by bureaucrats and enterprise directors with access to funds that can be invested, even if for a short term.[47]

The primary focus of this chapter—and of most Western analyses of parliamentary politics in Russia—has been on the lower house, the Duma. Under the constitution of the Second Russian Republic, the Duma appears the more politically weighty of the two chambers by virtue of its ability to express no confidence in the Government and to override Federation Council decisions with a two-thirds majority vote. Furthermore, unlike the Federation Council, the Duma is a directly elected chamber; as a result, it is here that one finds the seeds of party development in Russia. It is also in the Duma that one sees most clearly the economic or class cleavages that have been the staple of politics in the West in the last two centuries. In short, the Duma exhibits features that Western political scientists regard as familiar and important in democratic assemblies. However, it is the Federation Council that may pose the more serious challenge to presidential rule in Yeltsin's second term and beyond. In contrast to the Duma's inability to reject or express no confidence in a prime minister, the Federation Council's power of confirmation over key judicial and executive appointments has constrained presidential appointment policy. But more important than the powers of the chamber is the political prominence of its members and the centrality of center-periphery issues to its debates. Most Duma deputies are what the British might call "lobby fodder," political followers who lack visibility and an institutional base. Half of the members of the Federation Council, on the other hand, are by constitutional provision governors of regions or presidents of republics, with their own bureaucratic bases outside of parliament; the other half are speakers of the provincial legislatures.[48] Generating support for the president in the Federation Council requires, therefore, different skills and a different currency of exchange than in the Duma. Because of the weakness of party factions in the Federation Council, it is not enough to win over the leaders of the chamber. Support must be built one member at a time.

Beginning in 1996, under pressure from provincial elites, the president permitted the direct election of regional governors, most of whom had previously been the appointees of the president. This change in the country's institutional design promises to alter the relations between executive and legislature, between Duma and Federation Council, and between center and periphery in Russia.[49] Although the appointed governors were never really the prefects of the president—to be effective, they also needed the support of local elites—in the new incentive structure they must work to secure their electoral base as well. This reorientation of political loyalties may present the greatest challenge yet to presidential rule. As members of the parliament in Moscow and as chief executives and legislative speakers in the country's eighty-nine subject territories, these regional elites are emerging as the brokers of Russia's political future.

7

The Presidency and the Provinces

Establishing the tenor of relations between levels of government is one of the essential tasks of state building. Just as new states must devise rules and conventions that regulate the countervailing ambitions of branches of government, and of state power and individual freedom, so they must craft a stable framework of relations between center and periphery. That this goal has proved so elusive in Yeltsin's Russia is due to the country's historical and demographic legacy, the peculiar circumstances of the transition from Communist to post-Communist rule, and the dearth of political leadership in Moscow.

Despite vigorous attempts to create a new Soviet civilization out of the diverse peoples and cultures of central Eurasia, the USSR retained many of the traditional features of empire at its demise.[1] In the wake of Gorbachev's glasnost campaign, carefully constructed Soviet identities began to give way to older ethnic and national loyalties, on which leaders of several republics built movements for political autonomy and later independence. Pressures to devolve political authority were not limited, however, to the fifteen constituent republics of the USSR. Some ethnic homelands within these republics—called "autonomous republics" in the Orwellian language of the Soviet era—also sought to join the "parade of sovereignties" that moved across the Soviet political landscape in the late 1980s. Among these were Tatarstan and Chechnia in the Russian Federation. Thus, in the "*matrioshka* nationalism" of the transition period, the fifteen ethnic republics nested within the Soviet Union proclaimed their sovereignty, followed by ethnic territories within these Union republics. Even some smaller, third-tier ethnic territories, lying within Russian regions, made bold claims for home rule. Among this last group was the Khanti-Mansi province in Russia's oil-rich Tiumen region.

Facilitating the rise of national movements was the political geography of the Soviet Union. Unlike the Kurds in southwest Asia, who lack a clearly delineated and recognized territory, all but the smallest nationalities in the Soviet Union received the symbols of statehood: their own territory, flag, political institutions, and unified political elite. A vestige of the early years of Soviet power, these concessions to ethnic identity served to legitimate the political order for a diverse population. They did not, of course, grant genuine autonomy from Moscow. Yet the very existence of ethnically defined territories—and the deepening expectation that indigenous rulers should occupy the most visible state posts in them—presented a new generation of nationalists in the late 1980s with a ready-made institutional base. In a word, the formal trappings of statehood were already in place. What had seemed in the 1920s a benign measure to accord nationalities a measure of symbolic recognition facilitated the growth of separatism at the end of the twentieth century. Again, institutional design mattered. Had the Soviet Union been divided into administrative units without regard to ethnicity, elites bent on separatism, or even cultural revival, would have waged their struggle on a different—and far less congenial—political battefield.[2]

When Gorbachev sought in 1990 to grant autonomous republics greater home rule as a means of binding them to the Soviet center, Boris Yeltsin had no choice but to publicly welcome the efforts of Russia's provinces to assert their autonomy. In a much-quoted remark, Yeltsin—then leader of the Russian Federation parliament—urged Russia's subject territories "to claim as much sovereignty as you can swallow." But by the summer of 1991, the centrifugal forces that challenged the integrity of the Soviet political community threatened to pull apart the Russian Federation itself. To stem the rising tide of regionalism and nationalism within Russia, Yeltsin—now the directly elected president of the republic—launched a campaign to regather power in Moscow, a campaign that occupied a central place in the politics of the transition. Put simply, presidential leadership in the Yeltsin years revolved around two major axes, the executive's relations with the legislature and Moscow's relations with the provinces.

In attempting to impose central control on the far-flung territories of the Russian Federation, Yeltsin encountered a host of obstacles. First, the most effective institution of rule in the country, the Communist Party, was disintegrating by the fall of 1991. The demise of the party was a political godsend for Yeltsin but an administrative nightmare. Gone was not only the party's vast apparatus, which had linked governments in the center and periphery, but its potent ideology, which had contained ethnic and local sentiment and legitimated Moscow-based rule. To be sure, President Yeltsin and his allies had their own ideas about replacement institutions and belief systems—some inchoate, others more fully formed. To begin the painstaking construction of a new vertical chain of command, with the presidency rather than the party at the apex, Yeltsin appointed presidential representatives to serve as his eyes and ears in Russia's subject territories in the aftermath of the August 1991 coup. But such measures soon met fierce resistance from regional executives as well as deputies in the central parliament, many of whom viewed a dominant presidency with suspicion, if not alarm. Taken together with the chaos of the transition and the immensity of the task of building a new state apparatus and ideology, the ability of Russia's regional elites to play presidency and parliament—and ministry and ministry—against each other ensured that political power would remain highly dispersed well into the post-Soviet era.[3]

Further complicating presidential leadership of Russia's subject territories were the market reforms launched in January 1992. Although halting and incomplete, the introduction of market mechanisms wrested control over most property from the central ministries in Moscow and placed it in the hands of diverse business and regional political elites. Thus, besides one-party rule and a single, pervasive ideology, the collapse of Communism removed another of the center's key levers over the periphery: the command economy.

How each of the eighty-nine republics and regions responded to the new political and economic calculus is obviously beyond the scope of the present work. The subject territories differed in their ethnic makeup, their historical relation to the Russian Empire, their proximity to Moscow, their economic resources, and the ambition of their elites—to mention only a few of the determinants of the evolving relations between federal and provincial governments. There are, therefore, eighty-nine different stories to tell if one views events from the provinces. Aware of the variety in Russian provincial politics, Yeltsin tailored his policies to reflect specific regional interests and demands. But while granting concessions to the regions, much as he had done to the parliament, Yeltsin was attempting to develop reliable levers of central control that would allow the presidency to regather much of the power that had flowed from Moscow to the provinces.

Redesigning Relations Among Levels of Government

When the outcome of a game is not to one's liking, it is always tempting to change the rules. Such was the sentiment of many Russian political actors, including the president, in the first years of the post-Soviet era. Among the many design changes considered by the presidency, perhaps none was more ambitious, or controversial, than redrawing the political map of Russia. In 1992, the young presidential counselor, Sergei Stankevich was one of several officials who revived the century-old idea of dividing Russia into provinces, or lands (*zemli*), without regard to ethnic settlement patterns. As one might expect, the proposal pleased Russian nationalists, who pointed out that ethnic Russians, who made up 82 percent of the country's population, formed a majority in sixteen of the twenty-one non-Russian republics, and a plurality in two of the remaining five republics. But the reform engendered little support in other circles and eventually faded from the political agenda as the drafting of a new constitution—one that required approval by popular referendum—reached its final stages.[4]

The constitution of December 1993 did contain, however, several provisions that appeared to strengthen the hand of the president in his relations with the provinces.[5] Although the document touted the federal character of the new Russian state, it failed to incorporate explicitly the Federal Treaty that had been signed in early 1992 with the ethnic republics. Moreover, despite assigning issues to federal, regional, or joint jurisdiction, numerous articles in the constitution undermined the logic of federalism. Principles of taxation and tax collection, for example, were to be established by federal law (article 75). The governments of the federation and the subject territories were "to form a single system of executive power" (article 77), with the president at the top of the pyramid. As we shall illustrate in detail below, the constitution also granted the Russian president important powers of patronage and pardon in an essentially unified legal system. Thus, in enacting the constitution of 1993, President Yeltsin sought to design a system of government that was federal in form but unitary in content.[6]

The best he could do in practice, however, was asymmetrical federalism, a pattern of center-periphery relations reminiscent of late imperial Russia. Whereas in a federal system like that of the United States, each of the fifty states enjoys equal legal status, in Russia's asymmetrical federalism some subject territories are more equal than others. Just as the tsar granted Poland special rights as a Russian territory in the early nineteenth century, so the Russian president at the end of the twentieth century accorded special privileges to some provinces, such as the republics of Tatarstan and Chechnia. How much power a subject territory enjoys depended not only on its constitutional status as a republic or region, but also on the specific provisions contained in bilateral agreements negotiated between the center and individual territories. These treaties supplemented, and in some cases super-

Map 7.1 The Russian Federation

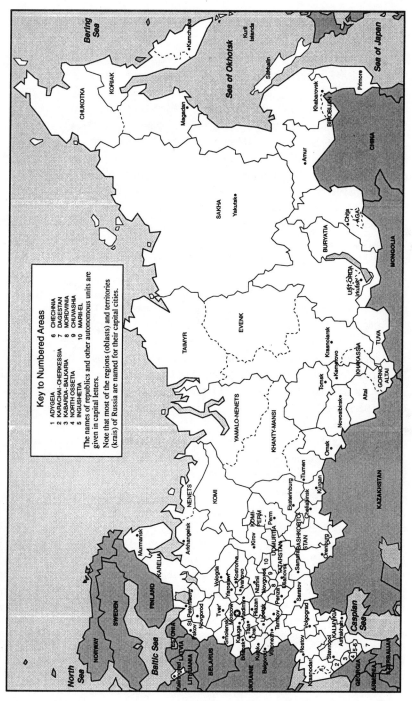

Key to Numbered Areas

1 ADYGEIA
2 KARACHAI-CHERKESSIA
3 KABARDA-BALKARIA
4 NORTH OSSETIA
5 INGUSHETIA
6 CHECHNIA
7 DAGESTAN
8 MORDVINIA
9 CHUVASHIA
10 MARII-EL

The names of republics and other autonomous units are given in capital letters.

Note that most of the regions (oblasts) and territories (krais) of Russia are named for their capital cities.

seded, the general language of the constitution on the jurisdictional boundaries between federal and republican or regional authority.

President Yeltsin signed the first such agreement, with Tatarstan, on 15 February 1994, barely six weeks after the enactment of the constitution. By the middle of 1998, just over half of the country's territories had negotiated and signed agreements with the center.[7] Judging by the similarities in the format and language of many documents, it appears that the presidency sought to impose on territories a template agreement that offered no guarantees beyond those contained in the constitution.[8] Some agreements, such as that concluded with the Orenburg region on 30 January 1996, fit this model: they were relatively brief and generic and offered no additional autonomy for the regions.[9] Most treaties, however, addressed specific concerns advanced during the negotiations with provincial elites. For example, the treaty between the Russian Federation and the mineral-rich republic of Sakha (Yakutia) guaranteed the Sakha government control over the Republic Fund of Precious Minerals, the organization that supervised the area's diamond and gold mines.[10] The northern territory of Komi, constantly in need of central subsidies to ensure adequate provisions for the winter, received treaty guarantees that recognized their special needs for "the timely delivery of goods" in the winter. The agreement between Komi and the Russian Federation also called for the center to maintain the wage supplements paid to persons working in the harsh climatic conditions of the Far North.[11] Regions such as Komi found it difficult to retain highly skilled workers without paying them the significantly higher wages to which they had become accustomed during the Soviet era—another reminder of the challenges posed by the transition to a market economy in Russia. In the case of the Buriat Republic, a historically Mongol region along the southern shore of Lake Baikal, one issue dominated the agreement with the center: cleaning up the polluted lake and its environs.[12] Understandably, the authorities in Buriatia did not wish to battle alone the environmental degradation caused by decades of centrally controlled paper production and other industrial activity in the area. Where some territories sought concessions from the center on financial or administrative matters, others fought for symbolic victories. The treaty with Bashkortostan recognized the republic as a "sovereign state" (*suverennoe gosudarstvo*)—a high-sounding phrase that in fact signified little in Russia, especially when followed, as it was here, by the words "within the Russian Federation" (*v sostav Rossiiskoi Federatsii*).[13]

Perhaps no territory rivaled Tatarstan for the generosity of concessions extracted from the center. A republic with extensive energy and industrial resources, a vigorous national movement, and an ambitious president,

Tatarstan was alone among Russian territories in obtaining for its citizens the right to pursue alternative service rather than submit themselves to military conscription. The agreement with Tatarstan also promised the republic a prominent role in the coordination of price and monetary policy, a concession that must have infuriated officials in the Ministry of Finance in Moscow. Along with several other republics, Tatarstan enjoyed greater influence over legal affairs and personnel selection in their territories. Finally, Tatarstan received the right to enter into direct relations with foreign states and international organizations.[14]

One can argue that because these bilateral agreements were not self-executing, the center lost little in granting some territories more formal autonomy than others. During a period when one of the country's republics, Chechnia, was engaged in a war of secession, the signing of bilateral treaties with other republics and regions could be viewed as a much-needed confirmation of the territorial integrity of the Russian Federation. And as the 1996 presidential elections approached, these "power-sharing agreements were [designed] . . . to appease oppositional provinces."[15] But resorting to such intrastate diplomacy invited a fresh round of center-periphery conflict and negotiations, what Steven Solnick has called "a competitive frenzy of deal-making."[16] Provinces receiving less generous concessions clamored for a more favorable relationship with the capital, while the privileged regions sought to hold Moscow to its word. Thus, these changes to the institutional design did not stabilize center-periphery relations. The ambiguities in the treaties merely allowed each side to feel that its position had been strengthened, while the struggle continued over the division of labor between levels of government in the making and execution of policy.

To this point, we have focused on the top two levels of government in Russia, those in Moscow and in the capitals of the subject territories. But within each of the subject territories there were districts and municipalities that formed a third administrative layer, that of local government (*mestnaia vlast'*). The presence of this third level created a triangular game in which Moscow often aligned itself with local governments. President Yeltsin personally chaired the Council on Local Self-Government, which sought to win the support of municipalities for his reform agenda.[17] In an exchange relationship full of paradox, the center was willing to expand the autonomy of local government—in part through the adoption of a federal law on local self-government—as a means of reducing the power of regional political elites. Like the autonomous republics in the late Soviet era, many local governments viewed the center as a shield against the high-handedness of their immediate superiors.[18] At a meeting of the newly formed Congress of

Municipal Associations at presidential headquarters in June 1998, mayors from around Russia hailed Yeltsin as their protector—the "patriarch of local government," in the words of one enthusiastic participant.[19] To cement political ties between cities and the center, executive agencies in Moscow at times granted important economic concessions to local authorities.[20] However, as Darrell Slider observes, the center failed to provide "adequate independent sources of financing to the heads of local government," thereby ensuring their continued dependence on provincial budgetary allocations.[21] In its relations with the periphery, the goal of the presidency was not just the immediate mobilization of local governments behind central policy and power but the nurturing of a new generation of reform-oriented political leaders who could eventually replace the conservative elites that dominated most provincial governments. In the words of the Japanese scholar Kimitaka Matsuzato, "[D]istricts and cities may not have been a school of democracy, but they served unquestionably as a school for the country's future leaders."[22]

Russia's provinces, of course, resented the attempts to sandwich them between federal and local power. In the most direct challenge to the presidency's emerging alliance with local governments, the republic of Udmurtia adopted its own law that eliminated all of its districts and municipalities, creating in their place a single "local" government at the regional level. When Boris Yeltsin criticized this move in a televised speech, the authorities in Udmurtia did not allow the president's comments to air in their region.[23] The bald-faced maneuver by Udmurtia to circumvent the provisions of the law on local self-government prompted an immediate challenge in the Constitutional Court. In a much-anticipated decision, the court ruled Udmurtia's actions unconstitutional and ordered the restoration of local governments in the republic.[24]

The presidency has also intervened directly in numerous conflicts between the leaders of regional and local governments. Typically, the mayor of a region's capital city becomes embroiled in a dispute with the regional governor, a dispute that is as likely to grow out of personal feuds as differences over policy. The presidency then aligns itself with the mayor, whose urban constituency has greater sympathy for Yeltsin's reform-oriented policies than the more rural social base of the governor.[25] But because Russia has not yet developed the single executive system mentioned in the constitution, the president does not have the power to resolve the dispute unilaterally in the mayor's favor. He must use instead various means of influence to support his ally, ranging from mobilizing public support to threats to withhold budgetary allocations from the regional government or even to employ emergency powers to dismiss the governor. Attempts by the president or officials in his administration to mediate such disputes usually fail, in part because regional elites do not regard the presidency as an honest broker.

Creating a Bureaucracy of *Kontrol'* over the Regions

In the Soviet era, the Communist Party's dominance of the periphery flowed from its ideological monopoly, its patronage powers in the so-called *nomenklatura* system, and its bureaucracy of supervision, or *kontrol'*, which monitored the behavior of provincial officials. Within the party's Central Committee apparatus in Moscow worked instructors and zonal inspectors who continually reviewed the operation of subordinate governments, whether by examining documents forwarded from the periphery or by conducting on-site inspections. The party also maintained, of course, its own extensive network of provincial and local organs, whose officials oversaw political, economic, and social life in their regions. Through its investigation and reporting up the line, the party's bureaucracy of *kontrol'* performed essential support services for the political leadership.

Although Boris Yeltsin had no intention of re-creating the full machinery of supervision maintained by the Communist Party, he did seek to establish presidential institutions that could provide reliable information from Russia's regions and then use that information to strengthen presidential leadership over the periphery. Creating a bureaucracy of *kontrol'* was especially important for Russia in transition, because unlike leaders in most democratic countries with federal systems, Yeltsin did not lead a national political party that could serve as a bridge uniting center and periphery.[26] The president preferred instead to use the institution of the presidency as his political as well as administrative base.

As we note earlier, one of the first steps in the establishment of a presidential bureaucracy of *kontrol'* was the appointment of Yeltsin's personal representatives to Russia's regions.[27] These representatives were not prefects—each republic or region already had its own chief executive—but rather officials whose task was to shadow the incumbent provincial leaders, to report on their rule, and to encourage local alliances that would be supportive of the presidency. It was yet another form of institutional redundancy, with parallels to the *namestniki* of the tsarist era and the *polpredy* of early Bolshevik rule. In each case, a fledgling central government placed personnel in the provinces to assist in the regathering of power. However, the evidence for the post-Soviet era suggests that most presidential representatives were not emissaries brought in from other areas of the country but rather local cadres enlisted by Moscow.

During Yeltsin's first term as president, the representatives were largely ineffectual. Not surprisingly, virtually all regional governors or republican presidents regarded the presidential representatives as interlopers and used every opportunity to marginalize them, at times by denying them the most basic courtesies, such as appropriate office space. There was not even what Americans would call a "federal building" in the provincial capitals to house them. Thus, when a representative began work in a province, he was at the mercy of the local chief executive, whose offices—much like the presidential administration in Moscow—distributed apartments, telephones, and automobiles. All that the representatives possessed—besides a staff of from four to six persons—was their titles, which meant little in areas where the provincial authorities were at odds with the president.[28]

Given the representatives' dependence on the regional governors and the presidents of republics for "social protection," it was not uncommon for them to "go native," that is, to exhibit greater loyalty to the provincial leaders than to the president of Russia. One Western observer has even claimed that "Yeltsin's representatives have been transformed from the president's watchdogs into the governors' emissaries to Moscow."[29] This assessment seems to be borne out by the comments of Aleksandr Kotenkov, a high-ranking official in the presidency who traveled throughout Russia's provinces in the mid-1990s. When encountering presidential representatives on their home turf, he often found that they did not have the time to meet with him because they were "organizing meetings of the governor with the public." When Kotenkov asked "what on earth for," they responded: "Otherwise, the governor won't like me."[30]

That such renegades often remained in their positions for long periods after passing to the other side was a measure of the president's, and his administration's, inattention to the work of the personal representatives in the regions. Whereas in 1992, Yeltsin met with his regional representatives once a month, by the end of his first term he had not met with them for more than a year.[31] The divided loyalties of representatives also resulted from a conscious change in personnel policy, which followed the Communist and nationalist successes in the December 1993 parliamentary elections. The first generation of presidential representatives had come to their posts with little or no experience in state administration. What recommended them to Yeltsin, or more precisely to presidential confidants such as Gennadii Burbulis, was their role as radical reformers in the parliaments of the late Soviet era. But by 1994, the presidency was shunting aside these activists in favor of more moderate or even conservative cadres with managerial experience. The Lipetsk region, south of Moscow, illustrates this trend well. There, the first presidential representative, Ravil Kasimov, was a coordinator of the local branch of Yegor Gaidar's party, Democratic Choice, and an implacable foe of the local governor, Mikhail Narolin, whose political biography included support for the August 1991 coup and consistent opposition to marketizing reforms. When Kasimov resigned his post in mid-1994, reportedly out of frustration with Yeltsin's unwillingness to heed his pleas to remove Narolin, he was succeeded by the deputy mayor of the city of Lipetsk, Anatolii Larin, an ally of the governor. On hearing of the appointment of Larin, Governor Narolin remarked that the new representative "will heed our opinion."[32] A similar shift in personnel occurred in the neighboring Penza region, where, in December 1993, the appointment of the former deputy procurator of the region as presidential representative "almost completely restored the political elite that had been removed from power on 31 October 1991."[33] In numerous cases in the mid-1990s, as Darrell Slider reports, the presidency appointed deputy governors of regions to serve as Yeltsin's representatives.[34] As prominent members themselves of regional cliques, such representatives were incapable of serving as effective watchdogs for the center.

President Yeltsin began to exhibit a renewed interest in his representatives early in his second term. During the previous three years, several changes in Russian politics had strengthened considerably the hand of the governors. First, the president's victory against the parliament in the autumn of 1993 led to the closure of regional legislatures as well as the national assembly. Like Yeltsin in the center, regional governors and republican presidents took advantage of the temporary absence of legislatures to further concentrate their hold on power in the provinces. Second, regional governors, who previously had been appointed by the president, began to submit themselves to direct election after December 1996.[35] Initially fearful of contested elections, the governors soon realized the advantages of incumbency during the campaign as well as the enhanced authority provided by a popular mandate. In the words of Vladimir Shpak, the direct gubernatorial elections "forced the Kremlin to think up all kinds of subtle methods for reestablishing control over disobedient governors."[36] Following the elections, a high-ranking official in the Kremlin admitted that "it was a mistake for Russia to start holding elections for governor."[37] Finally, the heads of republics and regions were becoming not only princes in their own domains but important actors in national politics by virtue of their membership in the upper house of the Federal Assembly, the Federation

Council.[38] Here again, institutional design had a profound effect on political outcomes. Imagine the consequences for American federalism if state governors and legislative speakers made up the United States Senate.

To limit the concentration of power in the hands of regional chief executives, Yeltsin issued a decree in the summer of 1997 that was designed to bolster the role of presidential representatives as outposts of federal authority in the provinces. Introduced over the objection of provincial elites and of Communists in the Duma,[39] the decree sought to turn the presidential representatives into powerful coordinators of the numerous federal agencies operating in Russia's republics and regions.[40] Despite the rise of vibrant and demanding regions, the federal government still employed more personnel in the provinces than their regional or republican counterparts, if one includes men and women in uniform. Thus, although there may not have been a landmark federal building in a typical provincial capital, scattered around the city were federal officials working in fields as diverse as finance and criminal prosecution.

Who ensured effective coordination among these discrete federal bureaucracies, and between them and provincial agencies working in related fields? In the Soviet era, the answer would have been the local Communist Party first secretary, who not only oversaw all provincial administration but influenced the hiring and firing of key federal officials working in their territories.[41] In theory, the end of the Soviet era eliminated the long-standing administrative tradition of "dual subordination" (*dvoinoe podchinenie*), where a federal government official in the provinces answered vertically to his technocratic superior in a Moscow ministry as well as horizontally to his political supervisor, whether the provincial party chief or a local government official. But in practice, some republican presidents and regional governors began to step into the breach to claim for themselves the power previously exercised by party officials.

To prevent newly elected provincial leaders from expanding their influence over the provincial branches of federal agencies, Yeltsin explicitly designated the presidential representatives as the senior federal officials in the provinces in July 1997.[42] As such, they were to preside over newly created cabinets (*kollegii*) composed of the heads of federal agencies in their provinces.[43] The decree also authorized the representatives to "take part in the meetings of the boards of [individual] federal executive agencies" in the provinces. Furthermore, the decree placed the representatives in charge of relations between federal officials and "the governments of the subject territories, the organs of local administration, political parties, [and] other social and religious organization" as well as citizens. Potentially even more threatening to provincial leaders were the decree's provisions expanding the prerogatives of the presidential representatives vis-à-vis the governments of the subject territories. They gave the representatives "unimpeded access to any state or municipal institution" in the subject territory as well as the right to "participate in the work of regional political institutions." Moreover, the July 1997 decree reiterated the obligations of the representatives to inform presidential officials, and in the first instance the presidency's Monitoring Administration, about the failure of federal or provincial agencies to carry out presidential directives or federal law. In cases where the actions of the government of the subject territories contradicted the constitution, federal law, or the rights of citizens, the representatives were to recommend to the president himself that the offending acts be suspended. Finally, according to Article 5 of the July decree, the presidential representatives were supposed to "agree on nominations [*soglasovyvat' kandidatur*] for leadership posts in federal executive agencies located in the provinces." In warning the presidential representatives that they should not "interfere in the everyday activity" of government institutions at the provincial and local levels, the decree employed language traditionally directed at lower-level Communist Party organs. In the Soviet era, the Central Committee apparatus continually advised provincial party officials against adopting an attitude of "petty daily tutelage" toward government institutions in their regions, an appeal that was frequently ignored.[44]

As Leonid Smirniagin and others have argued, the July decree represented a rejection of earlier presidential strategy toward the provinces, which had anticipated the creation of a single, unified executive branch, reaching from Moscow to local municipalities. When the direct election of governors rendered that strategy unviable, the president and his advisors opted instead for the coexistence of two separate executive hierarchies in the subject territories—one federal, the other provincial.[45] In essence, they abandoned a vision of a unitary Russian government for a quasi-federal one, not because they believed in federalism, but because they viewed it as a way of retaining some influence in provincial affairs. Better to maintain two discrete chains of command than to risk having branches of existing federal agencies dominated by regional political elites. If dual subordination was to be revived, the president seemed to be saying, let the responsibility for supervision and coordination at the provincial level lie with the presidential representatives rather than the elected chief executives, whose political loyalties rested with the periphery more than the center.

The provisions of the July 1997 decree reveal much about the goals and tactics of the Russian presidency in provincial affairs, but they are less reliable as indicators of the evolving relations between levels of government. As the Russian proverb has it, paper will stand anything. Issuing a decree is far easier than implementing it. Predictably, many Russian regional elites vigorously fought the president's attempt to use his representatives as levers in provincial politics. Nowhere was this resistance more acute than in the Maritime Province of Russia's Far East. Indeed, it was out of frustration with the behavior of the regional governor, Yevgenii Nazdratenko, that Yeltsin had issued a prototype of the July decree two months earlier and applied it to the Maritime Province alone.[46]

In the Far East, Nazdratenko had been engaged in a long-running feud with Viktor Cherepkov, the mayor of the regional capital, Vladivostok. The feud contributed to the grim economic conditions in the province, where residents often went without power for eight hours or more a day. Frustrated by Nazdratenko's mismanagement of local finances, his cultivation of Yeltsin's political opponents in Moscow, his unwillingness to implement market reform, and his interference in Russian-Chinese border negotiations—his populist motto was "Not an inch of Russian land to China"—officials in the presidency pressured Nazdratenko to resign in the spring of 1997.[47] When that effort failed, Yeltsin signed a decree in May that greatly expanded the powers of the presidential representative in the Maritime Province. In a move designed to humiliate the governor and lessen his authority, the decree empowered the presidential representative to supervise the disbursement of the substantial federal funds allocated to the region, funds that Nazdratenko had previously used to reward allies and punish opponents. In 1997, the largest portion of the 7.5 billion rubles in federal monies transferred to the Maritime Territory went to Dalnegorsk, the hometown of Nazdratenko and several of his political allies.[48] At the same time, Yeltsin replaced the sitting presidential representative, who had become an ally of Nazdratenko, with the head of the regional branch of the Federal Security Service, the successor to the KGB, General Viktor Kondratov. This challenge to Nazdratenko's authority unleashed a drama that threatened at times to descend into farce.

Visiting the province in early June 1997, the deputy head of the Executive Office of the President, Yevgenii Savostianov, held a press conference to accuse the governor and his regional bureaucracy of a litany of abuses, including "poor preparation for winter, the squandering [and diversion] of [federal] budget money, [and] disarray in the sphere of exporting seafood and timber." No sooner had Savostianov finished his indictment of the governor and his administration than Nazdratenko rushed the stage, amid shouts of encouragement from employees of the regional government brought in for the event. After reminding the visiting presidential official that "I am

Governor and you are a guest here," Nazdratenko claimed that he was a "victim of persecution by the Kremlin," or more precisely by Yeltsin's aides.[49] Like the tsar before the revolution, Yeltsin was said to be ignorant of the machinations of his subordinates.

In a move calculated to alert the presidency to the risks of attacking a governor elected in a landslide only eighteen months earlier, Nazdratenko threatened to resign his office and stand for reelection. Such an election would have served as a plebiscite on the feud between Nazdratenko, on one side, and the center and Vladivostok mayor Cherepkov, its ally, on the other. Although by no means a sure thing, a Nazdratenko victory would have inoculated the governor against further pressure from the presidency.[50] Among Nazdratenko's other provocative tactics was the appointment of governor's representatives to serve as his eyes and ears in each of the cities and districts of the Maritime Province.[51] Mockingly patterned after the presidential representatives in the subject territories, these emissaries of the governor promised to complicate the work of municipal leaders, in the first instance Cherepkov. An indication of the lengths to which Nazdratenko would go to embarrass and undercut the mayor occurred in July 1997 at the opening of the new police headquarters in Vladivostok, which had been funded from the city's budget. While Cherepkov was presiding over a dedication ceremony at the facility, the governor arrived uninvited and sought to take control of the event. To prevent the food and drink from falling into the hands of the governor and his large and insistent entourage, the mayor ordered the refreshments to be distributed at once to the police present, whereupon the governor physically assaulted a city employee—and World War II veteran—who was carrying out the mayor's directive.[52]

The conflict in the Maritime Province was further confirmation that in Russia, all local politics is national. Put more prosaically, provincial leaders seek their own advantage by attracting national actors to their cause. By the summer of 1997, Nazdratenko had become a poster boy for the anti-Yeltsin opposition in Moscow, which took turns traveling to the Far East to lay hands on the governor. The steady stream of visitors included Aleksandr Lebed, Lev Rokhlin, the dissident general who had stopped just short of calling for an army mutiny against Yeltsin, and Aleksandr Prokhanov, the editor of the radical nationalist newspaper *Zavtra* (Tomorrow).[53] Prokhanov urged the Maritime governor to persevere in what he labeled "a conflict between Russian distinctiveness and alien, aggressive Americanism. . . . Nazdratenko, be strong! You must not give yourself up to Moscow. Vladivostok, its ships, its mines, and the people who elected you are your base and your stronghold. Attack!"[54]

Nazdratenko also found support in the Federation Council in Moscow. Although many of the provincial chief executives and parliamentary speakers who made up the assembly may have been uncomfortable with Nazdratenko's flamboyance, they saw in the presidency's assault on his rule a threat to provincial autonomy nationwide. They adopted, therefore, a resolution in early August 1997 demanding that Yeltsin revise his May decree limiting Nazdratenko's authority. The appeal claimed that "the intrusion of the President's representative into the jurisdiction of the head of a Russian Federation member's executive branch will inevitably lead to a situation of dual power," a reference to the months before the October 1917 revolution, when two competing centers of authority—the Provisional Government and the workers' and peasants' soviets—coexisted uneasily.[55] The issue here was not just the precise share of power to be exercised by the center or periphery but the very governability of Russia's provinces.

Unable to topple Nazdratenko through political means, the president's men turned to a criminal investigation of the Maritime leader, a tactic with a long pedigree in the Soviet era, and one not unfamiliar to contemporary American politics. In the words of one journalist, "[T]he Kremlin had to concoct all sorts of sophisticated methods to re-establish oversight of the humble [*pokornii*] governor." In June 1997, during a search of Nazdratenko's offices, General Kondratov confiscated documents that allegedly "constitute[d] a threat to the constitutional system and civil rights." Among these materials was a memorandum entitled "Necessary Measures for Discrediting the Image of the Municipal Administration of the City of Vladivostok and of [Mayor] Viktor Cherepkov Personally."[56] Such documents subjected the governor to political embarrassment but not criminal prosecution. Neither legal investigations nor efforts by Kondratov to intervene in the disbursement of federal funds in the province were successful in forcing Nazdratenko out of office.

For his part, Nazdratenko continued his own assault on the Vladivostok mayor. In late September, while Cherepkov was visiting neighboring North Korea, the regional legislature issued a directive that replaced the mayor with a Nazdratenko supporter, Yurii Kopylov. The following Monday, a local correspondent for the Moscow-based business newspaper *Kommersant-Daily* wrote that "Cherepkov and Kopylov turned up at the mayor's office early in the morning, both claiming the mayoral chair."[57] After weeks during which the municipal administration was subjected to the "bizarre spectacle" of dueling mayors working on the same hall, Cherepkov called new elections for May 1998, left his post, and went on a hunger strike.[58] Predictably, Nazdratenko welcomed Cherepkov's depar-

ture, labeling it "a positive step for the city." He added that "it was probably motivated by his complete incompetence as an administrator."[59] The
Maritime governor could not savor his victory for long, however. On December 8, less than a month after Cherepkov's resignation, new elections
to the regional legislature turned out the pro-Nazdratenko majority.[60] In the
multilayered game that is Russian provincial politics, the wild card of popular elections had again revised the calculus of power.[61]

The events unfolding in the Maritime Province represented, to be sure,
the most dramatic clash between the presidency and a regional governor.
But while the tactics and personalities in the Far East may have been un-
usually colorful, the logic of center-periphery conflict on display there was
similar in other Russian provinces. Even presidential loyalists, such as
Governor Dmitrii Ayatskov of Saratov, "threatened to abolish the post of
Yeltsin's envoy [presidential representative] in the Saratov Region if the
envoy was given additional powers."[62] The furor created by the July 1997
decree on the presidential representatives confirmed the presence of two
distinct axes of conflict in Russian politics, one economic and the other
territorial. As Thomas Remington has argued convincingly, these two are-
nas of conflict became associated in central politics with the two chambers
of parliament, a Duma filled with deputies largely arrayed along a classic
European ideological spectrum, from advocates of laissez-faire to those
favoring economic statism, and a Federation Council filled with members
who were united in their opposition to the centralizing tendencies of the
Yeltsin administration. One could support vigorously the president's
marketizing reforms and yet resist just as tenaciously his initiatives that
threatened to erode the autonomy of the provinces.

Alongside the presidential representatives, the Monitoring Administration of the Executive Office of the President functioned as a parallel institution of *kontrol'* over the regions. This redundancy was not built into the
original design, however. Those responsible for the introduction of the representatives in 1991, Gennadii Burbulis and Valerii Makharadze, conceived
them, in effect, as the local agents of the Monitoring Administration, which
Makharadze then headed.[63] But unlike most officials in the Monitoring
Administration, who were auditors with legal or financial training, the first
group of presidential representatives consisted of pro-Yeltsin politicians
drawn mainly from the Russian or all-Union parliaments. They were unlikely foot soldiers in a bureaucracy whose major task was to conduct careful
inspections of public and private agencies in order to identify violations of
parliamentary statutes or of presidential decrees and assignments
(*porucheniia*). Unable to integrate the presidential representatives into their

operation, the Monitoring Administration gradually recruited its own team of local agents, first in eleven field offices scattered across the Russian Federation and then in individual regions and republics.[64]

Rather like the party and state *kontrol'* commissions of the Soviet era, the Monitoring Administration devoted part of its energies in the regions to routine sector-by-sector inspections and part to ad hoc investigations ordered by senior officials in the presidency.[65] In 1996, for example, then chief of staff Anatolii Chubais directed the Monitoring Administration to work alongside various federal agencies to uncover large-scale tax evasion. It was a familiar assignment for the Monitoring Administration, whose inspections each year had revealed widespread illegalities in the movement of capital and the privatization of state property. Immediately following his election to a second term, Boris Yeltsin instructed the Monitoring Administration to report on the extent to which his campaign promises made during trips to twenty-one of Russia's region were being carried out. According to the Monitoring Administration, 152 of 179 assignments had been fulfilled by the end of 1996 at a cost to the president's reserve fund of some 25 billion rubles.[66]

The results of the Monitoring Administration's inspections, therefore, served diverse ends: to cast the president in a favorable light, to identify resistance to the president's policy initiatives, whether in the capital or the provinces, and, without putting too fine a point on it, to collect dirt on the political opposition. Along with other federal agencies, the Monitoring Administration reported to the president on malfeasance in office by regional elites, information that could be used to pressure or even unseat those who grossly abused power or who opposed Yeltsin's leadership. In 1993 and 1994, on the basis of materials obtained in Monitoring Administration inspections, the president removed the governors in the Riazan, Belgorod, and Novosibirsk regions for wrongdoing.[67] According to Anatolii Chubais, the Monitoring Administration should develop into a "mini-IMF" for the regions, ensuring that the periphery carries out the terms of exchange with the center.[68] Thus, although the Monitoring Administration operates under considerable restraints, imposed by their small provincial staffs, by their status as an auditing and not a law enforcement body, and by the tendency of local inspectors to succumb at times to pressure from powerful regional elites, it serves nonetheless as an invaluable source of information for the presidency.

The Russian presidency also exercises supervision of the provinces through its Territorial Administration, known in Yeltsin's first term as the Administration for Work with Territories—or, less generously, as the Administration for Struggle with Territories, when Nikolai Medvedev was its head.[69] In addition to collecting and analyzing information from the subject territories, this subdivision of the Executive Office developed presidential policies for the regions and helped to identify and promote candidates for office who were loyal to the president. Its mission, therefore, was explicitly political rather than legal or administrative. With a staff of seventy-two persons, the Territorial Administration closely monitored political developments in the provinces. Just like the zonal inspectors in the old party Central Committee, officials of the Territorial Administration were assigned to supervise two or three regions each, an assignment that required frequent visits to the field.[70]

In June 1995, six months before the parliamentary elections, officials from the Administration for Work with Territories met in closed session in the cities of Ekaterinburg, Saratov, and Vladivostok with presidential representatives from the surrounding regions and republics. The purpose was to instruct the president's representatives in ways of assisting the party, Our Home Is Russia, in the upcoming elections.[71] In eleven instances, the representatives themselves stood for district seats in the Russian Duma, though only one was elected.[72] Thus, while the Russian president refused publicly to express a partisan preference, officials in his administration were working to elect candidates from Our Home Is Russia, the party associated with the prime minister, Viktor Chernomyrdin, and many other executive leaders in Moscow and the provinces.[73]

The Administration for Work with Territories also promoted candidates sympathetic to the president in the gubernatorial elections,[74] and in some cases even "dyed-in-the-wool Communists" sought the backing of the Executive Office of the President.[75] The presidency in Yeltsin's second term has taken an active role in regional legislative elections as well as the governors' races, not simply to influence politics in the provinces, but to affect the composition of the Federation Council, now composed of provincial chief executives and legislative speakers. In November 1997, when Yeltsin appointed Viktoria Mitina deputy head of the Executive Office of the President, he instructed her to assume responsibility for the forthcoming regional legislative elections in order to produce a Federation Council that is "effective and constructive," meaning more sympathetic to the president. Mitina also had the task of finding "interesting and promising regional leaders who could become leaders on a national scale."[76] There is little evidence, however, that the presidency was particularly successful in its recruitment efforts.

Another vital responsibility of the Administration for Work with Territories—and its successor, the Territorial Administration—was the introduction of consistency in federal and provincial laws on such potentially explosive issues as language use and education. The devolution of power to the subject territories in the early 1990s had produced a steady stream of new provincial legislation designed to revive non-Russian cultures, especially in ethnic republics. The presidential administration and the Government did not seek to halt this movement but rather to channel it into laws and policies that would not set ethnic group against ethnic group or region against region. Using a technique perfected in the Soviet era, the Ministry for Nationality Affairs and Federal Relations drafted model statutes (*makety*) on such questions and then circulated them to executive and legislative institutions in the provinces. In the case of laws on local self-government, some 70 percent of the provinces relied on the model statutes forwarded to them by the ministry.[77]

Finally, the Territorial Administration was an important point of contact for regional elites when they approached Moscow for information or assistance. Unless a governor visiting Moscow had direct access to the president in the Kremlin, he would visit the presidential offices on Old Square, including those of the Territorial Administration. There he received the latest information about the status of draft decrees or laws that could affect his republic or region.[78] He could also encourage the administration to intervene on his behalf with federal ministries and agencies from whom he desired assistance.

Law and Legal Institutions in the Center-Periphery Struggle

Although Boris Yeltsin lacked some of the levers of authority associated with strong federal rule, such as a national political party, he had every reason to believe that the legal system would serve as a defender of the interests of the center against the periphery. A unified legal system directed from the capital had been a tradition in Russia for centuries. At least in its basic structure, this unified legal order made the transition from the Soviet era intact. While Russia's nascent federalism offered regional political elites a substantial degree of autonomy from the center, it insisted on maintaining tight control over judges and prosecutors, who remained part of a single, integrated legal system.

Created by Peter the Great to operate as the "eyes of the tsar" (*gosudarevo oko*) in the country, the Procuracy was the institution responsible for criminal prosecution and "the general supervision of legality," the latter term having generated almost as much exegesis as the Holy Trinity. In the post-

Soviet era, the Procuracy retained its rigidly hierarchical structure, which required procurators to answer not to the political authorities on their administrative level but rather to their superiors at higher levels of the Procuracy. Interviewed in late 1996, the procurator general, Yurii Skuratov, claimed that "without a highly centralized Procuracy, separatism would seize Russia."[79] In its rigid chain of command and ranks, the Procuracy appeared to be akin to a military unit on the legal front. In some regions, procurators were willing to take on powerful governors when they abused their office—witness the protests lodged by the regional procurator against Aleksandr Rutskoi's behavior as the governor in Kursk.[80] Like the procurators, even the lowliest judges working in towns and rural districts were employees of the federal court system, whose judgments were to be based on the laws of the Russian Federation and the rulings of superior federal courts.

On the surface, then, it appeared that the president had, in legal personnel and institutions, natural allies in the struggle to contain the centrifugal forces unleashed at the breakup of the USSR. The reality, however, was decidedly more nuanced, especially by the mid-1990s. Conflict between executive and legislative institutions in the early 1990s for control of the legal system sent mixed signals to state jurists in Moscow and the provinces. With no clear mandate, some procurators began to insist on a special status for themselves as a fourth branch of government, a status for which the wording of the constitution—and Russian tradition—provided considerable support. Although the president could appoint the procurator general, with the consent of the Federation Council, he could not treat him and his twelve thousand personnel as administrative subordinates. Allegiances to parliament, the law, and their own professional and institutional traditions tempered the Procuracy's loyalty to the president. Moreover, the Procuracy's vertical chain of command did not always prevent regional political elites from enlisting local procurators to their cause. In the dismal economic and budgetary climate of the early and mid-1990s, procurators in the provinces found themselves more dependent than ever on in-kind subsistence offered by republic and regional governments.[81] As we have already seen, such financial and psychological dependency allowed the governor of the Maritime Province to recruit the regional procurator as an active participant in his campaign of intimidation against the mayor of Vladivostok and other political adversaries. By 1998, Procurator General Yurii Skuratov complained that

> we have to clear with the local authorities the appointment of procurators in subjects of the Federation. And what is the result of this? In a number of

subjects of the Federation the local procurators have fallen under the influence of the local governors and other officials. Moreover, we are underfinancing the system and eventually may lose it.[82]

A high-ranking official in the Federation Council in Moscow lamented this rise of "juridical separatism," which was transforming lawyers that had trained under a common curriculum in the Soviet era into "tools of juridical politics and hostages of local ambitions and local politicians."[83]

Although judges received several significant pay increases in the 1990s, they also remained dependent on provincial governments to provide adequate offices, housing, and security. As a result, they were at times creatures of regional as well as federal authority. At a meeting in the presidential administration in late 1996, a deputy chair of the Russian Supreme Court recounted a recent telephone conversation with the head of the provincial court in Krasnoiarsk, which ended abruptly when the Krasnoiarsk judge said that "they are cutting me off because the phone bills aren't being paid."[84] In Moscow, one official claimed that in 1996 the first deputy head of the Moscow city government conducted a meeting of local judges "as if he were the deputy head of a department in the local Communist Party apparatus. . . . You know, it was as if nothing had changed from 20 years ago."[85] In his usual measured language, Yeltsin's counselor for legal affairs, Mikhail Krasnov, complained that "the judiciary does not always stand on the side of federal interests."[86]

In order to check the power of what one observer called "regional-scale autocrats," it was essential for the presidency to help lower-level courts "acquire economic and administrative independence."[87] As a means of enhancing the loyalty of judges to the center, Yeltsin's team wrote a provision into the 1993 constitution that empowered the president to appoint all of the country's fifteen thousand judges. But as Chapter 5 illustrates, the presidency lacked the staff and the political authority to select candidates for the bench in every corner of the Russian Federation. In some cases, therefore, insistent republican presidents and regional governors appointed local judges and then waited for Yeltsin to formalize their status by issuing the requisite decree. In 1998, in the most remarkable instances of provincial self-assertion, the republican presidents of Bashkortostan and Ingushetia called for popular referendums in their territories that were designed to subordinate judges and all law enforcement officials to republican authority.[88]

Contrary to the hopes of Yeltsin loyalists, the passage of a new federal law on the court system did nothing to shore up presidential authority in judicial selection. Indeed, two of the statutes' provisions granted republics and regions their own embryonic court systems. The law revived a prerevolutionary legal institution, the justices of the peace, who would hear minor criminal and civil cases. It also authorized the republics and regions to create their own constitutional or "charter" courts (*ustavnye sudy*), with responsibility for interpreting the new provincial constitutions, or charters, enacted in the subject territories. Both justices of the peace and charter court judges were to be selected by republican presidents and regional governors rather than by the Russian president, though the justices of the peace were to be funded from the federal budget.

Intended as a minor concession to provincial elites who were dissatisfied with a unified national judiciary, these reforms laid the groundwork for parallel legal systems in Russia. Although dual court systems and discrete bodies of law are features of other federal governments, including that of the United States, it must be remembered that competition between state and federal laws in the early American experience escalated from the nullification controversy in the 1820s to a civil war forty years later. Likewise, in the declining years of the Soviet Union, conflict over jurisdictional boundaries between all-Union and republican authorities contributed to a "war of laws" and ultimately the demise of the Union. Thus, while by themselves provincial judiciaries and charters do not threaten the integrity of the federation, they serve as additional weapons in the arsenal of provincial elites intent on carving out greater autonomy from the center.[89]

By the end of 1996, Anatolii Chubais was complaining that the contradictions between federal statutes and the legal acts passed in the provinces had become "massive."[90] According to a later source:

> In the period from March 1995 through December 1997, the Russian Constitutional Court ruled on the constitutionality of 19 different legislative acts by Federation members and found only one of the disputed laws to be in line with the Russian Constitution. Since June 1995 the Ministry of Justice has reviewed 44,000 normative legal acts by Federation members and found a third of them to be out of compliance with federal legislation.[91]

These conflicts arose in spite of the formation in early 1996 of a presidential commission devoted to "assisting the subjects of the Russian Federation in their introduction of constitutional-legal reform."[92]

As we saw earlier in the case of Udmurtia, the Constitutional Court possessed the legal authority to arbitrate disputes between levels of government in Russia. Appointed by the president and comprised primarily of jurists with long experience in the capital, the Court has an interest in shoring up strong central authority, not unlike the United States Supreme Court. Moreover, the rules of standing allow the Russian president to seek remedies in the Constitutional Court by simply submitting a request (*zapros*).

At times, such requests have brought relief to the president. When the Tambov region enacted a statute that, in the opinion of the presidency, contained provisions in violation of the federal constitution, the very submission of a request to the Constitutional Court caused legislators in Tambov to remove the offending provisions.[93] But while the authority of the Constitutional Court is growing, it is not yet sufficient to ensure the compliance of either central or provincial executives—witness the unwillingness of Moscow's mayor, Yurii Luzhkov, to respect a recent court decision that declared unconstitutional Russia's long-standing system of residence permits.[94]

Regional Bargaining and Presidential Power

Despite the presidency's efforts to establish a stable legal and institutional framework that would govern center-periphery relations, bargaining remained the primary means of resolving conflict between Moscow and the provinces. In the nascent Russian federalism, politics, not law or administration, was in command. As in many other transition regimes, the absence in Russia of a broadly accepted division of authority between levels of government forces politicians to continually negotiate settlements of diverse claims made by regional leaders for financial, patronage, or symbolic advantage. In these negotiations, laws do matter, but the particular correlation of political forces between Moscow and individual provinces matters more.

One of the most fundamental questions to pose is: Why do the provinces ever obey Moscow? Why should they comply with the wishes of a weak central state? The reasons lie in two different realms: authority and power. For all of their separatist rhetoric, virtually all provincial leaders wish to remain part of the Russian state. This basic sense of political obligation to the center discourages them from pursuing strategies that would lead to warlordism or civil war. Most provincial leaders worked in the Soviet party or Government apparatus, where they imbued an attitude of deference toward higher-ranking officials. While the collapse of Communism may have diminished this element of elite political culture, it did not eliminate it. Let us recall that even under the Soviet regime, provincial officials combined a healthy respect for their superiors in Moscow with a willingness to bargain vigorously for scarce resources from the center. President Yeltsin, and the Russian central executive generally, remain beneficiaries of this residue of Soviet political culture.[95]

The Russian state also has available numerous sources of power that tend to restrain provincial demands. The first is armed force. As Thomas

Hobbes observed, when nothing else turns up, clubs are trumps. After lengthy negotiations with Chechnia failed to produce a settlement acceptable to the Kremlin, Yeltsin effectively declared war on the republic. Both the war in Chechnia and the president's earlier assault on the Russian parliament were designed in part to remind provincial elites of the costs of extended confrontation with presidential power. Unlike Gorbachev, Yeltsin has not shied away from the use of force in domestic politics. However, the ineffectiveness of the Russian armed forces in the Chechen war undermined to some extent the threat of force as an instrument of presidential rule.

During his first term, the Russian president enjoyed patronage powers that enabled him to hire and fire regional governors. The introduction of direct gubernatorial elections in the second half of the 1990s denied Yeltsin this prerogative, but the president continued to claim the right to remove provincial leaders if they violated constitutional norms or failed to implement parliamentary laws or presidential decrees. In 1998, Prime Ministers Kirienko and Primakov championed the adoption of legislation that promised to grant the president firm legal authority to remove miscreant governors—a bill that aroused protests among members of the Duma and Federation Council.[96] Yeltsin also annulled the acts of provincial executives if, in his view, they violated the constitution or federal laws. In June 1997, for example, Yeltsin struck down an order of the Kursk governor, Aleksandr Rutskoi, that impeded the free flow of goods out of the region.[97] Moreover, the presidency has assisted its regional allies in their election campaigns by providing media exposure, expertise, and funding.[98] Likewise, it has threatened to withhold support for campaigning presidents or governors if they resist overtures from Moscow. In an attempt to mediate a dispute between the neighboring northern Caucasian republics of Ingushetia and Northern Ossetia, Yeltsin warned the local presidents that he would deny them his support in their upcoming electoral campaigns if they did not cease their "undeclared war" against each other, which had heightened ethnic tensions between the populations of the two territories.[99]

It is financial power, however, that has emerged as the Russian president's weapon of choice during his second term. Whether in the form of direct transfers, favorable loans to local enterprises, or tax and import-export privileges, the center provides much-needed financial support to Russia's provincial governments. In the complex relationship of exchange that has developed between center and periphery, the promise of direct or indirect financial assistance serves as one of Moscow's most important bargaining chips. Russia's fiscal development since 1991 reveals several tendencies that would appear to enhance the center's ability to influence regional affairs.[100] First, only twenty of eighty-nine provinces were net recipients of federal funding in 1991, but that number had risen to eighty by 1997.[101] In the mid-1990s, federal transfers to the provinces accounted on average for 13 and 14 percent of regional and republican budgets, and the fifteen most dependent provinces received more than half of their budget revenues in the form of federal transfers. Furthermore, as Russia integrated itself more fully into the world economy, the presidency was in a position to offer—or withhold—support for the application of individual provinces to float bonds as a means of covering deficits, promoting investment, or renegotiating enterprise debt.

Although the presidency was only one of several actors involved in forming a budget at the federal level, it—along with the Government—played the decisive role in budgetary implementation, which assumed disproportionate importance in Russian politics because of the voodoo economics underpinning the annual Law on the Budget. At least at the beginning of Yeltsin's second term, according to Anatolii Chubais, work related to the "distribution of finances [to regions] . . . [could not] be performed anywhere but in the President's staff."[102] As noted in Chapter 5, budget revenues regularly fell so far behind expenditures that the executive was forced to sequester funds each year. This power of sequestration gave the executive broad discretion in doling out the remaining budgetary funds across the country's provinces. Recognizing the provinces' nervousness about the unpredictability of budgetary sequestration in 1998, Anatolii Chubais agreed to guarantee budgetary funding levels for the provinces—and to allow the Federation Council to participate for the first time in the initial drafting of the budget for 1998—if they would "make peace" with the Kremlin.[103]

Central executive institutions in Russia have been able to influence the timing as well as the amount of federal transfers to the provinces. For regions located in the Far North—a designation that embraces over half of Russia's territory—threats to delay winter provisioning concentrated the minds of regional leaders and made them especially anxious to reach accommodation with the center on outstanding disputes.[104] The center also sought to influence regional behavior by easing, or toughening, its approach to tax inspection, the payment of outstanding enterprise debt, wage arrears, and the amount of money that regional authorities could hold in their own bank accounts.[105] In November 1997, for example, Deputy Prime Minister Oleg Sysuev threatened to send "special brigades" (*spetsbrigady*) into the thirteen provinces with the worst records for delaying wage payments.[106] Simply put, the center wielded sufficient discretion in the implementation and oversight of fiscal policy to make life difficult for individual provinces. By modulating its approach to take account of the peculiarities of each region, the president and prime minister had the capacity to use the prerogatives of power to bargain for the compliance of provincial elites. And because, as Steven Solnick argues, many of the fiscal benefits directed toward specific regions are "invisible"—that is, they do not figure in public documents such as the federal budget—there was little cohesion among "those blocks of regions ostensibly either 'profiting' from preferential transfers or shouldering the burden of 'financing' the budgets of their neighbors."[107] In other words, lack of information discouraged collective action against the center.

But despite the levers of influence available to the Russian executive in Moscow, the president and prime minister failed to use the power of financial persuasion effectively. The reasons for the squandering of the center's political assets lay in the inconsistencies of Yeltsin's personal leadership as well as the divisions within and between the presidency and Government, which provincial elites exploited to their advantage. Furthermore, in the relationship of exchange between center and periphery, provincial leaders held their own trump cards. The first was their position as national legislators. Comparing the Federation Council to the upper house under the last tsar, a *Segodnia* correspondent noted that "the goal of regional leaders was simple and direct: expand the powers of the Ruling Senate in order to sell them to the Government for the highest price. . . . The desire to receive from federal authorities as much money as possible remains today one of the most important stimuli for the actions of the Federation Council."[108]

Second, the collapse of the old order brought an expansion of the taxing power of the provinces, which was part of a broader fiscal decentralization. By 1995, the regional governments' share of the consolidated national budget exceeded that of the federal government. Not only were the regions able to retain a greater share of the tax pie, on average 59 percent by 1995, including virtually all receipts for property and income tax, but some provinces struck informal agreements with the center that allowed them to withhold taxes normally transferred to the center, such as receipts for enterprises.[109] In the most extreme case, Sakha (Yakutia) stopped providing tax revenues altogether after 1992, a hefty economic price for the center to pay for political compliance. One observer remarked angrily that republics such as Sakha have openly blackmailed the center, vowing to leave the Union if they didn't get their way.[110] Shortly after becoming prime minister in the fall of 1998, Yevgenii Primakov lamented what he called the "fiefdom approach" to center-periphery relations. The provinces, he complained, "have gotten to the point that they don't want to transfer tax revenues [to Moscow] and don't allow food products to be taken out of their regions."[111]

The evidence is clear that President Yeltsin negotiated very different fiscal as well as constitutional arrangements with Russia's diverse provinces. What is less obvious are the reasons for the widely varying levels of financial concessions. Contrary to some expectations, Yeltsin has not rewarded the most financially needy or politically loyal provinces with the largest concessions. He appears instead to have been most generous with hostile regional elites governing in areas whose populations have voted against Yeltsin or other pro-reform candidates. In an important study of the politics of intergovernmental transfers, Daniel Triesman found that "challenging Moscow—whether by elite declaration, mass action, or public voting—paid off far better than compliance." Treisman concluded that "[w]hile this may be an effective means of defusing the most urgent regional crises, it creates conditions for an erosion of the governing regime's own support base, and for disillusion of previous democrats with democracy."[112] Rewarding disloyalty only breeds greater disloyalty.

There were signs by the spring of 1997 that Yeltsin was attempting to call a halt to the politics of fiscal capitulation, or what Treisman has called "selective appeasement."[113] Having lost his ability to appoint governors, the Russian president realized that he needed to use the fiscal weapon more effectively if he was to coordinate policy across Russia's varied regions. In part, this meant a dramatic reduction in the scale of federal largesse to the provinces, in part a changing of the terms of federal transfers to the periphery.[114] No longer would provinces receive federal funds primarily in the form of what American public administration would call revenue sharing, that is, money with no strings attached. For the first time, the center began to make federal transfers explicitly contingent on the faithful implementation of policies favored by the president.[115] If international financial institutions could impose "conditionality" on its aid to Russia, Chubais reasoned, the Russian state could also require that regional elites satisfy certain centrally imposed standards, all the more so because central money was often used by the provinces to maintain subsidies that the Kremlin had been seeking to reduce or eliminate.[116] Lev Freinkman and Michael Haney report that "a substantial portion of federal funds (30–40 percent of all disbursed transfers) is spent by the recipients on financing various local subsidy programs, primarily in housing."[117]

It was no surprise, then, when Prime Minister Chernomyrdin announced on 26 May 1997 that the first major experiment with conditionality in federal transfers would relate to housing and utility reform.[118] By reducing the vast subsidies paid out by the regions for housing and utilities, the center sought to force provincial governments to offload costs to consumers, thereby rationalizing resources. Artificially cheap energy has led to utility usage in Russian households that is two to three times greater than in comparable northern European climes.[119] Whether the leader of the Russian Government in the future is a westernizing reformer, like Sergei Kirienko, or a politician suspicious of open markets, like Yevgenii Primakov, the logic of tying federal funds to provincial support for the center's economic and political agenda will almost certainly prove compelling.

Conclusion

Relations between center and periphery and between presidency and provincial elites cannot be reduced to a neat equation that includes relatively stable variables such as the provinces' economic resources, their fiscal dependence on the center, their electoral behavior, the demandingness and political values of their elites, or the proximity of elections. Within an environment framed by these factors, a Russian president chooses how he will employ his diverse powers, ranging from persuasion through the media to tax privileges and armed force, in an effort to impose the center's will on the periphery. When and how he seeks compromise or confrontation is a function of presidential leadership, that slippery but vital term denoting the use of power and authority to meet challenges presented by continually changing circumstances.

As a leader, President Yeltsin has thus far been successful in maintaining regime stability but largely ineffectual in mobilizing provincial elites behind his policies. He has also failed to create the institutions of law and administration that would clearly delineate jurisdictional boundaries and resolve routine disputes between the center and periphery. If Russia is to consolidate its statehood, never mind its democracy, the unceasing negotiations between Moscow and the eighty-nine subject territories must yield to legitimate institutional arrangements that make contestation the exception rather than the rule. Democracy is as much about law and administration as politics.

8

Conclusion

Political philosophers from Plato to Rousseau exalted the role of the law-giver—a Solon or Lycurgus—who could deliver a legitimate and workable set of institutions to a country in crisis. In Russia's own history, the legendary Riurik arrived from Scandinavia in the ninth century to impose political order on warring Slavic tribes. But in contemporary politics, perhaps the closest equivalent to the deus ex machina are the postwar regimes in Germany and Japan—imposed by conquest—and the Fifth Republic constitution in France, crafted in a moment of crisis by Charles de Gaulle and Michel Debré. For other modern states in transition, the shaping of a new political and social system has been more protracted and painful. So it is with Russia at the new millennium.

To understand the trajectory of recent Russian political history, the comparative literature on transitions offers a useful starting point. Just as Aristotle uncovered the patterns of political change in the ancient world and Crane Brinton found the pathologies of the virus of revolution that infected modern European societies, so contemporary political scientists have revealed the logic of regime transformation and the stages through which societies pass in their escape from authoritarianism. Transitions from authoritarianism usually begin with a rift in the ruling elite and then proceed to a campaign of liberalization, the collapse of the old order, the crafting of new rules of the political game, and, in some cases, the consolidation of democracy. This paradigm of regime change, developed on the basis of the southern European and Latin American experiences in the 1970s and 1980s, fits the

Russian case in many respects. Yet as Valerie Bunce and others have argued, the East is not the South.[1] The lessons learned from the fledgling states of the former Soviet Union will be different from those gained in a study of societies with previous exposure to democratic rule. Thus, the parsimony and universalism of the comparative literature have their limits.

The most distinctive features of the Russian transition follow from the nature of the ancien regime. Put simply, Russia had a very different starting point than most other countries in transition at the end of the twentieth century. Leaving behind the communist and imperial Russian inheritances required negotiating several formidable hurdles at once. Whereas some countries' transitions involved only the accession to power of a new ruling elite and the refinement of institutional arrangements, Russia had to create a new national identity, recast relations between center and periphery, construct new national political institutions, dismantle a command economy, and redefine its world role. It was a task of staggering proportions, made all the more difficult by the humiliation associated with the descent from global power and a precipitous fall in living standards. No wonder that pessimistic observers such as Aleksandr Yanov compared post-Communist Russia to Weimar Germany.[2]

All transitions, then, are not alike; each represents a unique blend of "legacies, institutions, and decisions."[3] To borrow an ancient metaphor rediscovered by students of transitions, how one rebuilds the ship of state depends in large measure on the condition of the old vessel, the replacement materials at hand, and the pitch of the seas. In the language of Elster, Offe, and Preuss, "Virtually everything is affected by the long arm of the past and the ruinous conditions and habits the old regime has left behind."[4] Politics cannot escape circumstance, whether it is the slowly changing character of a country's culture or rapidly moving and unpredictable events such as the death of a leader. But politics is also about choice, about how—given a particular set of circumstances—elites and masses decide to behave in matters that affect the public realm. And of all the choices to be made in the transition period, the most important relate to a country's institutional design, which establishes the rules for making and implementing public policy.

In formal terms, the semipresidential arrangements in Russia are strikingly similar to the political architecture of the Soviet Union, only now the Russian presidency, rather than the Communist Party Politburo and Central Committee, stands above the parliament and Government. But because Boris Yeltsin and his entourage lack the party's patronage power, its vast organizational machine, its monopoly of discourse, and its historic achievements, such as the victory over the Nazis, even with the additional powers acquired in the December 1993 constitution, the Russian presidency must continually compromise with other institutional actors, whether parliament, ministries, courts, or regional authorities. Although Yeltsin designed the political system to be "superpresidential"—"democracy in its most anemic and tenuous incarnation," in Steven Fish's phrase—the cultural legacies and decisions of elites imposed severe constraints on the impressive formal powers of the presidency.[5] The result was the revival of politics in Russia, though politics of a particularly chaotic sort.[6]

Without a strong party or parties to integrate the varied forces in Russian politics, the country's institutional design contributed to a remarkable diffusion of power that has been the hallmark of Russian government during the transition. It is easy to forget that alongside the formidable prerogatives accorded to the presidency, the constitution of 1993 created an intricate institutional landscape, and therefore the potential for multiple and competing power centers. The extraordinary fragmentation of authority in contemporary Russia flows in part from the formal structures of power: a divided executive, a two-chamber parliament, four separate bases of representation for parliamentarians, three court systems, and the asymmetrical federalism governing relations between the center and the country's eighty-nine subject territories. Many other examples of institutional conflict and redundancy result from lower-order decisions that political scientists often refer to as elite tactics: the overlapping and competing departments in the presidential apparatus, especially pronounced during Yeltsin's first term; the multiple layers of oversight organs in the Government, which encourage department heads and deputy prime ministers to encroach on the authority of the ministers; two separate committees for foreign affairs in the Duma; two distinct bodies in the executive to combat tax evasion; and two discrete presidential reelection commissions operating in the spring of 1996.

Exacerbating the effects of this organizational parallelism have been Yeltsin's personnel appointments, which tend to favor political balance over cohesion. Just as institutions check each other, so do officials. This approach, much loved by Stalin, sets lieutenant against lieutenant. Such a "balancing" of cadres was especially evident during the Chernomyrdin era, when conservative figures, such as the head of the MVD, Anatolii Kulikov, worked to scuttle the initiatives of radical reformers in the Government, including those of the first deputy prime minister, Anatolii Chubais. In Chubais' own words, Yeltsin's personnel policy produced not a coalition government but a compromise Government. "The Chernomyrdin Government was seeking—and in a certain sense this was inevitable—a compromise position between the primary forces: the Communists in the Duma,

[the financier Boris] Berezovskii, and so forth, trying to please everyone."[7]
According to Timothy Colton,

> Russia's first president is temperamentally well suited to institutional redundancy. . . . He seems to thrive on inter-organization competition—competition, oftentimes, for his own ear and signature. Wanting passionately to modernize Russia and its government, he freely admits to being baffled by just what to do in many instances; this naturally tempts him to do more than one thing at once, and to create more than one organization to do the job(s).[8]

Russian voters have contributed to this splintering of political power as well. In the electoral contests in Russia during the last decade, the population has been reluctant to concentrate power in the hands of a single party or ruling group. In the parliamentary and presidential races, for example, the voters have opted for what Americans would call gridlock: the division of executive and legislative authority between two competing factions. They have also spread their votes among a dizzying array of parties, which has prevented the formation of a stable parliamentary majority in the Duma. Finally, the explosion of corruption in Russia has undermined the authority of the state, retarded economic development, and created new social networks that represent power centers in their own right.

Diffused power has its advantages, of course, both for society and its elites. Most obvious is that it prevents any single individual or institution from acquiring the means to tyrannize the population, a not inconsequential consideration for a country with Russia's history. Moreover, for the president, it can deflect criticism from the central leader and reduce his accountability—there are plenty of whipping boys about. It also discourages the formation of a united opposition. But more subtly, the proliferation of important institutional and individual actors expands the opportunities for political bargaining. The more participants in the game, the greater the number of negotiating options.[9] Such flexibility seemed especially important to Boris Yeltsin, who sat at the center of the state and relied on his Government, his advisors, and his personal representatives to the courts, the parliament, and the regions to forge the coalitions needed to further the interests of the presidency. As the economists might say, this was obviously a suboptimal solution for a president who would have preferred to rule by administrative fiat alone. But it is a measure of Yeltsin's adaptability that he learned how to employ to his advantage the many cleavages in the Russian political elite. There is no better example of this than the negotations that led a fragmented Duma in April 1998 to confirm as prime minister Sergei Kirienko, a young and inexperienced technocrat whose views clearly clashed with those of the Duma majority. Besides using the standard enticements of money, housing, and privilege, the president's men threatened to change the voting rules in ways that would have undermined the electoral chances of many Duma deputies.[10] The age-old tactic of divide and rule worked its magic.

Outside of the traditional institutions of state are many informal and often extraconstitutional forums for political negotiation, which represent a vital, and unappreciated, feature of Russian politics in transition. Students of political transitions, especially those in Eastern Europe, are familiar with the "roundtables" and other ad hoc venues where competing elites come together to steer the country through serious political crises or to establish a pact (or other broad-based political agreements) that lays the procedural foundation for a new political order. Such roundtables tend to close up shop once agreement is reached on the formal rules of the political game. In Russia, however, forums for mediating conflicts have flourished across the political landscape. At times, they emerge in response to a severe crisis. In December 1992, at the collapse of the Gaidar Government, the chairman of the Constitutional Court, Valerii Zorkin, sought to mediate the disputes between president and the legislature. Almost a year later, in October 1993, only days before relations between parliament and president descended into violence, the Patriarch of the Russian Orthodox Church organized negotiations between executive and legislative leaders.

Most forums, however, seek to overcome the regular stalemates created by the operation of formal institutions in an atmosphere of political polarization and ill will. Since the enactment of the constitution in December 1993, conciliation commissions have formed regularly to iron out differences among competing factions and institutions over pending legislation. Besides the more traditional intraparliamentary conference committees, there have been numerous interbranch conciliation committees that include representatives from the Government, presidency, and parliament. They often meet in informal sessions in dachas in the environs of Moscow. For example, at the end of 1997, Yeltsin formed an interbranch working group of twenty-five persons to develop legislation on land reform, an issue on which parliament had consistently opposed the liberalizing initiatives of the president.[11] Moreover, the bilateral agreements between Moscow and individual subject territories contain provisions for the use of "concilation procedures" to resolve disputes between center and periphery, an attempt to prevent the courts from assuming jurisdiction over the disputes. Finally, at the highest level of state power, the president, prime minister, Duma speaker, and chair of the Federation Council created the "Big Four" to reduce tension between legislative and executive authority.[12]

There is nothing unusual, of course, about the formation of ad hoc committees to resolve conflict. Indeed, alternative dispute resolution (ADR) has been all the rage in American legal circles, where informal mediation proceedings are replacing rigid, lengthy, and expensive judicial hearings. But in Russia, alternative venues for decision making have become so prevalent that they threaten to subvert the constitutional arrangements for governing. When the regular procedures produce stalemate, or outcomes that are not to the liking of key elites, in the first instance the Russian president, the temptation is to suspend the rules and negotiate a solution. Although functionally efficient over the short term, this approach prevents the development of an essential component of constitutional government: stable institutions. As Adam Przeworski has argued, "[T]he decisive step toward democracy is the devolution of power from a group of people to a set of rules."[13] Russian elites are as yet unwilling to submit themselves to a "dictatorship of law," which produces "institutionalized uncertainty." Constitutional democracy ensures a process, not an outcome.

Instead of a "pacted" transition, where a political agreement among a country's major competing groups serves to bridge the gap between the collapse of the old order and the introduction of stable institutional arrangements, Russia has had a permanently negotiated transition. In other words, informal bargaining continues over the full range of state policies. Although one can certainly overstate the degree of institutional flexibility—on some matters, the institutional design does hold—there is in Russian politics the penchant for *bespredel,* or the anything-goes mentality that one finds in other realms of contemporary life. Russia has yet to learn that unless tempered by law and administration, politics will inevitably descend into unlimited, and self-destructive, competition.

Why have these informal committees "secreted themselves in the interstices" of Russia's formal institutional arrangements? Why this parallel political universe alongside the constitutional order? Perhaps because the formal institutional design is simply incapable on its own of keeping key elites in the political game or of resolving disputes on highly contentious policy issues. In a country without a political consensus on issues as basic as property rights and the relationship between church and state, the consent of the population in a constitutional referendum—as Russia had in December 1993—is inadequate to bind strategic elites to a stable set of rules. The institutional design may be lawful but not legitimate—at least in the eyes of powerful opposition forces.

The proliferation of conciliation committees represents, therefore, a tempering of the formal powers accorded to the president and executive branch by the constitution of 1993. For opposition groups in the Duma, these multibranch working groups are welcome sources of information and influence over policy making. Functioning outside of the public eye, they allow opposition leaders to quietly compromise with the presidency and Government without alienating their constituents. A Communist deputy can make an angry speech in the Duma for the benefit of his electorate and then sit down with representatives of the president to calmly hammer out a compromise on a law desired by both executive and legislature. It is a pattern of behavior not unlike that found in other presidential systems, most notably that of the United States. For his part, the Russian president also gains from these informal committees, not just by avoiding a regime crisis but by co-opting members of the opposition into small groups where the authority and spoils of the presidency can be applied to maximum effect.

Summarizing the argument in its starkest form, Russia has a formal institutional design that is incompatible with its society. With a winner-take-all election for a powerful presidency, the losing side is bound to feel marginalized in politics, even if it wins an impressive share of the parliamentary seats. There is no evidence, however, that any other form of democratic government, such as parliamentarism, could have resolved more effectively the claims of political factions that are fundamentally intolerant of each other's views. Thus, the underlying problem, as Richard Pipes observes, is more the cultural legacy than the institutional design. Russian society is at the moment incompatible with itself: the minimum consensus necessary to sustain a stable political community is wanting. In Pipes' language, "the country is divided into two hostile blocs which find next to nothing in common with each other, and whose disagreements therefore concern not the best means of attaining common objectives but the objectives themselves."[14] In this climate, strict compliance with the formal rules of the political game would produce either perpetual stalemate or the exit of important groups into the political underground. To avoid the undesirable options of stalemate or subversion, Russia has developed ameliorating mechanisms that allow elites to move back and forth between formal and informal means of policy making. Diffusion of power, then, is a means of systemic self-preservation.[15]

If this analysis is correct, the very weakness of Yeltsin's leadership as president helped at times to maintain a relatively stable equilibrium among the myriad political forces in Russia. To sustain the atmosphere of compromise that characterized post-1993 Russia, there was no need for the strong hand so often invoked in casual conversations among Russians. Indeed, a vigorous and focused president who insisted on employing the full range of his prerogatives to promote westernizing reforms might have provoked another regime crisis, if not a civil war. Should we view Yeltsin's frequent disengagement from politics, then, as part of a grand strategy designed to ensure the survival of the realm? There is no compelling evidence to support this assertion. While Yeltsin no doubt compromised on many issues to preserve civic peace, and to avoid the risk that state officials would not carry out fiercely contested decrees, his irresoluteness stemmed from other causes, among them his fragile health, his mercurial character, and his lack of a personal understanding of, and commitment to, many of the reforms championed by his more radical advisors.[16] One has only to read the many memoirs of recent years, including Yeltsin's own, to appreciate the Russian president's disinterest in policy debates, especially on domestic affairs. He strove to retain a tsarlike distance from the everyday tasks of governing, and only at certain critical moments would he enter the fray with decisive measures.

Yeltsin's detachment as leader went far beyond what was necessary to avoid political stalemate or subversion. His failure to recruit or actively lead a disciplined team of officials in the presidency and Government invited administrative stalemate and strengthened unnecessarily the bargaining position of parliament, the regions, and financial-industrial groups, all of whom used the numerous political divisions in the executive to their own advantage. In some instances, Yeltsin tolerated public insults and open subordination from executive officials. It was as if the Russian president refused to recognize that modern democracies rest not only on diversity of opinion but also on rigid discipline, at least within the executive.

For all his attempts to invest the office of the president with gravity and dignity, Yeltsin often behaved in ways that were distinctly unpresidential. He managed at times to combine the boorishness of Khrushchev with the disorientedness of Brezhnev in his later years. When George Bush and his wife, Barbara, visited the Russian capital in June 1998, Yeltsin observed—upon receiving a cookbook compiled by the former First Lady—that "Americans cook badly and do not know how to eat."[17] Although this is a sentiment no doubt shared by most Russians as well as many others in the world, its expression in a public setting revealed a readiness to give offense that one normally associates with dictators rather than democrats. In dealing with subordinates, rather than visiting dignitaries, Yeltsin could exhibit the traits of a petty tyrant. In March 1998, apparently as a signal of his displeasure with the performance of the Government, Yeltsin ordered the removal of secret service protection from a dozen top executive officials, including Boris Nemtsov and Anatolii Chubais, who had many enemies among the country's new business elites.[18] Even in his second term, Yeltsin retained the personality of a political outsider.[19]

Where too much efficiency, resoluteness, and predictability in presidential rule may have invited stalemate or subversion, too little has left Russia with a weak state that cannot perform the most basic administrative tasks, such as tax collection. Such a state emboldens the representatives of "big capital" while it demoralizes ordinary citizens, who are subject to repeated wage arrears and other economic indignities. To be sure, enhancing state capacity in post-Communist Russia would have been a formidable challenge for any leader.[20] It required articulating a new national vision and identity, advancing successful public policies, and imposing a measure of discipline on state officials.[21] But Yeltsin enjoyed little success on any of these fronts. Perhaps most remarkably, he has not used his unrivaled access to the media or his powers over patronage and privilege to nurture a presidential party that could have encouraged the executive to speak with one voice. A presidential party need not have been a modern political party with deep social roots; it could well have been akin to a party of the king in early modern Europe. But some institution was required in order to integrate diverse state and social interests into a cohesive ruling elite. What Yeltsin sanctioned instead was the formation in 1995 of a "party of power," Our Home Is Russia, a loose collection of national and regional officials who were bound by little more than their desire to stay in office. It had neither a common ideology nor effective organizational means to reward loyalty and punish disobedience.

Reaching firm conclusions about Yeltsin's leadership is complicated, however, by what one observer called the president's "foreseeable unpredictability." Yeltsin seems to have understood instinctively Machiavelli's injunction that a prince must rule at times like a fox. Just as Russian politics was settling in comfortably to the pattern of a disengaged presidency and compromise cabinets, which characterized the Chernomyrdin governments from 1993 until 1998, Yeltsin formed a Government headed by Sergei Kirienko that boasted youth, energy, and political cohesion not seen since the prime ministership of Yegor Gaidar in 1992.[22] Almost without warning, Yeltsin abandoned the practice of political balance in the executive, opting instead for a more cohesive and efficient—but constituency-poor—Government. He was in effect proposing what political scientists call a "minimum winning majority" cabinet. That is, in forming the Government, Yeltsin granted only the minimum of personnel concessions necessary to achieve confirmation in the Duma. This meant removing the politician most detested by the parliament, Anatolii Chubais, but not placing ministers favored by the opposition in the cabinet, at least not in posts relating to the economy.[23] The result was a team of ministers firmly committed to economic reform.

As part of a broader campaign to downsize the bureaucracy, Yeltsin also approved measures in early 1998 to limit institutional redundancy. Targeted for elimination were numerous departments in the Government apparatus as well as some personnel in the presidential administration. Moreover, as we point out at the end of Chapter 3, a clearer division of labor began to emerge between the presidential apparatus and the Government. The presidency started to concentrate more fully on explicitly political assignments, such as relations with the media, the parliament, and the regions, leaving the Government to get on with the more technocratic tasks of economic management. An indication of the presidency's reduced oversight of everyday Government activity came in late April 1998, when President Yeltsin signed a decree that no longer required the Executive Office of the President to vet the draft directives of the prime minister and Government.[24] Upset by the election of unfriendly governors in many of Russia's regions, which meant heightened resistance to presidential initiatives in the center as well as the periphery—the governors were not just leaders of their regions but members of the Russian upper house—Yeltsin also made new appointments in the presidential administration that were designed to assure the formation of a bloc of presidential loyalists in the provinces. Finally, the Russian president exhibited a new visibility and vigor, staying on top of the financial crises in May and June 1998 in ways that befitted an American president or German chancellor. In short, Yeltsin adopted in the early summer of 1998 a leadership style that was closer to that of Charles de Gaulle than Nicholas II.

We now know that these developments in the first half of 1998 did not reflect a political epiphany but rather a temporary shift in Yeltsin's leadership tactics and a short-lived recovery from his debilitating illness. In August 1998, he abandoned Kirienko and returned for a time to the politics of compromise, eventually installing a critic of radical economic reform, Yevgenii Primakov, as the new prime minister. Then, in the middle of 1999, Yeltsin appointed two more prime ministers in rapid succession, Sergei Stepashin and Vladimir Putin, who, like Primakov, had backgrounds in the Security services. An enfeebled president seemed desperate to cling to what he believed Gorbachev had lost sight of at the end of Soviet rule: "the political game, the maneuver, the balancing act." In the twilight of the Yeltsin era, with the fundamental questions about the way forward in politics and the economy still essentially contested, presidential leadership had been reduced to the reshuffling of personnel.

Ruling the country in a time of troubles poses challenges that would try even the most tactically astute and politically engaged leader. Whether Yeltsin's successors can nurture reform while maintaining stability in Russia depends, however, on much more than their tactical skill and political energy. It depends on the performance of the economy, on the means and timing of assistance from the international community, on the organizational abilities of reformist and opposition forces (including those in the military), on the battle of ideas to redefine Russia's national identity and destiny, and on the response of the Russian public to all of the above, whether through the ballot box or direct action.

We began this book by observing that in the last decade, as in earlier episodes of reform and revolution in Russian history, the state has imposed change from above on a frightened and disoriented society. In some respects, the very quiescence of the Russian public has made it easier for leaders to administer the bitter medicine of transitional economics; in mobilized societies, a more potent dose of authoritianism would have been needed to maintain civic peace. But if economic and social conditions do not improve markedly, the continued disengagement of ordinary Russians from politics has the potential to lead to a sudden explosion of anger, either in the much-feared Russian *bunt* or in the election of an extremist outsider to the office of the presidency. Russia must develop vibrant parties, interest groups, or other institutions that bind the state to society, or else it will remain trapped in the cycle of reform and reaction that has plagued its history for centuries. As long as the Russian state remains "detached from the society it administers," the prospects for a constitutional and democratic order will remain precarious at best.[25]

Notes

Chapter 1: Introduction

1. I was fortunate that evening to have a seat two rows behind Yeltsin.

2. Natalya Timakova, "Deputy Chief of Staff Advises Yeltsin Against Running for Third Term," *Kommersant-Daily,* 10 July 1998, as printed in Johnson's Russia List, no. 2256, 10 July 1998.

3. See Alex Inkeles and Raymond Bauer, *The Soviet Citizen: Daily Life in a Totalitarian Society* (Cambridge, MA: Harvard University Press, 1959), and James R. Millar (ed.), *Politics, Work, and Daily Life in the USSR: A Survey of Former Soviet Citizens* (Cambridge: Cambridge University Press, 1987).

4. One of the first such studies was Ada W. Finifter and Ellen Mickiewicz, "Redefining the Political System of the USSR: Mass Support for Political Change," *American Political Science Review,* no. 4 (1992), pp. 857–874. A survey and analysis of the public opinion literature on Russia is available in F.J. Fleron Jr. and Richard Ahl, "Does the Public Matter? Public Opinion Surveys," in Harry Eckstein et al. (eds.), *Can Democracy Take Root in Post-Soviet Russia?* (Lanham, MD: Rowman and Littlefield, 1998), pp. 287–327.

5. See Stephen White, Richard Rose, and Ian McAllister, *How Russia Votes* (Chatham, NJ: Chatham House Publishers, Inc., 1997); Timothy J. Colton and Jerry F. Hough (eds.), *Growing Pains: Russian Democracy and the Elections of 1993* (Washington, DC: The Brookings Institution, 1998); Michael McFaul, *Russia's 1996 Presidential Elections: The End of Polarized Politics* (Stanford, CA: Hoover Institution Press, 1997); and Matthew Wyman, Stephen White, Bill Miller, and Paul Heywood, "Public Opinion, Parties and Voters in the December 1993 Russian Elections," *Europe-Asia Studies,* no. 4 (1995), pp. 591–614. Some of the finest voting studies have appeared in the journal *Post-Soviet Geography and Economics.*

6. James L. Gibson, Raymond M. Duch, and Kent L. Tedin, "Democratic Values and the Transformation of the Soviet Union," *Journal of Politics,* no. 2 (1992), pp. 329–371; Arthur H. Miller, Vicki L. Hesli, and William M. Reisinger, "Reassessing Mass Support for Political and Economic Change in the Former Soviet Union,"

American Political Science Review, no. 2 (1994), pp. 399–411. For a less sanguine view of Russia's democratic potential, see Stephen Whitefield and Geoffrey Evans, "Support for Democracy and Political Opposition in Russia, 1993–1995," *Post-Soviet Affairs,* no. 3 (1996), pp. 218–242.

7. One of the most important general works on this subject is Michael Urban, *The Rebirth of Politics in Russia* (Cambridge: Cambridge University Press, 1997). On the rise of parties in Russia, see M. Steven Fish, "The Advent of Multipartism in Russia, 1993–1995," *Post-Soviet Affairs,* no. 4 (1995), pp. 340–383; Stephen White, Matthew Wyman, and Sarah Oates, "Parties and Voters in the 1995 Russian Duma Elections," *Europe-Asia Studies,* no. 5 (1997), pp. 767–798, and the special issue "Party Politics in Post-Communist Russia" in *The Journal of Communist Studies and Transition Politics,* nos. 1–2 (1998).

8. See S. Frederick Starr, "Soviet Union: A Civil Society," *Foreign Policy,* no. 2 (1998), pp. 26–41; Gail W. Lapidus, "State and Society: Toward the Emergence of Civil Society in the Soviet Union," in Seweryn Bialer (ed.), *Politics, Society, and Nationality: Inside Gorbachev's Russia* (Boulder, CO: Westview Press, 1989), pp. 121–145; Marcia A. Weigle and Jim Butterfield, "Civil Society in Reforming Communist Regimes: The Logic of Emergence," *Comparative Politics,* no. 1 (1992), pp. 1–24; Vladimir Tismaneanu (ed.), *Political Culture and Civil Society in Russia and the New States of Eurasia* (Armonk, NY: M.E. Sharpe, 1995); Geoffrey Hosking, *The Awakening of the Soviet Union* (Cambridge, MA: Harvard University Press, 1991).

9. Jeffrey Hahn, "Changes in Contemporary Russian Political Culture," in Tismaneanu (ed.), *Political Culture and Civil Society in Russia and the New States of Eurasia,* p. 124, and Matthew Wyman, "Russian Political Culture: Evidence from Public Opinion Surveys," *Journal of Communist Studies and Transition Politics,* no. 1 (1994), pp. 31–32.

10. "The Image of Dual Russia," in Robert C. Tucker, *The Soviet Political Mind,* revised edition (New York: W.W. Norton, 1971), p. 123.

11. As Jerry Hough points out, deep and gradual changes in Soviet society and the world economy were pushing the USSR in a more liberal direction, but it was decisions at the top, within the state itself, that brought on a revolution and the collapse of the old order. See Hough, *Democratization and Revolution in the USSR, 1985–1991* (Washington, DC: The Brookings Institution, 1997), pp. 490 and passim. For a revisionist view of the social determinants of Gorbachev-era reforms, see Donna Bahry, "Society Transformed? Rethinking the Social Roots of Perestroika," *Slavic Review,* no. 3 (1993), pp. 512–554.

12. David Lane concludes that in the Gorbachev-era transformations, "political forces from society were minor actors." "The Transformation of Russia: The Role of the Political Elite," *Europe-Asia Studies,* no. 4 (1996), p. 545. To be sure, society did play a role in the late Gorbachev era in providing a constituency and power base for the counterelites that challenged traditional party rule and Russian dominance of non-Russian lands. On this see M. Steven Fish, *Democracy from Scratch; Opposition and Regime in the New Russian Revolution* (Princeton: Princeton University Press, 1995), Chapter II.

13. In a welcome development, by the mid-1990s an important component of the Russian state—the governments of its eighty-nine subject territories—became the subject of serious work by scholars representing every generation. Among the many works in this burgeoning literature are Mary McAuley, *The Politics of Uncertainty* (Cambridge: Cambridge University Press, 1997) and Kathryn Stoner-Weiss, *Local Heroes: The Political Economy of Russian Regional Governance* (Princeton: Princeton University Press, 1997).

14. On topics such as the presidency, evidence gathering requires qualitative research in widely scattered sources. There is very little to count in studies of the Russian state, save roll calls, decrees issued, rubles collected and expended, and the characteristics of elites. This shifts the focus of research—especially on a topic like the presidency—to nonquantifiable sources, such as those contained in legal acts on the organization and functions of institutions, memoirs and interviews, analytical and descriptive articles in contemporary newspapers and journals, and mundane, but important, materials such as in-house telephone directories that reveal the structure and ranking of executive offices.

15. Among the works that have taken Russian state institutions seriously are John Lowenhardt, *The Reincarnation of Russia: Struggling with the Legacy of Communism, 1990–1994* (Durham, NC: Duke University Press, 1995); Thomas F. Remington, "Democratization and the New Political Order in Russia," in Karen Dawisha and Bruce Parrott (eds.), *Democratic Changes and Authoritarian Reactions in Russian, Ukraine, Belarus, and Moldova* (Cambridge: Cambridge University Press, 1997), pp. 69–129; Robert Sharlet, "Transitional Constitutionalism: Politics and Law in the Second Russian Republic," *Wisconsin International Law Journal*, no. 3 (1996), pp. 495–521; Jeffrey W. Hahn (ed.), *Democratization in Russia: The Development of Legislative Institutions* (Armonk, NY: M.E. Sharpe, 1996); Philip G. Roeder, "Transitions from Communism: State-Centered Approaches," in Eckstein et al. (eds.), *Can Democracy Take Root in Post-Soviet Russia?* pp. 201–228; and Joel Ostrow, "Procedural Breakdown and Deadlock in the Russian State: The Problems of an Unlinked, Dual-channel Institutional Design," *Europe-Asia Studies*, no. 5 (1998), pp. 793–816. The journal *East European Constitutional Review* has also been an important source of articles on legal and political institutions.

On the nexus between society and a decaying Soviet and fledgling Russian state, see Fish, *Democracy from Scratch*, especially chapters III and VI, and Erik P. Hoffman, "The Dynamics of State-Society Relations in Post-Soviet Russia" and "State-Society Relations in the Soviet Union and Post-Soviet Russia," in Eckstein et al. (eds.), *Can Democracy Take Root in Post-Soviet Russia?* pp. 69–101 and 331–348.

There is only a handful of articles on the presidency itself. See Stephen White, "Russia: Presidential Leadership under Yeltsin," in Ray Taras (ed.), *Post-Communist Presidents* (Cambridge: Cambridge University Press, 1997), pp. 38–66; Timothy J. Colton, "Boris Yeltsin: Russia's All-Thumbs Democrat," in Colton and Robert C. Tucker (eds.), *Patterns in Post-Soviet Leadership* (Boulder, CO: Westview Press, 1995), pp. 49–74; Colton, "Superpresidentialism and Russia's Backward State," *Post-Soviet Affairs*, no. 2 (1995), pp. 144–148; Eugene Huskey, "Yeltsin as State Builder," *Soviet and Post-Soviet Review*, no. 1 (1994), pp. 56–62; Huskey, "The State-Legal Administration and the Politics of Redundancy," *Post-Soviet Affairs*, no. 2 (1995), pp. 115–143; Huskey, "Democracy and Institutional Design in Russia," *Demokratizatsiya*, no. 4 (1996), pp. 453–474; and Huskey, "The Making of Economic Policy in Russia: Changing Relations Between Presidency and Government," *Review of Central and East European Law*, no. 4 (1996), pp. 365–387.

16. For a discussion of what is meant by the term "Government" in Russia, see Chapter 4.

17. See Stephen K. Wegren, "Land Reform and the Land Market in Russia: Operation, Constraints, and Prospects," *Europe-Asia Studies*, no. 6 (1997), pp. 959–987.

18. Throughout Russian and Soviet history, rulers have rejected a neatly hierarchical form of political organization in favor of a more complex model with multiple supervisory organs. For a useful discussion of the *kontrol'*, or monitoring, function in

Russian and Soviet administrative history, see the articles by David Christian, Thomas F. Remington, and George Yaney in *Slavic Review,* no. 1 (1982), pp. 73–111. Yaney's *The Systemization of Russian Government: Social Evolution in the Domestic Administration of Imperial Russia, 1711–1905* (Urbana, IL: University of Illinois Press, 1973), remains the best introduction to prerevolutionary Russian government.

19. For an introduction to the now extensive literature on institutional design, see Giovanni Sartori, *Comparative Constitutional Engineering: An Inquiry into Structures, Incentives and Outcomes,* second edition (New York: New York University Press, 1997); and Sven Steinmo, Kathleen Thelen, and Frank Longstreth (eds.), *Structuring Politics: Historical Institutionalism in Comparative Analysis* (Cambridge: Cambridge University Press, 1992). For an introduction to the broader literature on the "rediscovery" of the state, see Peter B. Evans, Dietrich Rueschemeyer, and Theda Skocpol, *Bringing the State Back In* (Cambridge: Cambridge University Press, 1985), especially Skocpol's essay, pp. 3–37.

20. In indirect presidential elections, citizens elect a group of individuals that has the responsibility for choosing the president. The electoral college in the United States is one such system. Indirect presidential elections are likely to minimize institutional conflict by ensuring that a president enjoys the support of a majority of the country's key elites. Although this system filters popular preferences, and therefore appears to some insufficiently democratic, it encourages regime stability, a crucial value for new states. For a lucid analysis of electoral rules as they affect parliamentary seats in Russia, see Robert G. Moser, "The Impact of the Parliamentary Electoral System in Russia," *Post-Soviet Affairs,* no. 3 (1997), pp. 284–312.

21. According to the estimates of Olga Kryshtanovskaya and Stephen White, three-quarters of the Russian political elite in the mid-1990s had worked in the Soviet *nomenklatura.* "From Soviet *Nomenklatura* to Russian Elite," *Europe-Asia Studies,* no. 5 (1996), p. 729.

22. As Archie Brown points out, one of the most fateful personnel decisions made by Mikhail Gorbachev was the appointment of Boris Yeltsin to the post of party first secretary in Moscow, an appointment that Gorbachev made reluctantly, at the urging of Ligachev. "Politika liderstva v Rossii," *Vestnik Moskovskogo universiteta: Sotsiologiia i politologiia,* no. 2 (1998), p. 59.

23. "Duma Chairman Calls For Presidential Republic," Interfax, 20 July 1998, as printed in Johnson's Russia List, no. 2274, 20 July 1998.

Chapter 2: The Making of the Russian Presidency

1. V.I. Lenin, *The State and Revolution* (New York: International Publishers, 1932), pp. 35–44.

2. Egor L. Kuznetsov, *Sozdanie instituta Prezidenta SSSR. Politologicheskie aspekty.* Kandidat dissertation, Institute of State and Law, Moscow, 1994, p. 39.

3. *Ibid.,* pp. 40–41.

4. "We've Got a Special Way of Thinking: On the Establishment of the Soviet Presidency," *Demokratizatsiya,* no. 2 (Spring 1994), vol. II, pp. 228–229 (interview with Georgy Shakhnazarov).

5. Egor Kuznetsov, "The Making of a President: A Glimpse of the History of the Top Executive Post in the USSR," *Demokratizatsiya,* no. 2 (Spring 1994), vol. II, pp. 222–227.

6. *Ibid.,* pp. 224–225.

7. V.I. Boldin, *Krushenie p'edestala* (Moscow: Respublika, 1995), 219.

8. Whereas the Bolsheviks in 1917 employed the slogan "*vsia vlast' sovetam*" (all power to the soviets), Gorbachev used a more ambiguous formulation: "*polnevlastie sovetam*" (full power to the soviets). For the best political analysis of the Gorbachev era, see Archie Brown, *The Gorbachev Factor* (Oxford: Oxford University Press, 1996).

9. "We've Got a Special Way of Thinking," p. 230.

10. M. Nenashev, *Poslednee Pravitel'stvo SSSR* (Moscow: AO "Krym," 1993), p. 18.

11. "From the Archives," *Demokratizatsiya*, no. 2 (Spring 1994), vol. II, pp. 316–331.

12. On the emergence of a modern legislature in the USSR, see Robert T. Huber and Donald R. Kelley (eds.), *Perestroika-Era Politics: The New Soviet Legislature and Gorbachev's Political Reforms* (Armonk, NY: M.E. Sharpe, 1991).

13. *Ibid.*, pp. 330–331. See also Georgii Shakhnazarov, *Tsena svobody: reformatsiia Gorbacheva glazami ego pomoshchnika* (Moscow: Rossika, 1993), p. 136.

14. Kuznetsov, "The Making of a President," pp. 222–227.

15. Kuznetsov, *Sozdanie instituta Prezidenta SSSR*, p. 44. According to Shakhnazarov, "Lukianov combined the qualities of a professional jurist with a revolutionary romantic. He wrote a dissertation on the Congress of Soviets, and he was smitten by it." *Ibid.*

16. A.S. Cherniaev, *Shest' let s Gorbachevym: po dnevnikovym zapisiam* (Moscow: Kul'tura, 1993), p. 332.

17. Yegor Kuznetsov, "The Making of a President," pp. 222–227.

18. "Ob uchrezhdenii posta Prezidenta SSSR i vnesenii izmenenii i dopolnenii v Konstitutsiiu (Osnovnoi Zakon) SSSR," *Vedomosti S''ezda narodnykh deputatov SSSR i Verkhovnogo Soveta SSSR*, no. 12 (1990), st. 189.

19. Georgii Shakhnazarov claims that he championed the French model. Georgii Shakhnazarov, *Tsena svobody*, p. 138.

20. For an introduction to semipresidentialism, see Maurice Duverger, "A New Political System Model: Semi-Presidential Government," *European Journal of Political Research*, no. 2 , vol. 8 (1980), pp. 165–187.

21. The source of this description, made ironically after the collapse of the Soviet Union, is the former second secretary of the Communist Party, Yegor Ligachev. Ligachev, *Inside Gorbachev's Kremlin* (New York: Pantheon Books, 1993), p. 98.

22. "We've Got a Special Way of Thinking," p. 230.

23. Valentin Pavlov, *Upushchen li shans?* (Moscow: Terra, 1995), pp. 166–168.

24. Kuznetsov, *Sozdanie instituta Prezidenta SSSR*, p. 74. Kudriavtsev, among others, sought in vain to convince Gorbachev to accept the power of dissolution. *Ibid.*

25. For an analysis of the tensions between executive leaders in post-Communist Eastern Europe, see Thomas Baylis, "Presidents vs. Prime Ministers: Shaping Executive Authority in Eastern Europe," *World Politics*, no. 3 (1996), pp. 297–323.

26. Shakhnazarov, *Tsena svobody*, pp. 137–138.

27. "From the Archives," pp. 327–328. For insider accounts of the prime minister's office at the end of the Soviet era, see the interview with Nikolai Ryzhkov in Nenashev, *Poslednee Pravitel'stvo SSSR*, and Pavlov, *Upushchen li shans?*

28. For a critical assessment of this style, see the memoirs of Gorbachev's foreign policy advisor, Cherniaev, *Shest' let s Gorbachevym*, and Shakhnazarov, *Tsena svobody*.

29. "From the Archives," pp. 327–328.

30. Even reformists in Gorbachev's entourage, such as Georgii Shakhnazarov, did not initially favor direct *contested* elections for the presidency. He proposed instead that the Communist Party nominate a single candidate for the presidential "election." Kuznetsov, *Sozdanie instituta Prezidenta SSSR*, p. 51.

31. As Archie Brown notes, a "reason for going for the quick installation of presidential power was a widespread realization that, with the Baltic States intent on breaking away from the Soviet Union and economic difficulties worsening, the Soviet Union was reaching the point of crisis." Archie Brown, *The Gorbachev Factor* (Oxford: Oxford University Press, 1996), p. 203.

32. In this decision as well, he was following the precedent of the Fifth Republic in France. In France, however, the Fifth Republic's constitution envisioned the indirect election of the president as a permanent feature of the political system. In the Gaullist-inspired referendum of 1962, the French electorate approved the change to direct elections for the president. Shakhnazarov regarded Gorbachev's avoidance of direct elections as his "Achilles' heel." Shakhnazarov, *Tsena svobody,* p. 137.

33. Article 127.3 (15). Such extraordinary measures were to be introduced "at the request or with the consent of the supreme soviet presidium or the supreme organ of state power of the corresponding union republic." However, if such consent was not forthcoming, the revised constitution allowed the president to act if he received the support of two-thirds of the USSR Supreme Soviet. "Ob uchrezhdenii posta prezidenta SSSR i vnesenii izmenenii i dopol'nenii v Konstitutsiiu (Osnovnoi zakon) SSSR," *Vedomosti S"ezda narodnykh deputatov i Verkhovnogo soveta SSSR,* no. 12 (1990), st. 189.

34. The odd man out was Belarus, which retained the "speaker's parliamentarism" of the late Soviet era until the introduction of a presidential system in 1994. See Alexander Lukashuk, "Survey of Presidential Power: Belarus," *East European Constitutional Review* (Fall 1993–Winter 1994), pp. 58–61.

35. One of these was Sergei Stankevich, whose memo of 2 February 1990 warned of the consequences of introducing republican presidencies. Kuznetsov, *Sozdanie instituta Prezidenta SSSR,* p. 60.

36. According to one Russian observer, the system collapsed when the CPSU, which had been the central nervous system, shut down without something to take its place. Anatolii Utkin, "Piat' rokovykh shagov Gorbacheva," *Rossiiskaia Federatsiia,* no. 7 (1995), pp. 6–7. Thereafter, each economic leader in factories and farms felt himself "master in his own domain" (*svoego roda monarkhami v svoei votchine*). Ibid.

37. "Ukraine's Six Would-Be Presidents All Back Independence," 1 December 1991, Reuters Library Report. The winner of the Ukrainian presidential election, Leonid Kravchuk, had urged Ukrainians to vote to remain in the Union in a referendum organized by Gorbachev in March of that year.

38. For a lucid and compelling survey of the reasons for the collapse of the USSR, see Alexander Dallin, "The Causes of the Collapse of the USSR," *Post-Soviet Affairs,* no. 4 (1992), pp. 279–302.

39. N.I. Ryzhkov, *Ia iz partii po imeni "Rossiia"* (Moscow: Obozrevatel', 1995), p. 22.

40. Ibid., p. 48. When Gorbachev assumed the presidency in 1990, he reportedly stated that the country only needed five or six all-Union ministries to supervise areas such as defense, transportation, and economics. In his view, republic and local authorities could handle the remaining sectors. V.I. Boldin, *Krushenie p'edestala,* p. 369.

41. In his autobiography, Yeltsin observed that Gorbachev's descent from power began in early 1991, when, having thrown in his lot with only one pole, the right, "he was stripped of his chief weapon—the political game, the maneuver, the balancing act." Boris Yeltsin, *The Struggle for Russia* (New York: Random House, 1994), p. 24. On the role of the prime minister as "whipping boy" in post-Soviet Russia, see Vladimir Mironov, "Nuzhen li prezidentu 'mal'chik dlia bit'ia'? Bor'ba za pravitel'stvo prodolzhaetsia," *Vek,* no. 28 (1994), p. 3.

42. Nenashev, *Poslednee Pravitel'stvo SSSR*, p. 97.

43. For a bitter account of the removal of the Government, see the memoirs of the then prime minister, Pavlov, *Upushchen li shans?* pp. 157–159.

44. Shakhnazarov, *Tsena svobody*, pp. 143, 490.

45. *Ibid.*, p. 491.

46. *Ibid.*, p. 140.

47. Pavlov, *Upushchen li shans?* p. 103; Boldin, *Krushenie p'edestala*, p. 372; and Iu.M. Kozlov, "Ispolnitel'naia vlast': federal'nyi uroven'," *Vestnik MGU (Pravo)*, no. 6 (1992), p. 6.

48. Cherniaev, *Shest' let s Gorbachevym: po dnevnikovym zapisiam*, p. 337.

49. On the role of "pacted" transitions to democracy, see Guillermo O'Donnell and Philippe Schmitter (eds.), *Transitions from Authoritarian Rule: Tentative Conclusions About Uncertain Democracies* (Baltimore: Johns Hopkins University Press, 1986).

50. Pavlov, *Upushchen li shans?* pp. 11–12.

51. On this extraordinary episode in Russian history, see David Remnick, *Lenin's Tomb: The Last Days of the Soviet Empire* (New York: Vintage, 1994), pp. 448–490.

52. The periodization of post-Communist Russian history into distinct republics, along the French model, has been championed by Robert Sharlet. See, for example, his "Reinventing the Russian State: Problems of Constitutional Implementation," *The John Marshall Law Review*, no. 4 (1995), pp. 775–786. This approach has the advantage of alerting readers to the very different institutional arrangements in place before and after December 1993, when the adoption of the new constitution ushered in the Second Republic. The one disadvantage with this periodization is that it ignores the first Russian republic of this century, which separated the collapse of the autocracy in February 1917 and the Bolshevik Revolution of October 1917.

53. Kuznetsov, *Sozdanie instituta Prezidenta SSSR*, pp. 87–90.

54. Yeltsin, *The Struggle for Russia*, pp. 156–160.

55. *Ibid.*, pp. 155–160.

56. E. Gellner, "From the Ruins of the Great Contest: Civil Society, Nationalism, and Islam," *Times Literary Supplement*, 13 March 1992, p. 10.

57. Anders Aslund, *How Russia Became a Market Economy* (Washington, DC: The Brookings Institution, 1995), 88.

58. See, for example, A.A. Sobyanin, "Political Cleavages among the Russian Deputies," in Thomas F. Remington (ed.), *Parliaments in Transition* (Boulder, CO: Westview Press, 1994), pp. 181–216.

59. Lilia Shevtsova writes that "Russian development in these years became characterized by attempts on the part of all political actors and all political institutions to *monopolize* [her emphasis] power, instead of sharing it." She also contends that the deterioration in executive-legislative relations was due in part to the executive's use of parliament as a scapegoat for the country's declining fortunes. "Parliament and the Political Crisis in Russia, 1991–1993," in Jeffrey W. Hahn, *Democratization in Russia: The Development of Legislative Institutions* (Armonk, NY: M.E. Sharpe, 1996), pp. 38–40.

60. David Remnick, "Gorbachev's Last Hurrah," *New Yorker*, 11 March 1996, p. 77. On this point, see also Shakhnazarov, *Tsena svobody*, p. 222.

61. Yeltsin claims in his autobiography that he selected Rutskoi on the recommendation of two of his speechwriters. Khasbulatov's appointment was similarly "accidental," coming after three unsuccessful attempts to install Sergei Shakhrai as speaker. Yeltsin, *The Struggle for Russia*, pp. 31, 184.

62. *Ibid.*, pp. 168–169.

63. R. Khasbulatov, "The Congress of People's Deputies and Constitutional Reform," *Rossiiskaia gazeta,* 9 January 1993, as translated in *Foreign Broadcast Information Service,* 14 January 1993, p. 37.

64. The top three vote-getters, in declining order, were Yurii Skokov, Chernomyrdin, and Gaidar. Skokov's extensive support among Communist deputies angered Yeltsin and led to a rapid deterioration in their relations and, ultimately, the removal of Skokov from his post as head of the president's Security Council.

65. Chernomyrdin's original political base was with neither of the two major political forces in the parliament, Communists or Democratic Russia, but rather with a third force in Russian politics, the Civic Union. Although Civic Union had little popular support, it maintained close ties to leading state and economic institutions and sought to become what would later be called a "party of power," that is, a party of officialdom.

66. John Lowenhardt, *The Reincarnation of Russia: Struggling with the Legacy of Communism, 1990–1994* (Durham, NC: Duke University Press, 1995), p. 126.

67. "Prezidentskii proekt soglasheniia federal'nykh organov zakonodatel'noi i ispolnitel'noi vlastei RF po stabilizatsii konstitutsionnogo stroia na period do priniatiia novoi Konstitutsii RF," *Nezavisimaia gazeta,* 19 February 1993. This draft document gave the Constitutional Court the responsibility for enforcing the agreement.

68. "Chto predlagaet Prezident (iz Obrashcheniia k grazhdanam Rossii)," *Izvestia,* 23 March 1993, pp. 1–2.

69. Irina Savvateeva, "Vykhodiashchii iz teni," *Izvestia,* 15 March 1994, p. 5.

70. Sergei Filatov, *Na puti k demokratii* (Moscow: Moskovskii rabochii, 1995), p. 166. In his memoirs, Viacheslav Kostikov, Yeltsin's press secretary, reported that even in the Kremlin cafeteria, Rutskoi's contingent always ate separately from the president's entourage. Viacheslav Kostikov, *Roman s Prezidentom* (Moscow: Vagrius, 1997), p. 39.

71. *Aleksandr Rutskoi: Lefortovskie protokoly* (Moscow: Paleia, 1994), p. 33.

72. Yeltsin, *The Struggle for Russia,* p. 205.

73. *Ibid.,* p. 188.

74. *Ibid.,* p. 210.

75. Adam Przeworski, *Democracy and the Market: Political and Economic Reforms in Eastern Europe and Latin America* (Chicago: University of Chicago Press, 1991), p. 36.

76. Lowenhardt, *The Reincarnation of Russia,* pp. 128, 136.

77. For competing constitutions, advanced by presidency and parliament in the spring of 1993, see "Novaia konstitutsiia Rossii: dva proekta," *Konstitutsionnyi vestnik,* no. 16 (spetsial'nyi vypusk) (May 1993).

78. Filatov, *Na puti k demokratii,* p. 169.

79. "Nikolai Fedorov: Parlament dopuskaet antikonstitutsionnye deistviia," *Rossiiskie vesti,* 13 March 1993, p. 2.

80. Filatov, *Na puti k demokratii,* p. 178, 333. As his memoirs make clear, Yeltsin had no intention of resigning if impeached. Indeed, Yeltsin refused to accept the legitimacy or "seriousness" of such proceedings, believing that "a directly elected president could never by impeached." Yeltsin, *The Struggle for Russia,* p. 210.

81. Filatov, *Na puti k demokratii,* pp. 181–192. Filatov adds: "[W]e had information that in a number of ministries, including the State Customs Committee, people from the White House were already sitting with guns in their hands, de facto holding hostage all the activities of this committee." *Ibid.,* p. 180.

82. Aleksandr Korzhakov, *Boris El'tsin: ot rassveta do zakata* (Moscow: Interbuk, 1997), pp. 168–195; and Yeltsin, *The Struggle for Russia,* pp. 276–283. See also Veronika Kutsyllo, *Zapiski iz Belogo Doma* (Moscow: Kommersant, 1993).

83. Guillermo O'Donnell, "Delegative Democracy," *Journal of Democracy,* vol. 5, no. 1 (1994), p. 59.

84. David Remnick, *Lenin's Tomb: The Last Days of the Soviet Empire* (New York: Vintage Books, 1994), p. 536 (in afterword to the Vintage edition).

85. See, for example, the analyses of Aleksandr Sobianin, E. Gel'man, and O. Kaiunov, "The Political Climate of Russia's Regions: Voters and Deputies, 1991–1993," *The Soviet and Post-Soviet Review,* no. 1 (1994), pp. 63–84.

86. "Konstitutsiia Rossiiskoii Federatsii (proekt)," *Izvestia,* 10 November 1993, pp. 3–5.

87. Vladimir Kvasov, "Konflikta mezhdu pravitel'stvom i Prezidentom ne budet," *Rossiiskaia federatsiia,* no. 6 (1994), pp. 7–8.

88. The Duma and Government agreed to the following rules regarding the interpellation of ministers: they would invite members of Government to weekly question time at least three days in advance; they would invite no more than two ministers, and preferably only one; and they would make sure that deputies in the sector were prepared to ask informed, rather than childish (*detskie*), questions. Liubov' Vladimirova, "Deputaty prevrashchaiut 'Chas Pravitel'stva' v vecher voprosov i otvetov," *Rossiiskie vesti,* 21 June 1994, p. 1. See also I.P. Rybkin, *Gosudarstvennaia Duma: piataia popytka* (Moscow: International Humanitarian Fund "Znanie," 1994), p. 77. Earlier drafts of the 1993 constitution had envisioned Duma confirmation of all but the power ministries. Yeltsin returned to that idea in October 1994 in discussions with parliamentary factions. He never agreed, however, to this major concession to parliament. "Vyraziv votum nedoveriia pravitel'stvu, Gosduma mozhet postavit' pod udar sebia," *Izvestia,* 27 October 1994, p. 1.

89. Vladimir M. Lysenko, "Toward Presidential Rule," *Journal of Democracy,* no. 2 (1994), p. 11.

90. Konstitutsiia Rossiiskoi Federatsii, article 80/2–3.

91. On this point, see the comments of Sergei Filatov in "Chinovnik pod kolpakom," *Iuridicheskii vestnik,* nos. 11–12 (1995), p. 2.

92. In this and many other votes, many of Yeltsin's former democratic allies in the legislature joined the opposition. Aleksei Kiva, "Limit oshibok ischerpan," *Rossiiskie vesti,* 25 April 1995, p. 2.

93. Donald Barry, "Amnesty Under the Russian Constitution: Evolution of the Provision and Its Use in February 1994," *Parker School Journal of East European Law,* no. 1 (1994), pp. 437–461; Aleksandr Korzhakov, *Boris El'tsin: ot rassveta do zakata,* pp. 168–198. According to Korzhakov's account, the freeing of the prisoners would not have occurred if the prison housing the inmates, Lefortovo, had not been transferred from the MVD to the Procuracy two days before the release, on the orders of Yurii Baturin, the president's advisor on national security. *Ibid.,* p. 196.

94. "Democracy," Mainwaring notes, "presupposes the willingness of political actors to accept electoral and policy defeats. This willingness is enhanced when actors believe that defeats are reversible through the democratic struggle and that they are not catastrophic." Scott Mainwaring, "Presidentialism, Multipartism and Democracy: The Difficult Combination," *Comparative Political Studies,* vol. 26, no. 2 (1993), p. 219.

95. Although the 1993 constitution envisioned a four-year term for parliament, its transition provisions provided for an initial term of only two years. This exception was apparently designed to stifle legislative development and to prevent a recurrence of the executive-legislative stalemate that had characterized the first two years of post-Communist Russia.

96. Maksim Meier, "Duma mezhdu prezidentom, pravitel'stvom i konstitutsiei," *Novoe vremia,* no. 9 (1994), p. 6.

97. Rybkin and Yeltsin noted the "constructive dialogue" between president and speaker that characterized the first session of the Duma. Aleksei Kirpichnikov, "Duma: The President Approves of the Duma, and Its Chairman Approves of the President," *Segodnia,* 6 October 1994, p. 1, as translated in *Current Digest of the Post-Soviet Press,* no. 40 (1994), p. 1.

98. Mikhail Leont'ev, "Prem'er Skokovets [sic] kak produkt 'obshchestvennogo soglasiia,'" *Segodnia,* 25 October 1994, p. 1. For a revealing self-portrait, see Rybkin, *Gosudarstvennaia Duma: piataia popytka,* especially pp. 116–125.

99. Thomas F. Remington and Steven S. Smith conclude that Shumeiko's position in the Federation Council is more dominant than that of Rybkin in the Duma, where parties are more developed and deputies more active. "The Early Legislative Process in the Russian Federal Assembly," *Journal of Legislative Studies,* no. 1 (1996).

100. As of the beginning of 1995, there were three separate offices in the presidency with responsibilities for liaison with parties or the parliament. According to the head of the Administration for Relations with Parties, these bureaus were designed to bridge the "empty space" that exists between the executive and legislature. Anna Ostapchuk, "Proshlo soveshchanie dvukh vetvei vlasti," *Nezavisimaia gazeta,* 4 October 1994, p. 2.

101. The phrase is that of Mikhail Shchipanov in "Osoboi prezidentskoi partii ne budet," *Kuranty,* 7 April 1994, p. 4.

102. "Novaia nomenklatura ili novaia kadrovaia politika?" *Rossiiskie vesti,* 23 September 1994, p. 1.

103. Andrei Uglanov, "Ministry prikhodiat i ukhodiat, apparat ostaetsia," *Argumenty i fakty,* no. 20 (May 1994), p. 3. The Administration of Affairs is a powerful but little-studied arm of the Russian presidency, which now houses under one roof the remnants of the administrations of affairs of the Communist Party Central Committee and the Council of Ministers. See the next chapter for further analysis.

104. Robert Orttung, "Duma Seeks Financial Independence from Presidential Administration," *OMRI Daily Report,* 13 February 1996.

105. As is so often the case in Russian parliamentary votes, the motion failed because of high levels of tactical nonvoting by deputies. Nonvotes are counted as nay votes in the Duma. As Thomas F. Remington and Steven S. Smith point out, "for the January–July 1994 period, the mean number of 'yea' votes was 211 and the mean number of 'nay' votes was 49, so the typical motion was defeated (211 is less than a majority) because of nonvoting." "The Development of Parliamentary Parties in Russia," *Legislative Studies Quarterly,* no. 4 (1995).

106. Andranik Migranian, "Prezident dolzhen priniat' reshenie i naznachit' prem'erom cheloveka, kotoryi sposoben sozdat' pravitel'stvo natsional'nogo spaseniia," *Nezavisimaia gazeta,* 4 November 1994, pp. 1,3. This argument was first made by Sergei Chugaev, "Bol'shinstvo politikov zainteresovano v krakhe pravitel'stva," *Izvestia,* 27 January 1994, p. 2.

107. "U nas net bolee vazhnoi problemy, nezheli dogovorit'sia o pravilakh igry," *Posev,* no. 5 (1998) pp. 7–17. This is an interview with Gaidar.

108. Vladimir Kvasov, "Konflikta mezhdu pravitel'stvom i Prezidentom ne budet," *Rossiiskaia federatsiia,* no. 6 (1994), pp. 7–8.

109. The number of bureaucrats in Russia rose 1.7 times from 1989 to 1994, with local and regional government accounting for two-thirds of that increase. The total number of nonuniformed officials is 1.66 million, half of whom work in "organs of

state administration" and half in "other budgeted organizations" Aleksandr Bekker, "Pravitel'stvu predlagaiut samosokratit'sia," *Segodnia,* January 13, 1995, p. 2.

110. No one was more aware of this than Boris Yeltsin, who, as head of the Russian parliament before June 1991, struggled to obtain for himself decent living and working conditions. Yeltsin, *The Struggle for Russia,* pp. 19–20. According to Ligachev, provincial secretaries on short trips to Moscow struggled to get a meal, so the Central Committee set up a special canteen for them. Ligachev, *Inside Gorbachev's Kremlin,* p. 148. Western scholars ignore these cultural/economic conditions of politics at their peril.

111. Like most bosses everywhere, Yeltsin found it "easy to hire personnel and hard to fire them." This was especially true of subordinates whom he saw regularly. According to Aleksandr Korzhakov, Yeltsin resisted firing his defense minister, Andrei Grachev, because he lived in the same apartment building. Aleksandr Korzhakov, *Boris El'tsin: ot rassveta do zakata* (Moscow: Interbuk, 1997), p. 384. By his own admission, the head of the protocol section of the presidency, Vladimir Shevchenko, felt toward each of his staff "a moral, as well as a financial, obligation." "Vladimir Shevchenko: shef protokol'noi sluzhby vsegda pri prezidentakh," *Rossiiskaia gazeta,* 2 September 1994, p. 3. My contention is that such universal feelings are more pronounced in Russia than in the West, in part because of the conditions of Russian life, in part because of a cultural tradition with more feudal admixtures.

112. Iu.M. Kozlov, "Ispolnitel'naia vlast': federal'nyi uroven'," *Vestnik MGU (Pravo),* no. 6 (1992), p. 8.

113. Gavriil Popov, the former mayor of Moscow, argues forcefully that Yeltsin had no "team." Gavriil Popov, "Boris El'tsin i avtoritarnoe gosudarstvo," *Izvestia,* 24 December 1994, p. 5.

114. Tat'iana Malkina, "Aleksandr Korzhakov schitaet, chto prezidentskie vybory nuzhno otlozhit'," *Segodnia,* 6 May 1996, p. 1.

115. "Georgii Satarov: Prezidentu nado chashche ob"iasniat' svoiu pozitsiiu," *Argumenty i fakty,* no. 33 (1994), p. 3; and V.A. Mironov, "Rossiiskoe gosudarstvennoe stroitel'stvo v postsoiuznyi period (1991–1994 gg.)," *Kentavr,* no. 3 (1994), p. 11.

116. Elena Tregubova, "Administratsiia protiv prezidenta," *Izvestia,* 27 October 1998, p. 1, and Tregubova, "Neposlushnyi El'tsin," *Izvestia,* 15 October 1998, p. 1.

Chapter 3: The Institutional Presidency

1. Important exceptions to this rule include Richard E. Neustadt, *Presidential Power and the Modern Presidents. The Politics of Leadership from Roosevelt to Reagan* (New York: The Free Press, 1990); Stephen Hess, *Organizing the Presidency,* second edition (Washington, DC: The Brookings Institution; 1988), John P. Burke, *The Institutional Presidency* (Baltimore: Johns Hopkins University Press, 1992); and Charles E. Walcott and Karen M. Hult, *Governing the White House* (Lawrence, KS: University Press of Kansas, 1995). L.A. Okun'kov has written the only work on the Russian presidency to date. See *Prezident Rossiiskoi Federatsii—Konstitutsiia i politicheskaia praktika* (Moscow: INFRA M-NORMA, 1996), which offers considerable detail on the subdivisions of the presidency toward the end of Yeltsin's first term of office.

2. John P. Burke, *The Institutional Presidency,* p. 47.

3. Andrei Illarionov, "Uroki rossiiskikh reform," *Znamia,* no. 3 (1995), pp. 180. It is not known to what extent the elimination of the Communist Party apparatus helps to explain these figures.

4. Anatolii Utkin, "Piat' rokovykh shagov Gorbacheva," *Rossiiskaia Federatsiia,* no. 7 (1995), p. 6.

5. Egor Gaidar, *Gosudarstvo i evoliutsiia* (Moscow: Evraziia, 1995), p. 15.

6. See, for example, Lilia Shevtsova, "Parliament and the Political Crisis in Russia, 1991–1993," in Jeffrey W. Hahn, (ed.) *Democratization in Russia: The Development of Legislative Institutions* (Armonk, NY: M.E. Sharpe, 1996), p. 31.

7. Boris Yeltsin, *The Struggle for Russia* (New York: Random House, 1994), p. 6.

8. In early 1994, Yeltsin's extended family had three apartments in this building, one on the sixth floor and two on the fifth. Among the other notables in the building were Prime Minister Chernomyrdin, Kremlin security chiefs Korzhakov and Barsukov, MVD chief Yerin, Defense Minister Grachev, and Mayor Luzhkov. See "V nashem dome poselitsia zamechatel'nyi sosed," *Komsomol'skaia pravda,* 23 April 1994.

9. A native of the Sverdlovsk region, Petrov worked in responsible party positions in the area until 1977, when he was called to Moscow to assume leading posts in the Central Committee's Department for Organizational-Party Work. It was from there that he returned to Sverdlovsk in 1985 to replace Yeltsin as regional party first secretary. *Kto est' kto v Rossii i v blizhnem zarubezh'e* (Moscow: Novoe vremia, 1993), pp. 501–502.

10. "Security Council Secretary Lobov Interviewed," *Berlingske Tidende* (Copenhagen), 16 September 1995, p. 8, as translated in *Foreign Broadcast Information Service,* 21 September 1995, p. 34.

11. Indeed, some of his critics accused him of seeking to return the Ministry of Economics to its earlier incarnation as the State Planning Committee (Gosplan). Iurii Rytov, "Viktor Chernomyrdin: god u vlasti," *Rossiiskie vesti,* 14 December 1993, p. 3, and Dmitrii Lvov, "V obshchestve stress, a v Pravitel'stve—PRES," *Rossiiskie vesti,* 22 January 1994, p. 1.

12. As we shall see below, the firing of officials in the presidency did not mean the end of their political or administrative careers. The culture of guaranteed employment for high-ranking officials continued into the post-Communist era. Thus, Petrov moved immediately from his post as chief of staff into the directorship of a newly created Russian enterprise fund, which had hundreds of millions of dollars to distribute to upstart businesses. When I had dinner with Petrov at a Duke University seminar organized by Jerry Hough in the spring of 1993, he seemed slightly bemused by—but also proud of—his new status as one of Russia's most powerful CEOs. That Petrov retained an interest in politics is indicated by his inclusion on the party list of the Bloc of Ivan Rybkin in the December 1995 parliamentary elections.

13. According to Korzhakov, by 1993 Yeltsin had around him a team of political and social traditionalists with whom he felt close: Korzhakov (security chief), Borodin (business office), Soskovets (deputy prime minister), Yerin (MVD chief), and Tarpishchev (tennis coach). Aleksandr Korzhakov, *Boris El'tsin: ot rassveta do zakata* (Moscow: Interbuk, 1997), p. 155. Already in November 1992, Sergei Stankevich, the presidential counselor, was writing Yeltsin a memo in which he argued that "radical democrats can no longer serve as a base of support for the president." Viacheslav Kostikov, *Roman s Prezidentom* (Moscow: Vagrius, 1997), p. 135.

14. Yeltsin, *The Struggle for Russia,* p. 248.

15. Personal interviews in Moscow, September 1995.

16. Yeltsin offers a devastating assessment of Burbulis as a politician and a man in his *The Struggle for Russia,* pp. 31, 128, and 156–160.

17. See E. Huskey, "The State-Legal Administration and the Politics of Redundancy," *Post-Soviet Affairs,* no. 2 (1995), pp. 115–143.

18. See "Uvolen za chelovecheskoe otnoshenie k podsudimym," *Obshchaia gazeta,* 11–17 June 1998, pp. 1,6, and "Virtual'no-sudebnaia real'nost'," *Obshchaia gazeta,* 18–24 June 1998, p. 1.

19. "Yeltsin's 'Roller-Coaster' Method of Rule Eyed," *Kommersant-Daily,* 15 April 1995, p. 3, as translated in *Foreign Broadcast Information Service,* 18 April 1995, pp. 21–22.

20. According to Aleksandr Korzhakov, humiliating subordinates before their peers was a trait Yeltsin exhibited as party leader in the Soviet era. Aleksandr Korzhakov, *Boris El'tsin: Ot rassveta do zakata,* pp. 52–53.

21. Ibid., p. 316.

22. Ibid., p. 328.

23. On some personal matters, however, he took a lively interest. When he noticed that one of his young associates, the usually slim Vladimir Shumeiko, was developing a potbelly, he "knew that [he] would have to use the old Bolshevik methods to break this disrespectful attitude toward sports and physical exercise." Yeltsin, *The Struggle for Russia,* p. 234.

24. See, for example, the description of supplicants appearing before the Ethiopian emperor, Haile Selassie, in Ryszard Kapuscinski, *The Emperor* (New York: Vintage Books, 1984).

25. Roza Sergazieva, "Po stupeniam prezidentskoi 'piramidy.' Razgovor s khranitelem pechati," *Rossiiskie vesti,* 2 April 1993, p. 2. There was also within the presidency a separate office for heraldry. The herald master was responsible for developing and policing the use of the official symbols on state buildings, letterhead, and so forth. "O Gosudarstvennom geral'dicheskom registre RF," *Sobranie zakonodatel'stva,* no. 13 (1996), st. 1307.

26. For excellent introductions to this institution, see Denis Babichenko, "'Imperiia schast'ia' meniaet pravitelia," *Segodnia* online, 19 May 1998, and Valentin Nikolaev, "Chelovek vlasti: Upravliaiushchii delami Prezidenta Rossii," *Rossiiskie vesti* online, 23 January 1998.

27. See Yeltsin's 1995 tax return, reproduced in *Rossiiskie vesti,* 6 April 1996, p. 3. As the text below suggests, Yeltsin received far more than this in in-kind benefits provided by the Administration of Affairs. According to the tax return, the Russian president received in-kind benefits (*material'naia pomoshch'*) totaling 5 million rubles in 1995. By 1998, Yeltsin's salary had risen to 10,000 new rubles a month, or about $20,000 a year. This was still a small portion of his total earnings. He received, for example, royalties totaling more than $280,000 for his autobiography, *The Struggle for Russia.* See Natal'ia Konstantinova, "Na kakie den'gi zhivet Prezident," *Nezavisimaia gazeta,* 20 June 1998, p. 3.

28. A significant portion of the money received by the Administration of Affairs comes in the form of budgetary transfers from institutions serviced by the business office. "Ob Upravlenii delami Prezidenta Rossiiskoi Federatsii," *Sobranie zakonodatel'stva,* no. 32 (1995), st. 3288 (Article 8.a).

29. "Kto vy, 'tainyi' i 'samyi glavnyi' ministr?" *Rossiiskaia Federatsiia,* no. 24 (1995), p. 18.

30. Andrei Uglanov, "Ministry prikhodiat i ukhodiat, apparat ostaetsia," *Argumenty i fakty,* no. 20 (May 1994), p. 3.

31. Evgeniia Al'bats, "Vlast' taino sozdaet svoiu tenevuiu ekonomiku," *Izvestia,* 1 February 1995, p. 2.

32. A presidential decree updating the regulations governing the Administration of Affairs officially "confirmed" a list of its subordinate enterprises. Contrary to ordi-

nary practice, however, this list was not published in the official presidential register, a sign of the institution's desire to shield these businesses from public scrutiny. See "Ob Upravlenii delami Prezidenta Rossiiskoi Federatsii," *Sobranie zakonodatel'stva,* no. 32 (1995), st. 3288.

33. Andrei Uglanov, "Ministry prikhodiat i ukhodiat, apparat ostaetsia," *Argumenty i fakty,* no. 20 (May 1994), p. 3.

34. The Ministry of Finance, for its part, has been intent on establishing common salary levels in all ministries and state structures. Among the agencies most resistant to leveling of civil service wages are the tax police and tax inspectorate, whose nonbudgetary funds have apparently permitted them to hire more competent and less easily corrupted cadres. Svetlana Lolaeva, "Tamozhnia, nalogovaia sluzhba i nalogovaia politsiia lishaiutsia svoikh tselevykh fondov," *Segodnia,* 23 September 1995, p. 2. As Irina Savvateeva and others have argued, extrabudgetary funding continues the Soviet tradition of economic autarchy. For an introduction in English to extrabudgetary funds, see Eugene Huskey, "The Making of Economic Policy in Russia: Changing Relations Between Presidency and Government," *Review of Central and East European Law,* no. 4 (1996), pp. 365–387.

35. See James Kynge, James Harding, and John Riddy, "War by Other Means for Chinese Army Plc," *Financial Times,* 24 July 1998, p. 4.

36. See, for example, the information on special exporting licenses contained in Evgeniia Al'bats, "Vlast' taino sozdaet svoiu tenevuiu ekonomiku," *Izvestia,* 1 February 1995, pp. 1, 2, and the provisions contained in "Ob Upravlenii delami Prezidenta Rossiiskoi Federatsii," *Sobranie zakonodatel'stva,* no. 32 (1995), st. 3288. This decree orders the Government to consider granting investment tax credits to the Administration of Affairs as well as an exclusion from customs duties on goods used in production.

37. "Kto vy, 'tainyi' i 'samyi glavnyi' ministr?" *Rossiiskaia Federatsiia,* no. 24 (1995), pp. 17–19.

38. See "O perechniakh gosudarstvennykh dolzhnostei federal'noi gosudarstvennoi sluzhby kategorii 'B' i 'V' v Administratsii Prezidenta RF i apparate Soveta Bezopasnosti RF," *Sobranie zakonodatel'stva,* no. 16 (1996), no. 1833, and "O perechniakh gosudarstvennykh dolzhnostei federal'noi gosudarstvennoi sluzhby kategorii 'B' i 'V' v Upravlenii delami Prezidenta RF," *Sobranie zakonodatel'stva,* no. 16 (1996), st. 1834.

39. The notable exception to this rule is France, where *hautes fonctionnaires* may also serve as mayors of cities. They are not involved directly, however, in national party politics.

40. "Ob obespechenii deiatel'nosti Fonda prezidentskikh programm," *Sobranie zakonodatel'stva,* no. 25 (1995), st. 2377.

41. "O prezidentskikh programmakh," *Sobranie zakonodatel'stva,* no. 10 (1994), st. 1117.

42. In Yeltsin's second term, the Center for Presidential Programs was inexplicably folded into a new Economic Administration. "O merakh po sovershenstvovaniiu struktury Administratsii Prezidenta RF (s izmeneniiami na 28 marta 1998 goda)," ukaz Prezidenta RF no. 294, <www.inforis.ru>.

43. A discussion of the origins of the presidential counselors in the now abandoned State Council may be found in Richard Sakwa's *Russian Politics and Society* (London: Routledge, 1993), p. 50.

44. Vitalii Tretiakov, "Dvor plius apparat," *Nezavisimaia gazeta,* 25 December 1993, p. 1.

45. For a brief biography of Iliushin, see Kira Vladina, "Viktor Iliushin, pervyi pomoshchnik khoziania Kremlia," *Nezavisimaia gazeta,* 10 February 1994, p. 5. Perhaps because of his service in Afghanistan, Iliushin carried with him at all times a pistol that he had received when defending the White House in 1991. See Viacheslav Kostikov, *Roman s prezidentom* (Moscow: Vagrius, 1997), p. 21.

46. Igor Ryabov, "A Universal Soldier Without a Military Uniform," *New Times,* no. 8 (1994), pp. 14–15.

47. "Mikhail Krasnov: Kreml' sudami ne komanduet," *Iuridicheskii vestnik,* nos. 23–24 (1995), p. 3; "Novye naznacheniia," *Segodnia,* 10 February 1995, p. 2.

48. Huskey, "The Making of Economic Policy in Russia.

49. "Georgii Satarov: Prezidentu nado chashche ob"iasniat' svoiu pozitsiiu," *Argumenty i fakty,* no. 33 (1994), p. 3.

50. "Mikhail Krasnov: Kreml' sudami ne komanduet," p. 3.

51. Vasilii Kononenko, "Vozmozhny otstavki Egorova, Gracheva, Stepashina i dr. Poslanie El'tsina parlamentu budet reformatorskim," *Izvestia,* 2 February 1995, p. 1.

52. Denis Babichenko, "Prezidentskie broneviki otpraviatsia na zapasnyi put'," *Segodnia* online, 3 June 1998. There seemed to be virtually no limit on the money spent by the presidency. They stamped hundreds of thousands of medals that were given out to state employees, some of the most expensive costing $100 apiece. Ibid.

53. "Georgii Satarov: Prezidentu nado chashche ob"iasniat' svoiu pozitsiiu," p. 3.

54. When the journalist who conducted this interview turned off the tape recorder, Livshits discussed the massive theft that was plaguing economic development. He suggested that the topic of Yeltsin's knowledge of economics should be taken up only "when all present players are in retirement." "Aleksandr Livshits: Nizkaia infliatsiia tozhe opasna," *Literaturnaia gazeta,* no. 28 (1994), p. 10.

55. Maksim Meier, "Bor'ba v okruzhenii El'tsina obostriaetsia: chto stoit za reorganizatsiei apparata Prezidenta?" *Novoe vremia,* no. 7 (1994), p. 12; V.A. Mironov, "Rossiiskoe gosudarstvennoe stroitel'stvo v postsoiuznyi period (1991–1994 gg.)," *Kentavr,* no. 3 (1994), p. 11.

56. "Filatov Says Presidential Staff to Be Cut by 500," ITAR-TASS, 5 November 1994, 1657 GMT, as translated in *Foreign Broadcast Information Service,* 7 November 1994, p. 19.

57. Veronika Kutsyllo, "Personnel Cuts in President's Staff: No One Wants to Be Odd Man Out," *Kommersant-Daily,* 3 November 1994, p. 2, as translated in *Foreign Broadcast Information Service,* 3 November 1994, p. 18.

58. Vladimir Mironov, "U podnozhiia Olimpa: Administratsiia prezidenta RF vchera, segodnia, i zavtra," *Vek,* no. 24 (1994), p. 1.

59. Svetlana Alekseeva, "El'tsin: Popytka politicheskogo portreta," *Sovetskaia Rossiia,* 1 October 1994, p. 3. In contrast, this journalist characterized Chernomyrdin as a person who was more oriented toward "the real state of affairs in the country." Ibid.

60. Ibid.

61. "Novaia nomenklatura ili novaia kadrovaia politika?" *Rossiiskie vesti,* 23 September 1994, p. 1.

62. There was an effort, for example, to develop a gender-based quota to increase the percentage of women in the civil service. "Zhenshchiny i vlast'," *Rossiiskie vesti,* 2 July 1996, p. 1. Of the twenty-four members of this council, six each were appointed by the presidency, the Government, the parliament, and the country's highest courts. "O vnesenii izmenenii v Ukaz Prezidenta RF ot 1 dekabria 1995 g. No 1208 'O Sovete po voprosam gosudarstvennoi sluzhby pri Prezidente RF,'" *Sobranie zakonodatel'stva,* no. 7 (1996), st. 669.

63. See, for example, "Sila vlasti—v umenii naiti kompromiss," *Rossiiskie vesti,* 27 May 1994, pp. 1–2 (interview with Sergei Filatov), and Andrei Baiduzhii, "Kto kontroliruet kadrovuiu politiku v Kremle?" *Nezavisimaia gazeta,* 8 October 1994, pp. 1–2. The latter article detailed the objections of the power ministries to the involvement of the presidential staff in personnel decisions.

64. Nikolai Palagichev, "Chto chitaiut ministry," *Rossiiskie vesti,* 16 April 1993, p. 8.

65. The head of the presidential archives, Aleksandr Korotkov, reported that they contained more than eighty million files (*del*) from the Communist Party. A special commission, headed by the deputy leader of the Executive Office, Sergei Krasavchenko, began working on opening these files in the mid-1990s. See "Kak snimaiiut grif 'sekretno,' " *Rossiiskie vesti,* 23 January 1996, p. 3. This commission was part of a larger Interagency Commission for the Defense of State Secrets, consisting of approximately twenty executive officials, almost all of whom were the deputy heads of their organizations. See "Voprosy Mezhvedomstvennye komissii po zashchite gosudarstvennoi tainy," *Sobranie zakonodatel'stva,* no. 4 (1996), st. 268.

66. See "Esli ne vyslat', to soslat'. S MID SSSR soglasovano," *Izvestia,* 7 June 1996, p. 5.

67. See Alessandra Stanley, "The Americans Who Saved Yeltsin (Or Did They?)," *New York Times,* 9 July 1996, p. A3.

68. *Rossiiskie vesti,* 14 June 1996, p. 1. This paper broke with the presidency in the spring of 1998, apparently as a result of clashes with the passel of former journalists who at that time occupied key leadership positions in the presidency. It reopened as an independent paper in August 1998.

69. "O Press-sluzhbe Prezidenta RF," *Sobranie zakonodatel'stva,* no. 21 (1995), st. 1955.

70. Andrei Kozyrev, "Diplomatiia i gosudarstvo," *Segodnia,* 17 January 1995, p. 10.

71. A detailed and generally sympathetic account of Poltoranin's work in the presidency may be found in Viacheslav Kostikov, *Roman s prezidentom.*

72. "Esli vy trezvo myslite, to stanovites' radikalom," *Rossiiskie vesti,* 13 May 1994, p. 2.

73. "O vnesenii izmenenii i dopolnenii v Polozhenie ob Upravlenii informatsionnogo obespecheniia Administratsii Prezidenta RF," *Sobranie zakonodatel'stva,* no. 16 (1994), st. 1887.

74. "Sozdano Finansovo-biudzhetnoe upravlenie Prezidenta," *Rossiiskie vesti,* 2 March 1994, 1.

75. Vladimir Berezovskii, "Dva politicheskikh lageria federal'noi elity Rossii," *Svobodnaia mysl',* no. 9 (1994), pp. 69.

76. "Ob Upravlenii Administratsii Prezidenta RF po vzaimodeistviiu s politicheskimi partiiami, obshchestvennymi ob"edineniiami, fraktsiiami i deputatami palat Federal'nogo Sobraniia," *Sobranie zakonodatel'stva,* no. 18 (1994), st. 2068 (ukaz 1724, 23 August).

77. Tat'iana Krasnova, "Gosudarstvo dolzhno pomoch' kazakam naiti sebia," *Nezavisimaia gazeta,* 14 July 1994, p. 3. In early 1996, Yeltsin sanctioned the formation within the presidency of a Main Administration for Cossacks, staffed by thirty-five persons. "O Glavnom upravlenii kazach'ikh voisk pri Prezidente RF," *Sobranie zakonodatel'stva,* no. 4 (1996), st. 266.

78. "Ob Upravlenii Administratsii Prezidenta RF po vzaimodeistviiu s politicheskimi partiiami, obshchestvennymi ob"edineniiami, fraktsiiami i deputatami palat Federal'nogo Sobraniia."

79. "Tsentr ukhodit ot diktata," *Rossiiskaia gazeta,* 9 February 1994, p. 1, 2.

80. In March 1996, the Executive Office formed a separate administration to coordinate relations with the president's regional representatives. See "Ob Upravlenii Administratsii Prezidenta RF po koordinatsii deiatel'nosti polnomochnykh predstavitelei Prezidenta RF v sub"ektakh RF," *Sobranie zakonodatel'stva,* no. 12 (1996), st. 1067.

81. In the summer of 1994, the president created a special commission to clarify the division of political labor between Moscow and the subject territories. Little came of this initiative, however. "Ob obrazovanii Komissii pri Prezidente RF po podgotovke dogovorov o razgranichenii predmetov vedeniia i polnomochii mezhdu federal'nymi organami gosudarstvennoi vlasti i organami gosudarstvennoi vlasti sub"ektov RF," *Sobranie zakonodatel'stva,* no. 13 (1994), st. 1475.

82. Vil' Dorofeev, " 'Asimmetriia' ne protivorechit konstitutsii," *Nezavisimaia gazeta,* 17 March 1994, p. 1.

83. "President's Staff Reacts to Coming Cuts," *Kommersant-Daily,* 3 November 1994, p. 2, as translated in *Foreign Broadcast Information Service,* 3 November 1994, p. 18.

84. "Ob Upravlenii Prezidenta RF po rabote s obrashcheniiami grazhdan," *Sobranie zakonodatel'stva,* no. 22 (1995), st. 2031. Despite the rise of regional political power, and the increasing prominence of governors and presidents in the provinces, the Russian population continued to send complaints in large numbers to the center. In a 1998 seminar that brought together staff personnel from the presidency and regional executive bodies, specialists noted that citizens in some regions sent more letters to the presidency in Moscow than to their own regional executive. "Ekskliuziv: Esli vy obratilis' v Kreml'. . . ," *Rossiiskie vesti* online, 27 January 1998.

85. "V tsentre vnimaniia," *Rossiiskie vesti,* 10 February 1994, p. 1.

86. Sergei Filatov, *Na puti k demokratii* (Moscow: Moskovskii rabochii, 1995), p. 340.

87. "O chem pisali grazhdane Rossii Prezidentu RF v 1994 g.," *Rossiiskie vesti,* 24 January 1995, p. 2.

88. *Ibid.*

89. The commission is headed by the writer Anatolii Pristavkin. The members of the commission regularly receive letters harshly critical of their "liberalism" toward criminals. Among the files reviewed are those concerning criminals awaiting execution, some of whom have their sentences commuted to life imprisonment. In a recommendation in early 1996, for example, the commission encouraged the president to spare a young man condemned to death for committing two murders. The mitigating circumstances in the commission's view: the murderer's mother was an alcoholic and his father abused him. "V povestke dnia—16 khodataistv o pomilovanii," *Rossiiskie vesti,* 28 February 1996, p. 1.

Although Russia is obligated by virtue of its entrance into the Council of Europe to abolish the death penalty, political authorities have been reluctant to move quickly on this issue, with public opinion decidedly against the elimination of capital punishment. See "Rassmotreno 106 khodataistv o pomilovanii," *Rossiiskie vesti,* 13 March 1996, p. 2. As of mid-1998, Russia had suspended the use of the death penalty but had not abolished it in law.

90. See Lowell Barrington, "The Domestic and International Consequences of Citizenship in the Soviet Successor States," *Europe-Asia Studies,* no. 4 (1995), pp. 731–764.

91. Sergei Shakhrai, "Chto takoe GPU?" *Izvestia,* 6 February 1992, p. 4.

92. The term is Aleksandr Kotenkov's. Andrei Stepanov, "Andrei Voikov rasskazyvaet 'MK' o pereezde dumy i o sebe," *Moskovskii komsomolets,* 2 March 1994, p. 3.

93. "O Kontrol'nom upravlenii Prezidenta RF," *Sobranie zakonodatel'stva*, no. 5 (1994), st. 402.

94. For reports on the activities of the Monitoring Administration in 1994, see "Korruptsiia—bolezn' gosudartvennaia," *Izvestia*, 15 February 1994, p. 4; "Proverok bydet stol'ko, skol'ko gosudarstvennykh reshenii," *Rossiiskie vesti*, 8 February 1995, p. 2; and "Predstoit' bol'shaia rabota," *Prezidentskii kontrol': informatsionnyi biulleten'*, no. 3 (1995), pp. 3–15. The last source is the official journal of the Monitoring Administration.

95. The head of the protocol service, Vladimir Shevchenko, enjoyed the rank of ambassador. He had been chief of protocol in the Gorbachev administration as well, a rare example of an official who worked under both the Soviet and Russian presidents. "Vladimir Shevchenko: shef protokol'noi sluzhby vsegda pri prezidentakh," *Rossiiskaia gazeta*, 2 September 1994, p. 3. See also "O rukovoditele protokola Prezidenta RF i Upravlenii protokola Prezidenta RF," *Sobranie zakonodatel'stva*, no. 28 (1995), st. 2638.

96. The best introduction to the Russian security services in the first years of the post-Soviet era is to be found in Amy Knight, *Spies Without Cloaks: The KGB's Successors* (Princeton: Princeton University Press, 1996).

97. Andrei Kirillov, "Razgovor po shifru," *Rossiiskaia gazeta*, 2 September 1994, p. 15.

98. Vasilii Kononenko, "Kto u kogo v Rossii 'pod kolpakom,' " *Izvestia*, 26 April 1995, p. 5.

99. Kostikov, *Roman s prezidentom*, p. 11.

100. "Ob utverzhdenii Polozheniia ob Informatsionno-tekhnicheskom tsentre analiticheskikh razrabotok Administratsii Prezidenta RF," *Sobranie zakonodatel'stva*, no. 7 (1994), st. 688.

101. Vera Selivanova, "I na FAPSI est' UIDO," *Segodnia*, 5 May 1995, p. 2. The main concern of this administration seems to have been data storage and copying. See "Ob utverzhdenii Polozheniia ob Upravlenii informatizatsii i dokkumentatsionnogo obespecheniia Administratsii Prezidenta RF," *Sobranie zakonodatel'stva*, no. 4 (1995), st. 283. The new administration did not handle legal databases, however, which had been for some time within the purview of the State-Legal Administration or various structures created by it.

102. Vladimir Berezovskii, "Dva politicheskikh lageria federal'noi elity Rossii," *Svobodnaia mysl'*, no. 9 (1994), p. 82.

103. Vasilii Kononenko, "Kto u kogo v Rossii 'pod kolpakom,' " *Izvestia*, 26 April 1995, p. 5. Its formal powers and responsibilities are set out in "Polozhenie o Glavnom upravlenii okhrany Rossiiskoi Federatsii," *Sobranie zakonodatel'stva*, no. 2 (1996), st. 63.

104. Mikhail Berger, "Denezhnye appetity kremlevskikh spetskhozsluzhb konkuriruiut s voennymi raskhodami," *Izvestia*, 8 February 1995, pp. 1, 4.

105. Ibid.

106. For critical accounts of Yeltsin by his former cook, photographer, and other members of the personal staff, see "Telo mertvogo Prezidenta," *Moskovskii komsomolets*, 20 June 1998, p. 4.

107. "O Glavnom upravlenii okhrany RF," *Sobranie zakonodatel'stva*, no. 31 (1995), st. 3099. Formally, the Security Guard was a part of the Executive Office of the President until early 1996, though it remained outside of the day-to-day supervision (*operativnoe rukovodstvo*) of the leader of the Executive Office. "Ob Administratsii Prezidenta RF," *Sobranie zakonodatel'stva*, no. 31 (1995), st. 3008. In fact, the Secu-

rity Guard was empowered to deal directly with the various divisions of the Executive Office without working through its leadership.

108. Sergei Parkhomenko, "Modern Day Rasputin," *Moscow News*, no. 16 (1995), pp. 1, 6. Perhaps he was influenced in the bed's placement by the president's tennis coach?

109. Irina Savvateeva, "Kto upravliaet stranoi—El'tsin, Chernomyrdin ili general Korzhakov," *Izvestia*, 22 December 1994, p. 1; Otto Latsis, "General Korzhakov upravliaet stranoi kak riadovoi grazhdanin," *Izvestia*, 28 December 1994, p. 2; Aleksei Portanskii, "Pis'mo generala Korzhakova priniato v pravitel'stve k ispolneniiu. . . ," *Izvestia*, 30 December 1994, p. 4. See also Amy Knight's lucid analysis on Korzhakov's role in the Yeltsin presidency in *Spies Without Cloaks: The KGB's Successors*, pp. 225–227. Korzhakov seems to have had a special fear of the power of multinational corporations to unduly influence Russian politics. See the comments contained in his lengthy resignation letter to Yeltsin, in Korzhakov, *Boris El'tsin: ot rassveta do zakata*, p. 459.

110. "Aleksandr Sterligov podderzhivaet generala Korzhakova," *Segodnia*, 2 February 1995, p. 2.

111. "Korzhakov Interviewed on Security Service, Politics," *Argumenty i fakty*, no. 3 (1995), p. 3, as translated in *Foreign Broadcast Information Service*, 19 January 1995, pp. 13–15.

112. Valeryi Vyzhutovich, "The President's Armed Escort," *Moskovskie novosti*, 25 December 1994–1 January 1995, p. 6, as translated in *Current Digest of the Post-Soviet Press*, no. 52 (1994), p. 13.

113. Valerii Vyshutovich, "Tenevye sovetniki Kremlia usilivaiut svoe vliianie," *Izvestia*, 24 January 1995, pp. 1, 2.

114. Latsis, "General Korzhakov upravliaet stranoi kak riadovoi grazhdanin."

115. For a brief history of the institution, see "Iz istorii Soveta Bezopasnosti," National News Service, <www.nns.ru>; "Security Council 'Temporary Structure' Set Up," Interfax, in English, 1634 GMT, 8 June 1992, as translated in *Foreign Broadcast Information Service*, 9 June 1992, p. 36; and Mikhail Lashch, "Security Council Changes Political Appearance," *Kommersant-Daily*, 10 August 1993, p. 3, as translated in *Foreign Broadcast Information Service*, 10 August 1993, pp. 17–18.

116. "Security Council Secretary Lobov Interviewed," *Berlingske Tidende* (Copenhagen), 16 September 1995, p. 8, as translated in *Foreign Broadcast Information Service*, 21 September 1995, p. 35.

117. "The Security Council and the Politburo Have Nothing in Common," *Izvestia*, 16 February 1995, p. 4, as translated in *Foreign Broadcast Information Service*, 17 February 1995, p. 17.

118. Three deputies worked directly under the Security Council secretary: Valerii Manilov (preparation of Security Council meetings), Vladimir Rubanov (information analysis), and Aleksandr Troshin (strategic appraisals and forecasting). Ilya Bulavinov, "Security Council's Restructuring," *Kommersant-Daily*, 17 January 1995, pp. 1, 3, as translated in *Foreign Broadcast Information Service*, 18 January 1995, p. 9.

119. "Security Council Secretary Lobov Interviewed," p. 34.

120. "Security Council Reform Seen Immensely Boosting Its Clout," *Kommersant-Daily*, 17 January 1995, pp. 1, 3, as translated in *Foreign Broadcast Information Service*, 18 January 1995, p. 9.

121. "Yury Skokov: The New Man at the Top," *Kommersant*, 6–13 July 1992, p. 2, as translated in *Current Digest of the Post-Soviet Press*, no. 28 (1992), p. 1; "Boris Yeltsin's Quiet Coup," *Moskovskiye novosti*, 19 July 1992, p. 4, as translated in

Current Digest of the Post-Soviet Press, no. 28 (1992), p. 2; and "Russia Needs Radical Reform and a Strong Government," *Izvestia,* 3 August 1992, p. 3, as translated in *Current Digest of the Post-Soviet Press,* no. 31 (1992), p. 7.

122. "Can the Chechen Wall Be Breached by the Lobov Method?" *Komsomol'skaia pravda,* 26 August 1995, pp. 1–2, as translated in *Foreign Broadcast Information Service,* 30 August 1995, p. 7.

123. For this reason, the Constitutional Conference refused to give the Security Council its own article in the draft constitution, as desired by Yeltsin. Tamara Zamyatina, "To Achieve a Balance Between the Interests of the Power-Wielding Departments and Those of the Civilian Departments," *Rossiiskie vesti,* 7 March 1995, p. 2, as translated in *Current Digest of the Post-Soviet Press,* no. 8 (1995), p. 8.

124. Vladimir Mironov, "U podnozhiia Olimpa: Administratsiia prezidenta RF vchera, segodnia, i zavtra," *Vek,* no. 24 (1994), pp. 1, 3.

125. "Shannon Airport: Yeltsin Sleeps, Soskovets Holds Talks," *Komsomol'skaia pravda,* 17–20 February 1995, p. 5, as translated in *Foreign Broadcast Information Service,* 22 February 1995, p. 19.

126. *Ibid.*

127. "Glavnoe, chtoby Rossiia okonchatel'no sdelala svoi vybor v pol'zu svobody," *Rossiiskie vesti,* 5 June 1996 (spetsial'nyi vypusk "Politicheskaia sreda," p. I). Skokov's party won five single-mandate seats.

128. On this point, see Irina Savvateeva, "Chelovek El'tsina," *Izvestia,* 13 May 1994, p. 5, and Vladimir Berezovskii, "Dva politicheskikh lageria federal'noi elity Rossii," *Svobodnaia mysl',* no. 9 (1994), p. 71. In his official capacity, Lobov reportedly met with Yeltsin at least once a week for thirty to forty minutes to discuss Security Council matters. "Shannon Airport: Yeltsin Sleeps, Soskovets Holds Talks," p. 18.

129. Vyzhutovich, "The President's Armed Escort," p. 13.

130. Appointed in January 1993, Nazarkin lost his post that August.

131. "Iz istorii Soveta Bezopasnosti," National News Service, <www.nns.ru>.

132. Kozyrev had nothing but contempt for presidential structures that meddled in international affairs—"incompetence multiplied by ambition," in his words. Andrei Kozyrev, *Preobrazhenie* (Moscow: Mezhdunarodnye otnosheniia, 1995), p. 301.

133. Andranik Migranyan, "Russia's Foreign Policy: Disastrous Results of Three Years," *Nezavisimaia gazeta,* 10 December 1994, p. 1, as translated in *Current Digest of the Post-Soviet Press,* no. 50 (1994), p. 16. When Skokov lost the premiership to Chernomyrdin, Yeltsin created for him a new commission within the Security Council with responsibilities for foreign affairs, the Interdepartmental Foreign Policy Commission. However, the IFPC never appears to have played a serious role in foreign-policy making. Petr Akopov, "New Security Council Structure Created," *Rossiiskie vesti,* 30 January 1993, p. 2, as translated in *Foreign Broadcast Information Service,* 1 February 1993, p. 25, and Vladimir Orlov, "Yuri Skokov Is Russia's Top Diplomat," *Moskovskie novosti,* 14 February 1993, p. A10, as translated in *Current Digest of the Post-Soviet Press,* no. 9 (1993), p. 25.

134. ITAR-TASS, 1249 GMT, 7 November 1994, as translated in *Foreign Broadcast Information Service,* 8 November 1994, pp. 21–22.

135. See "O neotlozhnykh merakh po realizatsii Federal'noi programmy RF po usileniiu bor'by s prestupnost'iu na 1994–1995 gody," *Sobranie zakonodatel'stva,* no. 5 (1994), st. 403. As regards the copiers, this decree appears never to have been enforced.

136. Boldyrev would later become the deputy head of the Accounting Chamber, the parliamentary equivalent to the presidency's Monitoring Administration. In that

position, he leveled serious charges of wrongdoing against Yeltsin and his associates. Boldyrev also played a leading role in local politics in St. Petersburg.

137. "The Security Council Votes First, Then Discusses," *Komsomol'skaia pravda,* 20 December 1995, p. 3, as translated in *Current Digest of the Post-Soviet Press,* no. 51 (1994), p. 12.

138. "Korzhakov Emerges from the Shadows," *Moskovskie novosti,* 17–24 December 1995, p. 6, as translated in *Current Digest of the Post-Soviet Press,* no. 50 (1995), p. 18.

139. "Ukrepit' bezopasnost' obshchestva i lichnosti," *Rossiiskie vesti,* 21 June 1996, p. 1. Like members of the old party *nomenklatura,* Lobov and Baturin moved immediately into jobs of similar standing, Lobov as first deputy prime minister and Baturin as presidential counselor without portfolio.

140. See, for example, "Who's Closer to the President's Body," *Moskovskii komsomolets,* 30 June 1994, p. 2, as translated in *Foreign Broadcast Information Service,* 1 July 1994, pp. 21–22.

141. The first occupants of these posts were, respectively, Aleksandr M. Yakovlev (Duma) and Valerii Savitskii (Constitutional Court), both respected scholars from the Institute of State and Law. Both left their positions in February 1996, apparently casualties of the purging of cadres associated with the reformist camp of Filatov. "Kadrovye peremeny," *Rossiiskie vesti,* 7 February 1996, p. 1; "Polozhenie o polnomochnykh predstaviteliakh Prezidenta RF v palatakh Federal'nogo Sobraniia RF," *Sobranie zakonodatel'stva,* no. 11 (1996), st. 1034.

142. This assignment for Chubais meant little more than granting a more lofty title for a job he was already doing. As a member of the Government, and more specifically as chair of the Interagency Commission on Cooperation with International Financial Institutions (from 18 December 1997), he had been carrying out these functions. See "Utverzhden sostav Mezhvedomstvennoi komissii," *Segodnia* online, 23 December 1997.

143. Representatives to the Constitutional Court have included Valerii Savitskii, Sergei Shakhrai, and Mikhail Mitiukov.

144. Stenogramma brifinga Press-sekretaria Prezidenta RV, S.V. Iastrzhembskogo, Moskva, Kreml', 2 June 1998, <www.maindir.gov.ru/Administration/Prespage>.

145. Commenting on the departure from the Council of Yegor Gaidar, Otto Latsis, Sergei Alekseev, and Sergei Kovalev, Yeltsin's press secretary claimed that these men had only been "nominal" members for some time, since they had not participated in recent meetings of the Council. "S chem prishli, s tem i ushli," *Rossiiskie vesti,* 25 January 1996, p. 1.

146. "Russia: Arrest of Sports Foundation Head Could Be 'True Scandal,' " Moscow NTV, 1800 GMT, 21 May 1996, as translated in *Foreign Broadcast Information Service,* 22 May 1996, p. 24. This story recounts the arrest of the head of the National Sports Foundation on drug charges. On Tarpishchev's background and his relations with the president, see "Ia s El'tsinym vsegda igraiiu po odnu storonu setki," *Rossiiskie vesti,* 10 February 1996, pp. 8–9.

147. See, for example, the impressive annual report on human rights abuses published by the Commission on Human Rights.

148. Political disagreements among deputies—and between the two legislative chambers—retarded the establishment of an ombudsman. Amid the effort to create an independent ombudsman's office, the presidency retained its Commission on Human Rights. In May 1996, its members included Vladimir Kartashkin (chair), commentator Aleksei Kiva, writer Andrei Nuikin, deputy minister of foreign affairs, Sergei Krylov,

and the defense lawyer Nikolai Monakhov. See "Komissiia po pravam cheloveka: novyi sostav," *Rossiiskie vesti,* 23 May 1996, p. 4.

149. Mironov resigned from the Communist Party shortly after assuming the post. Anton Medvedenko, "Russian Human Rights Ombudsman to Leave Communist Party," ITAR-TASS, 22 May 1998.

150. "O sokrashchenii chislennosti rabotnikov federal'nykh organov ispolnitel'noi vlasti i gosudarstvennykh organov pri Prezidente RF," *Sobranie zakonodatel'stva,* no. 11 (1996), st. 1035.

151. *Sudebnaia palata po informatsionnym sporam pri Prezidente Rossiiskoi Federatsii, 1994–1996* (Moscow: Pravo i zakon, 1997).

152. *Ibid.,* pp. 97–98. The many complaints brought by regional officials who were offended by press criticism revealed the difficulty post-communist leaders had in adjusting to the transparency of a liberal regime. Although the Chamber was never a crude instrument of presidential power, it did at times come to Yeltsin's defense. During the Chechen war, the Judicial Chamber condemned the impediments to press coverage of the war that were erected by the armed forces, but at the same time it reminded journalists of their obligations to mention the efforts of Yeltsin to restore a constitutional order there. "Judicial Chamber Voices Support for Free Press," ITAR-TASS, 26 December 1994, 1355 GMT, as translated in *Foreign Broadcast Information Service,* 27 December 1994, p. 15.

153. Aleksandr Korzhakov, *Boris El'tsin: ot rassveta do zakata,* p. 322.

154. On the role of television in the 1996 Russian presidential election, see Ellen Mickiewicz, *Changing Channels: Television and the Struggle for Power in Russia* (Oxford: Oxford University Press, 1997), p. 167–189. The presidency remained immediately involved in questions of financing and regulating television and radio. See, for example, Stenogramma brifinga Press-secretaria Prezidenta RF, D.D. Iakushkina, Moskva, Kreml', 25 dekabria 1998, <www.maindir.gov.ru/Administration/Prespage>.

155. Nikita Vainonen, "Regional'noi presse otkryt dostup k informatsii o deiatel'nosti vlasti," *Rossiiskie vesti,* 24 April 1996, p. iii (spetsial'nyi vypusk '*Politicheskaia sreda*').

156. See "O chem pishut v Kreml'," *Rossiiskie vesti,* 5 March 1996, p. 1.

157. According to Yurii Boldyrev, in exchange for campaign contributions, "Yeltsin authorized the transfer of a 33 percent stake in [the natural gas monopoly] Gazprom from the government to the company's chairman for management under proxy. . . ." "Big Companies Accused of Funding Yeltsin," *Moscow Times,* 22 December 1998, as printed in Johnson's List, no. 2529, 21 [sic] December 1998.

158. Although the appointment of Yegorov was made official on January 15, 1996, he had been serving for several weeks as the de facto head of the Executive Office. According to one report, while Filatov was on vacation in the fall of 1995, the president took away his security detail, his dacha, and his office on Old Square. Yegorov moved into this office while Filatov was away, and well before the issuing of the decrees formalizing the personnel changes in January 1996. "S. Filatova vytesniaiut," *Argumenty i fakty,* no. 37 (1995), p. 2.

159. For a full list of the offices within each of the main administrations, see "Voprosy Administratsii Prezidenta RF," *Sobranie zakonodatel'stva,* no. 6 (1996), st. 532.

160. The official organizational chart of the presidency also made public for the first time the existence of a Main Administration for Special Presidential Programs, which answered directly to Yeltsin. This bureau had responsibility for mobilizing the bureaucracy for war and apparently managing the special facilities constructed for nuclear war. Among its 250 staff were 20 officials seconded to the center from mili-

tary and law enforcement personnel organizations. "Voprosy Glavnogo upravleniia spetsial'nykh programm Prezidenta RF," *Sobranie zakonodatel'stva*, no. 11 (1996), st. 1033.

161. Nikita Vainonen, "Useknovenie smysla," *Rossiiskie vesti*, 19 January 1996, p. 1.

162. "Ukaz Prezidenta RF o Chubaise, A.B.," *Rossiiskie vesti*, 18 January 1996, p. 1.

163. The best single work on the presidential election of 1996 is the official report of the Central Election Commission, *Vybory Prezidenta Rossiiskoi Federatsii* (Moscow: Ves' mir, 1996), which contains district-level voting results, electoral analysis, and overviews of the campaigns waged by the candidates. My thanks to Aleksandr Fetisov and Bruce Bradford for providing me a copy of this book.

164. These dismissals followed immediately after a bizarre late-night detention of Yeltsin campaign aides by Korzhakov's Kremlin guard, an incident that Anatolii Chubais sought to portray as a dangerous bid for power by Korzhakov. "Intsident s korobkoi valiuty," *Rossiiskie vesti*, 21 June 1996, pp. 1–2. The aides were removing hundreds of thousands of dollars in cash contributed to the presidential election campaign, reportedly for official purposes. On the dramatic days surrounding the presidential elections, see David Remnick, "The War for the Kremlin," *The New Yorker*, 22 July 1996, pp. 40–57.

165. Less than a week after assuming his post, Lebed launched an assault on organized crime in the Moscow region. "We'll see," he boasted, "who will defeat whom [*posmotrim, kto kogo*]." Feliks Babitskii, "U novoi idei est' budushchee," *Rossiiskie vesti*, 28 June 1996, p. 1.

166. Michael Specter, "Yeltsin's New Kremlin," *New York Times*, 18 July 1996, p. A1.

167. "Ob utverzhdenii Polozheniia ob Administratsii Prezidenta RF," *Sobranie zakonodatel'stva*, no. 41 (1996), st. 4689. The dismantling of the Yegorov apparatus was authorized by the following decree: "O merakh po sovershenstvovaniiu struktury Administratsii Prezidenta RF," *Rossiiskie vesti*, 27 July 1996, p. 3.

168. "Filatov Comments on Chubais, Korzhakov," *Kuranty*, 4 February 1997, as translated in *Foreign Broadcast Information Service* online, 4 February 1997.

169. See Pavel Chinkarenko, "Chetvertaia perestroika Administratsii Prezidenta RF," *Rossiiskie vesti*, 18 September 1996, pp. 1, 3.

170. See "Na staroi ploshchadi—novoe popolnenie: pervyi chekist-demokrat budet kurirovat' kadry. . . ," *Rossiiskie vesti*, 6 August 1996, p. 1.

171. Aleksandr Kinsbursky, "100 Leading Russian Politicians in July," *Nezavisimaia gazeta*, 1 August 1997, p. 1, as translated in *Russian Press Digest*, 1 August 1997. Just over a year later, it should be noted, Yumashev had risen to number four in this poll, which placed Yeltsin behind the new prime minister, Primakov, as the country's most influential politician, a reflection of Yeltsin's fading health and political engagement and Primakov's experience and authority with the Duma. Aleksandr Kinsbursky, "100 Leading Politicians of Russia in September," *Nezavisimaia gazeta*, 14 October 1998, p. 11, as translated in *Russian Press Digest*, 14 October 1998.

172. For a brief biography of Yumashev, see Veronika Kutsyllo, "Yumashev Is Certainly No Chubais," *Kommersant-Daily*, 12 March 1997, p. 1, as translated in *Current Digest of the Post-Soviet Press*, no. 10 (1997), p. 8.

173. For a sketch of Berezovskii, who worked for a time in the Security Council and in the committee for overseeing Russia's relations with the Commonwealth for Independent States, see Alessandra Stanley, "A Russian's Rise from Car Dealer to Tycoon," *New York Times*, 14 June 1997, p. 3. Berezovskii reportedly had at various times close relations with presidential officials such as Georgii Satarov, Tatiana

Diachenko, Anatolii Chubais, and Valentin Yumashev, and served as a freelance advisor for the latter in 1998. Stenogramma brifinga press-sekretaria Prezidenta RF S.V. Iastrzhembskogo, Moskva, Kreml', 23 marta 1998, <www.maindir.gov.ru/Administration/Prespage>.

174. Yumashev lives in Yeltsin's apartment building on Osennaia Street, and his sixteen-year-old daughter is reported to be attending the same British public school as Yeltsin's grandson. Olga Gerasimenko and Vasily Ustyuzhanin, "Komsomol'skaia Pravda's Ex-Probationer Appointed Chubais," Komsomol'skaia pravda, 12 March 1997, p. 1, as translated in Russian Press Digest, 12 March 1997.

175. One other presidential staff member apparently "made" by Diachenko was Viktoria Mitina, a local government official from a Moscow suburb who was promoted to the post of deputy leader of the Executive Office of the President in late 1997. Mitina noted that she has "been on good terms with Tatiana. One can say that we are sisters, or rather, that Tatiana is my niece." Maksim Zhukov, "Viktoria Mitina: 'I Have Always Been Close to the Powers that Be,' " Kommersant-Daily, 25 November 1997, p. 2, as translated in Russian Press Digest, 25 November 1997. Another reported friend of Diachenko who joined the presidency during the second term was Denis Molchanov, a public relations specialist. Natalya Timakova, "The President's Molchanov," Kommersant-Daily, 9 April 1998, p. 3, as translated in Current Digest of the Post-Soviet Press, no. 14 (1998), p. 15.

176. Kutsyllo, "Yumashev is Certainly no Chubais," p. 8.

177. While citing a figure of 200 persons removed from the presidency, Denis Babichenko points to inconsistent information emanating from the presidency on the size of its bureaucracy. Whereas the presidency claimed that it had a staff of 1,700 persons in 1997, the figure for 1998—after the cutbacks—was 1,945. Denis Babichenko, "V Kremle igraiut 'Bol'shoi perepolokh,' " Segodnia online, 16 February 1998. It is likely that the earlier figure included only the Executive Office and the latter additional structures such as the Security Council.

178. Denis Babichenko, " 'Kremlevskii organizm' ochishchaetsia," Segodnia online, 26 May 1998.

179. In the event, Yegorov chose to return to his home region of Krasnodar. He was by that time "convinced that a minister or even a deputy prime minister can do very little." "Nikolai Egorov: The Country Urgently Needs a Functioning President," Komsomol'skaia pravda, 22 October 1996, p. 3, as translated in Current Digest of the Post-Soviet Press, no. 44 (1996), p. 14. For his part, Yurii Baturin left the Kremlin to join the Russian space program and travel to the space station MIR in 1998.

180. See Tat'iana Sadkovskaia, "Kadry: Novaia apparatnaia logika Staroi Ploshchadi," Rossiiskie vesti online, 14 February 1998; and Denis Babichenko, "Kazhdyi sed'moi 'administrator' mozhet pokinut' Kreml'," Segodnia online, 4 December 1997.

181. For a list of the offices in the presidency, the best source is the full Spisok telefonov rabotnikov Administratsii Prezidenta Rossiiskoi Federatsii, published periodically in Moscow for internal use only. The author is in possession of the full list for April 1997 as well as a May 1998 abbreviated list.

182. Veronika Kutsyllo, "Komissar on the President's Staff," Kommersant-Daily, 15 August 1997, p. 1, as translated in Russian Press Digest, 15 August 1997.

183. Kostikov, Roman s prezidentom, p. 155.

184. Pavel Felgengauer, "A 'Hero of Our Time' Becomes Secretary of the Security Council," Segodnia, as translated in Current Digest of the Post-Soviet Press, no. 9 (1998), p. 5. Kokoshin was apparently a protege of Yurii Baturin who was placed in the Ministry of Defense to reform it but who became mired in its bureaucracy.

185. Ibid. More generally, see "Sovet bezopasnosti: ot Skokova do Kokoshina," *Rossiiskie vesti* online, 4 March 1998. For an organizational chart of the Security Council, see *Sobranie zakonodatel'stva,* no. 31 (1997), st. 3673. Although the presidency did not actively seek in this period to interpose itself between Yeltsin and the security wing of the Government, it did attempt under Kokoshin to eliminate a weaker parallel agency in the Government, though without success. The presidency also served as a training ground for at least one head of a power ministry. In July 1998, forty-five-year-old Vladimir Putin, who led the Monitoring Administration and served briefly as first deputy leader of the Executive Office under Yumashev, was appointed head of the Federal Security Service, the successor to the KGB. A longtime KGB operative who was recruited into the secret service during his last year of law school in Leningrad, Putin had worked for several years in the office of the St. Petersburg mayor, Anatolii Sobchak, before being invited to the presidency by Pavel Borodin. An instructive interview with Putin, conducted shortly after his appointment to the FSB, may be found in "First Interview with Federal Security Director Vladimir Putin," Official Kremlin International News Broadcast Online, 30 July 1998 (Federal Information Systems Corporation). In this transcript, Putin argued that in the Soviet era, the presence of KGB personnel in every organization "was justified at the time because it contributed to stability." He goes to say that "now there is no need for it." He also distinguishes sharply here between the polished and intellectual recruits to the KGB, and its successors, and the rougher and less well-educated beat cops in the MVD. This difference in backgrounds, he argues, would make a merger of the institutions extremely difficult.

186. Margelov lost his post in the presidency in April 1998, reportedly because of his tendency to provide information to journalists. He was known in media circles as the "leak man." "Nedelia v reitingakh 'RV': Samaia razreklamirovannaia otstavka," *Rossiiskie vesti* online, 8 April 1998.

187. Yelena Dikun, "Not Everything in the Kremlin Is Divided Among Three Persons," *Obshchaia gazeta,* 18 June 1998, p. 7, as translated in *Russian Press Digest,* 18 June 1998. Yastrzhembsky had sufficient standing in foreign affairs to meet individually with visiting dignitaries.

188. Detailed analysis of the reasons for this move must await a fuller historical record, but it appears that Yeltsin acted in part out of anger at comments made by his closest subordinates about the president's distancing himself from everyday governance of the country. On the surprisingly frank comments made by presidential officials about their boss's health and goals in the fall of 1998, see John Thornhill, "Russia: Yeltsin Gives Up Day-to-day Control," *Financial Times,* 29 October 1998, and *Izvestia,* 27 October 1998, in *BBC Summary of World Broadcasts,* 28 October 1998.

189. As early as June 1998, Yeltsin had made several appointments in the security sector of the presidency that were designed to "flex the muscles" of the organization, that according to the presidential press secretary. Stenogramma brifinga press-sekretaria Prezidenta RF S.V. Iastrzhembskogo, Moskva, Kreml', 2 iiunia 1998, <www.maindir.gov.ru/Administration/Prespage>.

190. Stenogramma brifinga Press-sekretaria Prezidenta RV, D.D. Iakushkina, Moskva, Kreml', 7 dekiabria 1998, <www.maindir.gov.ru/Administration/Prespage>.

Notes to Chapter 4

1. We would do well, however, to recall the anxiety that seized the French political elite in the months before the fateful parliamentary elections in 1986. The French

press was filled with widely divergent articles about how to manage cohabitation. Thus, a consensus had to be forged; it did not exist before the fact.

2. Ezra N. Suleiman, "Presidentialism and Political Stability in France," in Juan J. Linz and Arturo Valenzuela (eds.), *The Failure of Presidential Democracy: Comparative Perspectives*, vol. 1 (Baltimore: The Johns Hopkins University Press, 1994), p. 151.

3. See Chapter 2.

4. See article 31 of "Zakon o pravitel'stve," *Sobranie zakonodatel'stva*, no. 51 (1997), st. 5712.

5. "Press Conference with Representatives of Our Home Is Russia Faction," Official Kremlin International News Broadcast, 6 May 1998.

6. Irina Savvateeva, "Zakrytyi Sovmin: Vse tainoe stanovitsia iavnym," *Izvestia*, 7 May 1994, p. 2.

7. "Yeltsin's, Chernomyrdin's Roles in Budennovsk Crisis Assessed," *Moskovskii komsomolets*, 20 June 1995, pp. 1, 3, as translated in *Foreign Broadcast Information Service*, 6 July 1995 [supplement], p. 15. Yeltsin's inaction in the Budennovsk crisis was but the latest example of a Russian leader attempting to remain above the crush of events and human suffering, whether Tsar Nicholas II on Bloody Sunday, Mikhail Gorbachev during the Chernobyl tragedy, or Yeltsin himself following a devastating earthquake on Sakhalin Island. Americans have quite different expectations of their president during times of crisis, but then he is both head of state and head of government. Russian leaders have a prime minister to run interference for them at moments of tragedy.

8. "S kem Prezident khodit v baniu?" *Komsomol'skaia pravda*, 24 February 1994, p. 3.

9. Russians themselves are not altogether consistent in their use of the term *Government (pravitel'stvo)*. In the narrowest sense, it includes the prime minister, deputy ministers, and the highest-ranking ministers, in 1998 approximately twenty of the sixty-odd heads of ministries and state committees. But it is also used more inclusively to cover all of the "federal organs of executive power," a term embracing ministries, state committees, and agencies.

10. For a brief survey of the Government in Russian and Soviet history, see M.N. Korchagova and L.M. Lysenko, "Pravitel'stvo Rossii (istoricheskii ocherk)," in Lysenko, *Vlast': Pravitel'stvo Rossii* (Moscow: Institut sovremennoi politiki, 1997), pp. 19–46. This publication, funded by a number of prominent financial-industrial groups, also contains excellent short biographies of Government members in 1997 as well as an appendix listing all ministers since 1802.

11. "Zakon o pravitel'stve," *Sobranie zakonodatel'stva*, no. 51 (1997), st. 5712.

12. Irina Savvateeva, "V dome Pravitel'stva Pravitel'stvu tesno," *Izvestia*, 5 October 1994, p. 4.

13. "O preobrazovanii i reorganizatsii Soveta ministrov-Pravitel'stva Rossiiskoi federatsii," (no. 2277 ot 23 dekabria 1993), reprinted in *Pravitel'stvo Rossii* (Moscow: Informatsionno-ekspertnaia gruppa Panorama, July 1995), p. 183. This booklet provides a detailed breakdown of the subdivisions of the Russian Government. On the merger of ministries, see "O strukture federal'nykh organov ispolnitel'noi vlasti," *Sobranie zakonodatel'stva*, no. 34 (1996), st. 4082.

14. "Shatalin Claims Bureaucracy Hampers Reform," *Izvestia*, 29 April 1992, p. 3, as translated in *Foreign Broadcast Information Service*, 30 April 1992, p. 33.

15. "O sisteme federal'nykh organov ispolnitel'noi vlasti," *Sobranie zakonodatel'stva*, no. 34 (1996), st. 4081.

16. Stenogramma brifinga press-sekretaria Prezidenta RF, S.V. Iastrzhembskogo, Moskva, Kreml', 19 marta 1998, <www.maindir.gov.ru/Administration/Prespage>.

17. The term is Peter Stavrakis's. See his "State-Building in Post-Soviet Russia: The Chicago Boys and the Decline of Administrative Capacity," Occasional Papers no. 254, Kennan Institute for Advanced Russian Studies, Washington, DC, October 1993, p. 18.

18. One should note that there were at times serious political conflicts within ministries as well as between ministries.

19. "Okopnaia voina v apparate: kto komu roem iamu?" *Segodnia* online, 5 April 1997. In April 1998, Sergei Kirienko may have had a somewhat freer hand in selecting his team. He noted that while he was "absolutely free to propose candidates," the president insisted on personally selecting the nominee from among several alternative candidates for each ministerial post. "Sergei Kirienko: 'Ia lichno nikomu, krome prezidenta, nichem ne obiazan,' " *Nezavisimaia gazeta* online, 24 April 1998.

20. Private correspondence with the author.

21. "Pravitel'stvo vyigralo bitvu za kurs reform," *Rossiiskie vesti,* 29 October 1994, p. 1.

22. "Shatalin Claims Bureaucracy Hampers Reform," *Izvestia,* 29 April 1992, p. 3, as translated in *Foreign Broadcast Information Service,* 30 April 1992, p. 35.

23. During many years of research on the Russian executive, I have never encountered any detailed references to the operation of the Government presidium.

24. "Sovmin Rossii: chto sdelano?" *Rossiiskie vesti,* 29 April 1993, p. 2; "Tsifry i fakty," *Rossiiskie vesti,* 3 April 1993, p. 1. In his autobiography *The Struggle for Russia* (Moscow: Random House, 1994), p. 168, Yeltsin reports that in 1992 he met with the ministers every Thursday, presumably during the session of the presidium. This intense involvement does not seem to have continued for long, however.

25. Irina Savvateeva, "Zasedanie pravitel'stva: muzhskoi razgovor na intimnye temy," *Izvestia,* 6 May 1994, p. 2.

26. See Peter H. Solomon Jr., *Soviet Criminal Justice Under Stalin* (Cambridge University Press, 1997), p. 402, for a discussion of the blame culture in the Stalin era.

27. One might have added here, of course, "and members of the United States Congress."

28. *Izvestia,* 30 April 1994, p. 2. For a humorous account of a reprimand issued to Sergei Dubinin, the finance minister, by Yeltsin, see Rustam Arifdzhanov, "Proshy Prezidenta ob"iavit' vygovor moei zhene," *Izvestia,* 26 May 1994, p. 4.

29. Natalia Gurushina, "Chernomyrdin Slams Livshits, Yasin," *OMRI Daily Digest,* 24 January 1997. Following this episode, one observer noted that "according to the Russian administrative tradition, the prime minister had resorted to the knout for do-nothing [*bezdeiatel'nykh*] subordinates." Elmar Murtazaev, "Viktor Chernomyrdin kak khranitel' liberal'nykh tsennostei," *Segodnia* online, 27 January 1997.

30. *Kommersant-Daily,* 13 October 1994, pp. 1, 3, as translated in *Foreign Broadcast Information Service,* 14 October 1994, p. 13.

31. David Remnick, "The First and the Last," *The New Yorker,* 18 November 1996, p. 122.

32. Under Chernomyrdin, the head of the prime minister's personal secretariat was Gennadii Petelin, a man of considerable influence.

33. "U vitse-prem'erov teper' budet poriadok zameshchanie," *Rossiiskie vesti,* 9 December 1994, p. 1.

34. "Discusses Budget Issues, Reform," NTV, 1800 GMT, 13 November 1994, as translated in *Foreign Broadcast Information Service,* 14 November 1994, p. 22.

35. Mikhail Leont'ev, "Neiarkii kabinet," *Segodnia,* 16 August 1996, p. 1.

36. Fred Hiatt, "Yeltsin's New Cabinet: Reformers In—and Out—and Ideology Unclear," *Washington Post,* 20 November 1994, p. A37.

37. The head of the Government Secretariat did not retain that lofty post, however, under Prime Minister Sergei Kirienko.

38. "Gosapparat zhdet mini-reformu," *Rossiiskie vesti,* 21 December 1994, p. 2. The formal training of these officials was impressive, with 115 possessing advanced degrees. Aleksandr Bekker, "Boris El'tsin vyvel ez stroia motor prem'era," *Segodnia,* 15 November 1994, p. 2.

39. "Reglament zasedanii Soveta ministerstv i Pravitel'stva Rossiiskoi Federatsii i ego Prezidiuma," *Vlast': Pravitel'stvo Rossii,* p. 178, art. 2.

40. Aleksandr Bekker, "Boris El'tsin vyvel ez stroia motor prem'era," *Segodnia,* 15 November 1994, p. 2. Under Yegor Gaidar, the post was held by Alexei Golovkov.

41. Irina Savvateeva, "Komanda Chernomyrdina v politicheskom inter'ere," *Izvestia,* 14 April 1994, p. 4.

42. Babichev began his career as a foreman in Kalmykia. After a period in soviet work in the republican capital, Elista, he moved to the republic's party apparatus as second secretary. Following training in Moscow at the party's Academy for Social Sciences, he spent six years as head of the regional party organization in Astrakhan, where he became acquainted with "all the present and future members of the gas complex." From Astrakhan, he moved in 1986 to Moscow to work in the apparatus of the Communist Party Central Committee. At the very end of the Soviet era, he was assigned the task of turning the Communist Party into an effective parliamentary party. "Gosapparat zhdet mini-reforma, a chinovnikov—sokrashchenie," *Rossiiskie vesti,* 21 December 1994, pp. 1–2.

43. *Ibid.*

44. Irina Savvateeva, "Zakrytyi Sovmin: vse tainoe stanovitsia iavnym," *Izvestia,* 7 May 1994, p. 2.

45. Aleksandr Bekker, "Chubais' Third Attempt to Gain Control of the Apparatus," *Segodnia,* 22 April 1997, pp. 1, 6, as translated in *Current Digest of the Post-Soviet Press,* no. 17 (1997), p. 10.

46. *Ibid.*

47. "Gosapparat zhdet mini-reforma, a chinovnikov—sokrashchenie."

48. "O pervoocherednikh merakh po realizatsii federal'nogo zakona `Ob organakh federal'noi sluzhby besopasnosti v Rossiiskoi Federatsii,' " *Sobranie zakonodatel'stva,* no. 26 (1995), st. 2453.

49. "Number of Civil Servants Increasing," *OMRI Daily Digest—Russia,* 4 March 1996. For figures comparing the size of the federal, regional, and local executive bureaucracies in 1991 and 1993, see "Ob izmenenii chislennosti rabotnikov apparata organov gosudarstvennoi vlasti i upravleniia v RF," *Rossiiskie vesti,* 31 March 1994, p. 1. In some areas, the size of the regional bureaucracy was staggering. Thirty-six thousand federal and regional bureaucrats worked in Kalmykia, a southern republic with only 350,000 persons. Tat'iana Sadkovskaia, "Upravlencheskaia revoliutsiia nachalas'?" *Rossiiskie vesti* online, 26 February 1998.

50. "Shatalin Claims Bureaucracy Hampers Reform," *Izvestia,* 29 April 1992, p. 3, as translated in *Foreign Broadcast Information Service,* 30 April 1992, p. 34.

51. Liudmila Biriukova, "Kogda gosapparat razbukhaet, tuda vnedriaetsia massa neprofessionalov," *Rossiiskie vesti,* 20 January 1995, p. 3.

52. A presidential decree of 1996 that listed the federal organs of state power specified those that were subordinate directly to the president. Besides the ministries

of defense, internal affairs, and foreign affairs, they included the federal services for archives, border troops, security, foreign intelligence, railway police, radio and television, and Kremlin security, the Federal Agency for Government Communications and Information (FAPSI), and the Federal Inspectorate for Nuclear and Radiation Security. "O strukture federal'nykh organov ispolnitel'noi vlasti," *Sobranie zakonodatel'stva,* no. 34 (1996), st. 4082.

53. Viktor Mal'nev, "Apparat upravleniia: ot kolichestvu k kachestvu," *Rossiiskaia federatsiia,* no. 5 (1995), pp. 7–8.

54. "Raspredelenie assignovanii iz federal'nogo biudzheta na 1994 god po ministerstvam, vedomstvam i organizatsiiam RF," *Rossiiskie vesti,* 6 July 1994, p. 6.

55. Stephen Fortescue, "The Industry Policy Institutions of the Russian Government," paper presented to the Fifth World Congress of Central and East European Studies, Warsaw, 6–11 August 1995, p. 8. Peter Rutland argues that "the creation of specialized bureaucracies was a way of avoiding the problems caused by the lack of an efficient and corruption-free civil service and legal system." Peter Rutland, "Privatization in East Europe: Another Case of Words that Succeed and Policies that Fail," paper presented to the Fifth World Congress of Central and East European Studies, Warsaw, 6–11 August 1995, p. 16.

56. See A.G. Barabashev, "Formirovanie sistemy ispolnitel'noi vlasti RF (1989–1991)," *Konstitutsionnyi stroi Rossii,* vypusk 1 (Moscow, 1992), p. 86.

57. Personal interview with Irina Savvateeva, *Izvestia* correspondent, 27 September 1995, Moscow.

58. "U vitse-prem'erov teper' budet poriadok zameshchanie," *Rossiiskie vesti,* 9 December 1994, p. 1.

59. See, for example, Aleksandr Bekker, "The Cabinet's Future and Financial Stabilization Are Discussed at Volynskoe," *Segodnia,* 13 July 1996, as translated in *Current Digest of the Post-Soviet Press,* 21 August 1996, pp. 1–2.

60. "Yeltsin Addresses Academy of Civil Service," Russian public television, 1740 GMT, 6 September 1995, as translated in *Foreign Broadcast Information Service,* 7 September 1995, p. 28. On recent changes in Russian public administration, see Eugene Huskey and Sergei Porshakov, "The Russian Civil Service in Transition, 1985–1998," *Jahrbuch für europäische Verwaltungsgeschichte,* vol. 10 (1998), pp. 205–220.

61. *Ibid.*

62. "Yeltsin Attacks Civil Servants, Urges Reforms," ITAR-TASS in English, 1214 GMT, 6 September 1995, as translated in *Foreign Broadcast Information Service,* 6 September 1995, p. 19.

63. Sergei Filatov, "Kto pridet zavtra v organy vlasti," *Rossiiskie vesti,* 13 September 1994, pp. 1–2.

64. "Yeltsin Attacks Civil Servants, Urges Reforms."

65. "Yeltsin Addresses Academy of Civil Service," Russian public television, 1740 GMT, 6 September 1995, as translated in *Foreign Broadcast Information Service,* 7 September 1995, p. 28.

66. Writing in the semiofficial paper of the Russian presidency, Pavel Anokhin complained that deputies sought to make the country's civil service dependent on the parliament. "Chinovnikov teper' budut ne tol'ko sokrashchat', no i uchit'," *Rossiiskie vesti,* 2 September 1994, p. 1. For differences in the Government and parliamentary drafts of the civil service law, see "Parliament, Government on Civil Service Law," Interfax, 1246 GMT, 2 September 1992, as translated in *Foreign Broadcast Information Service,* 3 September 1992, p. 22. See also Sergey Vedeneyev, "To

Whom Is the Public Servant Subject?" *Nezavisimaia gazeta,* 5 January 1994, p. 1, as translated in *Foreign Broadcast Information Service,* 9 February 1994, pp. 4–5.

67. "Polozhenie o federal'noi gosudarstvennoi sluzhbe," *Rossiiskie vesti,* 19 January 1994, p. 6.

68. Indeed, until the issuance of a decree on a bureaucratic register (*reestr*) in early 1995, no one could say legally who was a civil servant. Pavel Anokhin, "Chinovnikov vystroiiat po ranzhiru," *Rossiiskie vesti,* 1 February 1995, p. 2.

69. Sergei Chugaev, "Rossiiskoe pravitel'stvo prishlo v dvizhenie," *Izvestia,* 5 January 1994, p. 1.

70. Even as early as the mid-1980s, some Soviet legal scholars were advancing proposals for a broad-based reform of the civil service. See Viktor Mal'nev, "Apparat upravleniia: ot kolichestvu k kachestvu," *Rossiiskaia federatsiia,* no. 5 (1995), p. 7.

71. Sergei Filatov, *Na puti k demokratii* (Moscow: Moskovskii rabochii, 1995), p. 305.

72. Vil' Dorofeev, "Gosudarstvennye sluzhashchie—osnova stabil'nosti strany," *Nezavisimaia gazeta,* 30 June 1994, p. 1–2.

73. "O Rossiiskoi akademii gosudarstvennoi sluzhbe pri Prezidente RF," *Sobranie zakonodatel'stva,* no. 7 (1994), st. 685.

74. "Voprosy Rossiiskoi akademii gosudarstvennoi sluzhby pri Prezidente RF," *Sobranie zakonodatel'stva,* no. 18 (1995), st. 1646.

75. New texts used in civil service training by the late 1990s included E.V. Okhotskii (ed.), *Sluzhebnaia karera* (Moscow: Ekonomika, 1998); A.I. Turchinov, *Professionalizatsiia i kadrovaia politika* (Moscow: Flinta, 1998); and E.V. Okhotskii, *Upravlenie personalom gosudarstvennoi sluzhby* (Moscow: RAGS, 1997).

76. "Yeltsin Addresses Academy of Civil Service," Russian public television, 1740 GMT, 6 September 1995, as translated in *Foreign Broadcast Information Service,* 7 September 1995, p. 28.

77. See *Sobranie zakonodatel'stva,* no. 3 (1995), st. 174.

78. See the commentary by the leader of the Government Secretariat in "Kvasov Interviewed on Civil Service Edict," *Rossiiskaia gazeta,* 30 December 1993, pp. 1–2, as translated in *Foreign Broadcast Information Service,* 3 January 1994, p. 23–24.

79. "O perechniakh gosudarstvennykh dolzhnostei federal'noi gosudarstvennoi sluzhby kategorii 'B' i 'V' v Administratsii Prezidenta RF i apparate Soveta Bezopasnosti RF," *Sobranie zakonodatel'stva,* no. 16 (1996), st. 1833.

80. "Polozhenie o federal'noi gosudarstvennoi sluzhbe," *Rossiiskie vesti,* 19 January 1994, p. 6.

81. *Ibid.*

82. See Anders Aslund, "Reform vs. 'Rent-Seeking' in Russia's Economic Transformation," *Transition,* 26 January 1996, pp. 12–16. It should also be noted that bureaucrats receive other advantages not available to the public, including preferential housing placement and, in some instances, preferential loans. In Bashkortostan, the speaker of the republic's parliament issued an edict granting low-interest long-term loans to all civil servants—a windfall given the high rates of inflation. "Kvasov Interviewed on Civil Service Edict," *Rossiiskaia gazeta,* 30 December 1993, pp. 1–2, as translated in *Foreign Broadcast Information Service,* 3 January 1994, p. 24.

83. See the "Polozhenie o Glavnom upravlenii Prezidenta RF po voprosam gosudarstvennoi sluzhby i kadrov," *Sobranie zakonodatel'stva,* no. 11 (1996), st. 1032.

84. "Novaia nomenklatura ili novaia kadrovaia politika?" *Rossiiskie vesti,* 23 September 1994, p. 1, and "O vnesenii izmenenii v Ukaz Prezidenta RF ot 1 dekabria

1995g. No. 1208 'O Sovete po voprosam gosudarstvennoi sluzhby pri Prezidente RF,' " *Sobranie zakonodatel'stva,* no. 7 (1996), st. 669.

85. An example of this is the recertification—or "attestation"—of existing civil servants. For the rules on these procedures, developed in the presidency, see "Ob utverzhdenii Polozheniia o provedenii attestatsii federal'nogo gosudarstvennogo sluzhashchego," *Sobranie zakonodatel'stva,* no. 11 (1996), st. 1036. For the twenty-point program to improve the civil service, see Yeltsin's decree of 6 September 1996, "O pervoocherednykh merakh po uluchsheniiu raboty s kadrami v sisteme gosudarstvennoi sluzhbe i realizatsii Federal'nogo zakona 'Ob osnovakh gosudarstvennoi sluzhby RF,' " *Sobranie zakonodatel'stva,* no. 37 (1996), st. 3588.

86. Ernst Chernyi, "Chinovnik mozhet s'est' Rossiiu," *Kuranty,* 3 August 1994, p. 4.

87. Viktor Mal'nev, "Apparat upravleniia: ot kolichestvu k kachestvu," *Rossiiskaia federatsiia,* no. 5 (1995), pp. 7–8.

88. Rod Hague and Martin Harrop, *Comparative Government and Politics: An Introduction* (London: Macmillan, 1987), p. 241.

89. *Ibid.*

90. Ferrel Heady, *Public Administration: A Comparative Perspective* (Englewood Cliffs, NJ: Prentice Hall, 1966), p. 42.

91. On bureaucracies in new states, see Fred W. Riggs, *Administration in Developing Countries: The Theory of Prismatic Society* (Boston: Houghton Mifflin, 1964).

92. "Kogda pravitel'stvo pravit," *Rossiiskie vesti,* 19 September 1993, p. 3.

93. F. Burlatskii, "Vozrodit' pravitel'stvo Rossii," *Nezavisimaia gazeta,* 12 February 1993, p. 2.

94. Samuel Huntington, *Political Order in Changing Societies* (New Haven: Yale University Press, 1968), p. 1.

95. Mikhail Berger, "The Government Could Change Beyond Recognition," *Izvestia,* 23 July 1996, p. 1, as translated in *Current Digest of the Post-Soviet Press,* no. 30 (1996), pp. 2–3.

96. *Ibid.;* Leonid Brodsky and Irina Savvateyeva, "Sound Conservatism Will Always be in Fashion," *Kommersant-Daily,* as translated in *Current Digest of the Post-Soviet Press,* no. 30 (1996), pp. 3–4.

97. For more on the Kirienko Government, see Chapter 8.

98. Fred W. Riggs, "Bureaucrats and Political Development: A Paradoxical View," in Joseph LaPalombara (ed.), *Bureaucracy and Political Development* (Princeton: Princeton University Press, 1963), p. 129.

99. *Ibid.,* p. 120.

Chapter 5: The Politics of the Dual Executive

1. Andrei Kozyrev, *Preobrazhenie* (Moscow: Mezhdunarodnye otnosheniia, 1995), p. 302.

2. Andrei Kozyrev, "Diplomatiia i gosudarstvo," *Segodnia,* 17 January 1995, p. 10.

3. The classic American examples of strong national security advisors undermining the authority of the secretaries of state are Henry Kissinger in Nixon's first term and Zbigniew Brzezinski in the Carter presidency. A revealing account of Kissinger's manuevers to weaken Secretary of State William Rodgers may be found in Anatolii Dobrynin, *In Confidence: Moscow's Ambassador to America's Six Cold War Presidents* (New York: Random House, 1995), especially pp. 204–206.

4. Stephen Foye, "A Hardened Stance on Foreign Policy," *Transition,* 9 June 1996,

p. 36, quoting *Nezavisimaia gazeta*, 10 December 1994, as translated in *Current Digest of the Post-Soviet Press*, no. 50 (1994).

5. Scott Parrish, "Chaos in Foreign-Policy Decision-Making," *Transition*, 17 May 1996, p. 32.

6. See Pavel Felgengauer, "Appointment: Igor Rodionov Becomes Minister of Defense," *Segodnia*, 18 July 1996, p. 1, as translated in *Current Digest of the Post-Soviet Press*, no. 29 (1996), pp. 1–2.

7. Leonid Brodsky, "Lebed Loses Weight," *Kommersant-Daily*, 4 October 1996, p. 3, as translated in *Current Digest of the Post-Soviet Press*, no. 40 (1996), p. 1.

8. Doug Clarke, "Tension Reported Between Lebed, Rodionov," *OMRI Daily Digest*, 15 August 1996.

9. For all his talents, Lebed remained a novice in the game of high-level bureaucratic politics. After one hundred days in office, he declared that he "has not been able to find out how things are done." Ivan Rodin, "Security: Aleksandr Lebed Sums Up His First 100 Days," *Nezavisimaia gazeta*, as translated in *Current Digest of the Post-Soviet Press*, no. 39 (1996), p. 1. Part of the problem was that Lebed was unable to bring his own deputies into the Security Council, apparently as a result of resistance from Anatolii Chubais. See Yelena Dikun, "Lebed's Swan Song Has Not Yet Been Sung," *Obshchaia gazeta*, 1–7 August 1996, p. 8, as translated in *Current Digest of the Post-Soviet Press*, no. 31 (1996), p. 12.

10. Protesting its formation, Lebed failed to attend the first meeting of the Defense Council. Ilya Bulavinov, "Every Secretary Wants to Be a First Secretary," *Kommersant-Daily*, 5 October 1996, pp. 1, 3, as translated in *Current Digest of the Post-Soviet Press*, no. 40 (1996), p. 8.

11. The presidential decree of 14 August assigning Lebed primary responsibility for ending the Chechen war also dissolved the prime minister's State Commission for Regulating the Chechen Conflict. Scott Parrish, "Yeltsin Orders Lebed to Resolve Chechen Conflict," *OMRI Daily Digest*, 15 August 1996. One may, of course, regard this assignment as rather like the portfolio for agriculture in the old Soviet era— where intractable problems often devoured its *responsable*. But Yeltsin did appear committed to ending the Chechen debacle, and entrusting the peacemaking to Lebed was a sign of his confidence in the abilities of his Security Council chief rather than an attempt to discredit him.

12. As one observer noted, "[To] many officers and generals in the Russian Federation Ministry of Defense and the Armed Forces General Staff . . . Lebed's talks with the separatists resembles a surrender." Sergei Arbuzov, "Opinion: Chechnya and the Army," *Nezavisimaia gazeta*, 23 August 1996, p. 2, as translated in *Current Digest of the Post-Soviet Press*, no. 34 (1996), p. 6.

13. "Everything Is Built on Lies and Ambiguity," *Sovetskaia Rossiia*, 5 October 1996, p. 2, as translated in *Current Digest of the Post-Soviet Press*, no. 40 (1996), p. 4.

14. "Lebed Says Chechen Orders Were Fakes," *Russia Today*, 20 August 1996. Lebed also accused Kulikov of involvement in the fabrication of a presidential decree authorizing the bombardment of the Chechen capital, Groznyi, at a crucial moment in the peace negotiations.

15. "Press Conference with Anatoly Kulikov, Russian Interior Minister," Official Kremlin International News Broadcast, 16 October 1996. This is a remarkable public condemnation of Lebed by Kulikov.

16. Tatiana Malkina, "Anatolii Kulikov: Aleksandr Lebed' gotovit miatezh," *Segodnia*, 17 October 1996, p. 1.

17. Leonid Brodsky, "Lebed Loses Weight," *Kommersant-Daily*, 4 October 1996, p. 3, as translated in *Current Digest of the Post-Soviet Press*, no. 40 (1996), p. 1.

18. Dmitry Volkov, "The Security Council Secretary Comes Up Against the 'Will of the State,' " *Segodnia*, 4 October 1996, p. 1, as translated in *Current Digest of the Post-Soviet Press*, no. 40 (1996), p. 2.

19. On the role of Yeltsin's daughter, Tatiana Diachenko, in high-level Russian politics, see Alessandra Stanley, "New Close Yeltsin Aide: His Daughter," *New York Times*, 3 November 1996, p. 4. In this account, Lebed attributed his firing to the intervention of Diachenko, who exercised influence on her "gullible" father.

20. Accusing Korzhakov of slandering his family and violating his trust, Yeltsin ordered that the general be stripped of his military rank and pension. Laura Belin, "Yeltsin Orders Documents Prepared for Korzhakov's Dismissal," *OMRI Daily Digest*, 29 October 1996.

21. See *OMRI Daily Digest* of 5 November 1996. This decree was sure to anger the defense minister, Rodionov, who had himself been trying to revive the Soviet system of military command, where the General Staff—operating under the defense ministry—assumed responsibility for all men and women under arms. See Scott Parrish, "Yeltsin Replaces Chief of General Staff," *OMRI Daily Digest*, 22 October 1996. The State Inspectorate accomplished this centralization, but with a civilian rather than a military commander at the top of the hierarchy.

22. Chubais alarmed the Russian political establishment by securing the appointment of a protege, Boris Berezovskii, as deputy chair of the Security Council. Berezovskii, a Jewish businessman with dual Russian-Israeli citizenship, had been a major contributor to Yeltsin's reelection campaign.

23. Among the many perils of presidentialism is the political role usually assumed by leading generals. Latin American presidential systems offer the most compelling evidence of this tendency. As Juan Linz points out, parliamentary systems insist on granting a civilian the defense portfolio. Juan Linz, "Presidential or Parliamentary Democracy: Does It Make a Difference?" in Juan J. Linz and Arturo Valenzuela (eds.), *The Failure of Presidential Democracy* (Baltimore: Johns Hopkins University Press, 1994).

24. The Government—and presumably this means the prime minister and finance minister—was far more likely to short the wages fund of the Defense Ministry than the smaller or more elite services. Thus, for the months of July and August 1996, the share of the budgeted wage funds received by power ministries was as follows: MVD (96 percent and 5 percent), Border troops (100 percent and 95 percent), FAPSI (100 percent and 90 percent), and the Defense Ministry (4.4 percent and 0 percent). Anatoly Krivolapov, "Protest," *Nezavisimaia gazeta*, 19 September 1996, p. 1, as translated in *Current Digest of the Post-Soviet Press*, no. 38 (1996), p. 17.

25. Pavel Fel'gengauer, "Igor' Rodionov v krugovoi oborone," *Segodnia* online, 14 January 1997.

26. Peter Rutland, "Rodionov vs. Baturin," *OMRI Daily Digest*, 26 February 1997.

27. Pavel Anokhin, "Armiia sbrasyvaet s plech 'zhirnykh' generalov," *Rossiiskie vesti*, 23 May 1997, p. 1.

28. Aleksandr Koretskii and Evgenii Krutikov, "Otstupat' nekuda: vperedu—Chernomyrdin, pozadi—Chubais," *Segodnia* online, 7 June 1997; "Iz ukaza prezidenta o novykh polnomochiiakh Soveta oborony," *Segodnia* online, 7 June 1997.

29. Defense Minister Igor Sergeev reported that the state was to give the armed forces 23,300 apartments by mid-1998 to house decommissioned officers. "First Stage in Military Reform Completed in Russia," *Interfax News Agency*, 22 February 1998.

30. See Tony Barber, "Reform Rattles Through the Ranks," *Financial Times*, 15 April 1998, p. 5. There were also disagreements about whether the armed forces would be able to privatize part of their supplies and resources as a way of funding reform. See "Defence Minister Sergeyev on How Military Blueprint Will Unify Armed Forces," Federal News Service, Moscow, 1634 GMT, 12 August 1998, in *BBC Summary of World Broadcasts*, 14 August 1998.

31. Aleksandr Zhilin, "Military Reform Lacks Strategy," Moscow News online, 19 March 1998.

32. The ultimate goal, Sergeev noted, was to create only three military services: ground, sea, and air. "Defence Minister Discusses Military Reform with Top Commanders," Russia TV, 0350 GMT, 29 March 1998, in *BBC Summary of World Broadcasts*, 31 March 1998.

33. Barber, "Reform Rattles Through the Ranks."

34. The same budgetary problems recurred in 1997. For the revisions to the budget, issued administratively by the prime minister as a Government directive (*rasporiazhenie*), see "Orientirovochnye minimal'nye pokazateli po finansirovaniiu raskhodov federal'nogo biudzheta v 1997 godu," *Sobranie zakonodatel'stva*, no. 20 (1997), st. 2310.

35. Iuliia Latynina, "Anatolii Chubais: sobiratel' zemli russkoi," *Izvestia*, 16 May 1997, p. 2.

36. Konstantin Levin, "Prem'er neset minimal'nye potery," *Vlast'*, no. 21 (1998), p. 11.

37. The reason: the country's employers owed the Pension Fund 51 trillion rubles (almost $10 billion), or about a third of the fund's annual budget. Aleksandr Bekker, "Pensionery budut molit'sia za zdorov'e VChK," *Segodnia*, 27 December 1996, p. 1.

38. Konstantin Katanyan, "The President's Message Is Indeed Innovative," *Nezavisimaia gazeta*, 7 March 1997, pp. 1–2, as translated in *Current Digest of the Post-Soviet Press*, no. 10 (1997), p. 6.

39. "Boris Nemtsov nadeetsia restavrirovat' Mintop," *Segodnia*, 16 May 1997.

40. Dmitrii Kokuchaev and Iuliia Ul'ianova, "Ne ver,' ne boisia, ne plati. . . ," *Izvestia*, 15 May 1997, p. 2.

41. See Adam Przeworski, *Democracy and the Market: Political and Economic Reform in Eastern Europe and Latin America* (Cambridge: Cambridge University Press, 1991).

42. "Nash lobbizm—samyi ot'iavlennyi v mire," *Rossiiskie vesti*, 14 April 1995, p. 3.

43. See Anders Aslund, "Reform vs. 'Rent-Seeking' in Russia's Economic Transformation," *Transition*, 26 January 1996, pp. 12–16. For an excellent survey of Russia's new business oligarchies, see Juliet Johnson, "Russia's Emerging Financial-Industrial Groups," *Post-Soviet Affairs*, no. 4 (1997), pp. 333–365.

44. Aleksandr Bekker, "Imperia nanosit otvetnyi udar," *Segodnia* online, 16 April 1997.

45. This situation led President Yeltsin to issue a decree that began to reclaim a vodka monopoly for the state beginning in the summer of 1997. See "S 1 iulia vodka v Rossii budet odnogo sorta—'monopol'naia,' " *Izvestia*, 5 May 1997, p. 1.

46. Elena Tregubova, "Evgenii Iasin: zakonodateli opiat' podstavili prezidenta," *Segodnia*, 14 February 1995, p. 2; "Aleksandr Livshits: Nizkaia inflatsiia tozhe opasna," *Literaturnaia gazeta*, no. 28 (1994), p. 10.

47. Aleksey Portanskiy, "Reform from Above Not Being arried Out in Russia, Aleksandr Livshits, Leader of the Russian Federation President's Group of Experts, Claims," *Izvestia*, 20 April 1994, as translated in *Foreign Broadcast Information Service*, 22 April 1994, p. 29.

48. "O priznanii utrativshimi silu i ob otmene reshenii Prezidenta RF v chasti predostavleniia tamozhennykh l'got," *Sobranie zakonodatel'stva*, no. 11 (1995), st. 967; Nikolai Gorlov, "Kak gotoviatsia Ukazy Prezidenta," *Rossiiskie vesti,* 27 May 1994, p. 1; and Irina Savvateeva, "Prezident pokonchil s privilegiiami," *Izvestia*, 10 March 1995, p. 1. On the same day that Yeltsin signed the 1995 "antiprivilege" decree, he issued another decree granting a refrigerator factory a special exception from rules on hard currency receipts. "Ob osvobozhdenii zavoda kholodil'nikov 'Stinol' aktsionernogo obshchestva 'Novolipetskii metallurgicheskii kombinat' ot obiazatel'noi prodazhi chasti valiutnoi vyruchki," *Sobranie zakonodatel'stva*, no. 11 (1995), st. 964.

49. Aleksandr Bekker, "V pokhod za l'gotami," *Segodnia*, 23 March 1995, p. 1.

50. Ibid.

51. For an introduction to this sector of the economy, see Peter Rutland, "Russia's Energy Empire Under Strain," *Transition*, 3 May 1996, pp. 6–11.

52. This accusation was made by Andrei Illarionov, the former economic advisor to the Chernomyrdin Government. Andrei Illarionov, "Uroki rossiiskikh reform," *Znamia*, no. 3 (1995), p. 174. The willingness of Yeltsin to accede to Chernomyrdin on questions of energy policy appears to have been confirmed in a 1 April 1995 decree on the oil sector. "O pervoocherednykh merakh po sovershenstvovaniiu deiatel'nosti neftianykh kompanii," *Sobranie zakonodatel'stva*, no. 15 (1995), st. 1284.

53. "Gosapparat zhdet mini-reforma, a chinovnikov—sokrashchenie," *Rossiiskie vesti*, 21 December 1994, pp. 1–2.

54. The newspaper *Izvestia* reported that five regional subdivisions of the LUKoil holding company owed more than a trillion rubles in taxes by late 1996. *Izvestia*, it should be noted, had every reason to highlight the delinquency of LUKoil, since the latter was attempting an unfriendly takeover of the newspaper, which had been critical of companies in the energy sector for some time. " 'LUKoil': politika i biznes," *Izvestia*, 15 May 1997, p. 5.

55. Except for Murmansk and the Volga region, the other areas were non-Russian republics (Chuvashia, Udmurtia, Komi, Karelia, Buriatia, Dagestan, Adegei, Sakha). See "O priznanii utrativshimi silu i ob otmene reshenii Prezidenta RF v chasti predostavleniia tamozhennykh l'got," *Sobranie zakonodatel'stva*, no. 11 (1995), st. 967.

56. "Hearings on Kaliningrad Province: The Amber Enclave Is Not Being Allowed to Become a Gold Mine," *Kommersant-Daily*, 8 June 1995, p. 2, as translated in *Current Digest of the Post-Soviet Press*, no. 23 (1995), p. 4.

57. Aleksandr Bekker, "Chubais's Attempt," *Segodnia*, 16 January 1996, p. 3, as translated in *Current Digest of the Post-Soviet Press*, no. 2 (1996), p. 22.

58. Aleksandr Bekker, "Nationwide Milking," *Segodnia*, 10 July 1996, p. 2, as translated in *Current Digest of the Post-Soviet Press*, no. 28 (1996), p. 17.

59. Yulia Latynina, "Prime Minister Promises to Eliminate Tax Breaks," *Segodnia*, 14 August 1996, p. 1, as translated in *Current Digest of the Post-Soviet Press*, no. 33 (1996), p. 18. Reportedly, the original impetus for such IOUs came from the energy and agricultural lobbies. Sergei Chugaev, "Biudzhet v obmen na golovu ministra," *Izvestia*, 2 November 1996, p. 3.

60. Aleksandr Bekker, "Stanley Fischer Looks into the Abyss," *Segodnia*, 19 July 1996, p. 1, as translated in *Current Digest of the Post-Soviet Press*, no. 29 (1996), p. 8. On the dangers for the Russian economy of financing the tax debt through the issuance of state bonds, see Daniel Treisman, "Contemplating a Postelection Financial Crisis," *Transition*, 27 June 1996, pp. 30–33, 64.

61. Aleksandr Bekker, "All the Federal Legions Take Up Arms Against Debtors,"

Segodnia, 17 July 1996, p. 2, as translated in *Current Digest of the Post-Soviet Press*, no. 29 (1996), p. 21.

62. Just as the Communist Party Central Committee received state cadres on secondment, and after a period of socialization returned them to their state institution, so the Russian presidency was engaged in this political training, especially in the realm of finance. Sergei Ignatiev followed the route of deputy minister of finance to assistant to the president to first deputy minister of finance; this is akin to the old path of deputy minister to party apparatchik to first deputy prime minister. "Iakov Urinson—razrushitel' nomenklaturnogo kapitalizma," *Segodnia* online, 8 April 1997.

63. "The Extraordinary Situation with Respect to the Collection of Taxes Calls for Extraordinary Measures," *Rossiiskie vesti*, 12 October 1996, p. 3, as translated in *Current Digest of the Post-Soviet Press*, no. 41 (1996), p. 5.

64. This comment was made by Viktor Iliushin, who, after several months as deputy prime minister in charge of the social sector, was frustrated that he was out of the decision-making loop. Tatyana Koskharyova, "Who's Running the Economy?" *Nezavisimaia gazeta*, 16 October 1996, p. 2, as translated in *Current Digest of the Post-Soviet Press*, no. 42 (1996), p. 13.

65. Andrei Uglanov, "Forward—To a State of Emergency?" *Argumenty i fakty*, no. 42 (1996), p. 2, as translated in *Current Digest of the Post-Soviet Press*, no. 41 (1996), p. 5.

66. Roman Artemyev, "On the Wings of the Latest Revolution," *Kommersant-Daily*, 16 October 1996, p. 11, as translated in *Current Digest of the Post-Soviet Press*, no. 41 (1996), pp. 3–4.

67. Uglanov, "Forward—To a State of Emergency?"

68. Komsomolskaia pravda, 8 October 1996, p. 3, as translated in *Current Digest of the Post-Soviet Press*, no. 41, (1996), p. 4–5.

69. For the court's decision in this case, see Dmitrii Kamyshev, "Nich'ia v pol'zu prezidenta," *Segodnia* online, 30 May 1997.

70. Viktor Melnikov and Viktor Ivanov, "The Government Resorts to Emergency Measures," *Kommersant-Daily*, 23 July 1996, pp. 1–2, as translated in *Current Digest of the Post-Soviet Press*, no. 29 (1996), p. 9.

71. "Nalogi sobiraiut bednye bogachi," *Rossiiskie vesti*, 15 March 1997, p. 3.

72. Interfax report, *Segodnia* online, 13 May 1997.

73. Natalya Varnavskaya, "Vitaly Artyukhov: Russia Needs a System in Which Failing to Pay Taxes Would Be Frightening, Ruinous, and Shameful," *Kommersant-Daily*, 8 April 1997, p. 5, as translated in *Current Digest of the Post-Soviet Press*, no. 16 (1997), p. 8. But see *Segodnia* online, 13 May 1997.

74. Evgenii Ivanov, " 'Otmyval'shchiki' deneg skoro okazhutsia vne zakona," *Rossiiskie vesti*, 22 April 1997, p. 2. Without firm information about this activity, the estimates naturally varied widely, depending the political viewpoint of the investigator. Citing "informed Cabinet members," one journalist reported that illicit trade accounted for 20 percent of the national income. Ingard Shula, "Gen. Kulikov Has Worked out a New Tax-Collection Plan," *Kommersant-Daily*, 15 February 1997, p. 1, as translated in *Current Digest of the Post-Soviet Press*, no. 7 (1997), p. 4.

75. Elmar Murtazayev, "Pyramid: Yeltsin 'Commissions' the Budget Task Force," *Segodnia*, 12 October 1996, p. 2, as translated in *Current Digest of the Post-Soviet Press*, no. 41 (1996), p. 6.

76. Vladimir Mikheev and Gennadii Charodeev, "4,2 milliona dollarov, vydelennykh na prokorm soldat, okazalis' . . . v offshornoi zone Gibraltara," *Izvestia*, 14 May 1997, p. 1.

77. Elena Stepanova, "Dume posovetovali zaniat'sia delom," *Segodnia* online, 7 June 1997.

78. Ten subject territories accounted for more than half of this "intrastate" debt, with the largest arrears owed by the Khanti-Mansi Autonomous Region, a poor, sparsely settled northern territory. Yelena Vishnevskaya, "Enlist the Intelligence Services in Tax Collection—That's Just What Russia Needs Today," *Izvestia*, 14 February 1997, p. 1, as translated in *Current Digest of the Post-Soviet Press*, no. 7 (1997), p. 2.

79. Ingard Shula, "Gen. Kulikov Has Worked Out a New Tax Collection Plan," *Kommersant-Daily*, 15 February 1997, p. 1, as translated in *Current Digest of the Post-Soviet Press*, no. 7 (1997), p. 4.

80. Vladimir Kucherenko, "A Tax 'Manhunt' Is Declared," *Rossiiskaia gazeta*, 22 October 1996, pp. 1, 3, as translated in *Current Digest of the Post-Soviet Press*, no. 42 (1996), p. 12.

81. Elena Ishkova, "Bremia nalogov budet oblegcheno, kontrol' za ikh sborom— uzhestochen," *Rossiiskie vesti*, 24 April 1997, p. 1.

82. For a critical account of Chubais' relations with USAID and the Harvard Institute for Institutional Development, see Janine R. Wedel, *Collision and Collusion: The Strange Case of Western Aid to Eastern Europe, 1989–1998* (New York: St. Martins Press, 1998).

83. "VChK vplotnuiu zaimetsia dokhodami grazhdan," *Segodnia*, 29 October 1996, p. 1.

84. "Anatolii Chubais—narody: zhdite arestov," *Segodnia* online, 23 April 1997.

85. Interfax report, *Segodnia* online, 13 May 1997.

86. Marina Kriuchkova, "70 trillionov rublei za schet l'gotnikov," *Rossiiskie vesti*, 20 February 1997, p. 1.

87. Nikolai Ivanov, "Therapy Is Powerless—A Scalpel Is Needed," *Segodnia*, 18 April 1997, p. 1, and Konstantin Katanyan, "The Current Budget Cannot Possibly Be Met," *Nezavisimaia gazeta*, 18 April 1997, pp. 1–2, both as translated in *Current Digest of the Post-Soviet Press*, no. 16 (1997), pp. 1–2.

88. Shula, "Gen. Kulikov Has Worked Out a New Tax Collection Plan."

89. Elena Lebedeva, "Nalogi i demokratiia—Pochti odno i to zhe," *Segodnia* online, 29 May 1997. See also "Kolichestvo deklaratsii" in the same issue. For an account of the indignities encountered in paying personal taxes in Moscow, see Gennadii Mikhailov, "A ty zaplatil nalogi?" *Rossiiskie vesti*, 6 March 1997, p. 2.

90. Aleksandr Bekker, "Aleksandr Livshits Takes His Place at the 'Cash Register,' " *Segodnia*, 15 February 1997, p. 1, 3, as translated in *Current Digest of the Post-Soviet Press*, no. 7 (1997), p. 4; Boris Fedorov, "Na razdache l'got—'temnye' sily?" *Rossiiskie vesti*, 21 February 1997, p. 1.

91. Tatyana Malkina, "Anatoly Kulikov Gets Carte Blanche from the President," *Segodnia*, 14 February 1997, p. 1, as translated in *Current Digest of the Post-Soviet Press*, no. 7 (1997), p. 2.

92. The phrase is Roman Artemev's. See his "On the Wings of the Latest October Revolution," *Kommersant-Daily*, 16 October 1996, p. 11, as translated in *Current Digest of the Post-Soviet Press*, no. 41 (1996), p. 4.

93. Georgii Osipov, "Chubais pozval bankirov v proizvodstvo," *Segodnia* online, 6 June 1997. "Khochesh' deklarirui, khochesh'—net," *Ogonek*, no. 21 (1997), pp. 20–22. This is an interview with Boris Nadezhdin, Boris Nemtsov's assistant for legal affairs.

94. For a text of the speech, see *Rossiiskie vesti*, 11 March 1997, p. 2. Among the Government institutions eliminated were the Ministry of Industry and the Ministry of Defense Industry, whose responsibilities—and some of whose personnel—were trans-

ferred to the Ministry of Economics. "Novye rukovoditeli Pravitel'stva RF," *Rossiiskie vesti*, 19 March 1997, p. 1.

95. Aleksandr Bekker, "Perekroika pravitel'stva nachalas'," *Segodnia* online, 5 March 1997.

96. Tension between Chubais and Kulikov continued behind the scenes, however. According to Chubais, at the end of 1997 he and his team "became the target of quite a brazen attack . . . by a group of oligarchs who had the support of some senior officials in the law enforcement agencies." "Press Conference with the Former First Vice Premier Anatoly Chubais," Official Kremlin International News Broadcast, 23 March 1998.

97. Natalya Arkhangelskaya, "Trench Warfare in the Apparatus: Who's Digging a Pit for Whom?" *Segodnia*, 5 April 1997, p. 3, as translated in *Current Digest of the Post-Soviet Press*, no. 14 (1997), p. 10.

98. Iurii Nevezhin, "Zhilishchnaia reforma edva ne nachalas' s kommunal'noi ssory v Belom dome," *Izvestia*, 13 May 1997, p. 2.

99. See "Ob Osnovnykh polozheniiakh strukturnoi reformy v sferakh estestvennykh monopolii," *Sobranie zakonodatel'stva*, no. 18 (1997), st. 2132. This decree targeted several other sectors of the economy, including transportation and communications. In tackling the "regulated industries," Nemtsov was engaging "wealthy structures whose aggregate resources are substantially greater than the resources controlled by the Ministry of Finance and the Ministry of Economics." As a perceptive economic journalist observed, "Virtually all of our natural monopolies are like huge ministries that have been given free rein to eat their fill." Irina Savvateeva, "Natural Monopolies: The State Is Afraid of Them," *Izvestia*, 6 February 1997, p. 4, as translated in *Current Digest of the Post-Soviet Press*, no. 7 (1997), p. 6.

100. In Moscow, a city with 3 million apartments, there were a total of 3,624 apartments with heat meters in June 1997. The plan was to complete installation of meters on all utilities by 2003, though Mayor Luhzkov admitted that the high cost of installation made the plan's realization doubtful. "Vsekh nas 'postaviat na schetchik,'" *Segodnia* online, 4 June 1997.

101. Recognizing the political costs of housing reform, Moscow's mayor, Yurii Luzhkov, insisted on opting out of the national reform. That Yeltsin allowed Luzhkov to postpone the implementation of the policy in Moscow reflected, no doubt, the mayor's political standing as well as the desire of the federal authorities to maintain social peace in the capital. "Diskussiia Luzhkova i Nemtsova o reforme zhilkomkhoza obrela prikladnoi kharakter," *Segodnia* online, 31 May 1997, and Iuliia Ul'ianova, "Zhilishchno-kommunal'naia reforma—spory tol'ko nachinaiutsia," *Izvestia*, 14 May 1997, p. 1. It appears that Luzhkov may have also tried to influence Nemtsov by denying him a residence permit (propiska) when he first arrived from Nizhnii Novgorod.

102. One of Nemtsov's first measures was to reduce the housing subsidy for families of "labor veterans," an enormously unpopular move. He also pushed for a reduction in subsidies for the railways, which promised to raise considerably the cost of tickets on what had become—with the dramatic rise in airline ticket prices—the only affordable means of long-distance travel for the average Russian. Elena Stepanova, "Solo dlia kabineta ministrov," *Segodnia* online, 28 May 1997. The official decree outlining the reform of the housing sector may be found in "O reforme zhilishchno-kommunal'nogo khoziaistva v RF," *Sobranie zakonodatel'stva*, no. 18 (1997), st. 2131.

103. Aleksandr Bekker, "Roving Forward," *Segodnia*, 12 March 1997, p. 2, as translated in *Current Digest of the Post-Soviet Press*, no. 11 (1997), p. 7.

104. Nemtsov's unseating of Petr Rodionov as head of the Ministry of Fuel and

Energy is discussed in "Boris Nemtsov nadeetsia restavrirovat' Mintop," *Segodnia* online, 16 May 1997. For an introduction to Nemtsov's agenda, and his political style, see Mikhail Berger, "Boris Nemtsov: People Should Be Put in Jail for Deceiving the Tax Services," *Izvestia*, 19 March 1997, p. 2, as translated in *Current Digest of the Post-Soviet Press*, no. 11 (1997), pp. 6–7.

105. In June 1997, Yegor Gaidar would in fact claim that the Government was seeking to fulfill the 1992 program of his own party, Russia's Democratic Choice. ITAR-TASS, 16 June 1997, as printed in Johnson's Russia List, 16 June 1997.

106. For an analysis that regards the prospects for this Government as more propitious than its liberal predecessor, see Vyacheslav Nikonov, "The Second Liberal Revolution," *Nezavisimaia gazeta*, 10 April 1997, pp. 1–2, as translated in *Current Digest of the Post-Soviet Press*, no. 15 (1997), pp. 1–3.

107. "State Tax Service Chief Declares War on Tax Evaders," Russia TV, 1000 GMT, 7 August 1998, as translated in *BBC Summary of World Broadcasts*, 8 August 1998.

108. "Gazprom Gas Monopoly Pays July Taxes in Full to Avoid Sanctions," Interfax in English, 0618 GMT, 2 August 1998, as translated in *BBC Summary of World Broadcasts*, 3 August 1998. Gazprom argued that government-financed institutions owed it an amount that offset its tax bill.

109. John Starrels, "Priorities for Russian Reform," *IMF Survey*, vol. 26, no. 10 (26 May 1997), pp. 153, 164. A highly placed official in the Russian executive made a similar point, noting that "this is the last major Government reshuffle in a Government of this type. Its radicalism gives it a long-term potential, if, of course, there's sufficient social and economic slack." Andrei Kolesnikov, "Utrom—poslanie, vecherom—stul'ia," *Segodnia* online, 5 March 1997.

110. For a discussion of "market fundamentalism" and a description of the August financial collapse in Russia, see George Soros, *The Crisis of Global Capitalism* (New York: Public Affairs, 1998).

111. On the course of the campaign for a law-based state, see Donald Barry (ed.), *Toward the "Rule of Law" in Russia? Political and Legal Reform in the Transition Period* (Armonk, NY: M.E. Sharpe, 1992), especially pp. 257–275.

112. This section draws heavily on my chapter "Russian Judicial Reform After Communism," in Peter Solomon (ed.), *Politics, Power, and Culture: Reforming Justice in Russia, 1864–1994* (Armonk, NY: M.E. Sharpe, 1997).

113. As Anatolii Chubais observed, it was not unusual in the mid-1990s for criminal groups to physically block the entrance of hostile witnesses to the court in order to protect their members from conviction. See "S"ezd sudei Rossii," *Rossiiskaia iustitsiia*, no. 2 (1997), p. 4.

114. "O Kontseptsii sudebnoi reformy v RSFSR," *Vedomosti S"ezda narodnykh deputatov i Verkhovnogo Soveta RSFSR*, no. 44 (1991), st. 1435.

115. Peter Solomon, "The Limits of Legal Order in Post-Soviet Russia," *Post-Soviet Affairs*, no. 2 (1995), p. 107.

116. "Sergei Pashin: Chinovnik, dalekii ot chinovnichestva," *Stolitsa*, no. 9 (1993), p. 8.

117. In the courts of general jurisdiction alone there were 12,740 judges at the district level, 2,824 judges in regional-level courts, and more than 100 justices on the Supreme Court. For statistics on the courts at the end of 1997, see "Rabota sudov Rossiiskoi Federatsii v 1997 godu," *Rossiiskaia iustitsiia*, no. 6 (1998), pp. 55–58.

118. These commissions, known in Russian as *kvalifikatsionnye kollegii*, do more than vet judicial candidates. They also hear ethical complaints against judges and

review proposals to remove judges from office for malfeasance. In at least one instance, the highest-level judicial nominating commission resisted attempts by executive officials to remove a judge in Rostov. "Polozhenie o kvalifikatsionnykh kollegiiakh sudei trebuet utochneniia," *Rossiiskaia iustitsiia*, no. 2 (1994), p. 1.

119. Yury Feofanov, "Neither the Police nor the State Likes Independent Judges," *Izvestia*, 25 August 1994, p. 5, as translated in *Current Digest of the Post-Soviet Press*, no. 34 (1994), pp. 10–11.

120. "Text of Yeltsin's Letter on Powers of Judges," *Rossiiskie vesti*, 9 November 1994, p. 1, as translated in *Foreign Broadcast Information Service*, 9 November 1994, p. 8.

121. "S″ezd sudei Rossii," *Rossiiskaia iustitsiia*, no. 2 (1997), p. 5.

122. Leading the opposition to the law was Tatarstan. See "Zakon o sudebnoi sisteme—Osnova sudbednoi reformy," *Rossiiskaia iustitsiia*, no. 2 (1997), p. 2.

123. With 134 votes needed to pass the law in the Federation Council, the bill received 140 votes, with 18 voting against and 3 abstaining, an impressive set of figures given the usual turnout of no more than 130–135 senators. "Zakon 'O sudenoi sisteme RF' priniat," *Rossiiskaia iustitsiia*, no. 2 (1997), p. 1.

124. See article 13 in "O sudebnoi sisteme Rossiiskoi Federatsii," *Sobranie zakonodatel'stva*, no. 1 (1997), st. 1.

125. It is unclear, for example, why there should be a federal constitutional law on the justices of the peace courts if they are to be "regional" judicial institutions. See the draft approved by the presidency's Council on Judicial Reform on 9 October 1996 in *Rossiiskaia iustitsiia*, no. 1 (1997), pp. 54–55.

126. For an assessment of the institutional barriers to judicial reform at the end of the Soviet era, see Eugene Huskey, "The Administration of Justice: Courts, Procuracy, and Ministry of Justice," in Huskey (ed.), *Executive Power and Soviet Politics* (Armonk, NY: M.E. Sharpe, 1992), pp. 221–246.

127. For a perceptive assessment of the relations between courts and their institutional overseers in the Soviet era, see Todd S. Foglesong, "The Politics of Judicial Independence and the Administration of Criminal Justice in Soviet Russia, 1982–1992," doctoral dissertation, University of Toronto, 1995.

128. The attempts to introduce a Judicial Department responsible for the administration of the judiciary, and subordinate to higher courts, encountered what one judge called "behind-the-scenes maneuvers and resistance . . . from the Ministry of Justice as well as, unfortunately, some officials in the presidency." See "Iz otcheta Iuriia Sidorenko o rabote Soveta sudei RF," *Rossiiskaia iustitsiia*, no. 2 (1997), p. 6, as well as criticisms of the ministry's actions by the Council of Judges in March 1996, "Postanovlenie Soveta sudei RF 'O sudebnom departmente,' " *Rossiiskaia iustitsiia*, no. 6 (1996), p. 2.

129. See, for example, Anatolii Babenko, "Sudy okazalis' 'na zadvorkakh' finansirovaniia," *Rossiiskaia iustitsiia*, no. 9 (1995), p. 13.

130. The passage of the Law on the Status of Judges in June 1992 limited the dependence of the courts on the Ministry of Justice.

131. George P. Fletcher, "The Presumption of Innocence in the Soviet Union," *UCLA Law Review*, vol. 15 (1968), pp. 1201–1225. As V. Rudnev has argued, "[C]ourt reform goes against the interests of the Procuracy of the Stalinist-Brezhnev type." "General'nyi prokuror protiv suda prisiazhnykh," *Izvestia*, 10 March 1993, quoted in A.D. Boikov, "Sudebnaia reforma: obreteniia i proschety," *Gosudarstvo i pravo*, no. 6 (1994), p. 21. Likewise, the liberal jurist Valerii Savitskii has labeled the Procuracy "a rudiment of the totalitarian system of the Soviet period." *Rossiiskai iustitsiia*, no. 10

(1994), p. 24. It was outspoken comments such as this that contributed to the defeat of Savitskii's nomination for a place on the Constitutional Court.

In a penetrating analysis of the Procuracy written in the mid-1980s, George Ginsburgs argued that "the party, for various motives, desires a strong Procuracy in order to ensure a built-in check on the judiciary's official performance and, to do so, has to portray the Procuracy as more than just the 'voice of the state,' or it would be tilting the balance in the courtroom in such a way as to destroy the credibility of the judicial proceedings." George Ginsburgs, "The Soviet Judicial Elite: Is It?" *Review of Socialist Law*, no. 2 (1985), p. 304. It may now be asked, in the absence of the Communist Party, whose interests the Procuracy is serving.

132. Valerii Rudnev, "Sudy narashchivaiut vlast': obshchestvo ot etogo luchshe," *Izvestia*, 30 May 1995, p. 4. Procurators have worked themselves into a fury against the efforts of reformers to create an independent judiciary. A district procurator complained that "the attempts of the courts to become independent not only of everyone and everything [vsekh i vsia] but of the law itself are alarming." "U prokurora i sud'i raznye funktsii," *Rossiiskaia iustitsiia*, no. 9 (1995), p. 51.

133. Never mind that Peter the Great borrowed the institution of the Procuracy from Sweden in 1722. On the power of Russian exceptionalism as a mode of thought, see Tim McDaniels, *The Agony of the Russian Idea* (Princeton: Princeton University Press, 1996).

134. Adding to the insult was a last-minute decision of personnel close to Yeltsin to drop wording acceptable to the Procuracy from the final version of the constitution. Personal interview with Ivan Kliver, head of department, Procuracy Institute of the Russian Federation, Washington, DC, 21 February 1995.

135. N. Kostenko, "Prokuratura—opora prezidentskoi vlasti," *Rossiiskaia iustitsiia*, no. 11 (1994), pp. 25–27. Responding to the shift of institutional power in Russia after October 1993, this same procurator sought to defend the Procuracy by linking its fate to that of the presidency. The Procuracy, in his view, "should become an important and necessary support [opora] for presidential power, which is particularly necessary in the developing conditions of unstable legal relations in society." *Ibid.*, p. 26. Andrei Vyshinsky employed a similar tactic in the mid-1930s as a means of promoting the institutional interests of the Procuracy against the Ministry of Justice and the NKVD.

136. If the judiciary is independent, why do representatives from executive legal institutions, such as the Procuracy, the MVD, and the Ministry of Justice, continue to attend plenums of the Supreme Court? Is the chair of the Supreme Court present at the meetings of the MVD Collegium? That questions such as these have not traditionally been posed in Russia reveals much about the assumptions underlying the relationship between executive and judicial power. According to Viacheslav Kostikov, "The entire system of the Procuracy is a nest of opponents of reform." *Roman s prezidentom* (Moscow: Vagrius, 1997), p. 181.

137. "MVD Minister's List of 'Unreliable Judges' Scored," *Izvestia*, 18 November 1993, p. 1, as translated in *Foreign Broadcast Information Service*, 22 November 1993, p. 18.

138. *Ibid.*; "Judiciary's Role in Anticrime Work Studied," *Literaturnaia gazeta*, 3 August 1994, p. 13, as translated in *Foreign Broadcast Information Service*, 21 August 1994, pp. 23–25. As Yurii Feofanov has argued, law enforcement officials have been frustrated by article 16 of the Law on the Status of Judges, which states that "under no circumstances may a judge be detained, or forcibly taken to any state agency during proceedings involving cases of administrative law-breaking. . . . [A] judge who is detained and taken to an internal affairs agency . . . must be released immediately

after his identity has been established." "Revamped Judicial System Suffers Birth Pangs," *Izvestia*, 25 August 1994, p. 5, as translated in *Current Digest of the Post-Soviet Press*, no. 34 (1994), p. 10.

139. "O neotlozhnykh merakh po realizatsii Federal'noi programmy Rossiiskoi Federatsii po usileniiu bor'by s prestupnost'iu na 1994–1995 gody," *Sobranie zakonodatel'stva*, no. 5 (1994), st. 403. For reaction to the decree, see the selections in "Yeltsin's Anticrime Decree Draws Flood of Protests," *Current Digest of the Post-Soviet Press*, no. 24 (1994), pp. 1–7.

140. John Lloyd, "Anti-crime Measures Split Russians," *Financial Times*, 27 June 1994, p. 3.

141. For an excellent account of the German judiciary, see David P. Currie, "Separation of Powers in the Federal Republic of Germany," *American Journal of Comparative Law*, vol. 41 (1993), pp. 239–259.

142. See Sarah J. Reynolds, "Jury Trials in Modern Russia," in Solomon (ed.), *Politics, Power, and Culture: Reforming Justice in Russia, 1864–1994*, p. 379.

143. On the politics of jury reform, and on the course of its implementation through the mid-1990s, see the seminal article by Stephen C. Thaman, "The Resurrection of Trial by Jury in Russia," *Stanford International Law Review*, no. 1 (1995), pp. 61–274.

144. The so-called Law on the Jury was in fact a set of interrelated amendments to existing laws on court organization, criminal law, criminal procedure, and administrative sanctions, amendments contained in a single parliamentary "law" or *zakon*. "O vnesenii izmenenii i dopolnenii v Zakon RSFSR 'O sudoustroistve RSFSR,' Ugolovno-protsessual'nyi kodeks RSFSR, Ugolovnyi kodeks RSFSR i Kodeks RSFSR ob administrativnykh pravonarusheniiakh," *Vedomosti S"ezda narodnykh deputatov i Verkhovnogo soveta RSFSR*, no. 33 (1993), st. 1313.

145. *Vedomosti S"ezda narodnykh deputatov i Verkhovnogo soveta RSFSR*, no. 33 (1993), st. 1314.

146. By the end of 1995, there had been almost five hundred jury cases heard in nine Russian regions. "Letopis' suda prisiazhnykh (pretsedenty i fakty)," *Rossiiskaia iustitsiia*, no. 3 (1996), p. 5.

147. Acquittal rates in jury trials were far higher than those in regular court proceedings. See Thaman, "The Resurrection of Trial by Jury in Russia," p. 270.

148. For a typical response to the jury trial by a procurator, see Feliks Sadykov, "Ia—protiv suda prisiazhnykh," *Rossiiskaia iustitsiia*, no. 1 (1997), pp. 7–8. Sadykov, a procuracy official from Moscow, cannot resist a reference to the O.J. Simpson trial as proof of the bankruptcy of the American jury system.

149. In the opinion of the Government, the introduction of juries to twelve additional regions in 1996 would require an additional 220 judges, 193 procuracy officials, 24 officials in the Supreme Court, and 990 MVD personnel. The total cost for 1996 to expand the experiment in these twelve regions was estimated to be 177.5 billion rubles, though the Finance Ministry seemed willing to assign only 98 billion rubles. "Priostanovit li sud prisiazhnykh svoe dvizhenie po Rossii?" *Rossiiskaia iustitsiia*, no. 2 (1996), p. 1.

150. Reynolds, "Jury Trials in Modern Russia," p. 387. The dilemma for reformists, according to Reynolds, was how to attract willing jurors without making the reform's cost prohibitive (pp. 383–384).

151. "Ministerstvo finansov v dolgu pered sudami," *Rossiiskaia iustitsiia*, no. 8 (1995), p. 3. On tensions between legal reformists and the Finance Ministry, see "Konstitutsiia i biudzhet o sudebnoi vlasti," *Rossiiskaia iustitsiia*, no. 3 (1996), p. 1.

152. Vladimir Tumanov, the chair of the Constitutional Court until his retirement

in 1997, complained that "judicial reform had unjustifiably devoted too much attention to the introduction of jury trials." This, as the progressive legal journalist Yurii Feofanov noted, was the view of a jurist of democratic convictions. "Kak u nikh sudiat," *Rossiiskaia iustitsiia*, no. 4 (1995), p. 7.

153. See, for example, Thaman, "The Resurrection of Trial by Jury in Russia," p. 139, and "Krizis sudebnoi sistemy ne preodolen . . . ," *Rossiiskaia iustitsiia*, no. 4 (1995), p. 1.

154. Comments made during press conference by Sergei Pashin, Radisson-Slavianskaia Hotel, Moscow, 27 September 1995, attended by the author. One liberal jurist noted, only half in jest, that Russia was again in a time of troubles, with a real Kovalev (Sergei, the human rights advocate) and a false Kovalev (Valentin the Pretender, the new minister of justice).

155. David Hoffman, "Jury Experiment Slow, Incomplete," *Washington Post,* 8 October 1995, p. A45. Pashin's pessimism reflected his lack of faith in democratic politicians, especially those in the Duma. With large numbers of democrats absent from the assembly when the law on the jury trial came up for a vote, it was left to Sergei Baburin, the Russian nationalist, to play the unlikely role of champion of the new law. Press conference by Sergei Pashin, Radisson-Slavianskaia Hotel, Moscow, 27 September 1995.

156. Press conference of Sergei Pashin, Radisson-Slavianskaia Hotel, Moscow, 27 September 1995, and edited remarks of Pashin printed in "Sudy prisiazhnykh i sudebnaia reforma 130 let spustia" (copy in possession of the author). Pashin noted that "the leadership of the GPU, which before [March] had not taken an active interest in our work, began to take measures to halt it." He recognized that his success with Yeltsin had attracted attention to his department that proved destructive (*gubitel'nym*).

157. More than a few Russian jurists accept the wisdom of the American judge Learned Hand, who "wonder[ed] if we don't place too much trust in the constitution, laws, and the court system. Such trust is misplaced, believe me. Freedom lives in the hearts of men. When freedom dies in the heart, no constitution, no law, no court is in a position to save it." Iurii Feofanov, "Kak u nas sudiat," *Rossiiskaia iustitsiia*, no. 4 (1995), p. 7.

158. For a sophisticated and carefully researched study of Russian law reform at the end of the 1990s, see Peter H. Solomon Jr. and Todd S. Foglesong, *The Challenges of Judicial Reform in Russia: A Policy Study* (forthcoming).

189. Mikhail Berger and Andrei Rumyantsev, "We're Not Idiots!" *Izvestia*, 24 August 1996, p. 2, as translated in *Current Digest of the Post-Soviet Press*, no. 34 (1996), p. 20.

160. Examples of this abound in Soviet criminal procedure reforms and even in the current jury reform. On the former, see E. Huskey, "The Politics of the Soviet Criminal Process," *American Journal of Comparative Law*, no. 1 (1986), pp. 93–112. As Stephen Thaman notes, procurators in Stavropol, a region participating in the second wave of the jury reform, responded to the mild verdicts given out by juries in the Moscow and Saratov regions by requalifying cases as simple murders in order to keep them out of the regional courts, and thus beyond the reach of juries. Thaman, "The Resurrection of Trial by Jury in Russia," p. 89, fn. 181.

161. Guillermo O'Donnell, "Delegative Democracy," *Journal of Democracy*, vol. 5. no. 1 (1994), p. 66. In the view of presidential advisors, the Russian bureaucracy is unable to work " 'in the automatic regime.' The apparatus must be constantly spurred up [sic] by presidential decrees. However, the frequent issuing of decrees devalues them." Andrei Kolesnikov and Dmitry Orlov, "Priority to Order and Reform," *New Times* (April 1997), p. 9.

162. Even Russian officials pushing for reform in the military can rely on the West for assistance. See, for example, "U.S. Ready to Help Russia with Military Reform," Reuters, 26 June 1997, as printed in Johnson's Russia List.

163. Stenogram, "Zasedanie Soveta po sudebnoi reforme pri Prezidente RF," 12 March 1997, pp. 3–35 (copy in possession of the author); "Trevozhnoe soveshchanie v kontse goda," *Rossiiskaia iustitsiia*, no. 12 (1996), p. 2. In this same meeting, the head of the State-Legal Administration, Ruslan Orekhov, commented on the $10 million for crime prevention to be provided to the Council on Judicial Reform by the United Nations. Ibid. See also *Rossiiskaia iustitsiia*, no. 4 (1996), which devotes several pages to the legal dimension of Russia's "return to Europe."

164. B. Fedorov, "Pravitel'stvennyi krizis," *Rossiiskie vesti*, 5 March 1997, p. 1.

Chapter 6: Presidency and Parliament

1. For a survey of the two-tiered assembly inherited from the Soviet era, see Thomas F. Remington, "The Evolution of Rules in the Russian Legislature" (manuscript, 1992). Remington and Stephen S. Smith provide an excellent overview of the legislature of the Second Russian Republic in "The Early Legislative Process in the Russian Federal Assembly," *Journal of Legislative Studies*, no. 1 (1996), pp. 161–192.

2. Eugene Huskey, "The Rebirth of the Russian State," in Huskey (ed.), *Executive Politics and Soviet Power: The Rise and Fall of the Soviet State* (Armonk, NY: M.E. Sharpe, 1992), p. 259.

3. "Executive-Legislative Relations in Post-Communist Europe," *Transition*, 13 December 1996, p. 11.

4. Our Home Is Russia has at times opposed the president on important issues. See Robert W. Orttung and Scott Parrish, "From Confrontation to Cooperation in Russia," *Transition*, 13 December 1996, pp. 17–18.

5. As noted in Chapter 3, Loginov was promoted in Yeltsin's second term to head the Domestic Policy Administration, which brought under its wing the Department for Relations with Parties and other political bureaus.

6. " 'Stabil'naia Rossiia' otritsaet svoiu sviaz' s administratsiei prezidenta," *Segodnia*, 12 April 1995, p. 2; "Boika Leads Business Bid for Political Clout," *Kommersant*, 14 March 1995, p. 3, as translated in *Current Digest of the Post-Soviet Press*, no. 11 (1995), p. 1. According to the latter source, Oleg Boiko and other prominent bankers launched the effort to unite centrist forces in the Duma.

7. "O realizatsii konstitutsionnykh prav grazhdan na zemliu," *Sobranie zakonodatel'stva*, no. 11 (1996), st. 1026; and "O prave sobstvennosti grazhdan i iuridicheskikh lits na zemel'nye uchastki pod ob"ektami nedvizhimosti v sel'skoi mestnosti," *Sobranie zakonodatel'stva*, no. 8 (1996), st. 740.

8. Thomas F. Remington and Steven S. Smith, "Theories of Legislative Institutions and the Organization of the Russian Duma," *American Journal of Political Science*, no. 2 (1998), pp. 545–572.

9. Joel M. Ostrow, "Procedural Breakdown and Deadlock in the Russian State Duma: The Problems of an Unlinked, Dual-channel Institutional Design," *Europe-Asia Studies*, no. 5 (1998), pp. 793–816.

10. Thomas F. Remington and Stephen S. Smith examine the consequences, and the politics behind the selection of, Russia's electoral rules in "Political Goals, Institutional Context, and the Choice of an Electoral System: The Russian Parliamentary Election Law," *American Journal of Political Science*, no. 4 (1996), pp. 1254–1279.

The correlation between the kind of seat occupied—PR or single-member-district—and the voting behavior of deputies is examined in Moshe Haspel, Thomas F. Remington, and Steven S. Smith, "Electoral Institutions and Party Cohesion in the Russian Duma," *Journal of Politics*, no. 2 (1998), pp. 417–439.

11. Stephen White, Richard Rose, and Ian McAllister, *How Russia Votes* (Chatham, NJ: Chatham House Publishers, 1997), pp. 198–204.

12. For a critique of what he calls Russia's "schizoid" electoral system, see Giovanni Sartori, *Comparative Constitutional Engineering: An Inquiry into Structures, Incentives and Outcomes*, second edition (New York: New York University Press, 1997), p. 74.

13. Interview with Liudmila Zavadskaia, DeLand, Florida, 15 April 1996.

14. In early February 1997, the Duma passed a resolution demanding that Yeltsin offer "the necessary legal conclusions" concerning Chubais's alleged attempts to avoid taxes on the receipt of several hundred thousand dollars. "K Prezidentu RF v sviazi s obnarodovaniem svedenii o narushenii Rukovoditelem Administratsii Prezidenta RF Chubaisom A.B. zakonodatel'stva RF," *Sobranie zakonodatel'stva*, no. 6 (1997), st. 715.

15. For a critique of this activity by the presidential representative in the Duma, Aleksandr Kotenkov, see "Russian Opposition Expected to Try Impeachment Next Fall," Interfax, 3 June 1998.

16. Peter Bachrach and Morton S. Baratz, *Power and Poverty: Theory and Practice* (New York: Oxford University Press, 1970), pp. 3–63.

17. Sergei Chugaev, "Kto voz'met na sebia grekh narushit' konstitutsiiu: prezident ili zakonodateli?" *Izvestia*, 12 May 1994, p. 1.

18. On the use of goods to encourage parliament to confirm Sergei Kirienko as prime minister, see Evgenii Iur'ev, "S tiazhelym serdtsem i ushchemlennym statusom," *Segodnia* online, 30 July 1998, and Celestine Bohlen, "Communists Risking Perks and Power in Yeltsin Battle," *New York Times*, 24 April 1998, pp. A1, A6.

19. Anatolii Stepovoi, "Access to Okhotnyi Row," *Izvestia*, 27 February 1997, pp. 1–2, as translated in *Current Digest of the Post-Soviet Press*, no. 9 (1997), p. 12. Vladimir Zhirinovskii was reported to have had over two hundred aides himself. Ibid.

20. Ibid.

21. Igor Vandenko, "We Say 'Deputy' but Mean Broker," *Izvestia*, 30 May 1997, pp. 1–2, as translated in *Current Digest of the Post-Soviet Press*, no. 22 (1997), p. 16.

22. Ibid.

23. V.A. Vinogradov, *Koordinatsiia pravotvorchestva v Rossiiskoi federatsii* (Moscow, 1996), p. 31. My thanks to Peter Reddaway for bringing this source to my attention.

24. For the statute governing this institution, see "O polnomochnykh predstaviteliakh Prezidenta RF v palatakh Federal'nogo Sobraniia RF," *Sobranie zakonodatel'stva*, no. 11 (1996), st. 1034. Presidential representatives insist that they are merely lawyers who ensure adherence to legal and constitutional norms. The reality is far more complex and more political.

25. A detailed description of the role and authority of presidential institutions in the legislative process may be found in "Polozhenie o poriadke vzaimodeistviia Prezidenta RF s palatami Federal'nogo Sobraniia RF v zakonotvorcheskom protsesse," *Sobranie zakonodatel'stva*, no. 16 (1996), st. 1842.

26. "V Kremle naiden instrument razresheniia politicheskikh protivorechii," *Rossiiskie vesti*, 29 April 1994, p. 1. It should be noted that the legislature does have institutions similar to the American conference committees, and they, confusingly, also bear the label *soglasitel'nye komissii*.

27. A subsequent "compromise" bill, passed overwhelmingly in the Duma, unanimously in the Federation Council, and signed into law by the president, did little to allay the fears of Western officials about restrictions on religion in Russia. The passage of the country's new Criminal Code also followed a presidential veto and the establishment of a conciliation commission. See "Rekomendatsii Prezidenta vypolneny, novyi UK Rossii priniat," *Rossiiskaia iustitsiia*, no. 7 (1996), p. 47.

28. See Robert W. Orttung and Scott Parrish, "From Confrontation to Cooperation in Russia," *Transition*, 13 December 1996, pp. 19–20.

29. Yeltsin had also sought unsuccessfully at the end of 1994 to create a commission for the coordination of legislation that would serve as a multibranch supercommittee for legislative drafting. According to Georgii Satarov, this commission would have included ten members each from the presidency, Government, Duma, Federation Council, Election Commission, and Social Chamber. Such a commission would have limited its work to major policy issues, such as the electoral law, the budget, tax and privatization policy, and "state construction." Andrei Kolesnikov, "Smozhet li 'trekhgolovyi Gaidar' spasti ekonomiku Rossii?" *Rossiiskie vesti*, 18 November 1994, p. 1. Rather than develop a strong presidential party, Satarov sought to create a consociational institution where members of the executive, legislative, and society would develop laws before they were presented to parliament. See "Effektivnost': 'te resheniia, kotorye liudi gotovy vypolnit,'" *Rossiiskie vesti*, 5 August 1994, p. 1; and Dmitrii Orlov, "Prezident prodolzhaet poisk mekhanizmov vzaimodeistviia s Federal'nym Sobraniem," *Rossiiskie vesti*, 18 November 1994, p. 1.

30. Presumably, these votes would occur within three weeks after the president first nominated the prime minister. Article 111 of the constitution states that the Duma must vote initially within a week of the submission of the prime minister's candidacy.

31. *Konstitutsiia Rossiiskoi Federatsii* (Moscow: Iuridicheskaia literatura,1994), Article 117.

32. "Yeltsin May Dissolve Duma if It Fails to Vote for Budget," *Interfax*, 1459 GMT, 21 November 1997.

33. Valery Vyzhutovich, "Bicameral Cabinet: The Government Is Split," *Izvestia*, 22 April 1997, p. 2, as translated in *Current Digest of the Post-Soviet Press*, no. 16 (1997), p. 5.

34. According to Sergei Chugaev, the Duma sought to use the threat of a no-confidence vote as a chip "in its trading with the president over changes in ministerial portfolios." "Duma predpochitaet otstavke pravitel'stva torgolviu s prezidentom," *Izvestia*, 19 October 1994, p. 4.

35. Fred Weir, *Hindustan Times*, 30 July 1997, as printed in Johnson's Russia List, 30 July 1997.

36. "Kotenkov Says Only 10 Deputies Deserve Ministerial Posts," ITAR-TASS in English, 1442 GMT, 27 April 1998, as printed in *BBC Summary of World Broadcasts*, 29 April 1998.

37. "Press Conference with Presidential Representative at the State Duma," Official Kremlin International News Broadcast, 29 September 1997; "Lower House Protests over Remarks by Yeltsin Representative," *Interfax*, 0725 GMT, 25 September 1997, as translated in *BBC Summary of World Broadcasts*, 26 September 1997.

38. The pace of parliamentary lawmaking slowed down markedly after the collapse of the First Russian Republic, only to pick up again by the end of Yeltsin's first term. During its first four months, the Duma elected in December 1993 did not pass a single law, save a technical statute on how laws should be published (a *zakon o zakonakh*). And before that bill was rejected by the upper house, Yeltsin published his

own decree regulating the publication of laws. Leonid Nikitinskii, "Sud'ba zakona o zakonakh," *Izvestia*, 26 April 1994, p. 2.

39. On the Latin American cases, see Guillermo O'Donnell, "Delegative Democracy," *Journal of Democracy*, no. 1 (1994), p. 66.

40. Robert W. Orttung and Scott Parrish, "From Confrontation to Cooperation in Russia," *Transition*, 13 December 1996, p. 17. Matthew Soberg Shugart makes a similar point in his "Executive-Legislative Relations in Post-Communist Europe," *Transition*, 13 December 1996, p. 9.

41. Data based on analysis of decrees published in *Sobranie zakonodatel'stva* for 1996. Thomas F. Remington, Steven S. Smith, and Moshe Haspel offer a detailed examination of decree-making in "Decrees, Laws, and Inter-Branch Relations in the Russian Federation," *Post-Soviet Affairs*, no. 4 (1998), pp. 287–322.

42. This act was revoked by a subsequent presidential decree in June 1997.

43. Viktor Khamraev, "Kreml' blokiruet Dumu: schitaet Gennadii Seleznev i podozrevaet kommunista Semago v sviaziakh s kremlevskimi 'intriganami,'" *Segodnia* online, 21 August 1997.

44. On interpellation of Government ministers, see Liubov' Vladimirova, "Deputaty prevrashchaiut 'Chas Pravitel'stva' v vecher voprosov i otvetov," *Rossiiskie vesti*, 21 June 1994, p. 1.

45. For a detailed study of the methods and institutions—including the White House's Office of Congressional Relations—used by American presidents to influence Congress, see Nigel Bowles, *The White House and Capitol Hill* (Oxford: Oxford University Press, 1987).

46. The involvement of the Duma in the sequestration of funds followed from a provision, article 69, in the 1997 Law on the Budget, which stated that the legislature should participate equally with the Government in decisions to reduce budgetary expenditures if the treasury received less than 90 percent of planned revenues. This provision directly contradicted, however, the law on the budget process, which holds that the executive is solely responsible for such midyear budgetary cutbacks. See Aleksandr Bekker, Nikolai Ivanov, and Igor' Moiseev, "Gosduma priachet golovu v pesok," *Segodnia* online, 22 May 1997, and "Chut'-chut' politicheskogo teatra, nemnozhko kompromissa i maksimum dokhodnykh," *Segodnia* online, 21 May 1997. As an article in the newspaper of the presidency indicated, the executive did not believe parliament could deal responsibly with a budget shortfall. Their instinct was either to "introduce emergency measures to resolve the crisis or to print 300 trillion rubles." Elena Ishkova, "Srazhenie za chestnyi biudzhet," *Rossiiskie vesti*, 22 May 1997, p. 1.

47. See the important article by Irina Savvateeva, "The Budget Debate Might End with New Elections to the Duma," *Izvestia*, 21 November 1996, pp. 1–2, as translated in *Current Digest of the Post-Soviet Press*, no. 47 (1996), p. 9.

48. In one of the many wrinkles in Russia's political transition, the initial elections for Federation Council seats, in December 1993, were direct contests in which voters cast ballots for two candidates in each region or republic. Beginning with the December 1995 elections, however, the constitutional provisions applied, and Federation Council members now hold their seats by virtue of their being the chief executive or legislative speaker of a region or republic.

49. It is in the interest of the Federation Council to change the electoral law to eliminate the 225 proportional representation seats in the Duma. If at the next election all seats were in single-member districts, where provincial elites have greater influence in the nomination of candidates, the regional governors and republican presi-

dents—and the chamber in which they sit—could dominate the lower house. See Aleksandr Trifonov, "Molchanie Kremlia," *Vlast'*, 16 June 1998, p. 23.

Chapter 7: Presidency and Provinces

1. On the legacy of empire, see Mark Beissinger, "The Persisting Ambiguity of Empire," *Post-Soviet Affairs*, no. 2 (1995), pp. 149–184.

2. This assumes, of course, that the Soviet Union could have so neglected the interests of ethnic groups, a questionable assumption at best.

3. For an example of the divisions within the Government on policy toward the northern Caucasus, and their implications, see Evgenii Krutikov, "Namestnichestvo uzhe est,' a politiki poka net," *Segodnia* online, 27 May 1998.

4. Steven L. Solnick, "Federal Bargaining in Russia," *East European Constitutional Review*, Fall 1995, p. 57. The idea of redrawing the boundaries among Russia's regions arose again in late 1998, when the governor of the Kemerovo region, Aman Tuleev, proposed consolidating the political-administrative structure into between twenty-five and thirty regions. Elizaveta Osetinskaia, "Primor'e i Kemerovo ostalis' nepokorennymi," *Segodnia* online, 23 September 1998.

5. Prior to December 1993, relations between the center and the ethnic republics were governed by the Federal Treaty, signed by eighteen of those republics in March 1992. For a lucid survey of federalism in Russia, see Joan DeBardeleben, "The Development of Federalism in Russia," in Peter J. Stavrakis, Joan DeBardeleben, and Larry Black (eds.), *Beyond the Monolith: The Emergence of Regionalism in Post-Soviet Russia* (Washington, DC, and Baltimore, MD: Woodrow Wilson Center Press and Johns Hopkins University Press, 1997), pp. 35–56.

6. As Richard P. Nathan and Erik P. Hoffman point out, modern federalism is not an all-or-nothing proposition but a sliding scale embracing at least six different dimensions. These are, in their view, historical/cultural, which addresses loyalties of citizens to regional units, often for ethnic reasons; political/constitution, which indicates the regions' ability to determine their own political structure; fiscal, relating to taxing powers; programmatic, which sets out the division of labor between center and periphery in various policy areas; representative/participation, which indicates the extent to which regional officials are represented in national institutions; and finally the extent to which regional governments control the local governments that operate within them. *Modern Federalism: Comparative Perspectives and Lessons for the Commonwealth of Independent States and Russia* (Albany, NY: Nelson Rockefeller Institute of Government, 1996).

7. "Yeltsin Focuses on Problems of Russia's Regions in Weekly Radio Address," Radio Russia, Moscow, 0600 GMT, 31 October 1997, in *BBC Summary of World Broadcasts*, 1 November 1997.

8. Sergei Shakhrai observed that by early 1996 the presidency had developed a "standard approach" (*model'nyi podkhod*) to the conclusion of bilateral treaties with provinces. "Dogovor—v upriazhku s konstitutsiei," *Prezidentskii kontrol'*, no. 1 (1997), p. 26.

9. "O razgranichenii predmetov vedeniia i polnomochii mezhdu organami gosudarstvennoi vlasti RF i organami gosudarstvennoi vlasti Orenburgskoi oblasti," *Rossiiskie vesti*, 14 March 1996, p. 3.

10. "O razgranichenii predmetov vedeniia i polnomochii mezhdu organami gosudarstvennoi vlasti RF i organami gosudarstvennoi vlasti Respubliki Sakha (Iakutiia)," *Rossiiskie vesti*, 14 March 1996, p. 3.

11. "O razgranichenii predmetov vedeniia i polnomochii mezhdu organami gosudarstvennoi vlasti RF i organami gosudarstvennoi vlasti Respubliki Komi," *Rossiiskie vesti*, 28 March 1996, p. 3.

12. "O razgranichenii predmetov vedeniia i polnomochii mezhdu organami gosudarstvennoi vlasti RF i organami gosudarstvennoi vlasti Respubliki Buriatiia," *Rossiiskie vesti*, 22 February 1996, p. 3.

13. "O razgranichenii predmetov vedeniia i vzaimnom delegirovanii polnomochii mezhdu organami gosudarstvennoi vlasti RF i organami gosudarstvennoi vlasti Respubliki Bashkortostan," *Rossiiskie vesti*, 22 February 1996, p. 3.

14. "O razgranichenii predmetov vedeniia i vzaimnom delegirovanii polnomochii mezhdu organami gosudarstvennoi vlasti RF i organami gosudarstvennoi vlasti Respubliki Tatarstan," *Rossiiskie vesti*, 22 February 1996, p. 3. The cities of Moscow and St. Petersburg were also subject territories. For an analysis of the treaty with the city of Moscow, see Natal'ia Konstantinova, "Pereros li Iurii Luzhkov uroven' stolichnogo mera?" *Nezavisimaia gazeta*, 17 June 1998, pp. 1–2.

15. Peter Kirkow, "Stumbling Leviathan: Conceptualizing Institutional Change of Russian Intragovernmental Relations," paper presented at the 29th AAASS Convention, Seattle, November 1997, p. 6.

16. Steven L. Solnick, "Federal Bargaining in Russia," *East European Constitutional Review*, Fall 1995, p. 58.

17. See Andrei Kolesnikov, "Kreml' nashchupal tochki rosta," *Segodnia* online, 11 June 1997. On the full-time department in the presidency responsible for liaison with local government, see "Ob utverzhdenii Polozheniia ob Upravlenii Prezidenta RF po voprosam mestnogo samoupravleniia," *Sobranie zakonodatel'stva*, no. 22 (1998), st. 2408.

18. See Ian Bremmer, "Post-Soviet Nationalies Theory: Past, Present, and Future," in Ian Bremmer and Raymond Taras (eds.), *New States, New Politics: Building the Post-Soviet Nations* (Cambridge: Cambridge University Press, 1997), pp. 3–26.

19. Irina Nagornykh, "Mery ob"ediniaiutsia pered vyborami-99," *Kommersant-Daily*, 20 June 1998, p. 3; Ekaterina Rybas, "Mery gorodov dobivaiutsia vliianiia na tsentr i gubernatorov," *Nezavisimaia gazeta*, 20 June 1998, p. 2. For a survey of local government issues, see Peter Kirkow, "Local Self-Government in Russia: Awakening from Slumber?" *Europe-Asia Studies*, no. 1 (1997), pp. 43–58, and John F. Young, "At the Bottom of the Heap: Local Self-Government and Regional Politics in the Russian Federation," in Stavrakis, DeBardeleben, and Black (eds.), *Beyond the Monolith*, pp. 81–102.

20. See Brian Whitmore, "Government Woos, Scares Governors," *St. Petersburg Times*, 23 June 1998, as printed in Johnson's Russia List, no. 2339, 25 June 1998.

21. Darrell Slider, "Can the Center Reassert Control? Institutional Development in Russian Federalism," paper presented at the annual conference of the AAASS, 26 September 1998, p. 3.

22. Kimitaka Matsuzato, "Subregional'naia politika v Rossii—metodika analiza," in Matsuzato, *Tret'e zveno gosudarstvennogo stroitel'stva Rossii* (Sapporo, Japan: Slavic Research Center, 1998), p. 15.

23. Liubov' Tsukanova, "Rukovodstvo Udmurtiia brosilo vyzov Konstitutsionnomu Sudu," *Rossiiskie vesti*, 12 March 1997, p. 1.

24. Veronika Kutsyllo, "Boris Yeltsin Summons Udmurtia to Prosecutor General's Office," *Kommersant-Daily*, 22 February 1997, p. 1, as translated in *Current Digest of the Post-Soviet Press*, no. 8 (1997), p. 11.

25. In a meeting with mayors from nineteen of Russia's largest cities, Anatolii Chubais noted that "their shoulders would bear the weight" of future reforms in the

country. Iuliia Latynina, "Nereal'nyi biudzhet vsekh razoriaet, a chinovnika obogashchaet," *Izvestia*, 17 May 1997, p. 2.

26. Peter Ordeshook argues that the impediments to the formation of national political parties in Russia had less to do with the voluntarism of the president than with Russia's institutional design—specifically the overly fragmented election schedule—and the failure of Moscow elites to recognize that in federal systems parties must be built from the ground up rather than from the capital down. See his "Russia's Party System: Is Russian Federalism Viable?" *Post-Soviet Affairs*, no. 3 (1996), pp. 195–217.

27. The best survey of the development of the president's representatives as an institution is Irina Busygina, "Predstaviteli Prezidenta: problemy stanovleniia i perspektivy razvitiia instituta," *Svobodnaia mysl'*, no. 4 (1996), pp. 52–61.

28. Ibid., p. 55. Lyubov Tsukanova, "Dotted Line Will Be Replaced by Solid Line of Demarcation of Powers," *Rossiiskie vesti*, 11 February 1997, pp. 1–2, as translated in *Current Digest of the Post-Soviet Press*, no. 6 (1997), p. 10.

29. Mark Zlotnick, "Russia's Governors and the Presidential Elections," *Post-Soviet Prospects*, no. 4 (1996). Busygina makes a similar point on p. 59 of "Predstaviteli Prezidenta: problemy stanovleniia perspektivy razvitiia instituta."

30. "Zakony pishet ne gubernator," *Prezidentskii kontrol'*, no. 1 (1997), p. 37.

31. Busygina, "Predstaviteli Prezidenta: problemy stanovleniia i perspektivy razvitiia instituta," p. 54. After March 1996, presidential representatives answered directly to a special Administration for the Coordination of the Activities of Authorized Representatives of the President, a subdivision of the Executive Office of the President. See "Ob upravlenie Prezidenta RF po koordinatsii deiatel'nosti polnomochnykh predstavitelei Prezidenta RF v regionakh RF," *Sobranie zakonodatel'stva*, no. 36 (1997), st. 4126.

32. Aleksandr Shatilov, "Lipetskaia oblast,'" in Kimitaka Matsuzato and Shatilov (eds.), *Regiony Rossii: khronika i rukovoditeli*, vol. 1 (Sapporo, Japan: Slavic Research Center, 1997), pp. 66 and passim. This work is part of an invaluable multivolume study of personnel in Russian regions, published in the Hokkaido University series Occasional Papers on Changes in the Slavic-Eurasian World.

33. German Titov, "Tambovskaia oblast'," in Matsuzato and Shatilov (eds.), *Regiony Rossii: khronika i rukovoditeli*, pp. 224–225.

34. Slider, "Can the Center Reassert Control? Institutional Development in Russian Federalism."

35. For an analysis of the results of gubernatorial elections, see Leonid Smirniagin, "Tainy gubernatorskikh vyborov," *Rossiiskie vesti*, 6 March 1997, pp. 1, 2, and Jeffrey W. Hahn, "Regional Elections and Political Stability in Russia," *Post-Soviet Geography and Economics*, no. 5 (1997), pp. 251–263.

36. Vladimir Shpak, "Pervyi raund voiny s regional'noi vol'nitsei ostalsia za provintsiei. Zhdem vtorogo," *Segodnia* online, 9 July 1997.

37. Lyubov Tsukanova, "Good Luck in Getting Elected!" *Rossiiskie vesti*, 22 January 1997, as translated in *Current Digest of the Post-Soviet Press*, no. 3 (1997), p. 14.

38. And in late 1998, governors promised to create their own deputies' group within the Duma as well. "Gubernatory namereny sozdat' v Dume regional'nuiu gruppu," *Segodnia* online, 18 November 1998. An exceptionally important article on the role of governors in the Federation Council is "Rossiiskaia 'palata lordov' zhelaet vlastvovat'," *Segodnia* online, 5 March 1997. According to the transition provisions of the 1993 constitution, from December 1995 the chief executives of regions and republics were to occupy, ex officio, half of the seats in the Federation Council, which, as the preced-

ing chapter illustrated, had the authority to reject many presidential nominees and to impede or alter legislative initiatives of the president.

39. In June 1998, Communists in the Duma ordered committee hearings designed to lead the elimination of the presidential representatives. One of the president's supporters in parliament labeled this initiative "anticonstitutional," noting that provisions of the 1993 Constitution specifically authorize such representatives. "Komitety Dumy izuchat vopros ob uprazdnenii dolhznosti predstavitelia prezidenta na mestakh," *Segodnia* online, 27 June 1998. See also Elena Kolokol'tseva, "Nadezhda na vstrechu s prem'erom umiraet poslednei," *Segodnia*, 18 June 1998, p. 3.

40. It also anticipated the formation of representatives who would supervise several regions at once. The only example of this as this book went to press was in the northern Caucasus. See "Ob organizatsii deiatel'nosti polnomochnogo predstavitelia Prezidenta RF v Respublike Adygeiia, Respublike Dagestan, Kabardino-Balkarskoi Respublike, Karachaevo-Cherkesskoi Respublike i Stavropol'skom krae," *Sobranie zakonodatel'stva*, no. 12 (1997), st. 1420.

41. On the role of the regional party secretaries in the Soviet era, see Jerry Hough's classic work, *The Soviet Prefects* (Cambridge, MA: Harvard University Press, 1969).

42. For an excellent analysis of the strategy of the presidency toward the regions in this period, see Anatoly Kostyukov, "The Gist of the Matter: Deputized to Do Someone Else's Job," *Obshchaia gazeta*, 10–16 July 1997, p. 8, as translated in *Current Digest of the Post-Soviet Press*, no. 27 (1997), pp. 8–9.

43. Ibid. See "O regional'noi kollegii federal'nykh organov ispolnitel'noi vlasti," *Sobranie zakonodatel'stva*, no. 22 (1998), st. 2407. On the initial operation of the collegium in Sverdlovsk region, see Iurii Glazkov, "Rosselia uravnovesiil kollegiei," *Obshchaia gazeta*, 18–24 June 1998, p. 7.

44. "O polnomochnom predstavitele Prezidenta RF v regione Rossiiskoi Federatsii," *Sobranie zakonodatel'stva*, no. 28 (1997), st. 3421.

45. Leonid Smirniagin, "Priorities: Boris Yeltsin Strengthens the Vertical Chain of Command," *Rossiiskie vesti*, 29 April 1997, pp. 1–2, as translated in *Current Digest of the Post-Soviet Press*, no. 17 (1997), p. 6. Separating the regional and republican leaders from the federal agencies in the territories raised the difficult question of how the center planned to make up for the significant financial support that the agencies had received from provincial governments.

46. The preparation of these decrees seems to go back at least as far as December 1996, when a conference organized by the presidency resolved to strengthen the role of the presidential representatives. See *Prezidentskii kontrol'*, no. 1 (1997), p. 41.

47. "'I'm One of Yours,' Nazdratenko Says, Trying to Convince Boris Yeltsin, and He Asks for a Meeting," Izvestia, 10 June 1997, p. 5, as translated in *Current Digest of the Post-Soviet Press*, no. 24 (1997), p. 7.

48. Denis Dyomkin, "Nazdratenko Doesn't Fear President's Representative—He Now Has Plenty of Representatives of His Own," *Kommersant-Daily*, 23 July 1997, p. 3, as translated in *Current Digest of the Post-Soviet Press*, no. 29 (1997), p. 12.

49. Denis Dyomkin, "Nazdratenko Is Not Leaving without a Fight," *Kommersant-Daily*, 7 June 1997, p. 1, as translated in *Current Digest of the Post-Soviet Press*, no. 24 (1997), pp. 6–7.

50. See Irina Nagornykh and Vladimir Shpak, "Nazdratenko's Second Coming Would Be Judgment Day for Moscow," *Segodnia*, 18 June 1997, p. 3, as translated in *Current Digest of the Post-Soviet Press*, no. 24 (1997), p. 8.

51. Dyomkin, "Nazdratenko Doesn't Fear President's Representative—He Now Has Plenty of Representatives of His Own."

52. Yevgenia Lents, "Maritime Governor Beats Up Vladivostok Mayor Office Staffer," ITAR-TASS News Agency, 24 November 1997.

53. NTV, Moscow, 11 GMT, 6 January 1998, in *BBC Summary of World Broadcasts*, 7 January 1998, SU/D3118/B. See also Denis Dyomkin and Veronika Kutsyllo, "The President Will Have to Make Peace with the Governors," *Kommersant-Daily*, 25 June 1997, p. 1, as translated in *Current Digest of the Post-Soviet Press*, no. 25 (1997), p. 5.

54. Aleksandr Prokhanov, "Nazdratenko—Be Lukashenko!" *Zavtra*, 24 June 1997, p. 1, as translated in *Current Digest of the Post-Soviet Press*, no. 25 (1997), p. 5.

55. Sergei Nikodimov, "Governors Support Yevgeny Nazdratenko," *Kommersant-Daily*, 5 July 1997, p. 1, as translated in *Current Digest of the Post-Soviet Press*, no. 27 (19897), p. 7.

56. Denis Dyomkin, "Maritime Territory Authorities Say: 'It Was a Search, Plain and Simple,'" *Kommersant-Daily*, 11 June 1997, pp. 1, 3, as translated in *Current Digest of the Post-Soviet Press*, no. 24 (1997), p. 7.

57. Denis Dyomkin, "Mayor Comes Back from Pyongyang," *Kommersant-Daily*, 30 September 1997, p. 2, as printed in *Russian Press Digest*, 30 September 1997.

58. "Vladivostok Mayor Declares Hunger Strike in Protest at 'Systematic Persecution,'" *Interfax*, Moscow, 0204 GMT, 17 November 1997, in *BBC Summary of World Broadcasts*, 18 November 1997.

59. Christian Lowe, "Mayor Vows to Resign Amid Far East Feuding," *Moscow Times*, 12 November 1997.

60. See *Russkii Telegraf*, Moscow, 9 December 1997, in *BBC Summary of World Broadcasts*, 12 December 1997, SU/D3100/B; Denis Dyomkin, "Anti-Nazdratenko Opposition Takes Power in Maritime Territory," *Kommersant-Daily*, 9 December 1997, p. 3, as translated in *Current Digest of the Post-Soviet Press*, no. 49 (1997), p. 13.

61. When elections for mayor of Vladivostok were finally held in September 1998, the local election commission—allied to Nazdratenko—removed Cherepkov's name from the ballot on the night before the election. Angered by this move, more than half the voters marked through all the remaining names on the ballot, thereby invalidating the election. "Yeltsin's Man in Far East says Vladivostok Election Chaos Cost R3.5m," ITAR-TASS, 0452 GMT, 28 September 1998, in *BBC Summary of World Broadcasts*, 29 September 1998.

62. Yekaterina Deinego, "New Challenge to Country's Unity," *Vek*, 29 August 1997, pp. 1, 3, as printed in *Russian Press Digest*, 29 August 1997. On Ayatskov's special relationship to the Kremlin, see Tatiana Malkina, "Gubernskie vybory kak zerkalo russkoi evoliutsii," *Segodnia*, 3 September 1996, pp. 2–3.

63. Busygina, "Predstaviteli Prezidenta: Problemy stanovleniia i perspektivy razvitiia instituta," p. 53.

64. "Proverok bydet stol'ko, skol'ko gosudarstvennykh reshenii," *Rossiiskie vesti*, 8 February 1995, p. 2.

65. For a summary of the activities of the administration in 1994, see "Predstoit bol'shaia rabota," *Prezidentskii kontrol'*, no. 3 (1995), pp. 3–15.

66. "Tverdoe slovo," *Prezidentskii kontrol'*, no. 1 (1997), pp. 45–46.

67. "Proverok bydet stol'ko, skol'ko gosudarstvennykh reshenii"; "Korruptsiia—bolezn' gosudarstvennaia," *Izvestia*, 15 February 1994, p. 4.

68. Andrei Kolesnikov, "Aleksei Kudrin Bequeaths His Post to Vladimir Putin," *Segodnia*, 28 March 1997, p. 2, as translated in *Current Digest of the Post-Soviet Press*, no. 13 (1997), p. 4.

69. Busygina, "Predstaviteli Prezidenta: problemy stanovleniia i perspektivy razvitiia instituta," p. 56.

70. Denis Babichenko, "Izbirateli predpochitaiut tsentristov," *Segodnia* online, 9 January 1998. The head of this administration was Sergei Samoilov, a former director of a children's home in the Siberian city of Chita, who came to Moscow in 1990 as a people's deputy in the Russian parliament.

71. Busygina, "Predstaviteli Prezidenta: problemy stanoveleniia i perspektivy razvitiia instituta," p. 56.

72. Ibid., p. 59. Busygina notes that the only victorious presidential representative in the 1995 parliamentary election stood in the Koriak Autonomous Region, an area of northeastern Siberia where there was little competition.

73. Aleksandr Kazakov, the deputy head of the Executive Office of the President, maintained that "in the overwhelming majority of cases, the President's staff is successfully performing the function of a political arbiter," and is not putting its weight behind either the Communists or the democrats. That is because the candidates preferred by the presidency tended to lie between these two poles. "Regional Elections Through the Kremlin's Eyes," *Nezavisimaia gazeta*, 22 November 1996, p. 2, as translated in *Current Digest of the Post-Soviet Press*, no. 46 (1996), p. 5.

74. For an assessment of the varied tactics used by the presidency to influence gubernatorial elections, see Gleb Cherkasov and Vladimir Shpak, "Regional Elections: Everyone is Celebrating Victory," *Segodnia*, 26 December 1996, p. 2, as translated in *Current Digest of the Post-Soviet Press*, no. 52 (1996), pp. 4–5.

75. Natalya Arkhangelskaya and Dmitry Kamyshev, "Both the Whites and the Reds Are Centrists," *Kommersant-Daily*, 24 December 1996, p. 3, as translated in *Current Digest of the Post-Soviet Press*, no. 51 (1996), pp. 6–7. As one Russian study showed, the candidates for gubernatorial elections tended to avoid the ideological distinctions drawn during the elections for the Duma. Leonid Smirnyagin, "In the Gubernatorial Elections, the Russian Voter is the Winner," *Rossiiskie vesti*, 3 December 1997, pp. 1–2, as translated in *Current Digest of the Post-Soviet Press*, no. 48 (1996), p. 1.

76. "Regions Have a New Supervisor from the [President's] Staff," *Rossiiskie vesti*, 25 November 1997, p. 1, as translated in *Current Digest of the Post-Soviet Press*, no. 47 (1997), p. 8.

77. "Narushitelia vidim, a nakazat´ ne mozhem," *Prezidentskii kontrol´*, no. 1 (1997), p. 20.

78. Anna Ostapchuk, "Power: With Whom Are the 'Intransigents' Making Friends?" *Moskovskie novosti*, no. 18 (1997), p. 6, as translated in *Current Digest of the Post-Soviet Press*, no. 17 (1997), p. 7.

79. *Ogonek*, October 1996, p. 14.

80. Vladislav Pavlenko, "Idol with a Saber: Aleksandr Rutskoi's First 100 Days as Governor," *Trud*, 4 February 1997, p. 2, as translated in *Current Digest of the Post-Soviet Press*, no. 5 (1997), p. 13. The regional procurator would later bring charges against two of Rutskoi's deputies, which infuriated the governor. See Alla Barakhova and Dmitrii Khakhalev, "Rutskoi ishchet v Moskve druzei i vragov," *Kommersant-Daily*, 20 June 1998, p. 2.

81. For a complaint on this score by the deputy procurator general of the Russian Federation, see *Prezidentskii kontrol´*, no. 1 (1997), p. 24.

82. "Press Conference with Prosecutor General Yuri Skuratov," Official Kremlin International News Broadcast, 2 July 1998.

83. "Esli iuristy—zalozhniki mestnykh ambitsii. . . ," *Prezidentskii kontrol´*, no. 1 (1997), p. 18.

84. "Sudu ne vse iasno," *Prezidentskii kontrol´*, no. 1 (1997), p. 28.

85. Stenogram, Zasedanie Soveta po sudebnoi reforme pri Prezidente RF, 12 March 1997, p. 57 (copy in possession of the author).

86. "Problemu mozhno reshat' tol'ko v komplekse," *Prezidentskii kontrol'*, no. 1 (1997), p. 39.

87. Anatoly Kostyukov, "The Gist of the Matter: Deputized to Do Someone Else's Job," *Obshchaia gazeta*, 10–16 July 1997, p. 8, as translated in *Current Digest of the Post-Soviet Press*, no. 27 (1997), pp. 8–9.

88. "Sudebnaia reforma ne mozhet idti beskonechno," *Rossiiskie vesti* online, 12 February 1998.

89. As a means of limiting separatist tendencies in the charter courts, the Russian Constitutional Court organized a congress of constitutional courts throughout the country. Sensitive to the feelings of regional-level judges, the chair of the Russian constitutional court asserted that "no one has any intention of institutionalizing a hierarchy of constitutional courts; we're merely creating a way to discuss a broad range of problems, including demarcation of the jurisdiction of various courts." Maksim Zhukov, "Russia's Constitutional Courts Attempt to Reach Agreement," *Kommersant-Daily*, 22 April 1998, p. 2, as translated in *Current Digest of the Post-Soviet Press*, no. 50 (1998), p. 14.

90. "Nachinat' nam sleduet s sebia," *Prezidentskii kontrol'*, no. 1 (1997), p. 10. Federal authorities struggled to find an institution that could alert Moscow to conflicts between the laws of the provinces and those of the Russian Federation.

91. Zhukov, "Russia's Constitutional Courts Attempt to Reach Agreement," p. 14. "In 1996–1997 about 20 percent of the Federation members refused to submit their normative acts for review by the Justice Ministry. During the past two years, prosecutor's offices at the republic, territory and province levels have challenged over 1,400 laws and resolutions enacted by the state authorities of Russian Federation members." Ibid. The importance of having federal authorities able to prosecute crimes was evident in the republic of Kalmykia in June 1998, when a local opposition journalist was murdered, apparently by two former aides to the Kalmyk president. German Aleksandrov, "Prezident ne doveriaet Kalmytskoi militsii," *Nezavisimaia gazeta*, 16 June 1998, p. 2. See also "Genprokuratora i Miniust kontroliruiut normotvorchestvo sub"ektov RF," *Segodnia* online, 25 December 1998.

92. "O Komissii pri Prezidente RF po vzaimodeistviiu federal'nykh organov gosudarstvennoi vlasti i organov gosudarstvennoi vlasti sub"ektov RF pri provedenii konstitutsionno-pravovoi reformy v sub"ektakh Rossiiskoi Federatsii," *Sobranie zakonodatel'stva*, no. 5 (1996), st. 461.

93. On this, see the comments of the Constitutional Court chairman at a meeting in the presidency in December 1996. "Ia poka ne vizhu sistemy, kotoraia ostanovila by narusheniia," *Prezidentskii kontrol'*, no. 1 (1997), pp. 12–13.

94. David Hoffman, "Moscow Mayor Defies Court on Residence Rights," *Washington Post*, 13 March 1998, as printed in Johnson's Russia List, no. 2107, 13 March 1998.

95. Gerald Easter makes this point convincingly in his "Redefining Centre-Regional Relations in the Russian Federation: Sverdlovsk Oblast'," *Europe-Asia Studies*, no. 4 (1997), p. 631. According to Easter, even the regionalist movement in Sverdlovsk "did not view the region as an independent entity, but rather as a 'subject of the Russian state.' Thus, their perceptions of their own roles as regional actors were derived from and constrained by a social identity of themselves as state actors. Separatism was never a serious option. . . . [T]he conflict with Moscow, instead, should be seen as an intra-state elite power struggle over political, economic, and status resources." *Ibid*.

96. Konstantin Katanian, "Gubernatory pod damoklovym mechom," *Izvestia*, 2 October 1998, p. 1.

97. "O normativnykh pravovykh aktakh gubernatora Kurskoi oblasti," *Sobranie zakonodatel'stva*, no. 51 (1997), st. 5745.

98. According to Aleksandr Kazakov, the deputy head of the Executive Office of the President, the election of Boris Govorin as governor of the Irkutsk region was attributable in part to the assistance provided by federal executive officials. "Irkutsk Election Viewed as Victory for Government," *RFE/RL Newsline*, 29 July 1997, as printed in Johnson's Russia List, no. 1097, 29 July 1997.

99. Aleksandr Koretskii, "Boris El'tsin ostavil Ausheva i Galazova 'pri svoikh,' " *Segodnia* online, 9 August 1997.

100. For a clear and brief introduction to Moscow's fiscal policy toward the regions, see Daniel Treisman, "Moscow's Struggle to Control Regions Through Taxation," *Transition*, 20 September 1996, pp. 45–49.

101. Elena Lebedeva, "Pravitel'stvo idet v regiony," *Segodnia* online, 28 May 1997. As Vladimir Shpak noted, however, "The increase in the number of recipient regions says less about the 'impoverishment of the masses' than the increasing influence of regional barons on federal rulers." "Pereraspredelenie vlasti," *Segodnia* online, 1 January 1997.

102. Yevgenia Albats, "Who Is Governing Russia?" *Izvestia*, 18 September 1996, as translated in *Current Digest of the Post-Soviet Press*, no. 37 (1996), p. 5.

103. Vladimir Shpak, "Senators' 'Holiday of Disobedience' Comes to an End," *Segodnia*, 23 April 1997, p. 3, as translated in *Current Digest of the Post-Soviet Press*, no. 17 (1997), pp. 6–7.

104. On the extraordinary inefficiencies and corruption built into the winter provisioning system, see Aleksandr Bekker, "A Big Regional Scam," *Segodnia*, 13 March 1997, pp. 1–2, as translated in *Current Digest of the Post-Soviet Press*, no. 11 (1997), p. 9.

105. On this last point, which promised strengthened fiscal discipline by holding all federal monies in provincial branches of the federal treasures until final disbursement, see Steven L. Solnick, "Territorial Coalitions in Transitional States: Russia in Comparative Perspective," paper presented at the annual meeting of the Midwest Political Science Association, Chicago, 24 April 1998, p. 22, and Slider, "Can the Center Reassert Control? Institutional Development in Russian Federalism," p. 10.

106. Iuliia Ulianova, "Pravitel'stvo formiruet spetsbrigady," *Segodnia* online, 26 November 1997.

107. Solnick, "Territorial Coalitions in Transitional States: Russia in Comparative Perspective," p. 21.

108. Vladimir Shpak, "Pereraspredelenie vlasti," *Segodnia* online, 30 January 1997.

109. Aleksei Lavrov, "Pochemu dotatsionnye regiony golosuiut za kommunistov, ili Mify Rossiiskogo biudzhetnogo federalizma," *Politicheskaia sreda*, p. III, a supplement to *Rossiiskie vesti*, 10 April 1996.

110. Elena Lebedeva, "Pravitel'stvo idet v regiony," *Segodnia* online, 28 May 1997. Not all recalcitrant regions got their way, of course. According to one report, threats from Procuracy and Finance Ministry officials in Moscow put an end to a tax revolt by the Irkutsk region in early 1997. Dmitryi Kamyshev and Irina Nagornykh, "Irkutsk Governor's 'Tax Putsch' Is Put Down," *Segodnia*, 5 March 1997, pp. 1, 3, as translated in *Current Digest of the Post-Soviet Press*, no. 9 (1997), p. 9. Moreover, even Sakha—labeled the "weakest link in the chair of Russian offshore [sic] territories"—came under pressure from the center in 1997 to relinquish some of its financial privileges. " 'Barkhatnaia revoliutsiia' idet s sibirskogo Sever," *Segodnia* online, 16 May 1997.

111. Aleksandr Batygin, "Money Is Already on its Way to the Regions," *Rossiiskaia gazeta*, 30 September 1998, p. 1, as translated in *Current Digest of the Post-Soviet Press*, no. 40 (1998), p. 10.

112. Daniel Treisman, "The Politics of Intergovernmental Transfers in Post-Soviet Russia," *British Journal of Political Science*, no. 2 (1996), pp. 322, 329–330. For a different interpretation of these findings, see Peter Rutland, "The Russian Elite and the Challenge of Regionalism," paper presented at the annual conference of the American Association for the Advancement of Slavic Studies, Seattle, 21 November 1997.

113. Treisman, "Moscow's Struggle to Control Regions through Taxation," p. 49.

114. The 1998 draft budget prepared by the Government envisioned a reduction in financial aid to the regions from 66 trillion to 38.5 trillion rubles, this at a time when regional leaders asked for an increase in federal aid. Irina Demchenko, "Russian Budget Could Spark Row with Regions," Reuters, 20 August 1997, as printed in Johnson's Russia List, no. 1134, 20 August 1997.

115. See Lev Freinkman and Michael Haney, "What Affects the Russian Regional Governments' Propensity to Subsidize?" Policy Research Working Paper 1818, The World Bank, August 1997, pp. 4–8.

116. *Ibid.*

117. *Ibid.*, p. 22.

118. Georgii Ivanov, "Nalogovyi kodeks s biudzhetom ili bez," *Segodnia* online, 28 May 1997.

119. See Freinkman and Haney, "What Affects the Russian Regional Governments' Propensity to Subsidize?" p. 8.

Chapter 8: Conclusion

1. Valerie Bunce, "Comparing East and South," *Journal of Democracy*, no. 3 (1995), pp. 87–100.

2. Aleksandr Yanov, *Posle El'tsina: "Veimarskaia" Rossiia* (Moscow: Moskovskaia gorodskaia tipografiia im. Pushkina, 1995). For a critique of this historical analogy, see Stephen E. Hanson and Jeffrey S. Kopstein, "The Weimar/Russia Comparison," *Post-Soviet Affairs*, no. 3 (1997), pp. 252–283.

3. Jon Elster, Claus Offe, and Ulrich K. Preuss, *Institutional Design in Post-Communist Societies: Rebuilding the Ship at Sea* (Cambridge: Cambridge University Press, 1998), p. 293.

4. *Ibid.*, p. 19. This work relates first and foremost to transitions in the Eastern European countries of Bulgaria, Czechoslovakia, and Hungary.

5. M. Steven Fish, "The Pitfalls of Superpresidentialism," *Current History* (October 1997), p. 326.

6. See A.J. Polan, *Lenin and the End of Politics* (Berkeley: University of California Press, 1984).

7. Andrei Kolesnikov, "Battle with Oligarchs Cannot Be Treated Like a Political Campaign," *Novoe vremia*, 3 May 1998, as printed in Johnson's Russia List, no. 2202, 31 May 1998.

8. Timothy J. Colton, "Superpresidentialism and Russia's Backward State," *Post-Soviet Affairs*, no. 2 (1995), p. 147.

9. My thanks to James Gibson, whose response to my remarks at a Kansas University forum in September 1996 first set me to thinking about this issue.

10. In early 1998, the president's representative in the Constitutional Court, Sergei

Shakhrai, floated the idea of abandoning the party list, or proportional representation, voting that filled half of the seats in the Duma in the 1993 and 1995 elections in favor of "majoritarian," or single-member-district, contests for all Duma members. This proposal would have devastated some factions, most notably the Liberal Democratic Party of Zhirinovskii, as well as threatening Moscow-based elites in other parties. "Sergei Shakhrai: Boris El'tsin zainteresovan v tom, chtoby navesti poriadok v protsesse priniatiia zakonov v strane," *Rossiiskie vesti* online, 17 January 1998.

11. "Prezident," *Rossiiskie vesti* online, 25 February 1998.

12. See, for example, "Sergei Shakhrai: Boris El'tsin zainteresovan v tom, chtoby navesti poriadok v protsesse priniatiia zakonov v strane." In the summer of 1998, there was also talk of inviting the leaders of financial-industrial groups to join a corporatist-like body chaired by the president. According to one source, a Group of Four was first formed in October 1996, shortly before the president's surgery. In July 1997, Yeltsin created a new Group of Four, made up exclusively of executive officials, before returning to the original membership in 1998. Mikhail Poletayev, "Boris Yeltsin Reshuffles the 'Group of Four,' " *Kommersant-Daily*, 2 July 1997, pp. 1–2, as translated in *Current Digest of the Post-Soviet Press*, no. 26 (1997), p. 7.

13. Adam Przeworski, *Democracy and the Market: Political and Economic Reforms in Eastern Europe and Latin America* (Cambridge: Cambridge University Press, 1991), p. 14. The classic work on this subject remains Samuel Huntington, *Political Order in Changing Societies* (New Haven: Yale University Press, 1968).

14. Richard Pipes, "Whither Russia?" *IntellectualCapital.com*, 25 September 1997.

15. Based on an analysis of the Latin American experience Terry Lynn Karl warns that the price of initial political survivability may be high: "The conditions that permit democracies to persist in the short run may constrain their potential for resolving the enormous problems of poverty and inequality." "Dilemmas of Democratization in Latin American," *Comparative Politics*, no. 1 (1990), p. 13. In Russia, the tension is not only between democracy and equity but between political stability, on the one hand, and administrative efficiency and legal integrity, on the other.

16. After writing these lines, I came upon an article by Viacheslav Nikonov that makes a somewhat similar point about a less dangerous Yeltsin in late 1998, when poor health prevented new and bold initiatives. "Slabyi El'tsin kak faktor stabil'nosti," *Izvestia*, 3 November 1998, p. 2.

17. Georgii Bovt, "Kak pensioner—prezidentu," *Segodnia*, 19 June 1998, p. 2.

18. It is tempting to compare the behavior of Yeltsin with that of Lyndon Johnson, another politician from the heartland whose antics could shock the sensibilities of the establishment. But unlike the earthy Texan, with his lengthy experience in a democratic legislature, Yeltsin was not a coalition builder or a massager of egos.

19. How much of Yeltsin's unpredictability and boorishness was due to drinking and health problems may be known only when a new set of memoirs appears by Yeltsin associates, probably after his departure or death. On the effects of drinking and illness on political leadership more generally, see Jerrold M. Post and Robert S. Robins, *When Illness Strikes the Leader* (New Haven: Yale University Press, 1993).

20. In the view of Peter Reddaway, given the divisions and crises facing the country, even a strong and effective leader could at best have helped Russia "muddle through" rather than "muddle down." "Possible Scenarios for Russia's Future," *Problems of Post-Communism* (September–October 1997), p. 42.

21. Yeltsin seemed uninterested in providing Russia with a replacement ideology. Only in the middle of his second term did he sanction the formation of a task force responsible for developing a "Russian idea." Judging by a conference on this project,

which I attended in June 1998, the organizers were intent on advancing a new "official ideology," which one leading participant likened to the teachings of the Orthodox Church before 1917 or Marxism-Leninism after it. William Zimmerman may be right in asserting that Russians of all backgrounds are rejecting "synoptic thinking," but some forces within the presidency appear intent on reviving it. See Zimmerman, "Synoptic Thinking and Political Culture in Post-Soviet Russia," *Slavic Review*, no. 3 (1995), pp. 630–641.

22. By appointing Kirienko, a young minister with little experience in national politics, Yeltsin virtually guaranteed that he would become, for a time, more politically active. As one observer noted, Kirienko couldn't deflect criticism from Yeltsin until he achieved "a minimal political weight. A scapegoat can't be a bunny." Vadim Komplektov, "Poslednee otstuplenie prezidenta," *Vlast'*, no. 21 (1998), p. 10.

23. It should be noted that only weeks after the Duma confirmed the Government of Kirienko, Yeltsin brought Chubais back into the presidency in the newly created post of presidential representative to international financial institutions.

24. Mikhail Berger, "Bol'she demokratii v biurokraticheskom protsesse," *Segodnia* online, 6 May 1998. For a brief official discussion of the new relationship between presidency and Government, see Stenogramma brifinga Press-sekretaria Prezidenta RF, S.V. Iastrzhembskogo, Moskva, Kreml,' 5 May 1998, <www.maindir.gov.ru/ Administration/Prespage>.

25. Pipes, "Whither Russia?"

Selected Bibliography

Aslund, Anders. *How Russia Became a Market Economy.* Washington, DC: The Brookings Institution, 1995.

Barry, Donald (ed.). *Toward the "Rule of Law" in Russia? Political and Legal Reform in the Transition Period.* Armonk, NY: M.E. Sharpe, 1992.

Bialer, Seweryn (ed.). *Politics, Society, and Nationality: Inside Gorbachev's Russia.* Boulder, CO: Westview Press, 1989.

Boldin, V.I. *Krushenie p'edestala.* Moscow: Respublika, 1995.

Bowles, Nigel. *The White House and Capitol Hill.* Oxford: Oxford University Press, 1987.

Bremmer, Ian, and Raymond Taras (eds.). *New States, New Politics: Building the Post-Soviet Nations.* Cambridge: Cambridge University Press, 1997.

Brown, Archie. *The Gorbachev Factor.* Oxford: Oxford University Press, 1996.

Burke, John P. *The Institutional Presidency.* Baltimore: Johns Hopkins University Press, 1992.

Cherniaev, A.S. *Shest' let s Gorbachevym: po dnevnikovym zapisiam.* Moscow: Kul'tura, 1993.

Colton, Timothy J., and Jerry F. Hough (eds). *Growing Pains: Russian Democracy and the Elections of 1993.* Washington, DC: The Brookings Institution, 1998.

Dawisha, Karen, and Bruce Parrott (eds.). *Democratic Changes and Authoritarian Reactions in Russian, Ukraine, Belarus, and Moldova.* Cambridge: Cambridge University Press, 1997.

Dobrynin, Anatolii. *In Confidence: Moscow's Ambassador to America's Six Cold War Presidents.* New York: Random House, 1995.

Eckstein, Harry, et al. (eds). *Can Democracy Take Root in Post-Soviet Russia?* Lanham, MD: Rowman and Littlefield, 1998.

Elster, Jon, Claus Offe, and Ulrich K. Preuss. *Institutional Design in Post-Communist Societies: Rebuilding the Ship at Sea.* Cambridge: Cambridge University Press, 1998.

Evans, Peter B., Dietrich Rueschemeyer, and Theda Skocpol. *Bringing the State Back In*. Cambridge: Cambridge University Press, 1985.

Filatov, Sergei. *Na puti k demokratii*. Moscow: Moskovskii rabochii, 1995.

Fish, M. Steven. *Democracy from Scratch: Opposition and Regime in the New Russian Revolution*. Princeton: Princeton University Press, 1995.

Foglesong, Todd S. *The Politics of Judicial Independence and the Administration of Criminal Justice in Soviet Russia, 1982–1992*. Doctoral dissertation, University of Toronto, 1995.

Gaidar, Yegor. *Gosudarstvo i evoliutsiia*. Moscow: Evraziia, 1995.

Glaz'ev, Sergei. *Ekonomika i politika: epizody bor'by*. Moscow: Gnozis, 1994.

Hahn, Jeffrey W. (ed.). *Democratization in Russia: The Development of Legislative Institutions*. Armonk, NY: M.E. Sharpe, 1996.

Hess, Stephen. *Organizing the Presidency*, second edition. Washington, DC: The Brookings Institution, 1988.

Hough, Jerry. *Democratization and Revolution in the USSR, 1985–1991*. Washington, DC: The Brookings Institution, 1997.

———. *The Soviet Prefects*. Cambridge, MA: Harvard University Press, 1969.

Huber, Robert T., and Donald R. Kelley. *Perestroika-Era Politics: The New Soviet Legislature and Gorbachev's Political Reforms*. Armonk, NY: M.E. Sharpe, 1991.

Huntington, Samuel. *Political Order in Changing Societies*. New Haven: Yale University Press, 1968.

———. *The Third Wave: Democratization in the Late Twentieth Century*. Norman, OK: University of Oklahoma Press, 1991.

Huskey, Eugene (ed.). *Executive Power and Soviet Politics*. Armonk, NY: M.E. Sharpe, 1992.

Kapuscinski, Ryszard. *The Emperor*. New York: Vintage Books, 1984.

Knight, Amy. *Spies Without Cloaks: The KGB's Successors*. Princeton: Princeton University Press, 1996.

Kostikov, Viacheslav. *Roman s Prezidentom*. Moscow: Vagrius, 1997.

Korzhakov, Aleksandr. *Boris El'tsin: ot rassveta do zakata*. Moscow: Interbuk, 1997.

Kozyrev, Andrei. *Preobrazhenie*. Moscow: Mezhdunarodnye otnosheniia, 1995.

Kutsyllo, Veronika. *Zapiski iz Belogo Doma*. Moscow: Kommersant, 1993.

Kuznetsov, Yegor L. *Sozdanie instituta Prezidenta SSSR. Politologicheskie aspekty*. Kandidat dissertation, Institute of State and Law, Moscow, 1994.

LaPalombara, Joseph (ed.). *Bureaucracy and Political Development*. Princeton: Princeton University Press, 1963.

Ligachev, Yegor. *Inside Gorbachev's Kremlin*. New York: Pantheon Books, 1993.

Linz, Juan J., and Alfred Stepan. *Problems of Democratic Transition and Consolidation: Southern Europe, South America, and Post-Communist Europe*. Baltimore: Johns Hopkins University Press, 1996.

Linz, Juan J., and Arturo Valenzuela. *The Failure of Presidential Democracy*. Baltimore: The Johns Hopkins University Press, 1994.

Lowenhardt, John. *The Reincarnation of Russia: Struggling with the Legacy of Communism, 1990–1994*. Durham, NC: Duke University Press, 1995.

Lysenko, L.M. *Vlast': Pravitel'stvo Rossii*. Moscow: Institut sovremennoi politiki, 1997.

Matlock, Jack. *Autopsy on an Empire*. New York: Random House, 1995.

Matsuzato, Kimitaka, and Aleksandr Shatilov (eds.). *Regiony Rossii: khronika i rukovoditeli*, vol. 1. Sapporo, Japan: Slavic Research Center, 1997.

McAuley, Mary. *The Politics of Uncertainty*. Cambridge: Cambridge University Press, 1997.

McDaniels, Tim. *The Agony of the Russian Idea.* Princeton: Princeton University Press, 1996.

McFaul, Michael. *Russia's 1996 Presidential Elections: The End of Polarized Politics.* Stanford, CA: Hoover Institution Press, 1997.

Mickiewicz, Ellen. *Changing Channels: Television and the Struggle for Power in Russia.* Oxford: Oxford University Press, 1997.

Nathan, Richard P., and Erik P. Hoffman. *Modern Federalism: Comparative Perspectives and Lessons for the Commonwealth of Independent States and Russia.* Albany, NY: Nelson Rockefeller Institute of Government, 1996.

Nenashev, M. *Poslednee Pravitel'stvo SSSR.* Moscow: AO "Krym," 1993.

Neustadt, Richard E. *Presidential Power and the Modern Presidents. The Politics of Leadership from Roosevelt to Reagan.* New York: The Free Press, 1990.

O'Donnell, Guillermo, and Philippe Schmitter (eds.). *Transitions from Authoritarian Rule: Tentative Conclusions about Uncertain Democracies.* Baltimore: Johns Hopkins University Press, 1986.

Okun'kov, L.A. *Prezident Rossiiskoi Federatsii—Konstitutsiia i politicheskaia praktika.* Moscow: INFRA M-NORMA, 1996.

Pavlov, Valentin. *Upushchen li shans?* Moscow: Terra, 1995.

Polan, A.J. *Lenin and the End of Politics.* Berkeley: University of California Press, 1984.

Przeworski, Adam. *Democracy and the Market: Political and Economic Reforms in Eastern Europe and Latin America.* Chicago: University of Chicago Press, 1991.

Remington, Thomas F. (ed.). *Parliaments in Transition.* Boulder, CO: Westview Press, 1994.

———. *Politics in Russia.* New York: Longman, 1999.

Remnick, David. *Lenin's Tomb: The Last Days of the Soviet Empire.* New York: Vintage, 1994.

———. *Resurrection: The Struggle for a New Russia.* New York: Vintage, 1998.

Riggs, Fred W. *Administration in Developing Countries: The Theory of Prismatic Society.* Boston: Houghton Mifflin, 1964.

Rutskoi, Aleksandr. *Lefortovskie protokoly.* Moscow: Paleia, 1994.

Rybkin, I.P. *Gosudarstvennaia Duma: piataia popytka.* Moscow: International Humanitarian Fund "Znanie," 1994.

Ryzhkov, N.I. *Ia iz partii po imeni "Rossiia."* Moscow: Obozrevatel', 1995.

Sakwa, Richard. *Russian Politics and Society.* London: Routledge, 1993.

Sartori, Giovanni. *Comparative Constitutional Engineering: An Inquiry into Structures, Incentives and Outcomes,* second edition. New York: New York University Press, 1997.

Shakhnazarov, Georgii. *Tsena svobody: reformatsiia Gorbacheva glazami ego pomoshchnika.* Moscow: Rossika, 1993.

Sobianin, A.A., and V.G. Sukhovol'skii. *Demokratiia, ogranichennaia fal'sifikatsiiami: vybory i referendumy v Rossii v 1991–1993gg.* Moscow: Proektnaia gruppa po pravam cheloveka, 1995.

Solomon, Peter (ed.). *Politics, Power, and Culture: Reforming Justice in Russia, 1864–1994.* Armonk, NY: M.E. Sharpe, 1997.

Soros, George. *The Crisis of Global Capitalism.* New York: Public Affairs, 1998.

Stavrakis, Peter J., Joan DeBardeleben, and Larry Black (eds.). *Beyond the Monolith: The Emergence of Regionalism in Post-Soviet Russia.* Washington, DC and Baltimore, MD: Woodrow Wilson Center Press and Johns Hopkins University Press, 1997.

Steinmo, Sven, Kathleen Thelen, and Frank Longstreth (eds). *Structuring Politics: Historical Institutionalism in Comparative Analysis.* Cambridge: Cambridge University Press, 1992.

Stoner-Weiss, Kathryn. *Local Heroes: The Political Economy of Russian Regional Governance.* Princeton: Princeton University Press, 1997.

Sudebnaia palata po informatsionnym sporam pri Prezidente Rossiiskoi Federatsii, 1994–1996. Moscow: Pravo i zakon, 1997.

Lev Sukhanov. *Tri goda s El'tsinym: zapiski pervogo pomoshchnika.* Riga: Vaga, 1992.

Taras, Ray (ed.). *Post-Communist Presidents.* Cambridge: Cambridge University Press, 1997.

Tismaneanu, Vladimir (ed.). *Political Culture and Civil Society in Russia and the New States of Eurasia.* Armonk, NY: M.E. Sharpe, 1995.

Tsentral'naia izbiratel'naia komissia. *Vybory Prezidenta Rossiiskoi Federatsii.* Moscow: Ves' mir, 1996.

Urban, Michael. *The Rebirth of Politics in Russia.* Cambridge: Cambridge University Press, 1997.

Walcott, Charles E., and Karen M. Hult. *Governing the White House.* Lawrence, Kansas: University Press of Kansas, 1995.

Wedel, Janine R. *Collision and Collusion: The Strange Case of Western Aid to Eastern Europe, 1989–1998.* New York: St. Martin's Press, 1998.

White, Stephen, Richard Rose, and Ian McAllister. *How Russia Votes.* Chatham, NJ: Chatham House Publishers, Inc., 1997.

Yakovlev, Alexander M. *Striving for Law in a Lawless Land: Memoirs of a Russian Reformer.* Armonk, NY: M.E. Sharpe, 1996.

Yaney, George. *The Systemization of Russian Government: Social Evolution in the Domestic Administration of Imperial Russia, 1711–1905.* Urbana, IL: University of Illinois Press, 1973.

Yanov, Aleksandr. *Posle El'tsina: "Veimarskaia" Rossiia.* Moscow: Moskovskaia gorodskaia tipografiia im. Pushkina, 1995.

Yeltsin, Boris. *Against the Grain: An Autobiography.* New York: Summit Books, 1990.

———. *The Struggle for Russia.* New York: Random House, 1994.

Index

About the Author

Eugene Huskey is professor of political science and director of Russian studies at Stetson University in DeLand, Florida. He received his Ph.D. in politics from the London School of Economics and Political Science in 1983 and taught at Colgate University and Bowdoin College before joining the Stetson faculty in 1989. He is author of two books and more than two dozen articles on politics and legal affairs in the Soviet Union and the successor states of Russia and Kyrgyzstan.